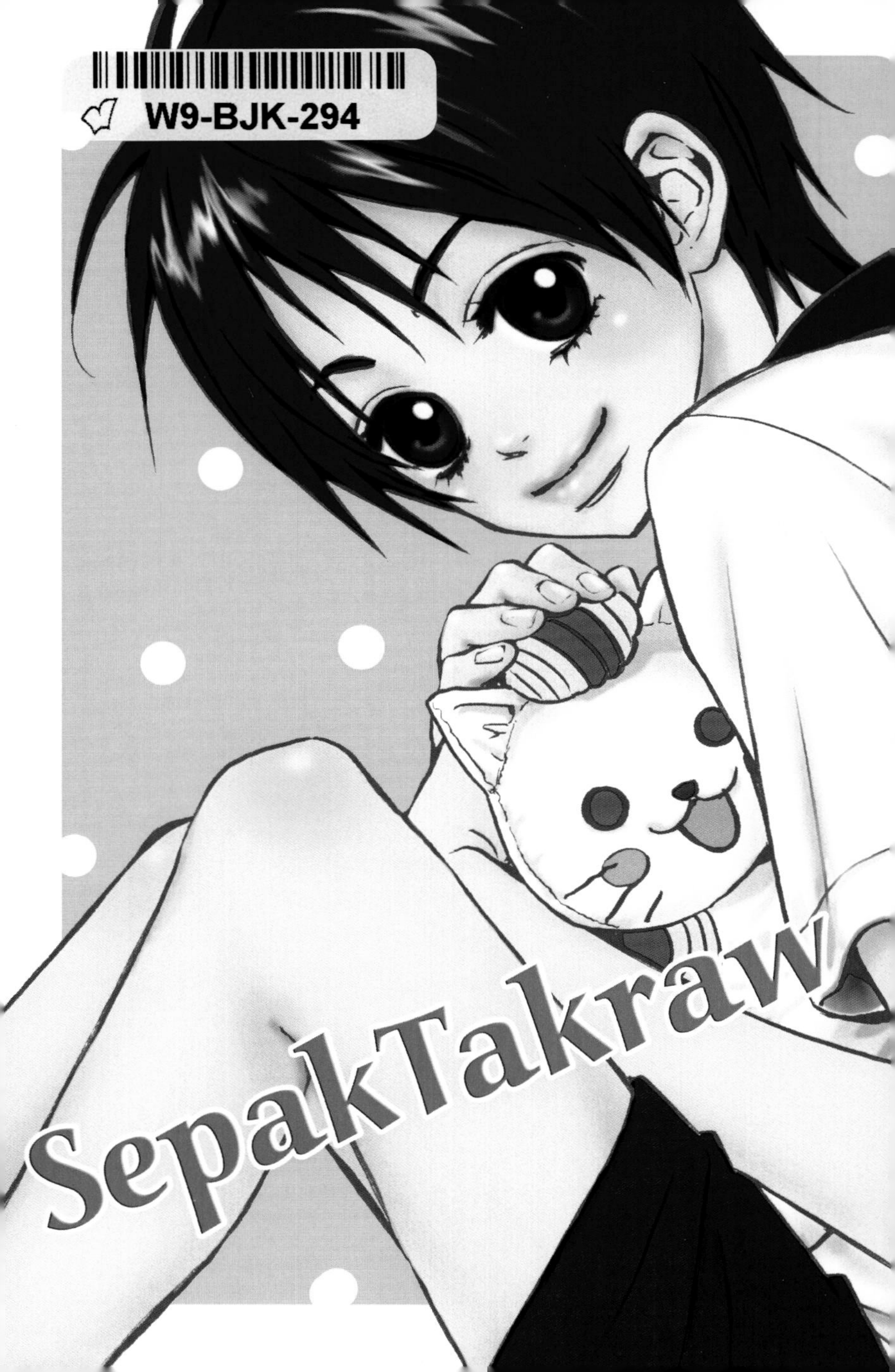
SepakTakraw

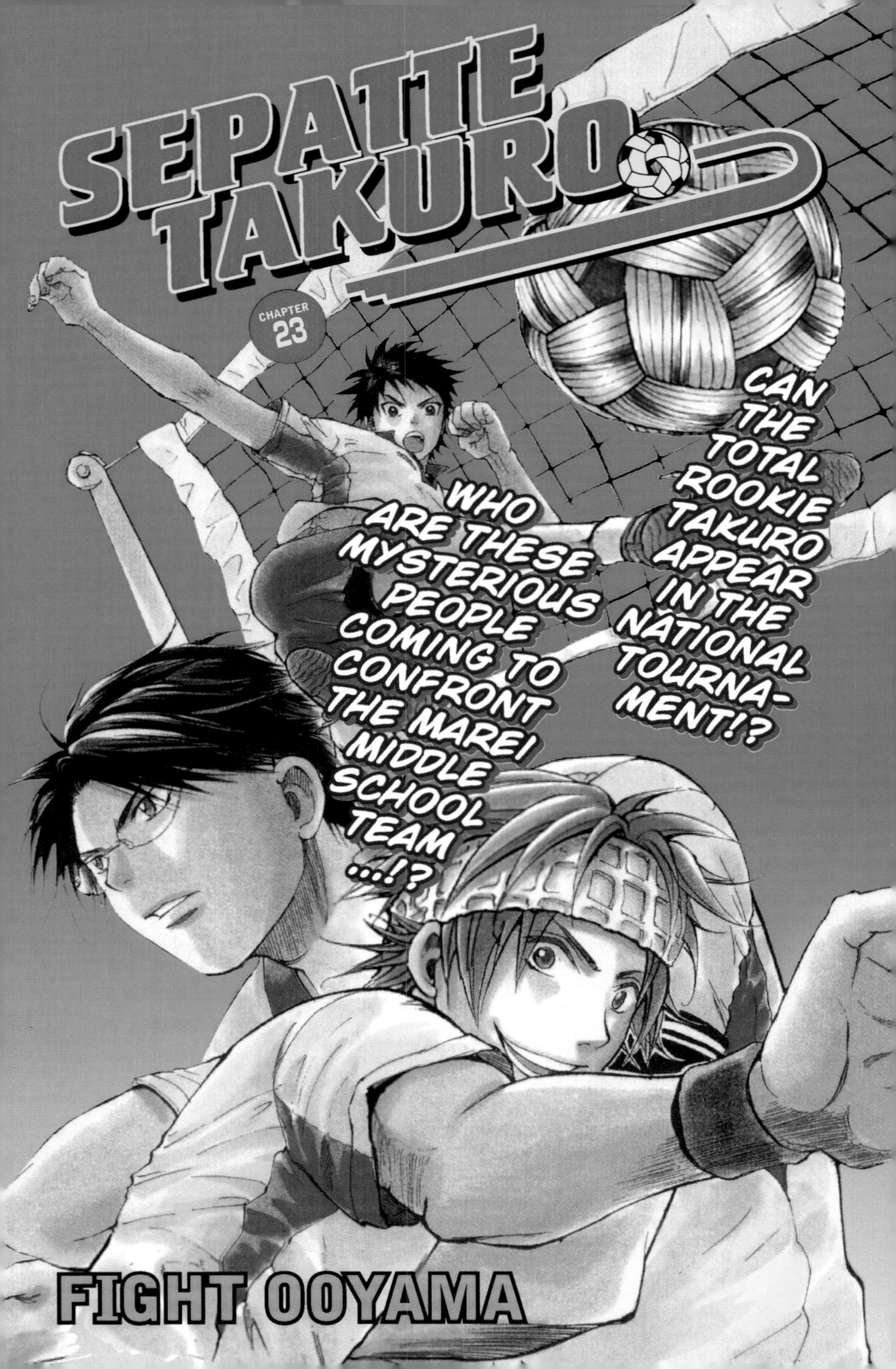
SEPATTE TAKURO
CHAPTER 23
CAN THE TOTAL ROOKIE TAKURO APPEAR IN THE NATIONAL TOURNA-MENT!?
WHO ARE THESE MYSTERIOUS PEOPLE COMING TO CONFRONT THE MAREI MIDDLE SCHOOL TEAM ...!?
FIGHT OOYAMA

My Girlfriend's a GEEK

3

RIZE SHINBA
STORY: PENTABU

My Girlfriend's a GEEK

AT A ★ GLANCE

♥THE STORY SO FAR♥

College student Taiga Mutou is in a loving relationship with his new, older girlfriend Yuiko-san . . . except for the fact that she's a *fujoshi*! First she starts calling him "Sebas" (short for "Sebastian") because he "feels like a butler," and before you know it, she's got him writing a Boys' Love novel based on her favorite coupling! Taiga's life is growing more "rotten" by the day! Next comes the introduction of an oddly classy rival for Yuiko's affections. Will Taiga's love life ever find peace and tranquility again!?

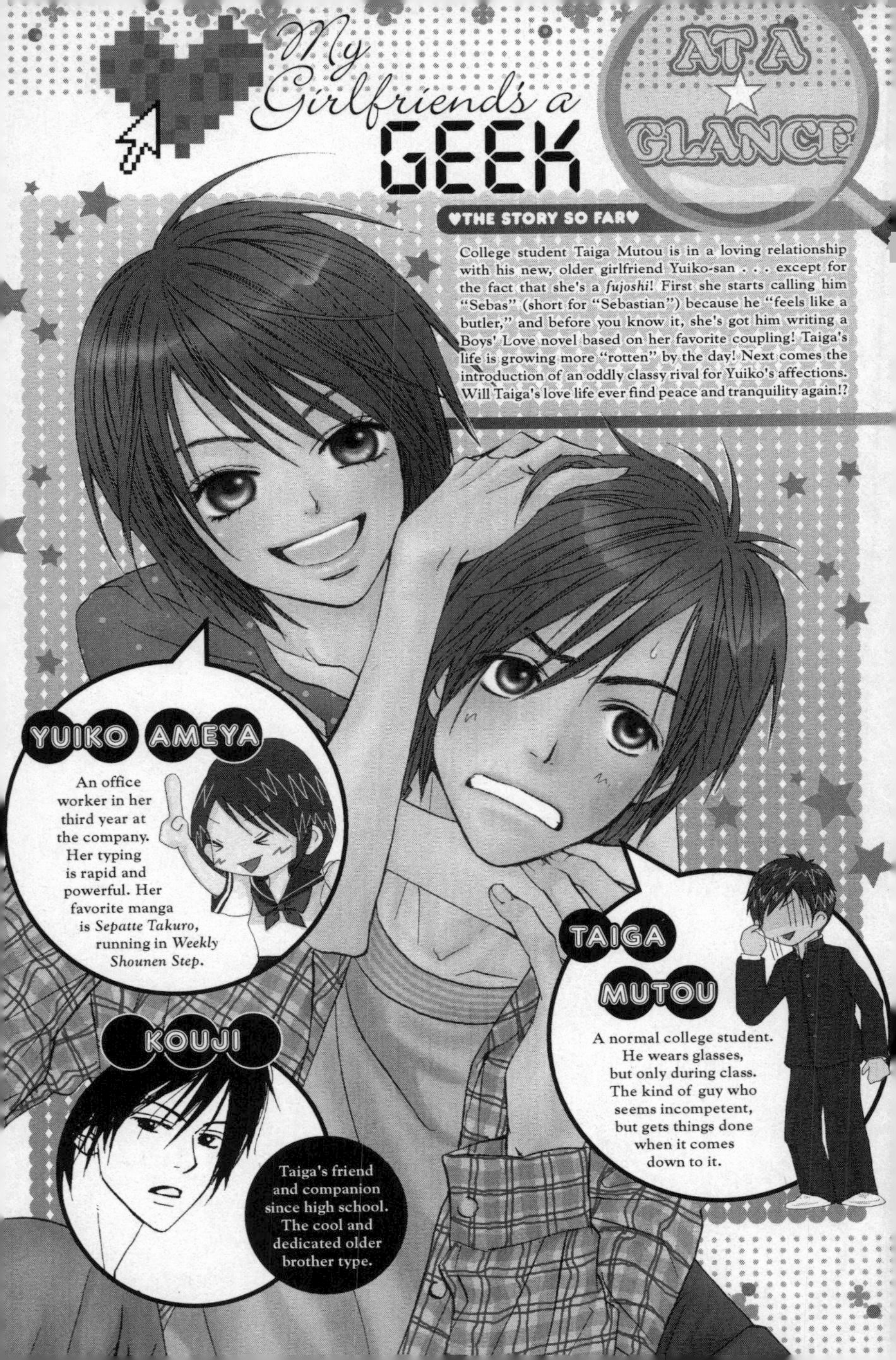

YUIKO AMEYA

An office worker in her third year at the company. Her typing is rapid and powerful. Her favorite manga is *Sepatte Takuro*, running in *Weekly Shounen Step*.

TAIGA MUTOU

A normal college student. He wears glasses, but only during class. The kind of guy who seems incompetent, but gets things done when it comes down to it.

KOUJI

Taiga's friend and companion since high school. The cool and dedicated older brother type.

FUJOSHI NEWS

YUIKO-SAN'S LATEST OBSESSIONS: A DIGEST♥

SHOUNEN MANGA

SEPATTE TAKURO

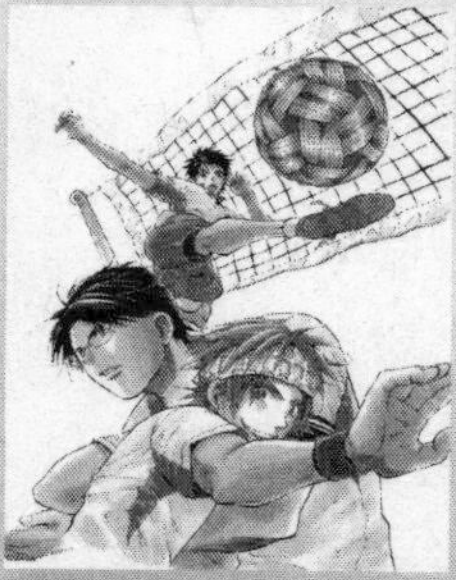

A SHOOTING STAR IN THE WORLD OF SHOUNEN MANGA CURRENTLY BEING SERIALIZED IN *WEEKLY SHOUNEN STEP*. GLOOMY AND WITHDRAWN MIDDLE SCHOOLER TAKURO SEBA IS POSSESSED BY THE MYSTERIOUS SEPA SPIRIT. WITH HIS CAPTAIN AND TEAMMATES OF THE MAREI MIDDLE SCHOOL SEPAK TAKRAW TEAM, HE SETS HIS SIGHTS ON THE NATIONAL TOURNAMENT. IT'S A PERFECTLY NORMAL AND TRADITIONAL SHOUNEN MANGA, BUT FOR SOME REASON, TAIGA IS BEING FORCED TO WRITE A CAPTAIN x TAKURO B.L. NOVEL.

GAME FOR GIRLS

DREAMING NOUVELLE MARIE

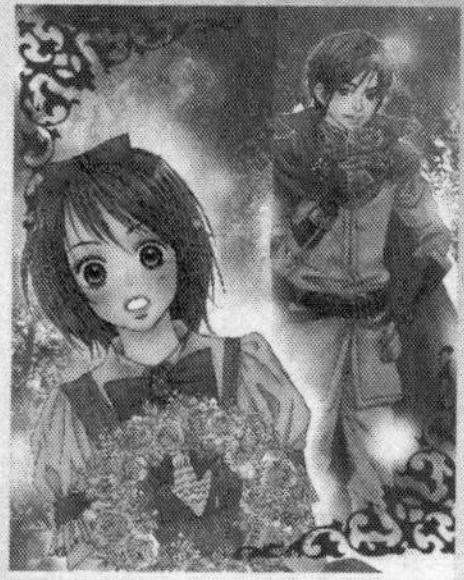

AN INSTALLMENT OF THE ETERNAL SWEET ROMANCE SERIES ("ESROMA" AMONG FANS), A WILDLY POPULAR LINE OF GAMES FOR GIRLS. THE HEROINE, MARIE HANABISHI, IS A POTENTIAL BRIDE FOR A LIST OF HANDSOME PRINCES FROM ANOTHER WORLD. YUIKO-SAN'S FAVORITE IS PRINCE MAXIMILLIAN. BUT HER TOP COUPLING IS ANSELM (THE SMART ONE WITH GLASSES) x HEROLD (THE DARK AND HANDSOME ONE).

THESE ARE BOTH ORIGINAL TO THE MANGA VERSION OF "MY GIRLFRIEND'S A GEEK"! YOU WON'T FIND THEM ANYWHERE ELSE! ♡

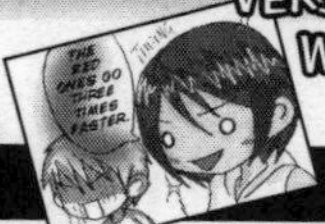
THE RED ONES GO THREE TIMES FASTER.

HERE'S THE ORIGINAL★

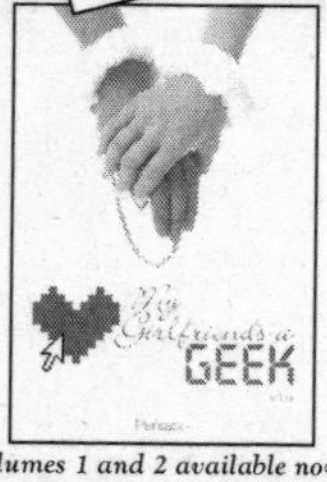

Volumes 1 and 2 available now!

MY GIRLFRIEND'S A GEEK
WRITTEN BY PENTABU

A love diary about a *fujoshi* and a normal man? The infamous blog has made the transition to paperback! Pentabu lovingly dishes out withering smackdowns to every nerdy *fujoshi* comment his girlfriend makes. Feel the sympathy course through your veins as you witness his daily struggles!
If you haven't checked out the inspiration for this manga, what are you waiting for?♥

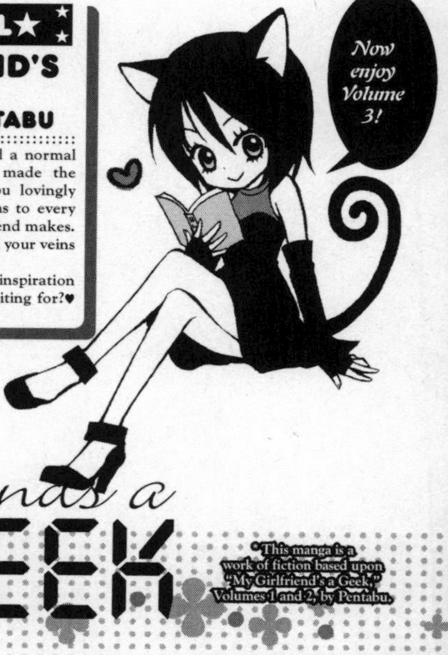
Now enjoy Volume 3!

My Girlfriend's a GEEK

*This manga is a work of fiction based upon "My Girlfriend's a Geek," Volumes 1 and 2, by Pentabu.

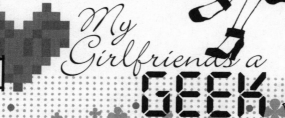

CONTENTS ♥

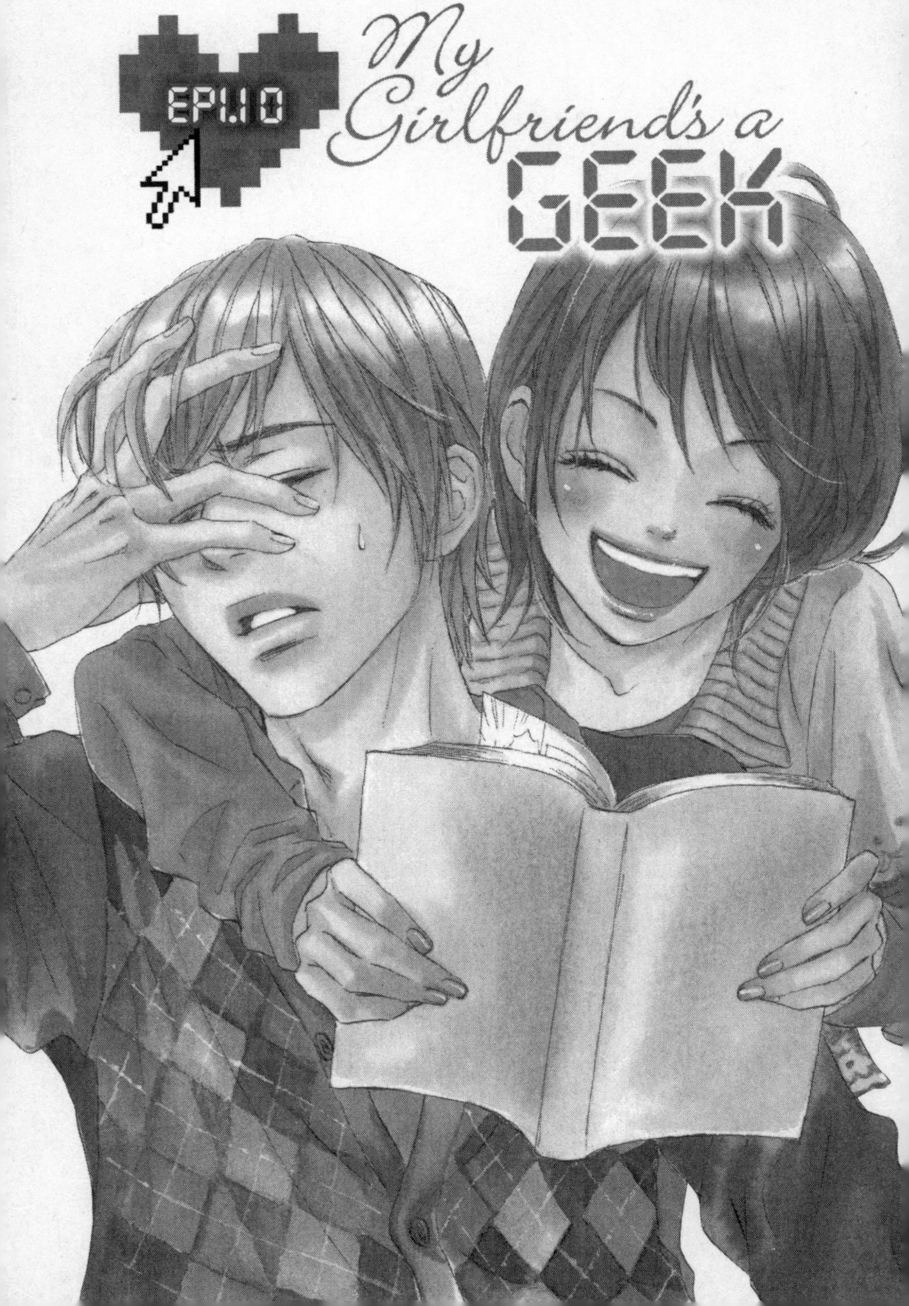
EPI.1 0
My Girlfriend's a GEEK

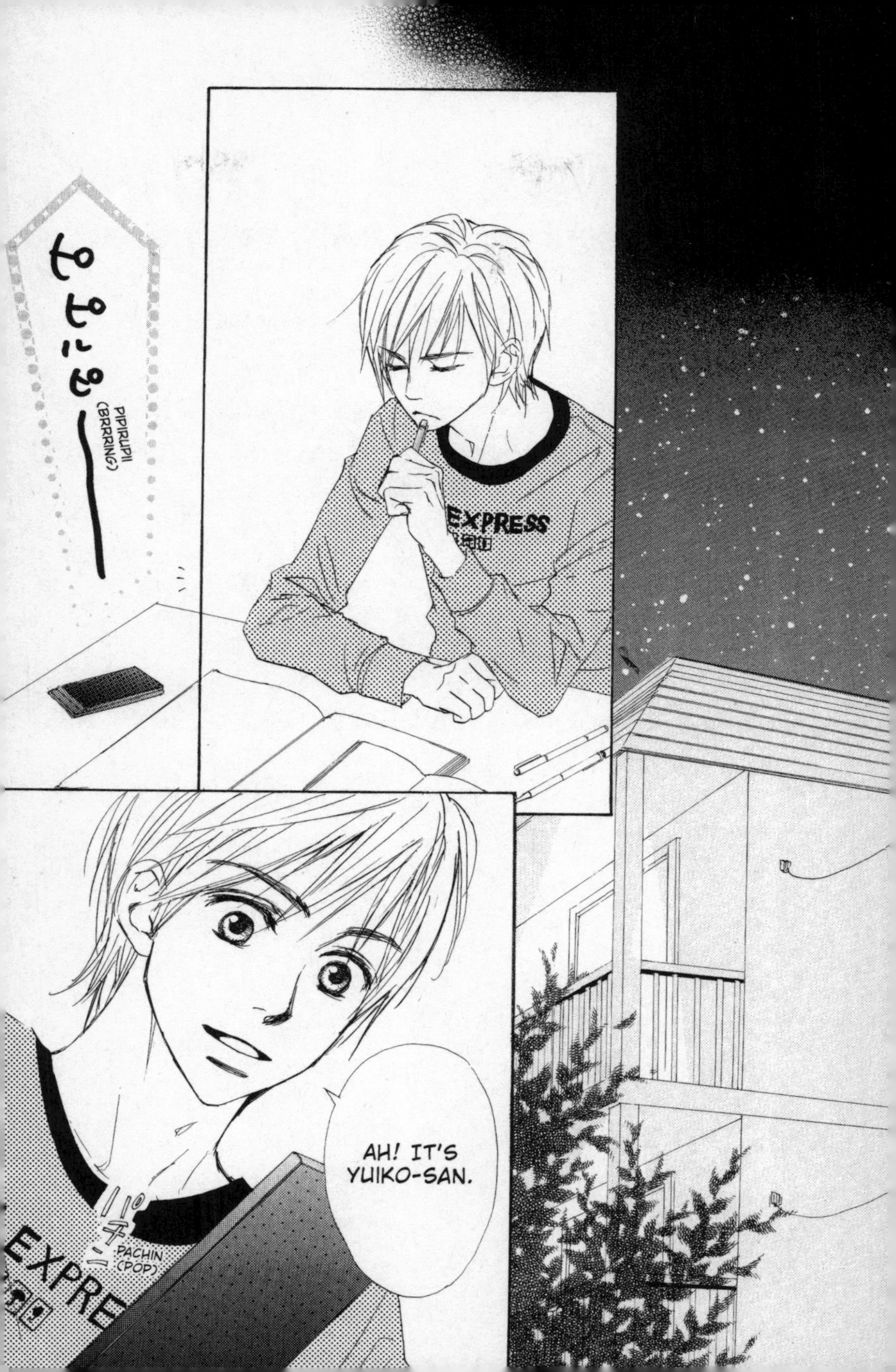
PIPIRUPII (BRRRING)
AH! IT'S YUIKO-SAN.
PACHIN (POP)

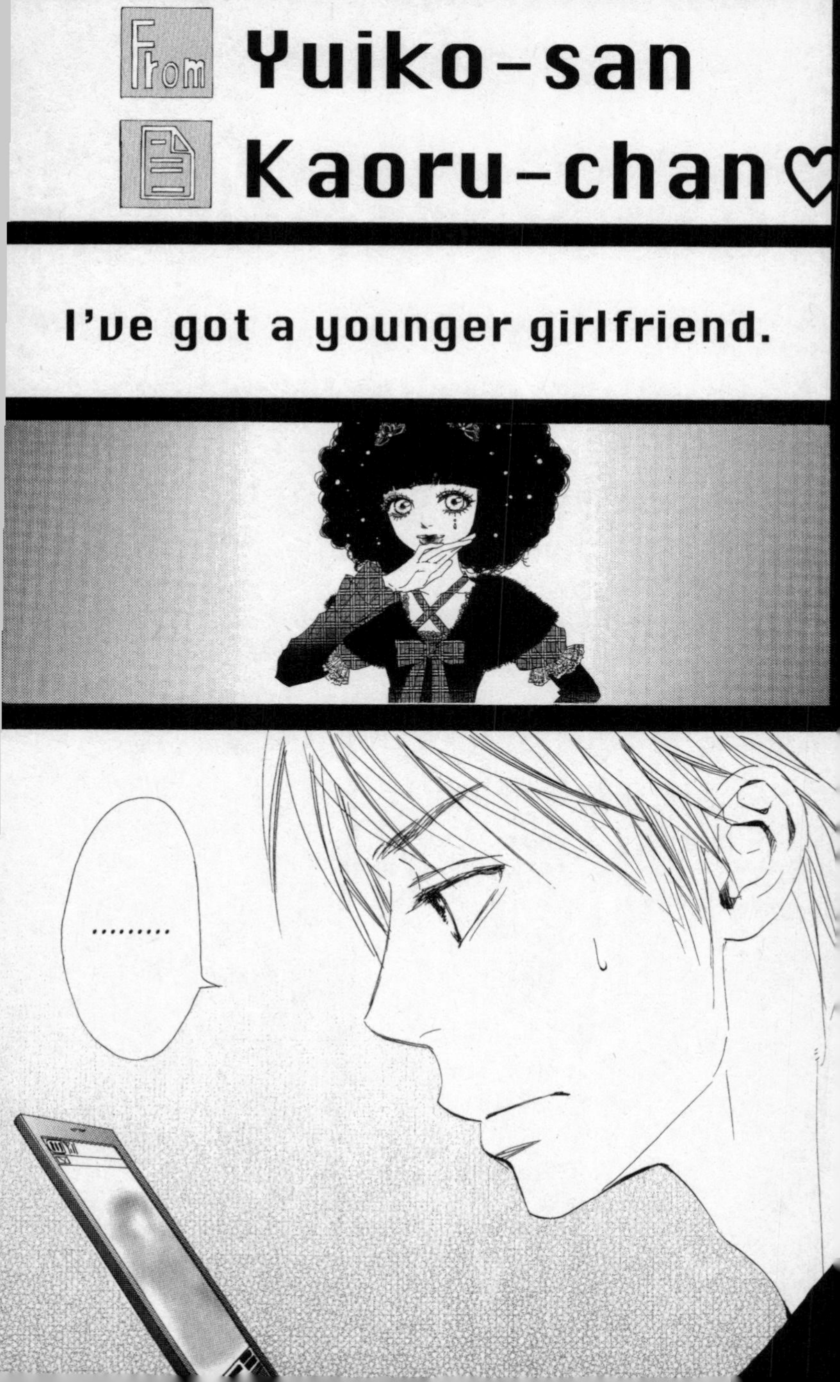
From Yuiko-san
Kaoru-chan♡
I've got a younger girlfriend.
....

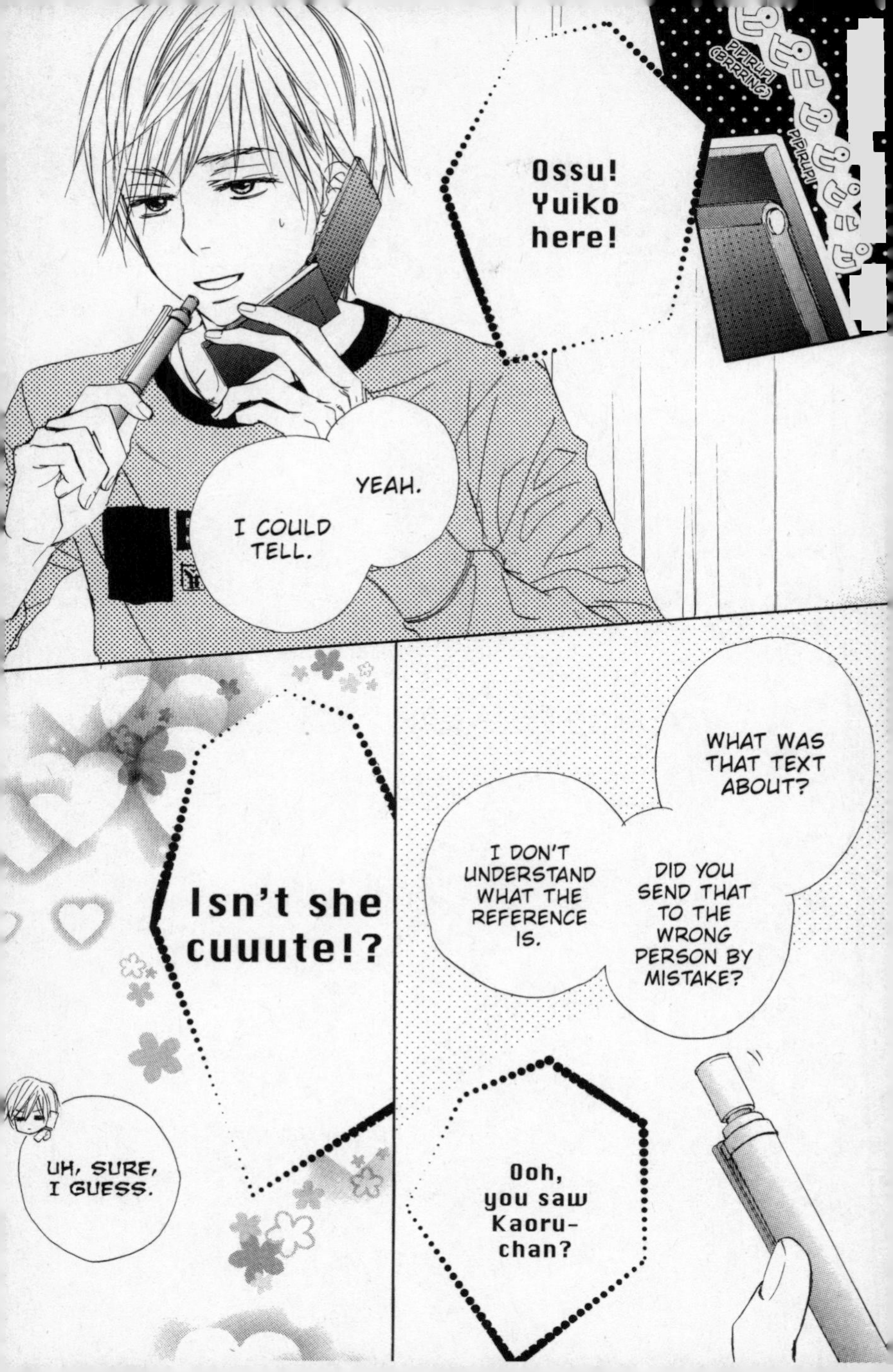

PIPIRUPI (BRRRING)
PIPIRUPI
Ossu! Yuiko here!
YEAH.
I COULD TELL.
WHAT WAS THAT TEXT ABOUT?
DID YOU SEND THAT TO THE WRONG PERSON BY MISTAKE?
I DON'T UNDERSTAND WHAT THE REFERENCE IS.
Ooh, you saw Kaoru-chan?
Isn't she cuuute!?
UH, SURE, I GUESS.

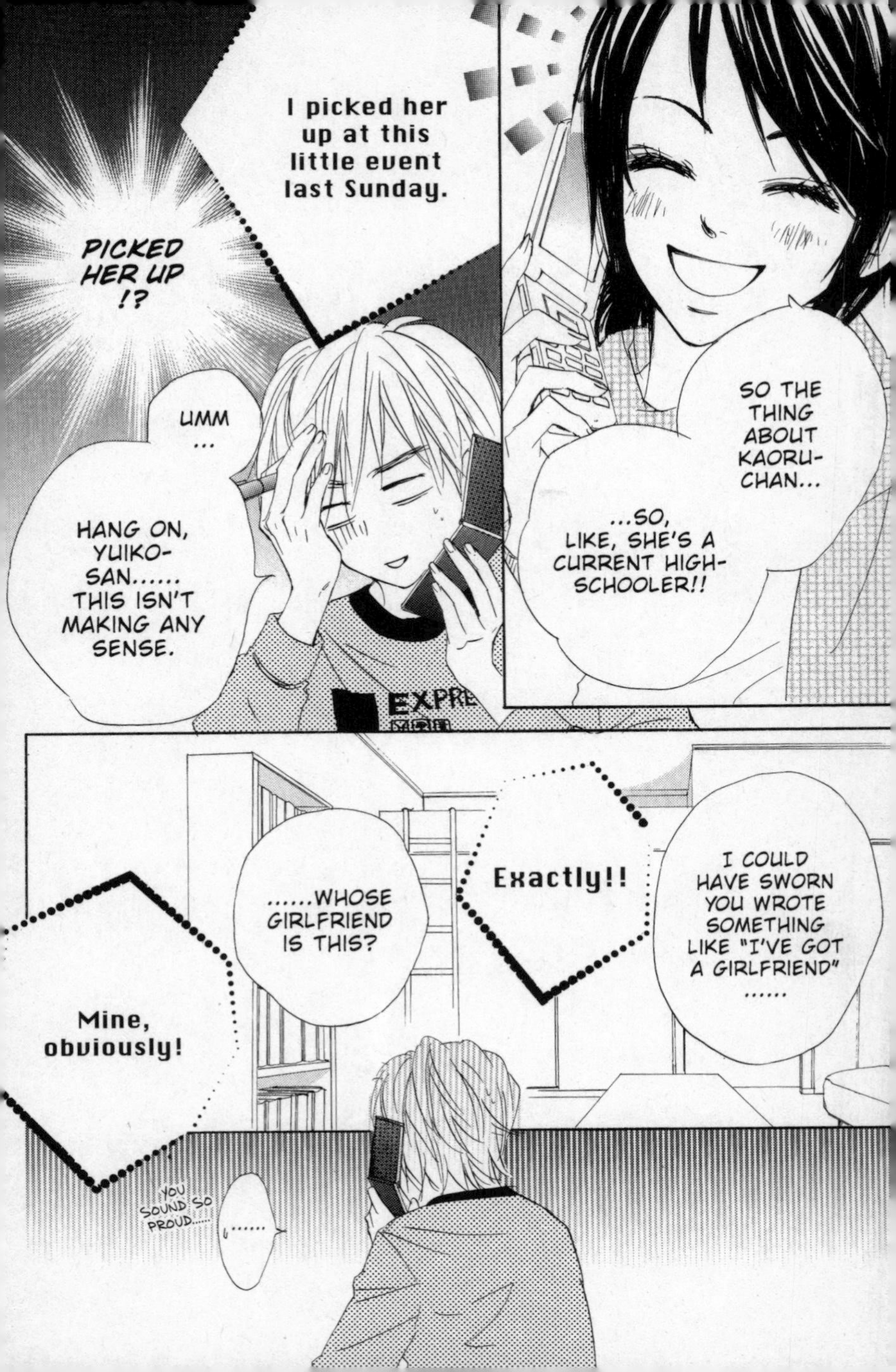
SO THE THING ABOUT KAORU-CHAN...
...SO, LIKE, SHE'S A CURRENT HIGH-SCHOOLER!!
I picked her up at this little event last Sunday.
PICKED HER UP !?
UMM ...
HANG ON, YUIKO-SAN...... THIS ISN'T MAKING ANY SENSE.
I COULD HAVE SWORN YOU WROTE SOMETHING LIKE "I'VE GOT A GIRLFRIEND" ......
Exactly!!
......WHOSE GIRLFRIEND IS THIS?
Mine, obviously!
YOU SOUND SO PROUD......
......

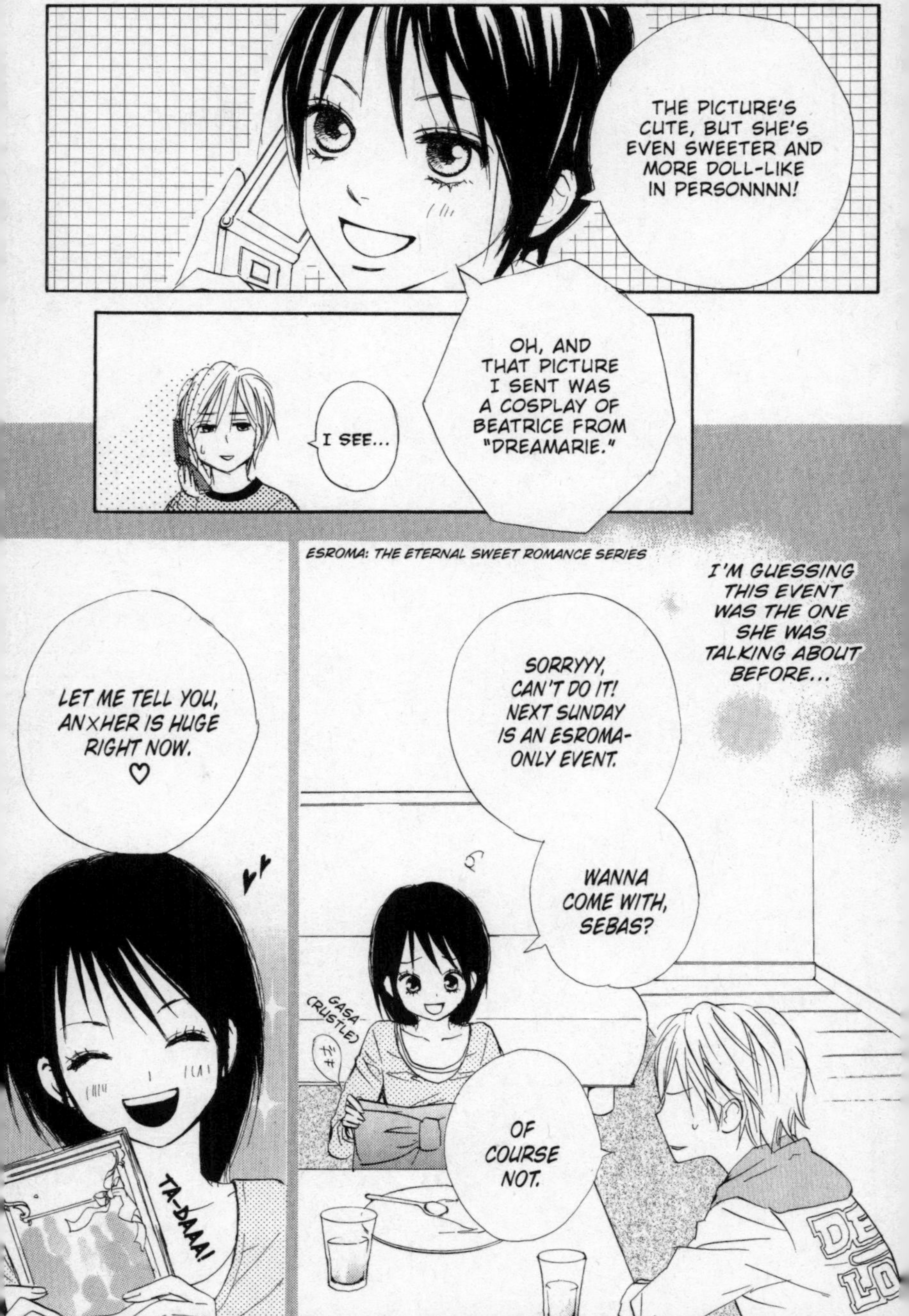
THE PICTURE'S CUTE, BUT SHE'S EVEN SWEETER AND MORE DOLL-LIKE IN PERSONNNN!
OH, AND THAT PICTURE I SENT WAS A COSPLAY OF BEATRICE FROM "DREAMARIE."
I SEE...
ESROMA: THE ETERNAL SWEET ROMANCE SERIES
I'M GUESSING THIS EVENT WAS THE ONE SHE WAS TALKING ABOUT BEFORE...
SORRYYY, CAN'T DO IT! NEXT SUNDAY IS AN ESROMA-ONLY EVENT.
WANNA COME WITH, SEBAS?
GASA (RUSTLE)
OF COURSE NOT.
LET ME TELL YOU, AN×HER IS HUGE RIGHT NOW. ♡
TA-DAAA!

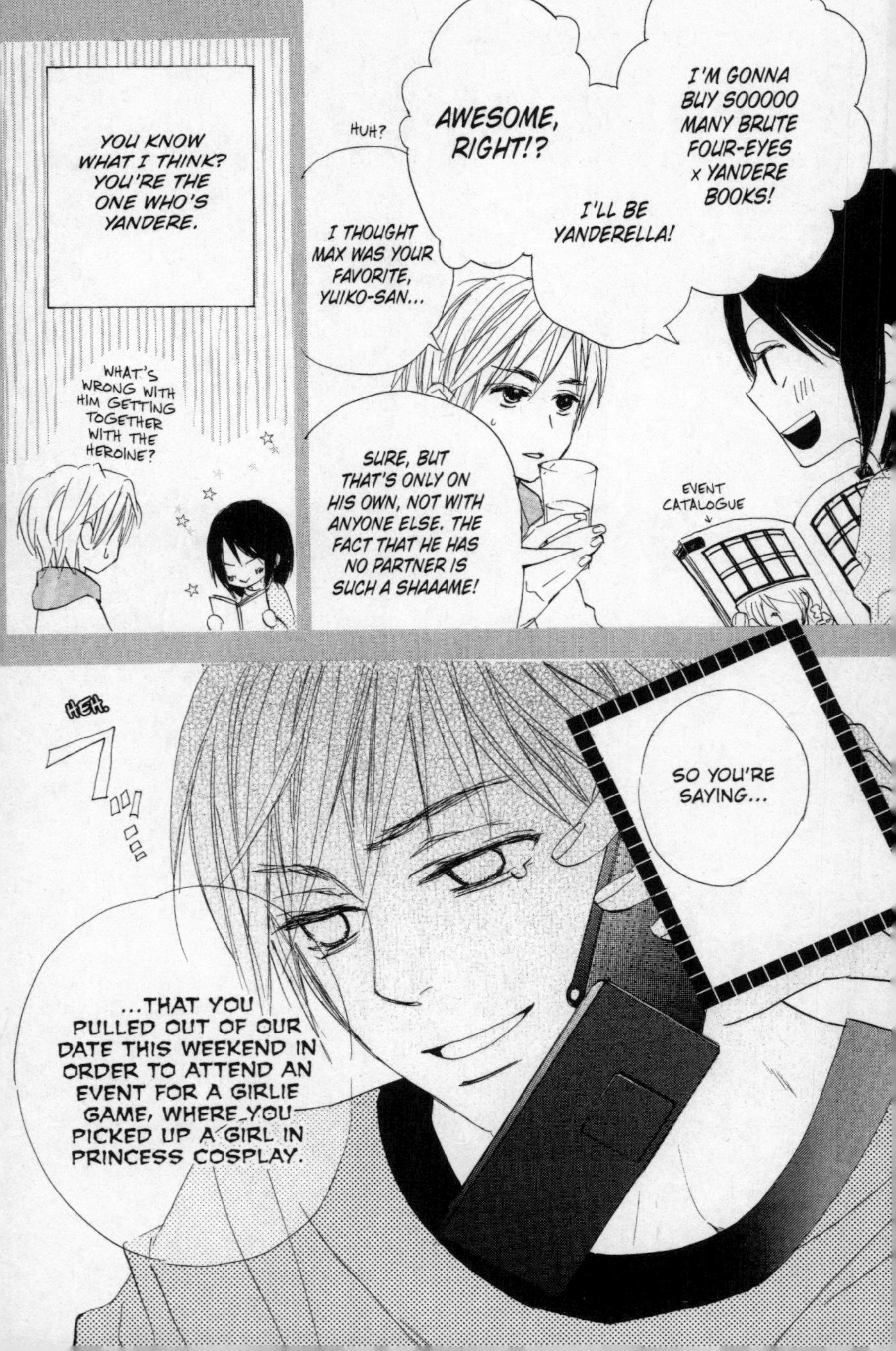
I'M GONNA BUY SOOOOO MANY BRUTE FOUR-EYES x YANDERE BOOKS!
AWESOME, RIGHT!?
I'LL BE YANDERELLA!
HUH?
I THOUGHT MAX WAS YOUR FAVORITE, YUIKO-SAN...
EVENT CATALOGUE
SURE, BUT THAT'S ONLY ON HIS OWN, NOT WITH ANYONE ELSE. THE FACT THAT HE HAS NO PARTNER IS SUCH A SHAAAME!
YOU KNOW WHAT I THINK? YOU'RE THE ONE WHO'S YANDERE.
WHAT'S WRONG WITH HIM GETTING TOGETHER WITH THE HEROINE?
SO YOU'RE SAYING...
HEH.
...THAT YOU PULLED OUT OF OUR DATE THIS WEEKEND IN ORDER TO ATTEND AN EVENT FOR A GIRLIE GAME, WHERE YOU PICKED UP A GIRL IN PRINCESS COSPLAY.

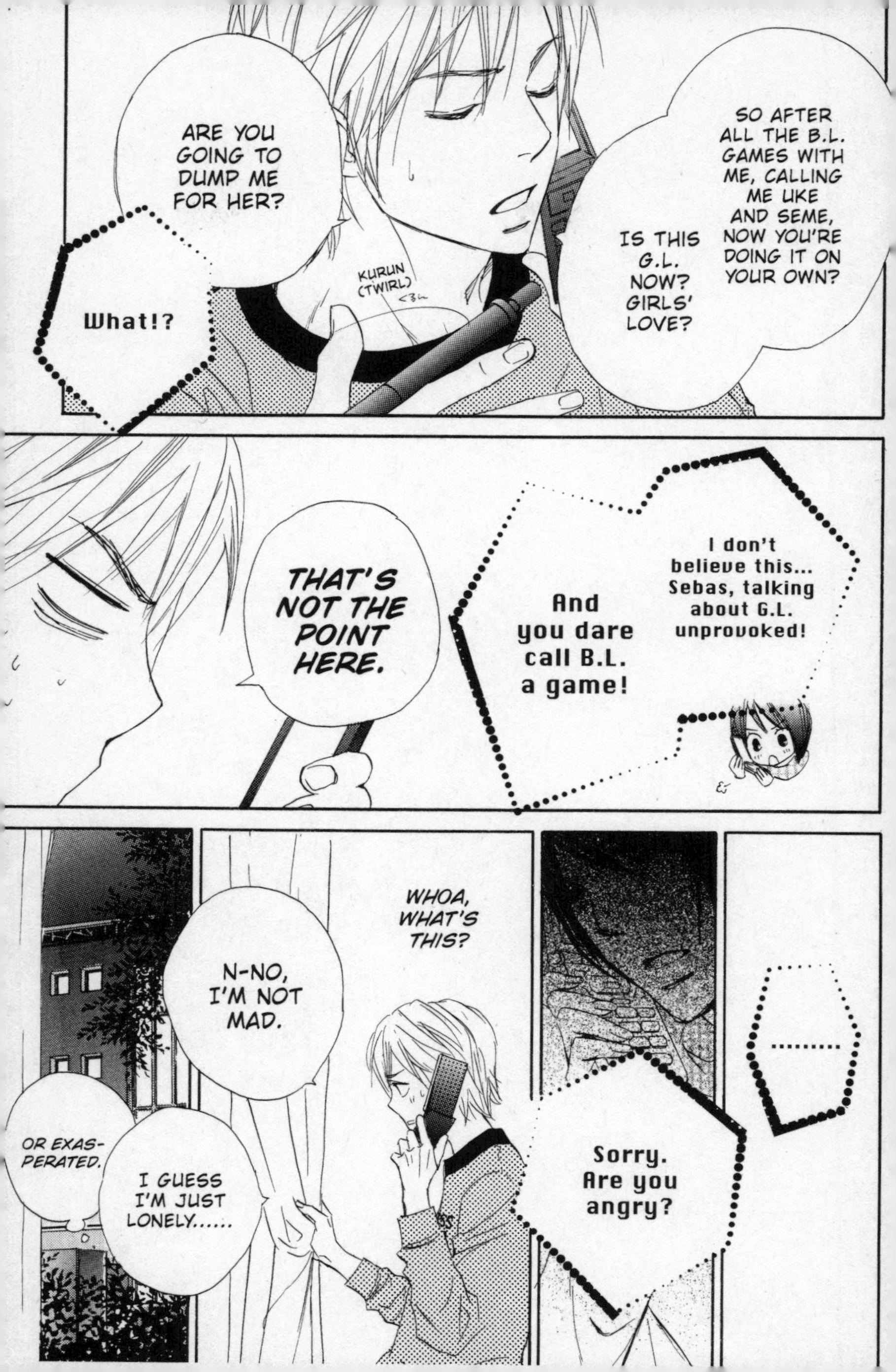
SO AFTER ALL THE B.L. GAMES WITH ME, CALLING ME UKE AND SEME, NOW YOU'RE DOING IT ON YOUR OWN?
IS THIS G.L. NOW? GIRLS' LOVE?
KURUN (TWIRL)
ARE YOU GOING TO DUMP ME FOR HER?
What!?
I don't believe this... Sebas, talking about G.L. unprovoked!
And you dare call B.L. a game!
THAT'S NOT THE POINT HERE.
....
Sorry. Are you angry?
WHOA, WHAT'S THIS?
N-NO, I'M NOT MAD.
I GUESS I'M JUST LONELY......
OR EXASPERATED.

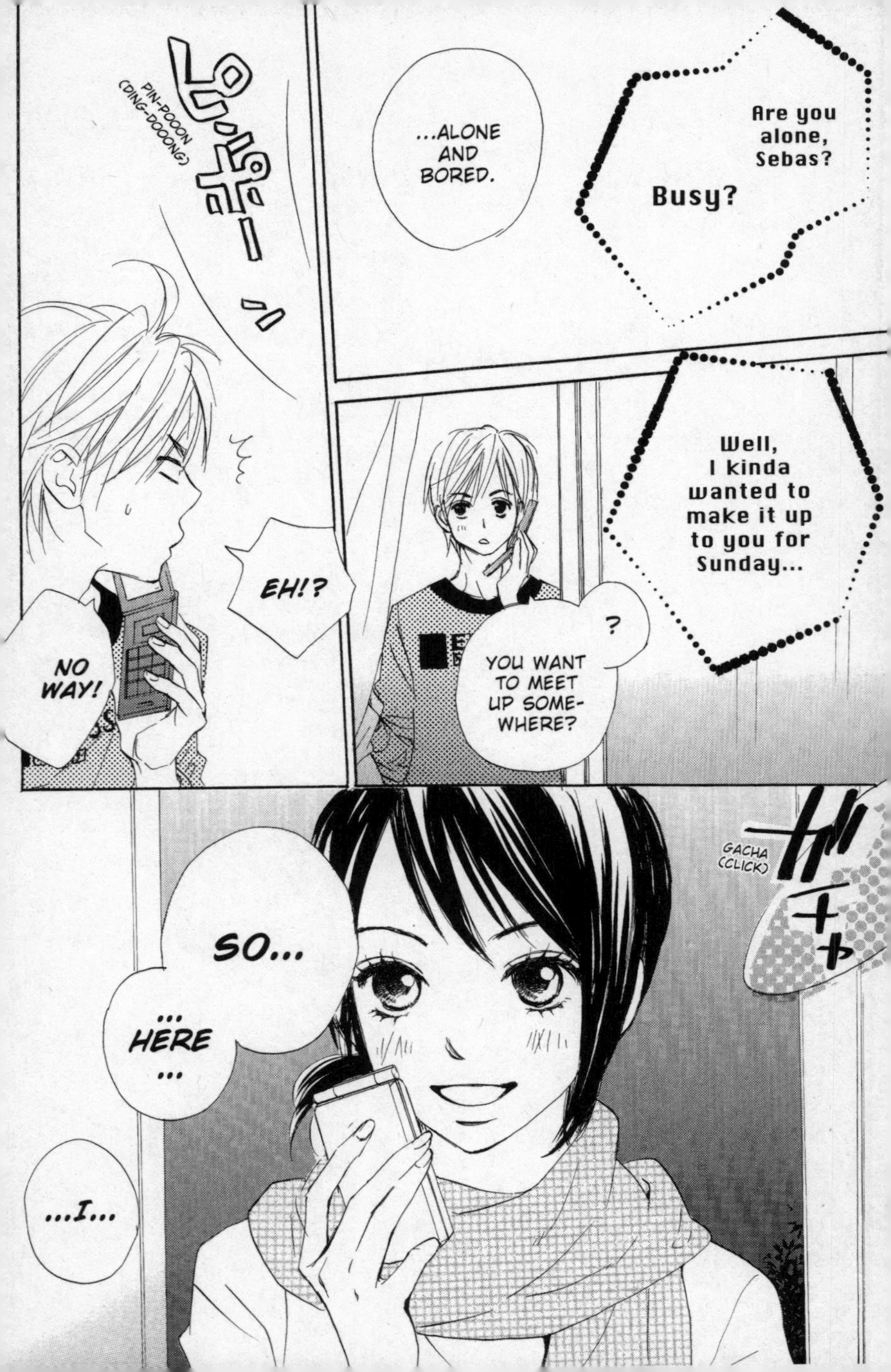
Are you alone, Sebas?
Busy?
...ALONE AND BORED.
Well, I kinda wanted to make it up to you for Sunday...
?
YOU WANT TO MEET UP SOME-WHERE?
PIN-POOON (DING-DOOONG)
EH!?
NO WAY!
GACHA (CLICK)
SO...
... HERE ...
...I...

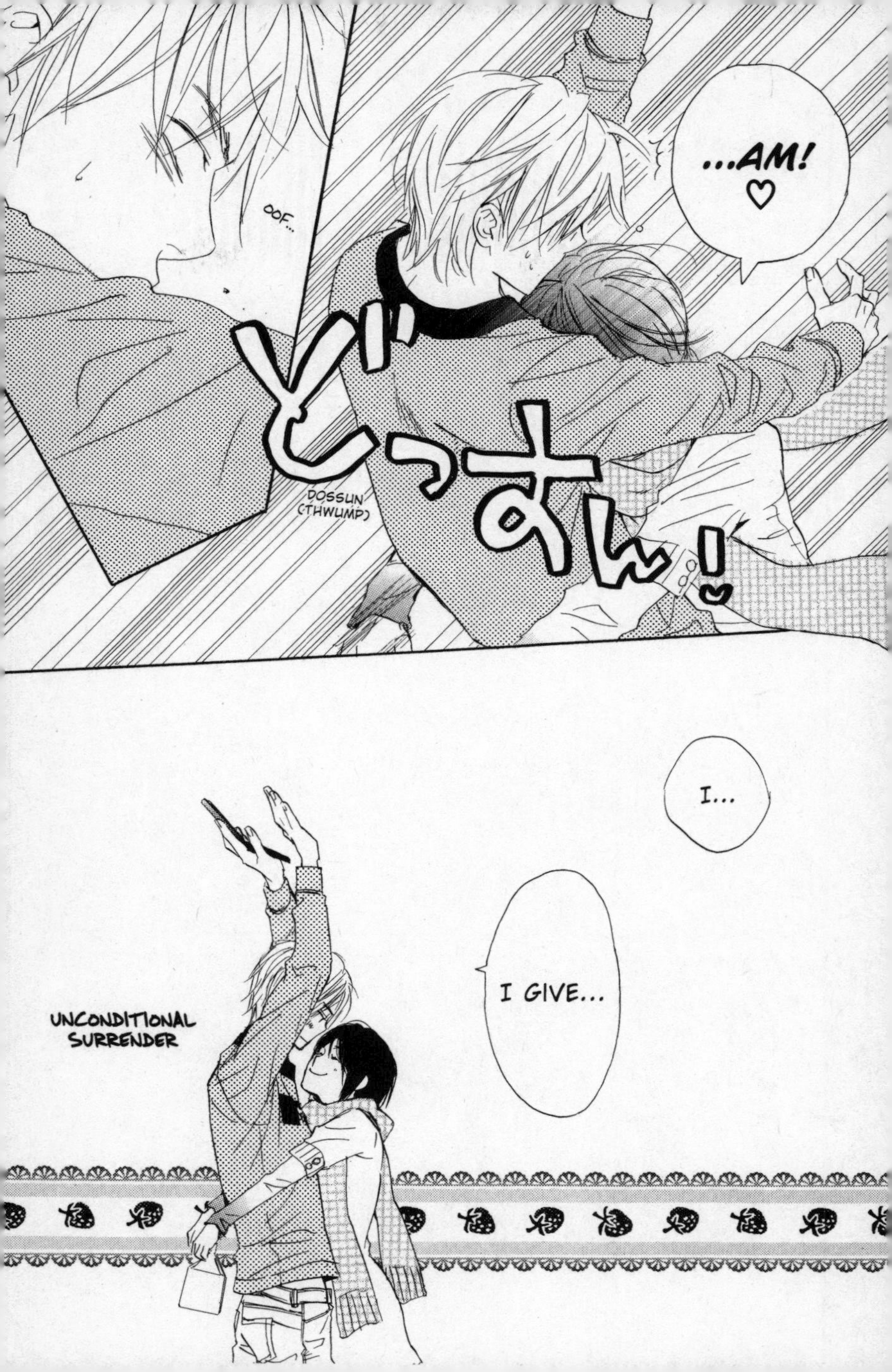
...AM! ♡
どっすん!
DOSSUN (THWUMP)
OOF...
I...
I GIVE...
UNCONDITIONAL SURRENDER

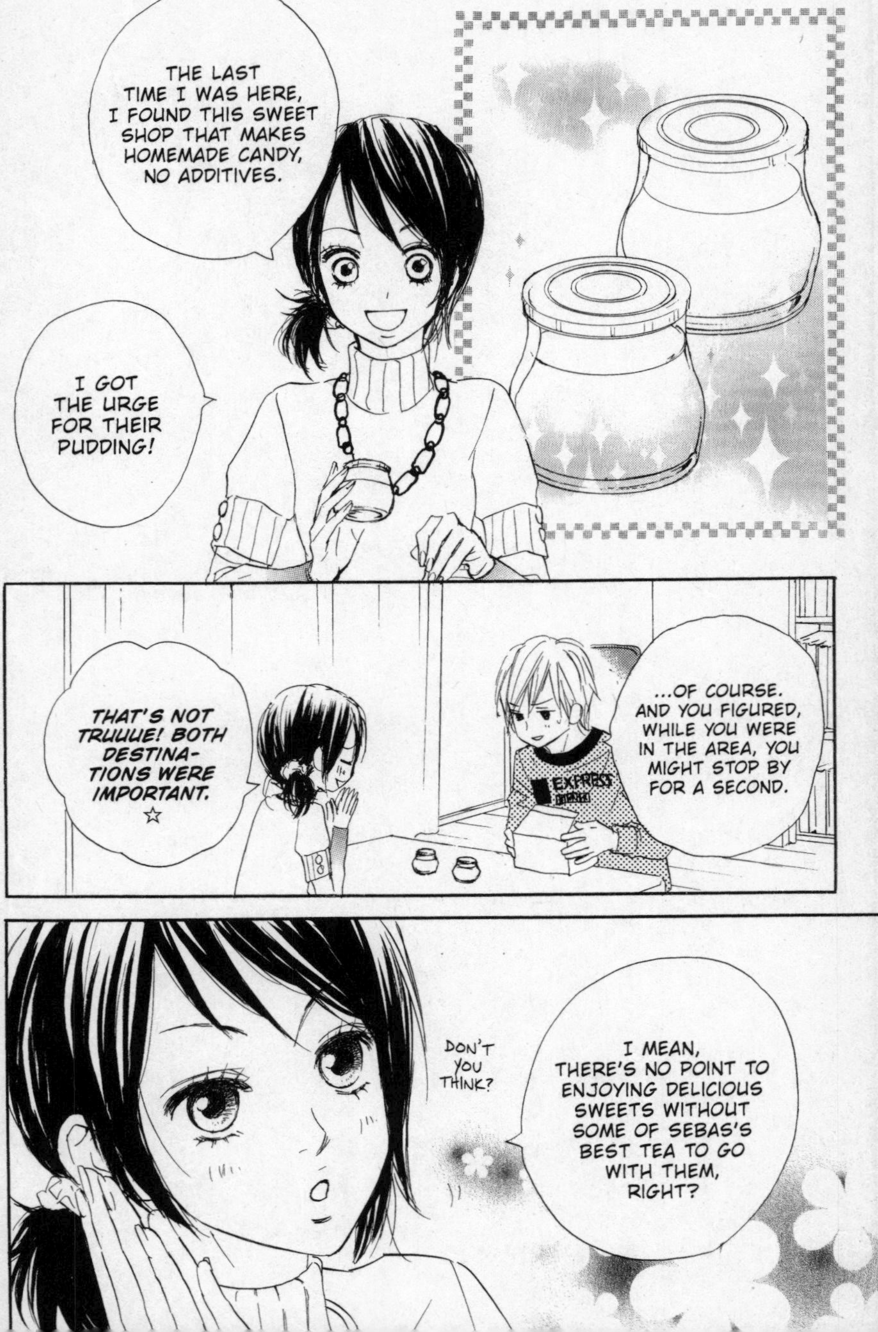
THE LAST TIME I WAS HERE, I FOUND THIS SWEET SHOP THAT MAKES HOMEMADE CANDY, NO ADDITIVES.
I GOT THE URGE FOR THEIR PUDDING!
...OF COURSE. AND YOU FIGURED, WHILE YOU WERE IN THE AREA, YOU MIGHT STOP BY FOR A SECOND.
EXPRESS
THAT'S NOT TRUUUE! BOTH DESTINATIONS WERE IMPORTANT. ☆
I MEAN, THERE'S NO POINT TO ENJOYING DELICIOUS SWEETS WITHOUT SOME OF SEBAS'S BEST TEA TO GO WITH THEM, RIGHT?
DON'T YOU THINK?

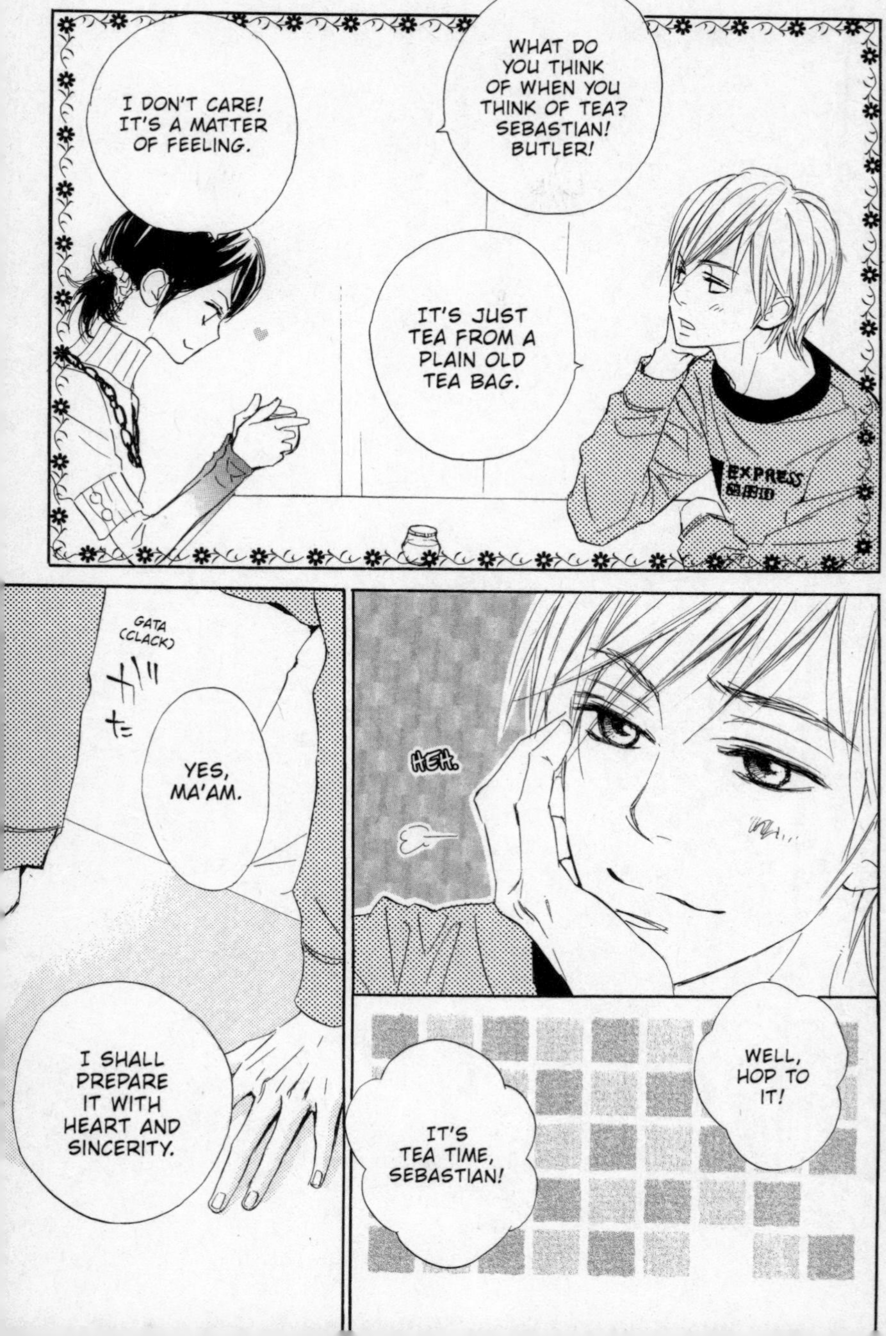
WHAT DO YOU THINK OF WHEN YOU THINK OF TEA? SEBASTIAN! BUTLER!
IT'S JUST TEA FROM A PLAIN OLD TEA BAG.
I DON'T CARE! IT'S A MATTER OF FEELING.
EXPRESS
HEH.
WELL, HOP TO IT!
IT'S TEA TIME, SEBASTIAN!
GATA (CLACK)
YES, MA'AM.
I SHALL PREPARE IT WITH HEART AND SINCERITY.

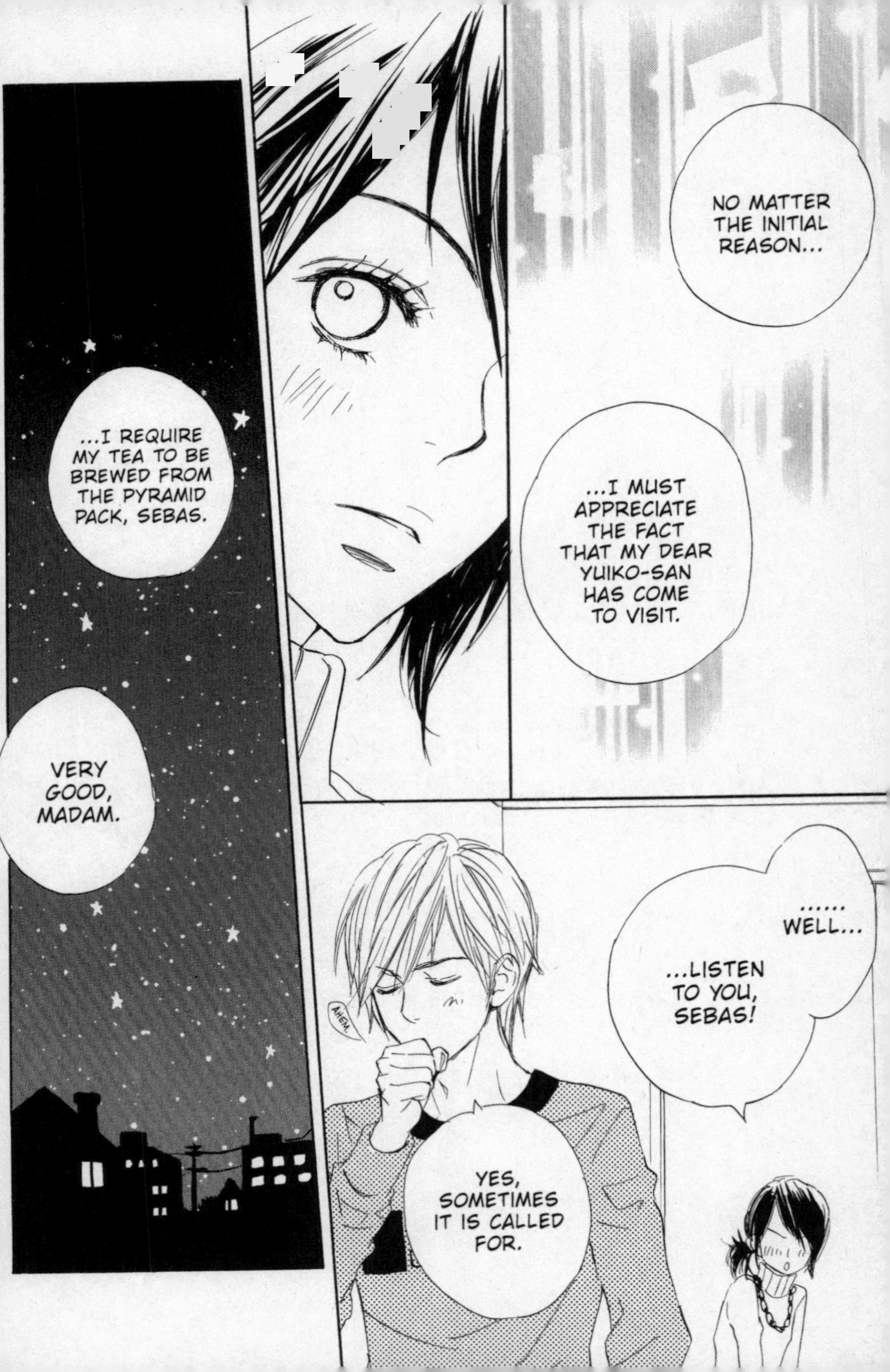
NO MATTER THE INITIAL REASON...
...I MUST APPRECIATE THE FACT THAT MY DEAR YUIKO-SAN HAS COME TO VISIT.
......WELL...
...LISTEN TO YOU, SEBAS!
AHEM
YES, SOMETIMES IT IS CALLED FOR.
...I REQUIRE MY TEA TO BE BREWED FROM THE PYRAMID PACK, SEBAS.
VERY GOOD, MADAM.

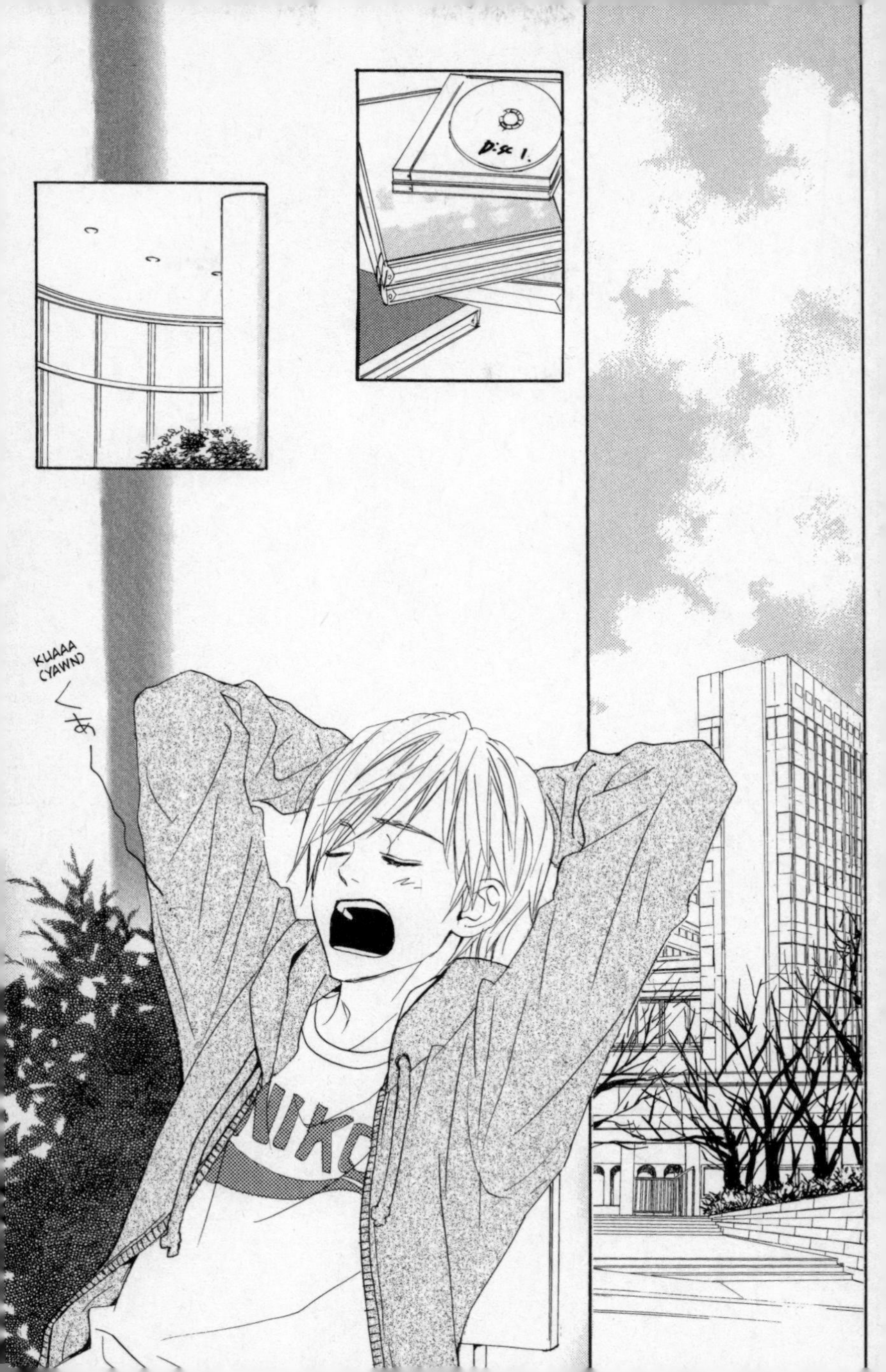
Disc 1.
KUAAA (YAWN)
くあー

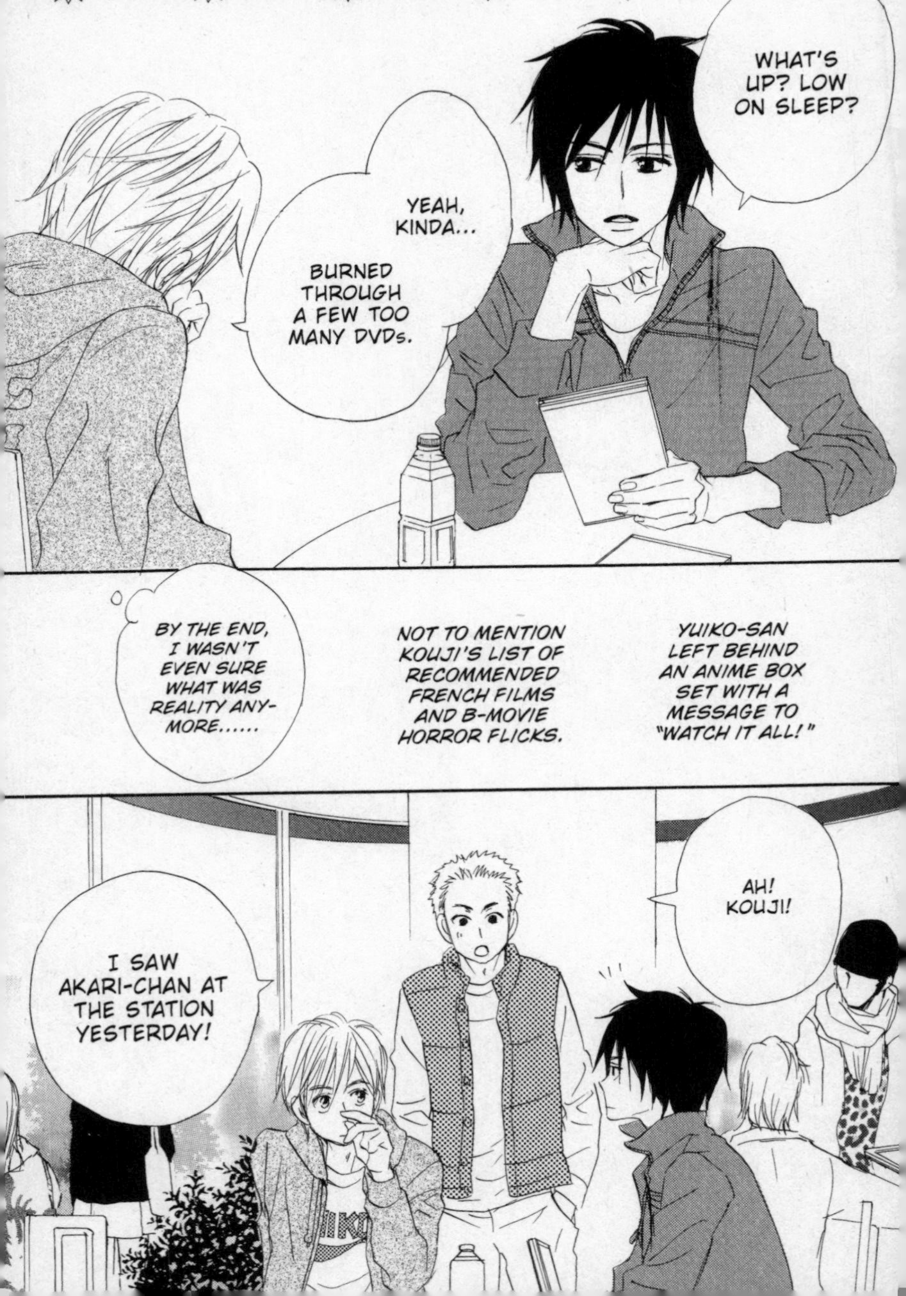
WHAT'S UP? LOW ON SLEEP?
YEAH, KINDA...
BURNED THROUGH A FEW TOO MANY DVDs.
YUIKO-SAN LEFT BEHIND AN ANIME BOX SET WITH A MESSAGE TO "WATCH IT ALL!"
NOT TO MENTION KOUJI'S LIST OF RECOMMENDED FRENCH FILMS AND B-MOVIE HORROR FLICKS.
BY THE END, I WASN'T EVEN SURE WHAT WAS REALITY ANY-MORE......
AH! KOUJI!
I SAW AKARI-CHAN AT THE STATION YESTERDAY!

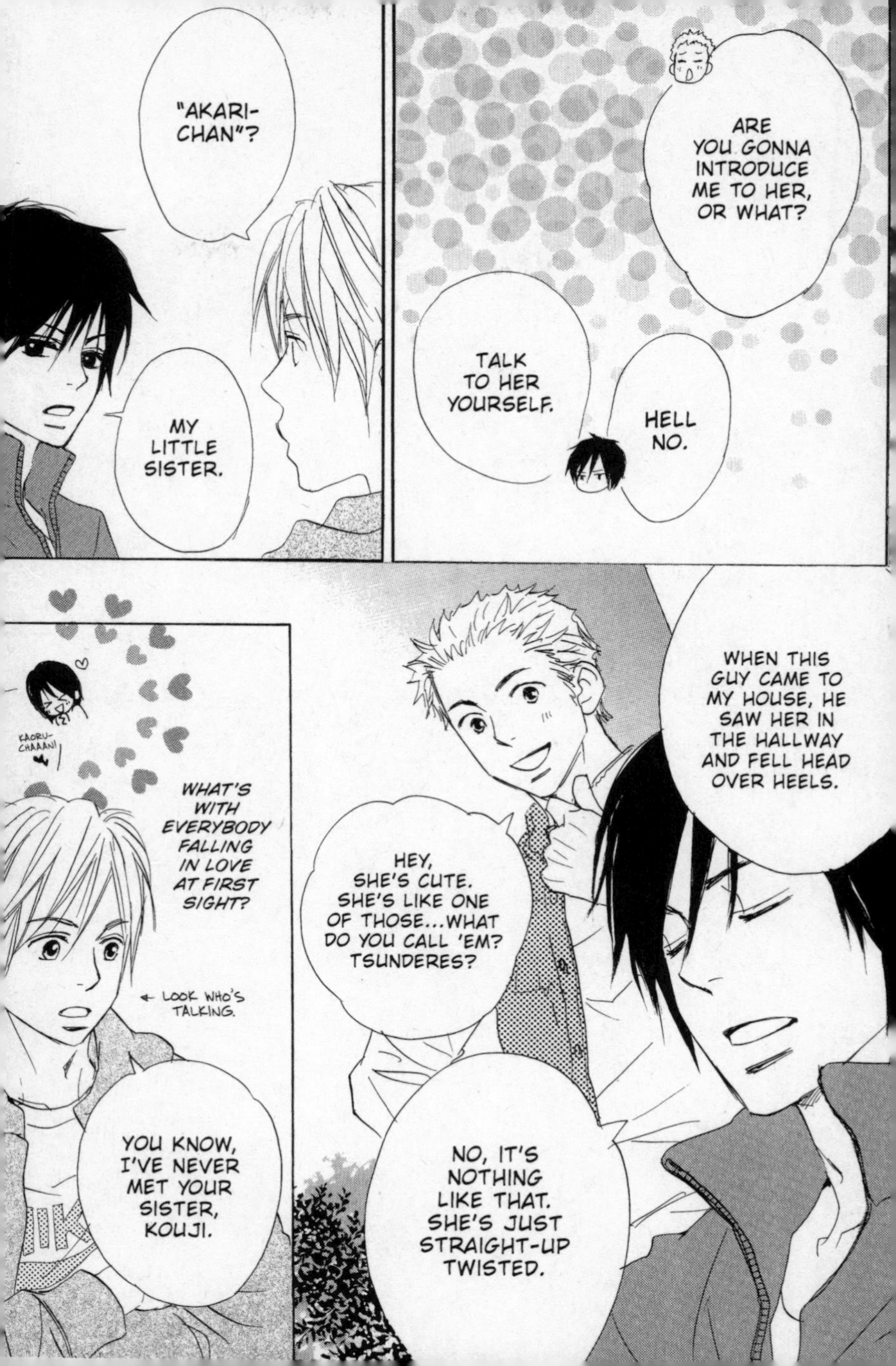
ARE YOU GONNA INTRODUCE ME TO HER, OR WHAT?
HELL NO.
TALK TO HER YOURSELF.
"AKARI-CHAN"?
MY LITTLE SISTER.
WHEN THIS GUY CAME TO MY HOUSE, HE SAW HER IN THE HALLWAY AND FELL HEAD OVER HEELS.
HEY, SHE'S CUTE. SHE'S LIKE ONE OF THOSE...WHAT DO YOU CALL 'EM? TSUNDERES?
NO, IT'S NOTHING LIKE THAT. SHE'S JUST STRAIGHT-UP TWISTED.
KAORU-CHAAAN!
WHAT'S WITH EVERYBODY FALLING IN LOVE AT FIRST SIGHT?
← LOOK WHO'S TALKING.
YOU KNOW, I'VE NEVER MET YOUR SISTER, KOUJI.

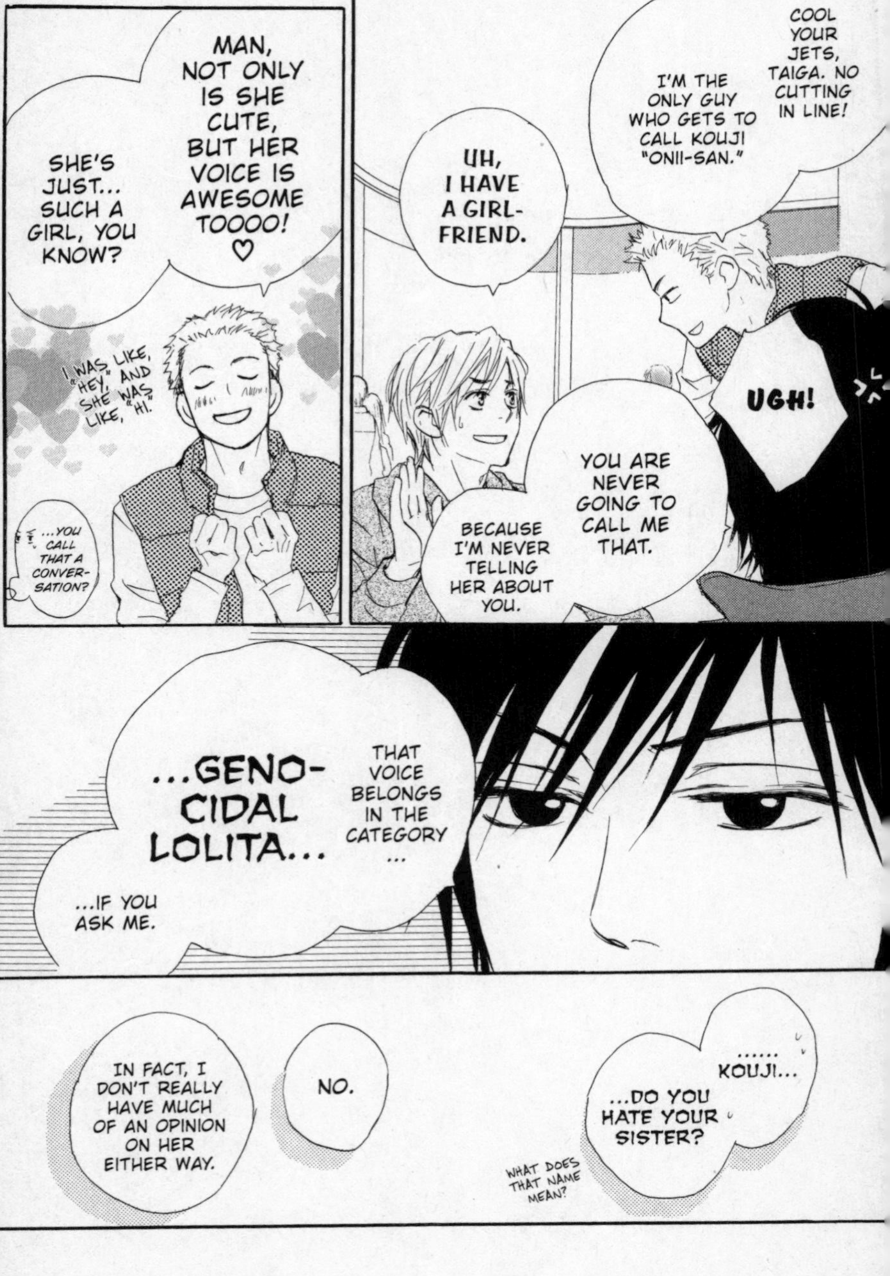
COOL YOUR JETS, TAIGA. NO CUTTING IN LINE!
I'M THE ONLY GUY WHO GETS TO CALL KOUJI "ONII-SAN."
UH, I HAVE A GIRL-FRIEND.
UGH!
YOU ARE NEVER GOING TO CALL ME THAT.
BECAUSE I'M NEVER TELLING HER ABOUT YOU.
MAN, NOT ONLY IS SHE CUTE, BUT HER VOICE IS AWESOME TOOOO! ♡
SHE'S JUST... SUCH A GIRL, YOU KNOW?
I WAS LIKE, "HEY," AND SHE WAS LIKE, "HI."
...YOU CALL THAT A CONVER-SATION?
THAT VOICE BELONGS IN THE CATEGORY ...
...GENO-CIDAL LOLITA...
...IF YOU ASK ME.
...... KOUJI...
...DO YOU HATE YOUR SISTER?
WHAT DOES THAT NAME MEAN?
NO.
IN FACT, I DON'T REALLY HAVE MUCH OF AN OPINION ON HER EITHER WAY.

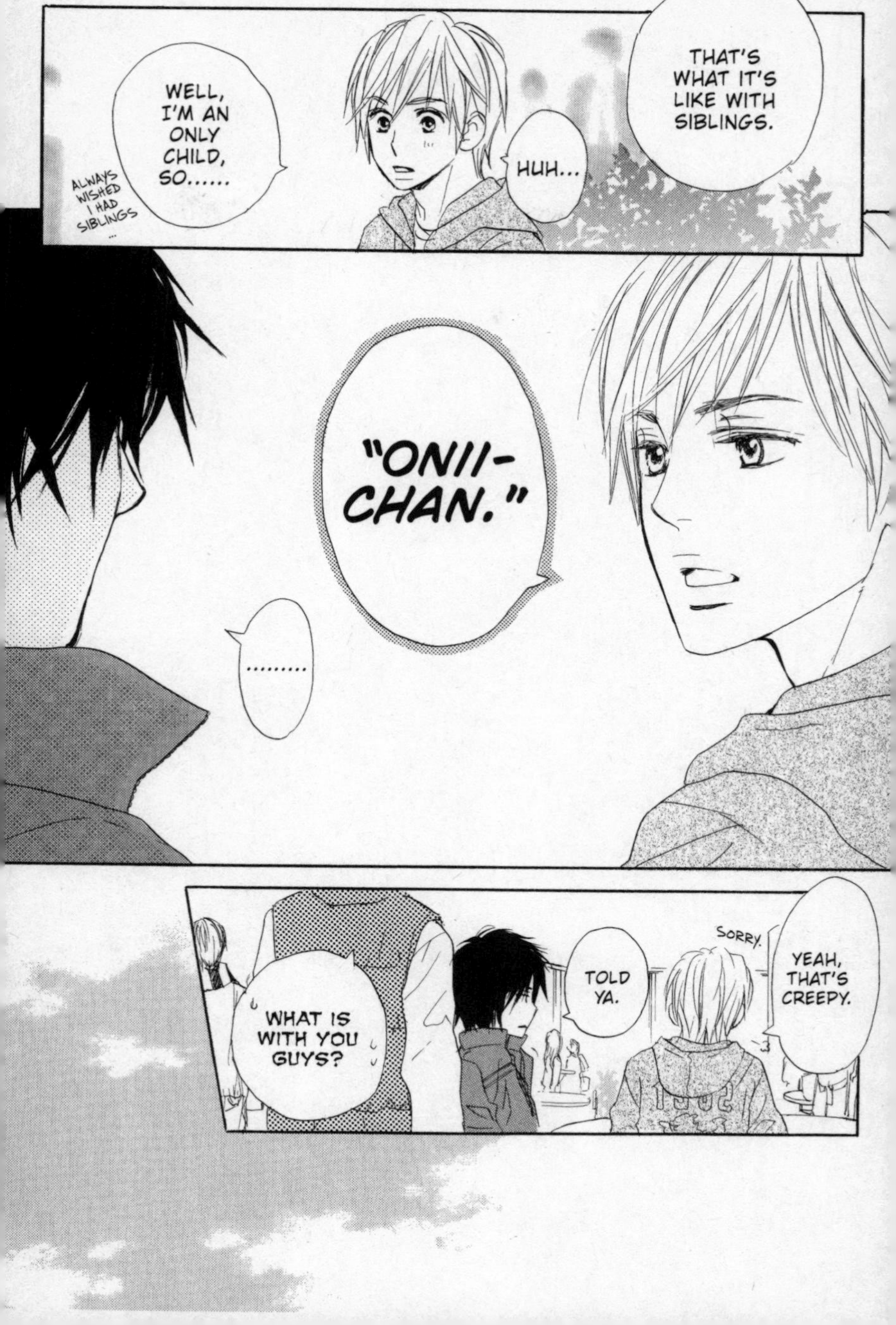
THAT'S WHAT IT'S LIKE WITH SIBLINGS.
HUH...
WELL, I'M AN ONLY CHILD, SO......
ALWAYS WISHED I HAD SIBLINGS ...
"ONII-CHAN."
....
YEAH, THAT'S CREEPY.
SORRY.
TOLD YA.
WHAT IS WITH YOU GUYS?

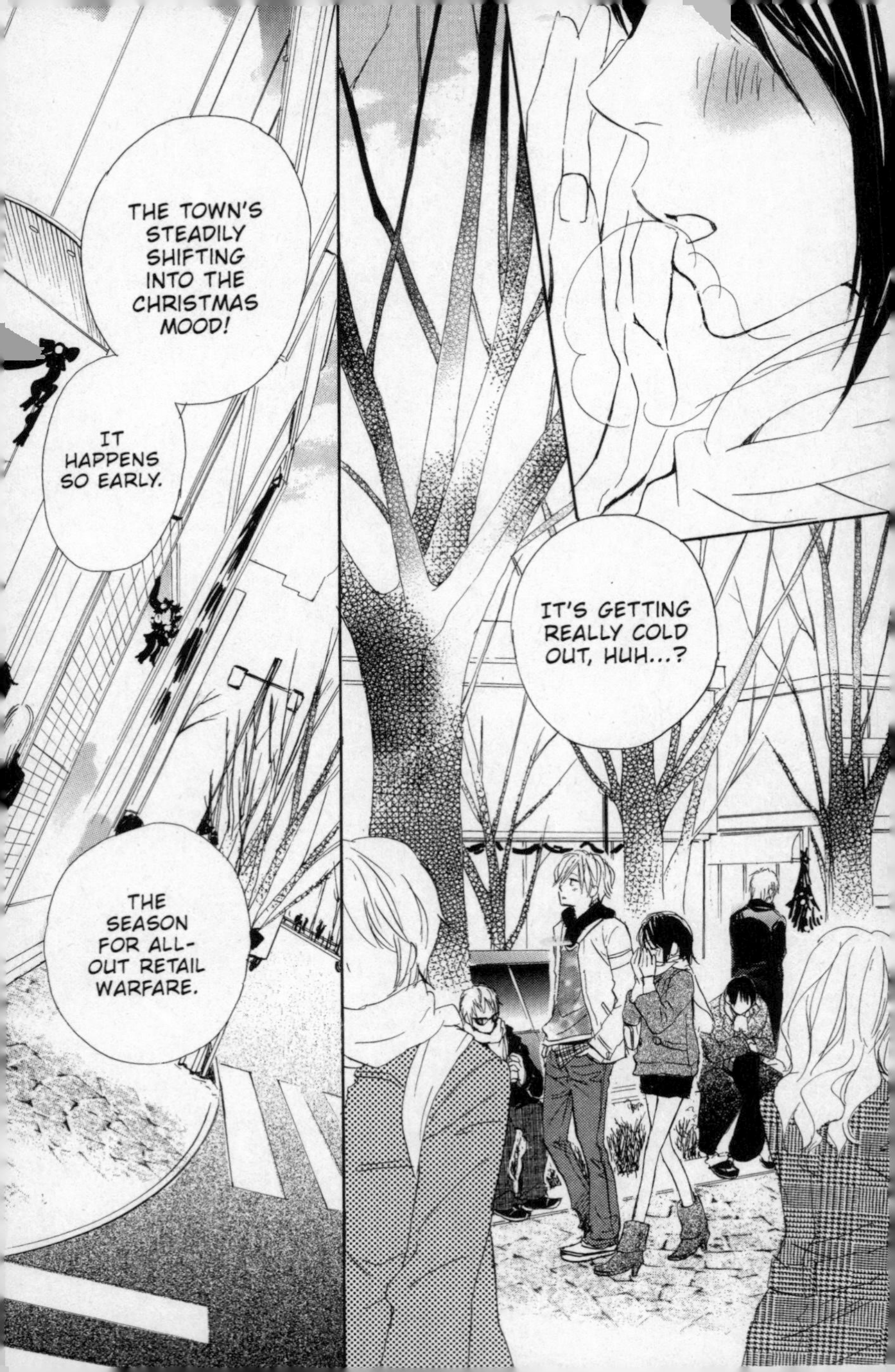
IT'S GETTING REALLY COLD OUT, HUH...?
THE TOWN'S STEADILY SHIFTING INTO THE CHRISTMAS MOOD!
IT HAPPENS SO EARLY.
THE SEASON FOR ALL-OUT RETAIL WARFARE.

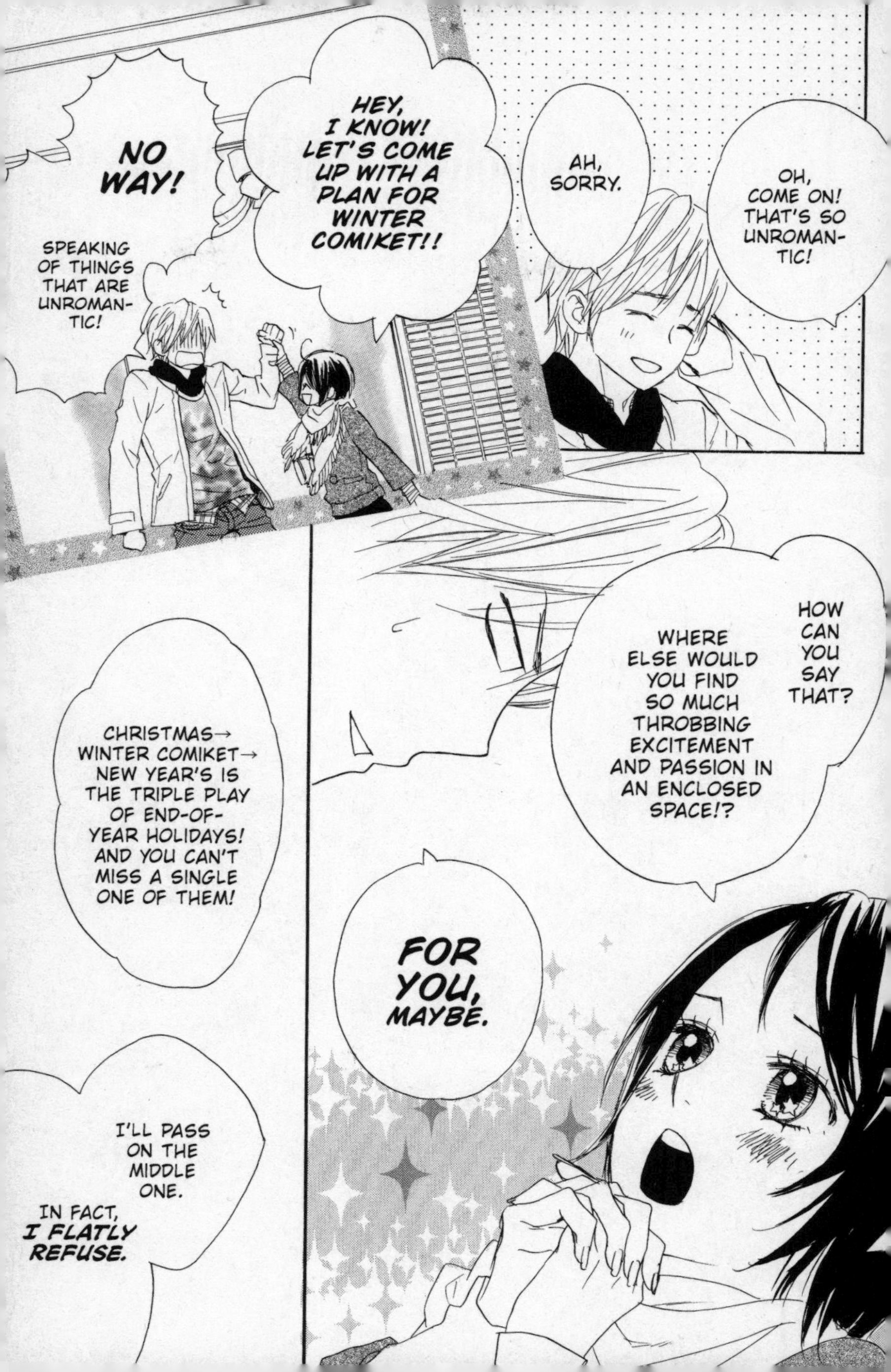
OH, COME ON! THAT'S SO UNROMANTIC!
AH, SORRY.
HEY, I KNOW! LET'S COME UP WITH A PLAN FOR WINTER COMIKET!!
NO WAY!
SPEAKING OF THINGS THAT ARE UNROMANTIC!
HOW CAN YOU SAY THAT?
WHERE ELSE WOULD YOU FIND SO MUCH THROBBING EXCITEMENT AND PASSION IN AN ENCLOSED SPACE!?
FOR YOU, MAYBE.
CHRISTMAS→ WINTER COMIKET→ NEW YEAR'S IS THE TRIPLE PLAY OF END-OF-YEAR HOLIDAYS! AND YOU CAN'T MISS A SINGLE ONE OF THEM!
I'LL PASS ON THE MIDDLE ONE.
IN FACT, I FLATLY REFUSE.

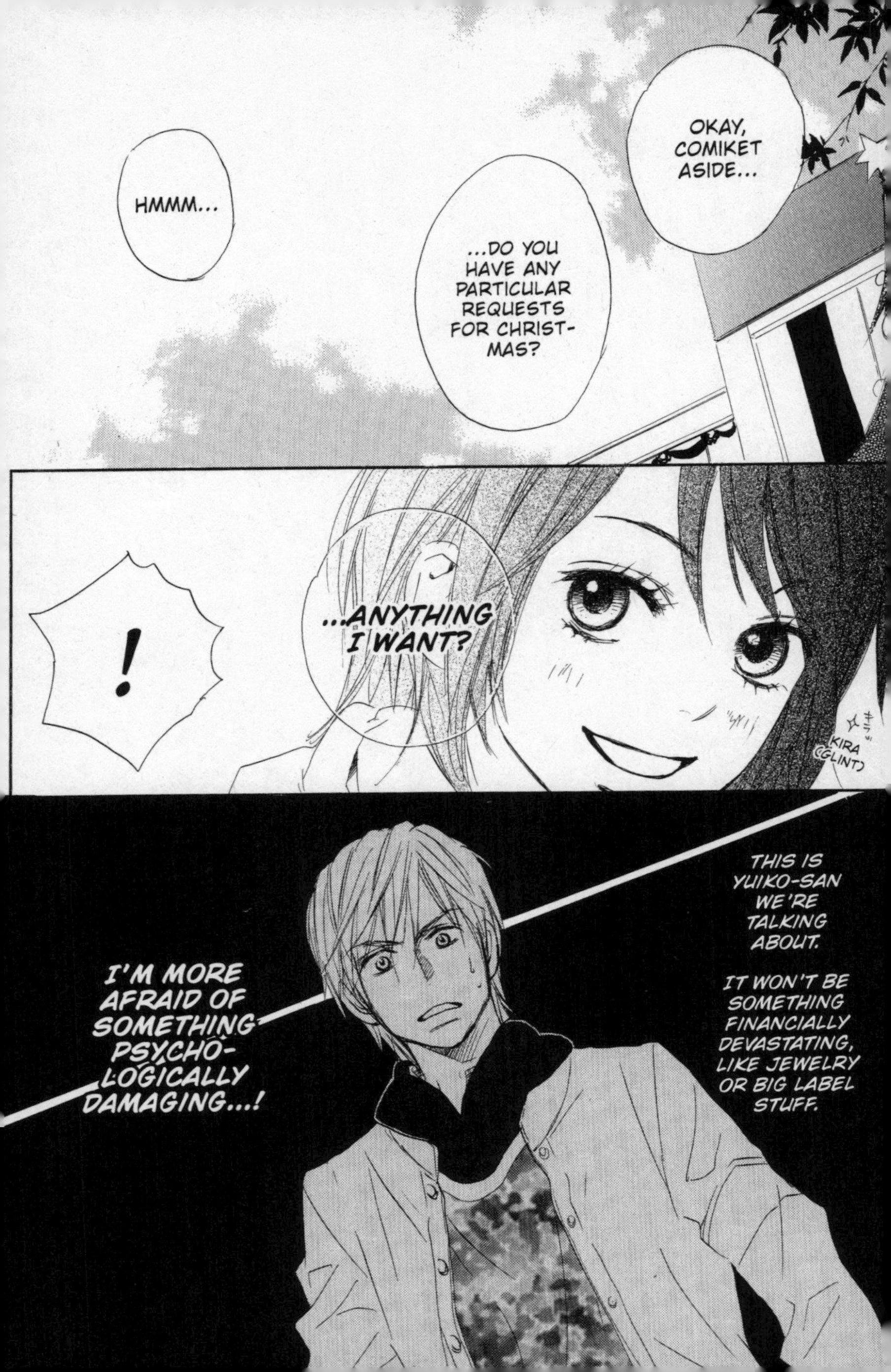
OKAY, COMIKET ASIDE...
...DO YOU HAVE ANY PARTICULAR REQUESTS FOR CHRIST-MAS?
HMMM...
KIRA (GLINT)
...ANYTHING I WANT?
!
THIS IS YUIKO-SAN WE'RE TALKING ABOUT.
IT WON'T BE SOMETHING FINANCIALLY DEVASTATING, LIKE JEWELRY OR BIG LABEL STUFF.
I'M MORE AFRAID OF SOMETHING PSYCHO-LOGICALLY DAMAGING...!

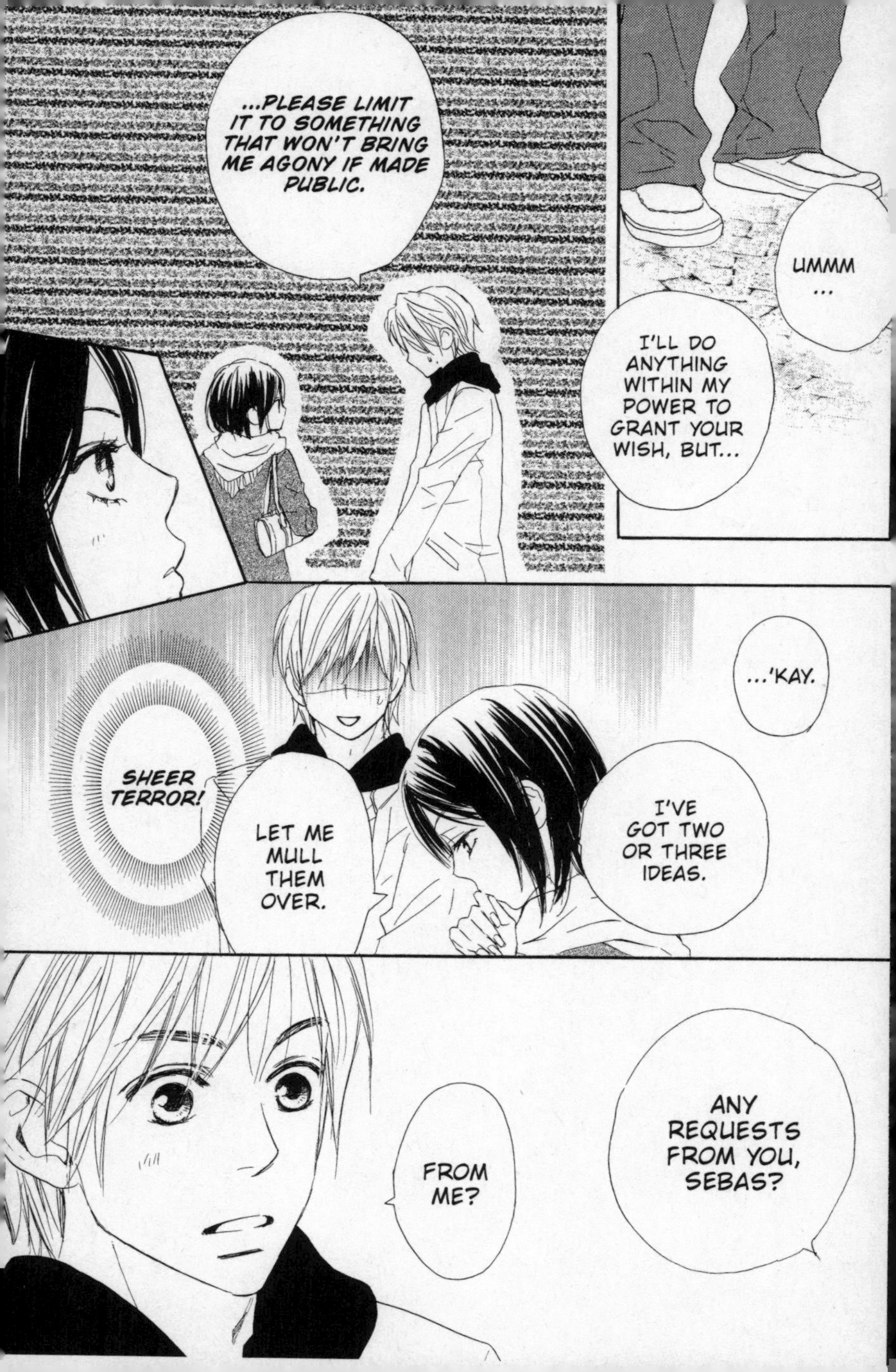
UMMM ...
I'LL DO ANYTHING WITHIN MY POWER TO GRANT YOUR WISH, BUT...
...PLEASE LIMIT IT TO SOMETHING THAT WON'T BRING ME AGONY IF MADE PUBLIC.
...'KAY.
I'VE GOT TWO OR THREE IDEAS.
LET ME MULL THEM OVER.
SHEER TERROR!
ANY REQUESTS FROM YOU, SEBAS?
FROM ME?

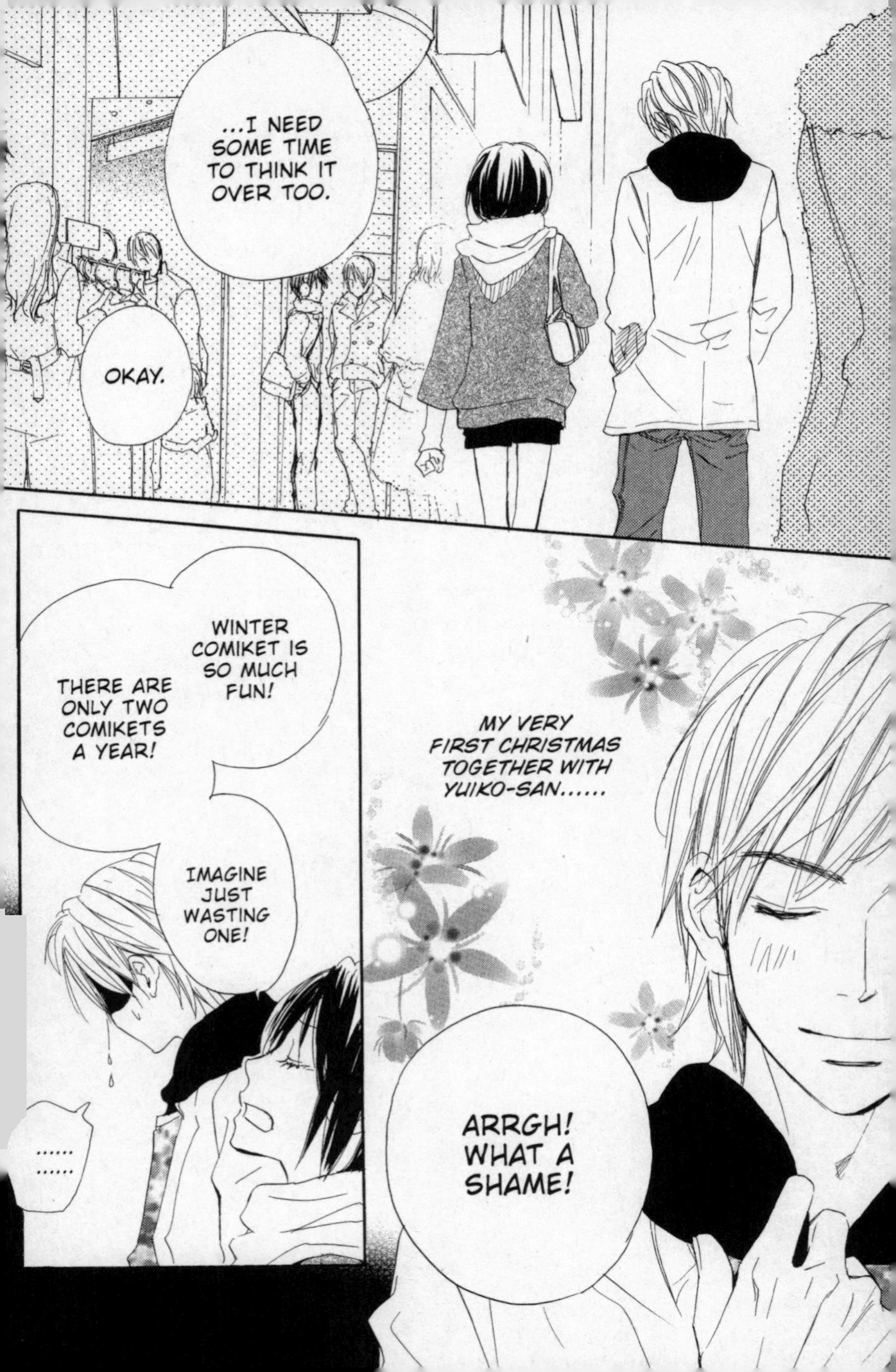
...I NEED SOME TIME TO THINK IT OVER TOO.
OKAY.
MY VERY FIRST CHRISTMAS TOGETHER WITH YUIKO-SAN......
ARRGH! WHAT A SHAME!
WINTER COMIKET IS SO MUCH FUN!
THERE ARE ONLY TWO COMIKETS A YEAR!
IMAGINE JUST WASTING ONE!
....

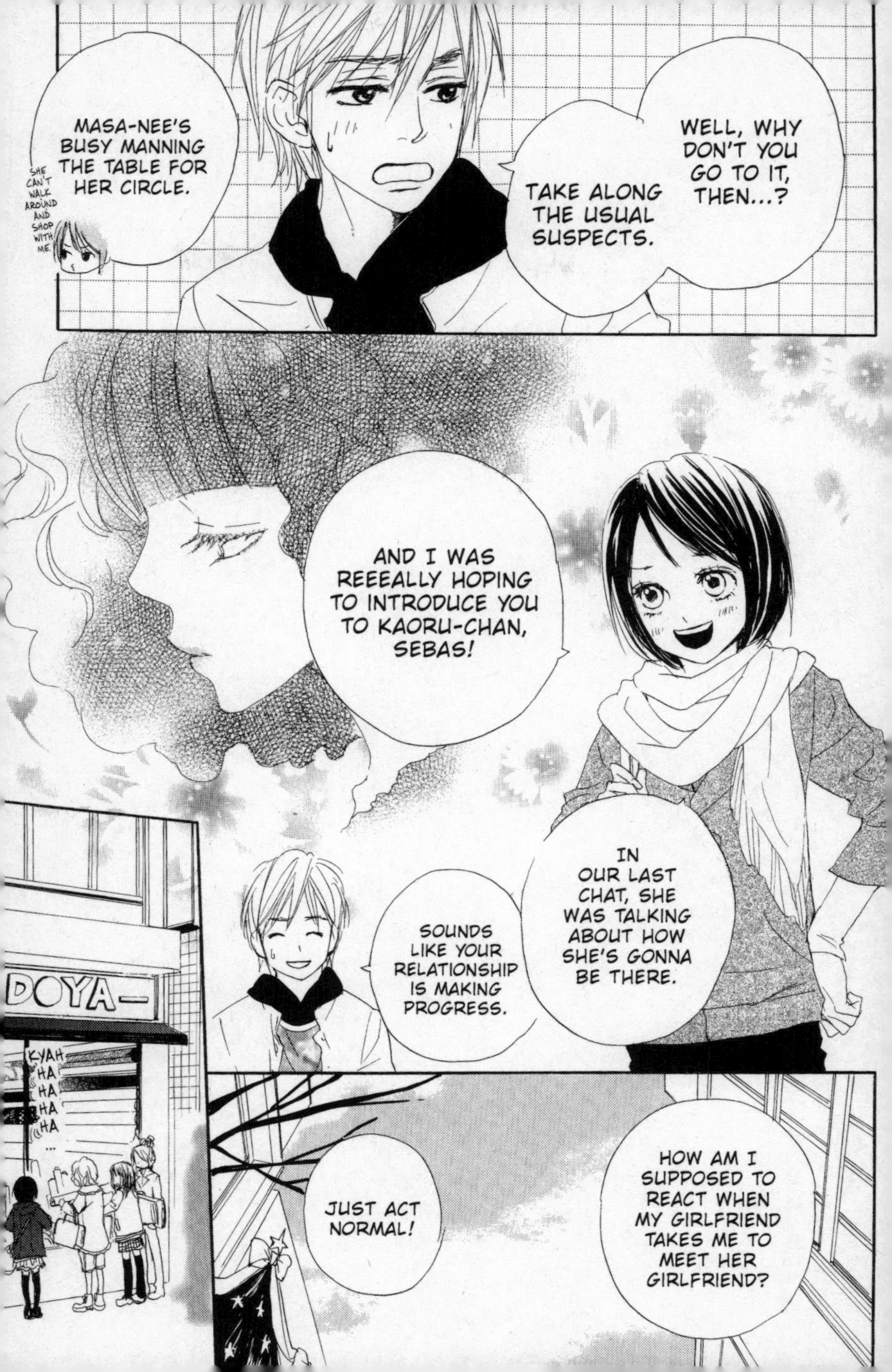
WELL, WHY DON'T YOU GO TO IT, THEN...?
TAKE ALONG THE USUAL SUSPECTS.
MASA-NEE'S BUSY MANNING THE TABLE FOR HER CIRCLE.
SHE CAN'T WALK AROUND AND SHOP WITH ME.
AND I WAS REEEALLY HOPING TO INTRODUCE YOU TO KAORU-CHAN, SEBAS!
IN OUR LAST CHAT, SHE WAS TALKING ABOUT HOW SHE'S GONNA BE THERE.
SOUNDS LIKE YOUR RELATIONSHIP IS MAKING PROGRESS.
HOW AM I SUPPOSED TO REACT WHEN MY GIRLFRIEND TAKES ME TO MEET HER GIRLFRIEND?
JUST ACT NORMAL!
DOYA-
KYAH HA HA HA HA ...

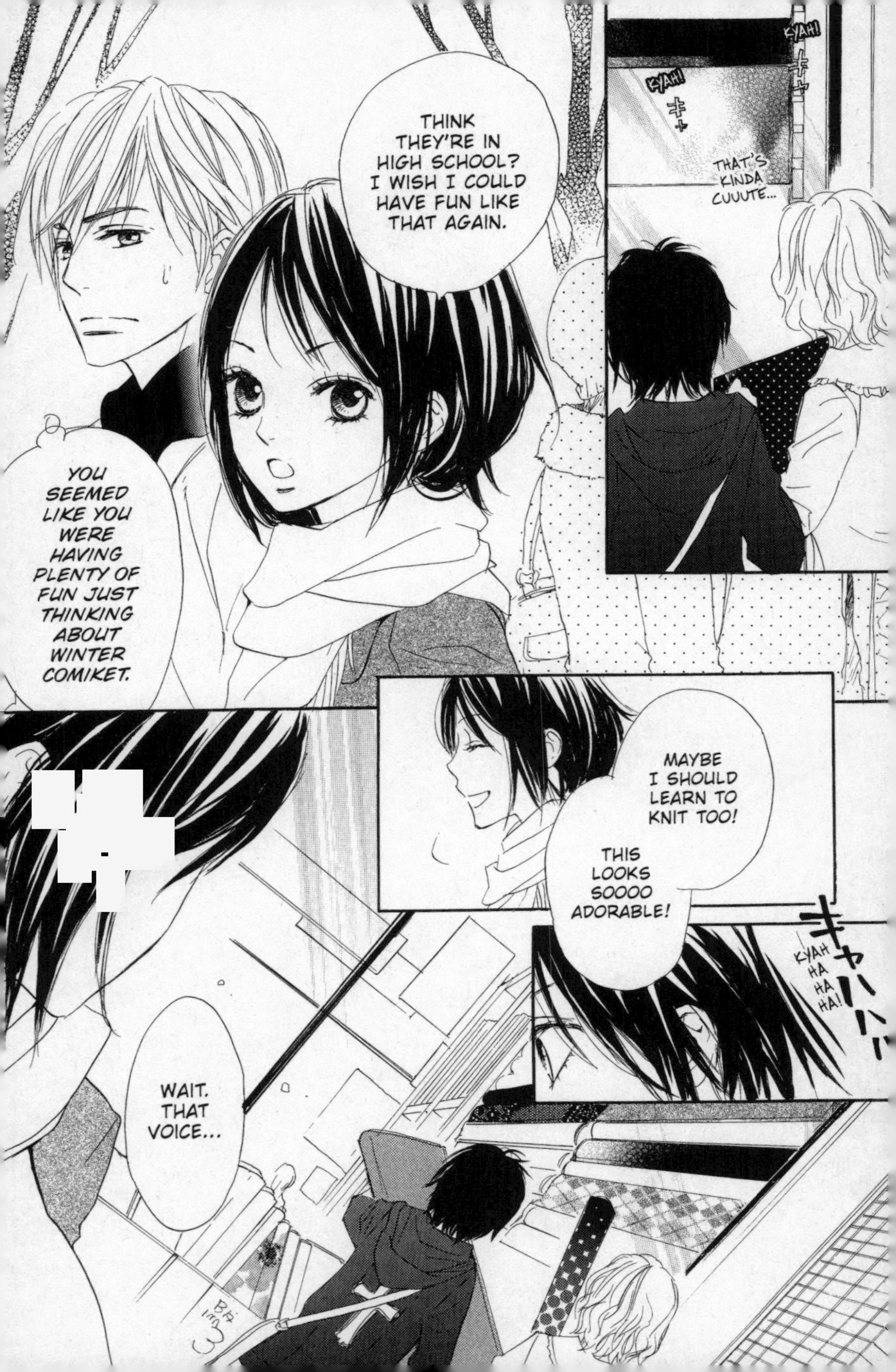
KYAH!
KYAH!
THAT'S KINDA CUUUTE...
THINK THEY'RE IN HIGH SCHOOL? I WISH I COULD HAVE FUN LIKE THAT AGAIN.
YOU SEEMED LIKE YOU WERE HAVING PLENTY OF FUN JUST THINKING ABOUT WINTER COMIKET.
MAYBE I SHOULD LEARN TO KNIT TOO!
THIS LOOKS SOOOO ADORABLE!
KYAH HA HA HA!
WAIT. THAT VOICE...

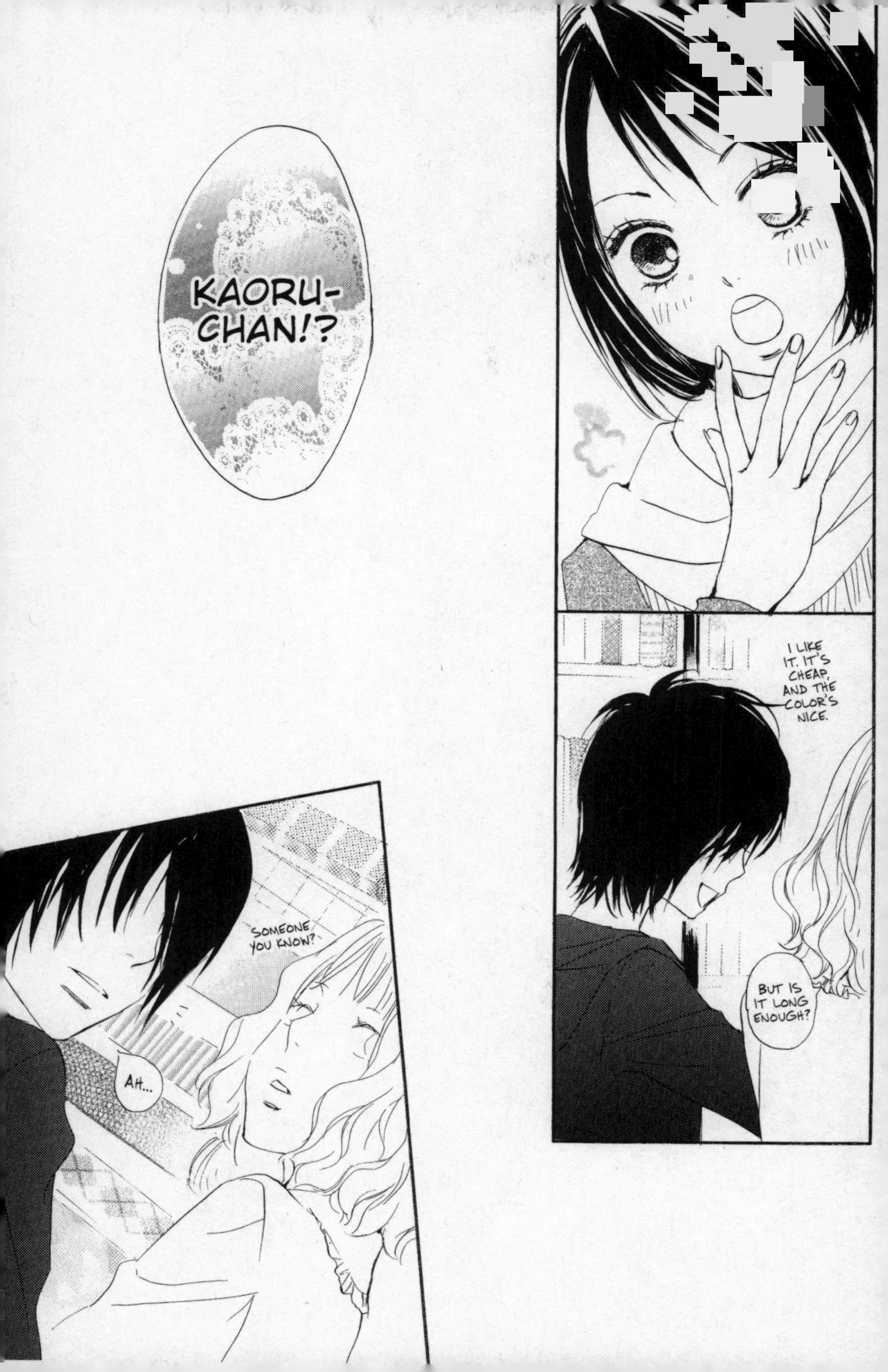
KAORU-CHAN!?
I LIKE IT. IT'S CHEAP, AND THE COLOR'S NICE.
BUT IS IT LONG ENOUGH?
SOMEONE YOU KNOW?
AH...

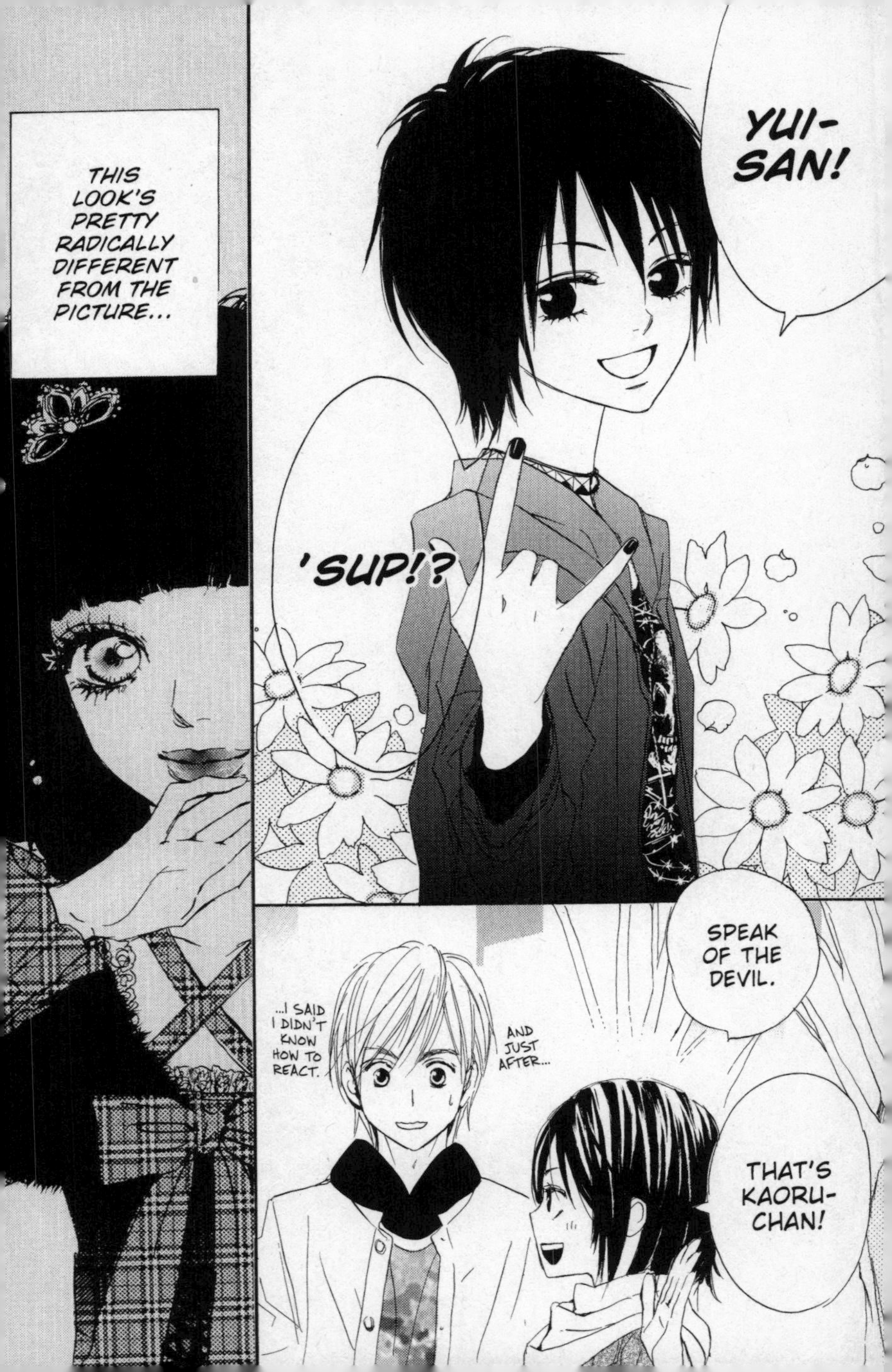
YUI-SAN!
'SUP!?
SPEAK OF THE DEVIL.
THAT'S KAORU-CHAN!
AND JUST AFTER...
...I SAID I DIDN'T KNOW HOW TO REACT.
THIS LOOK'S PRETTY RADICALLY DIFFERENT FROM THE PICTURE...

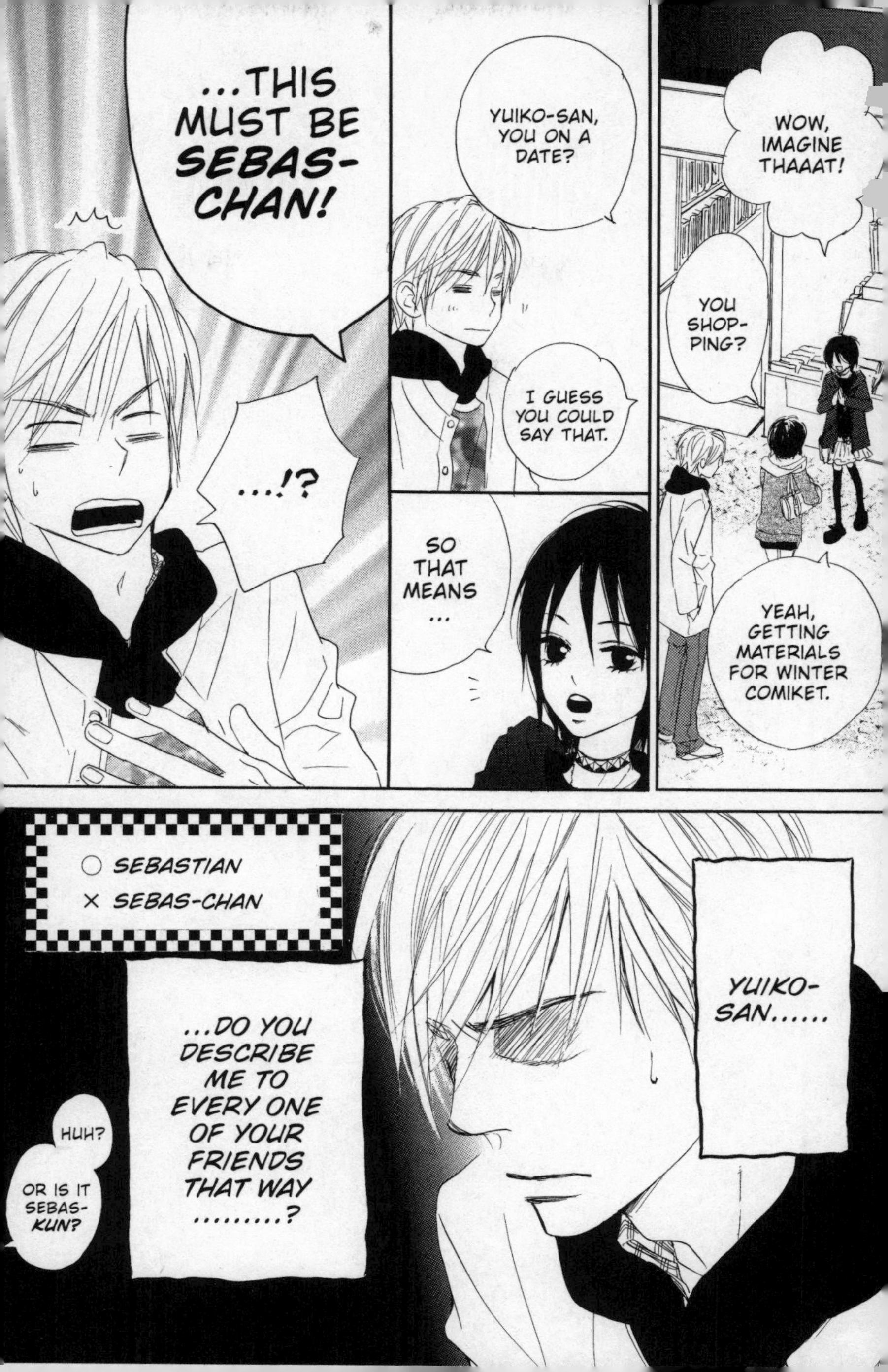
WOW, IMAGINE THAAAT!
YOU SHOPPING?
YEAH, GETTING MATERIALS FOR WINTER COMIKET.
YUIKO-SAN, YOU ON A DATE?
I GUESS YOU COULD SAY THAT.
SO THAT MEANS ...
...THIS MUST BE SEBAS-CHAN!
...!?
YUIKO-SAN......
○ SEBASTIAN
× SEBAS-CHAN
...DO YOU DESCRIBE ME TO EVERY ONE OF YOUR FRIENDS THAT WAY ....?
HUH?
OR IS IT SEBAS-KUN?

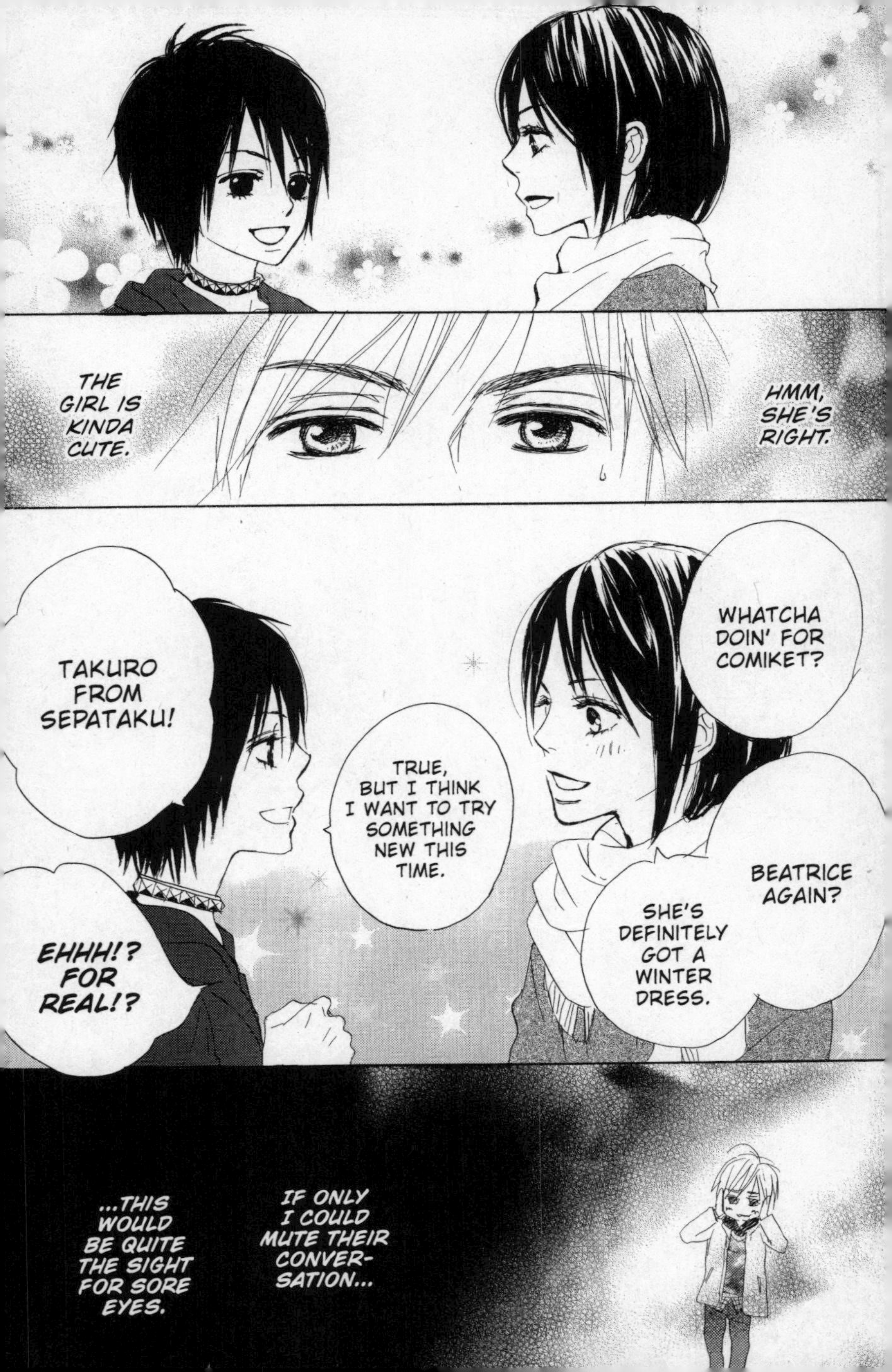
HMM, SHE'S RIGHT.
THE GIRL IS KINDA CUTE.
WHATCHA DOIN' FOR COMIKET?
TAKURO FROM SEPATAKU!
BEATRICE AGAIN?
SHE'S DEFINITELY GOT A WINTER DRESS.
TRUE, BUT I THINK I WANT TO TRY SOMETHING NEW THIS TIME.
EHHH!? FOR REAL!?
IF ONLY I COULD MUTE THEIR CONVER-SATION...
...THIS WOULD BE QUITE THE SIGHT FOR SORE EYES.

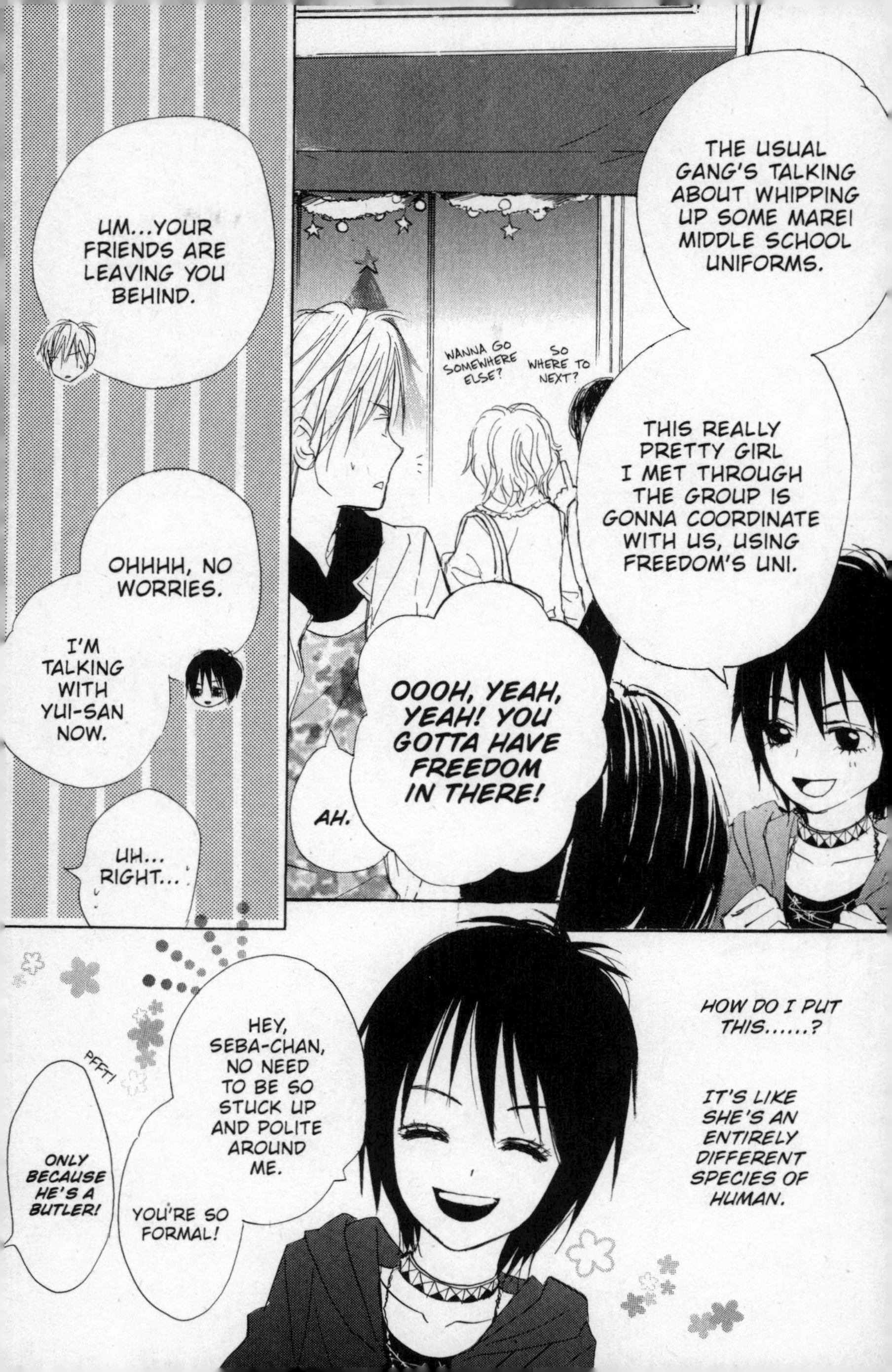
THE USUAL GANG'S TALKING ABOUT WHIPPING UP SOME MAREI MIDDLE SCHOOL UNIFORMS.
SO WHERE TO NEXT?
WANNA GO SOMEWHERE ELSE?
THIS REALLY PRETTY GIRL I MET THROUGH THE GROUP IS GONNA COORDINATE WITH US, USING FREEDOM'S UNI.
OOOH, YEAH, YEAH! YOU GOTTA HAVE FREEDOM IN THERE!
AH.
UM...YOUR FRIENDS ARE LEAVING YOU BEHIND.
OHHHH, NO WORRIES.
I'M TALKING WITH YUI-SAN NOW.
UH... RIGHT...
HOW DO I PUT THIS......?
IT'S LIKE SHE'S AN ENTIRELY DIFFERENT SPECIES OF HUMAN.
HEY, SEBA-CHAN, NO NEED TO BE SO STUCK UP AND POLITE AROUND ME.
YOU'RE SO FORMAL!
PFFT!
ONLY BECAUSE HE'S A BUTLER!

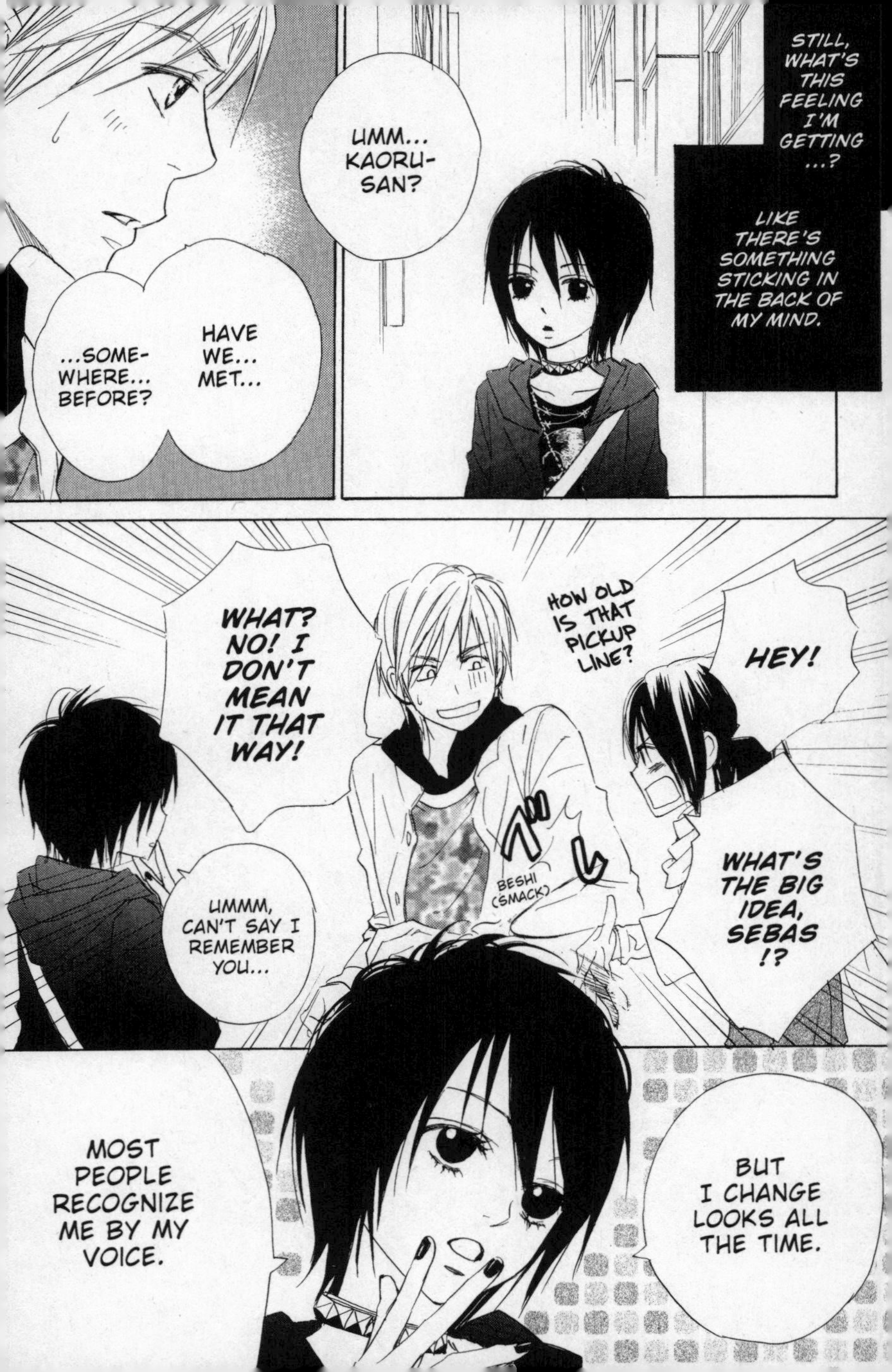
STILL, WHAT'S THIS FEELING I'M GETTING ...?
LIKE THERE'S SOMETHING STICKING IN THE BACK OF MY MIND.
UMM... KAORU-SAN?
HAVE WE... MET...
...SOME-WHERE... BEFORE?
HEY!
WHAT'S THE BIG IDEA, SEBAS !?
HOW OLD IS THAT PICKUP LINE?
BESHI (SMACK)
WHAT? NO! I DON'T MEAN IT THAT WAY!
UMMM, CAN'T SAY I REMEMBER YOU...
BUT I CHANGE LOOKS ALL THE TIME.
MOST PEOPLE RECOGNIZE ME BY MY VOICE.

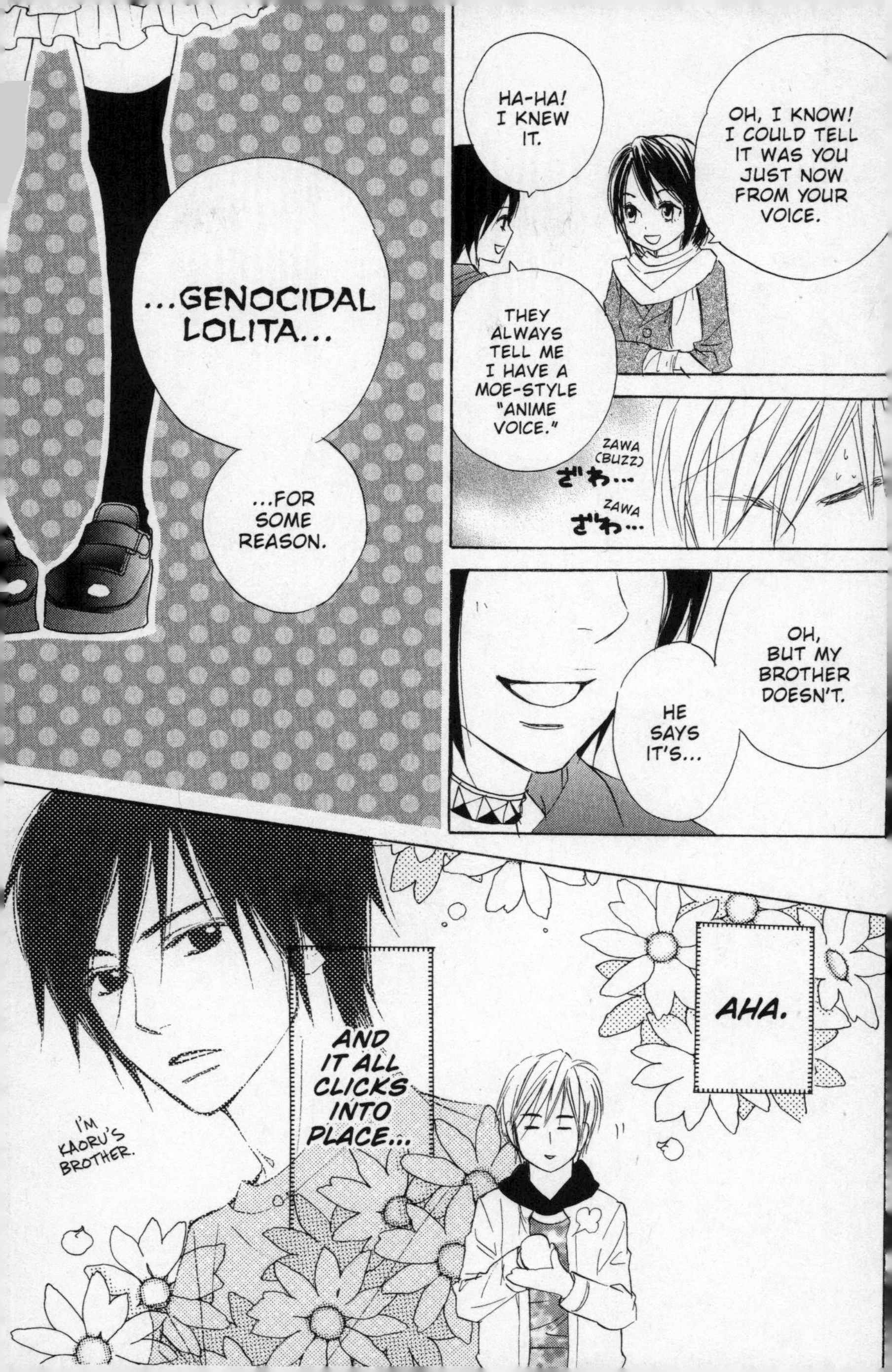
OH, I KNOW! I COULD TELL IT WAS YOU JUST NOW FROM YOUR VOICE.
HA-HA! I KNEW IT.
THEY ALWAYS TELL ME I HAVE A MOE-STYLE "ANIME VOICE."
ZAWA (BUZZ)
ざわ…
ZAWA
ざわ…
OH, BUT MY BROTHER DOESN'T.
HE SAYS IT'S...
...GENOCIDAL LOLITA...
...FOR SOME REASON.
AHA.
AND IT ALL CLICKS INTO PLACE...
I'M KAORU'S BROTHER.

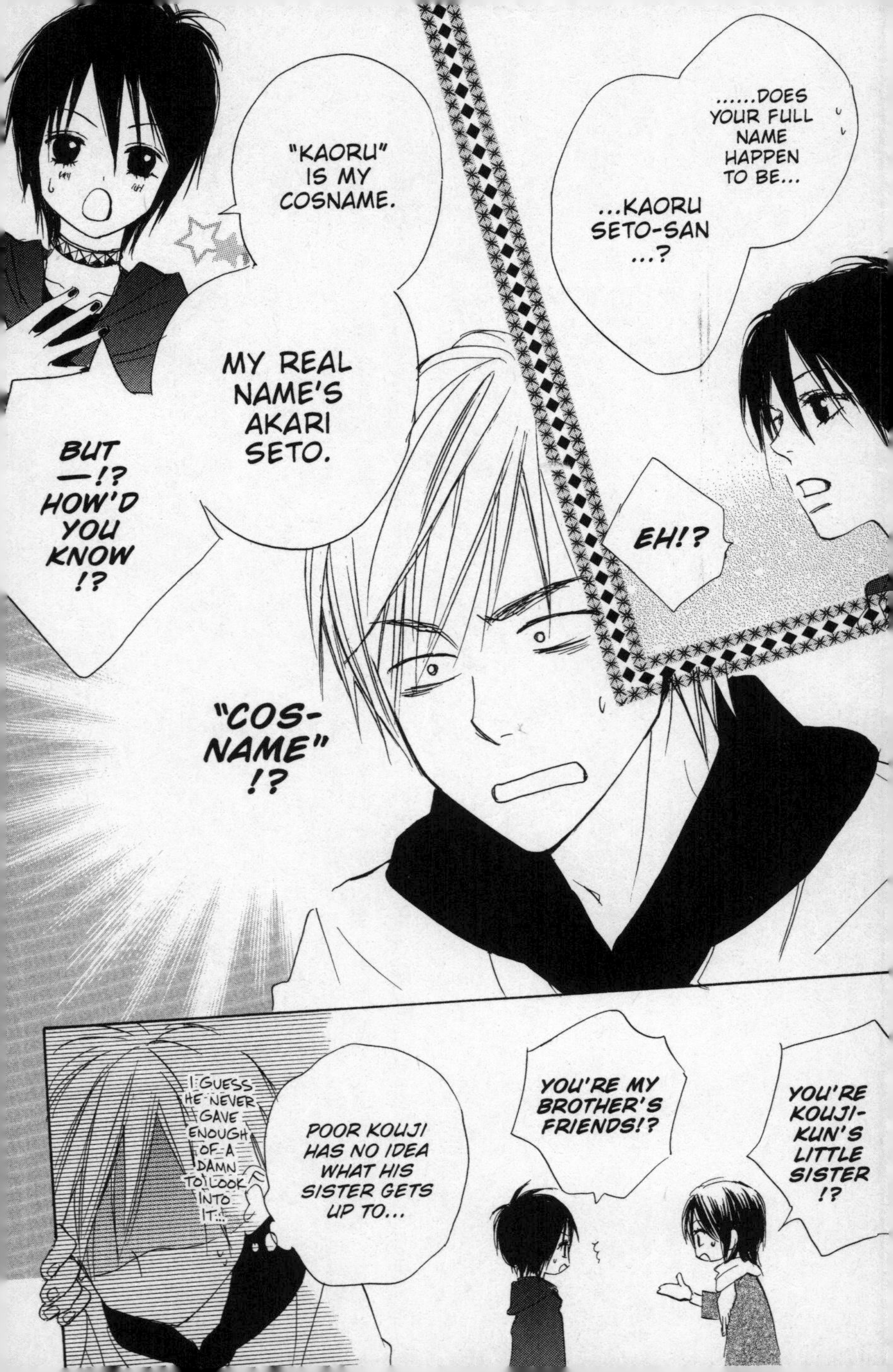
......DOES YOUR FULL NAME HAPPEN TO BE...
...KAORU SETO-SAN ...?
EH!?
"KAORU" IS MY COSNAME.
MY REAL NAME'S AKARI SETO.
BUT—!? HOW'D YOU KNOW !?
"COS-NAME" !?
YOU'RE KOUJI-KUN'S LITTLE SISTER !?
YOU'RE MY BROTHER'S FRIENDS!?
POOR KOUJI HAS NO IDEA WHAT HIS SISTER GETS UP TO...
I GUESS HE NEVER GAVE ENOUGH OF A DAMN TO LOOK INTO IT...

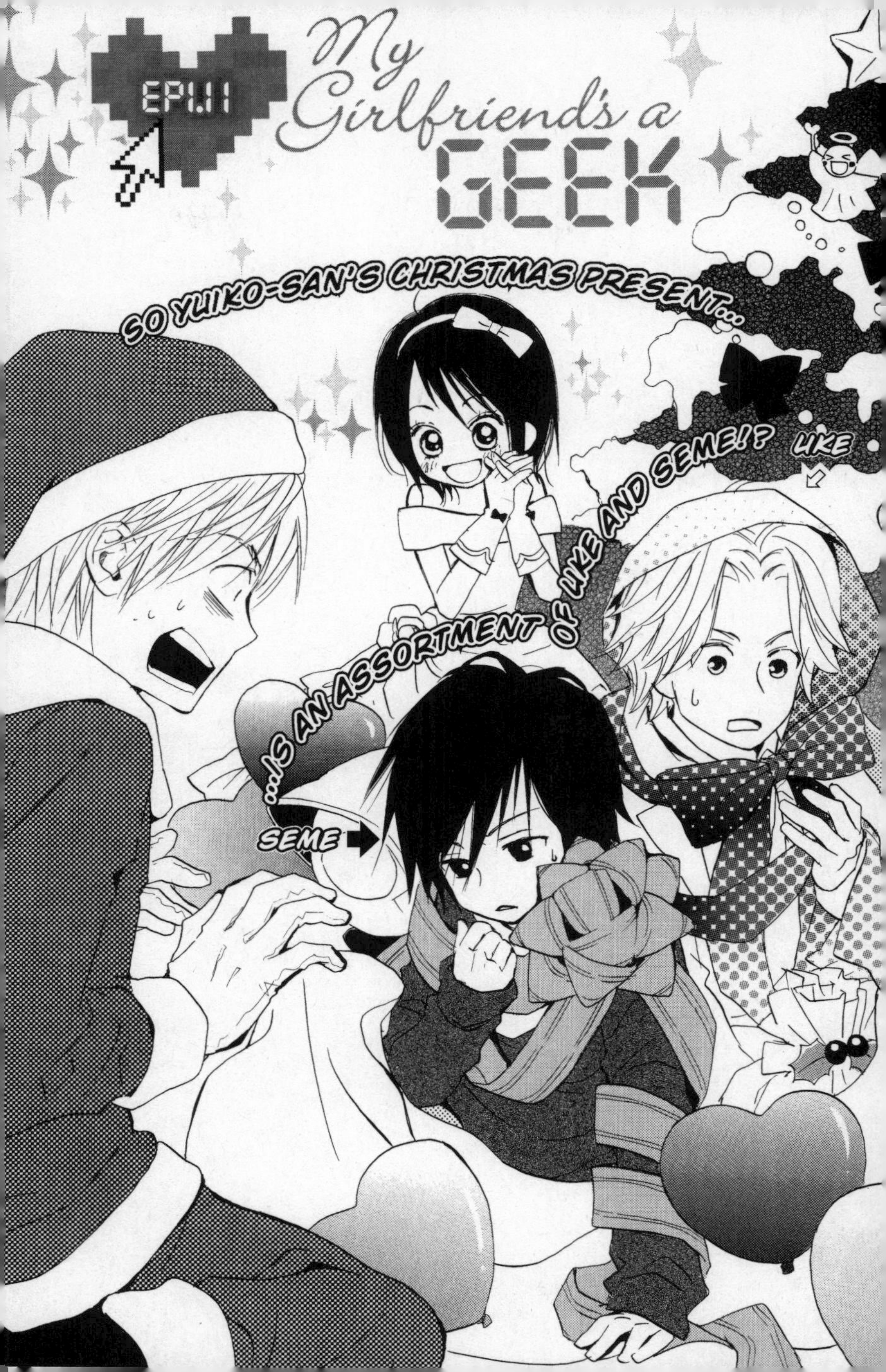
EP1.11
My Girlfriend's a GEEK
SO YUIKO-SAN'S CHRISTMAS PRESENT...
...IS AN ASSORTMENT OF UKE AND SEME!?
UKE
SEME

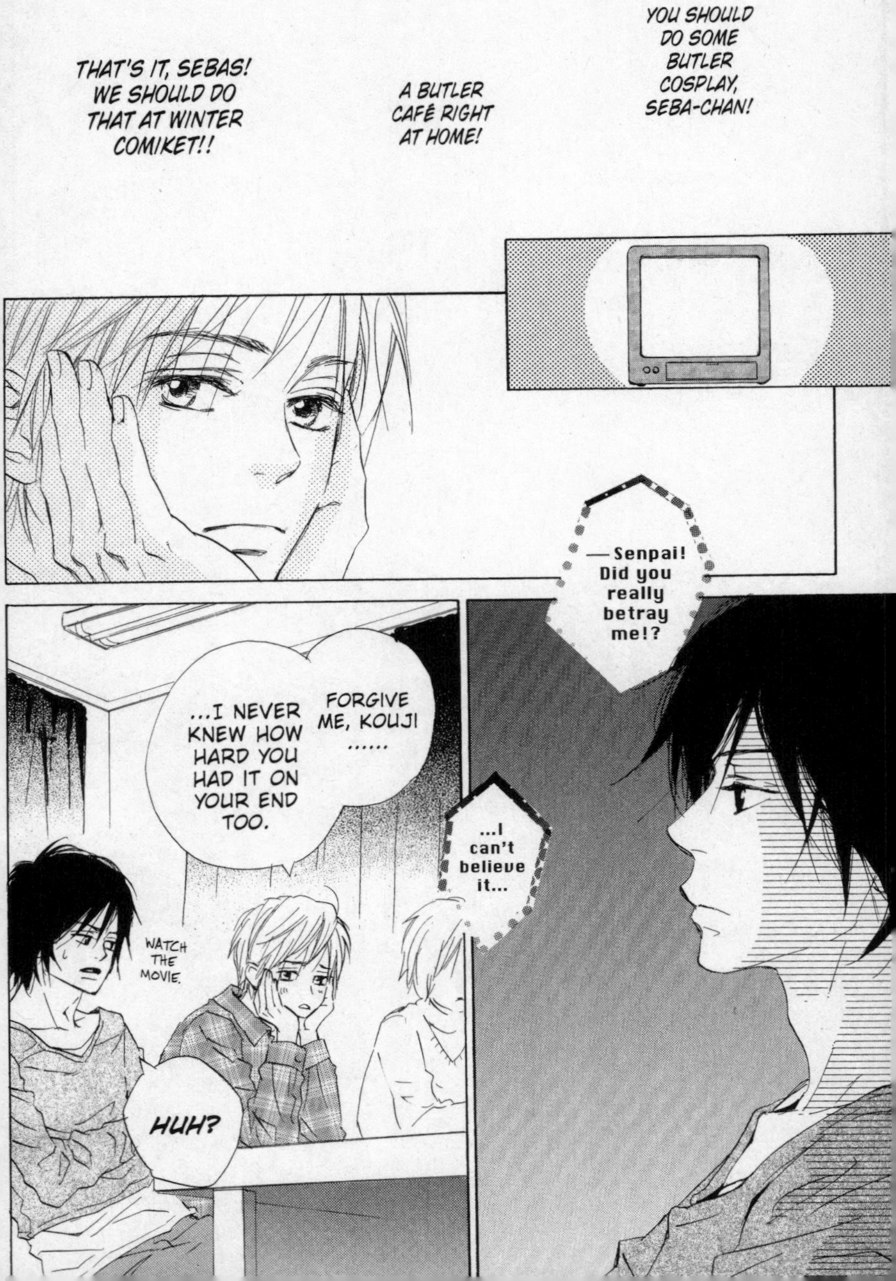
YOU SHOULD DO SOME BUTLER COSPLAY, SEBA-CHAN!
A BUTLER CAFÉ RIGHT AT HOME!
THAT'S IT, SEBAS! WE SHOULD DO THAT AT WINTER COMIKET!!
—Senpai! Did you really betray me!?
...I can't believe it...
FORGIVE ME, KOUJI ......
...I NEVER KNEW HOW HARD YOU HAD IT ON YOUR END TOO.
WATCH THE MOVIE.
HUH?

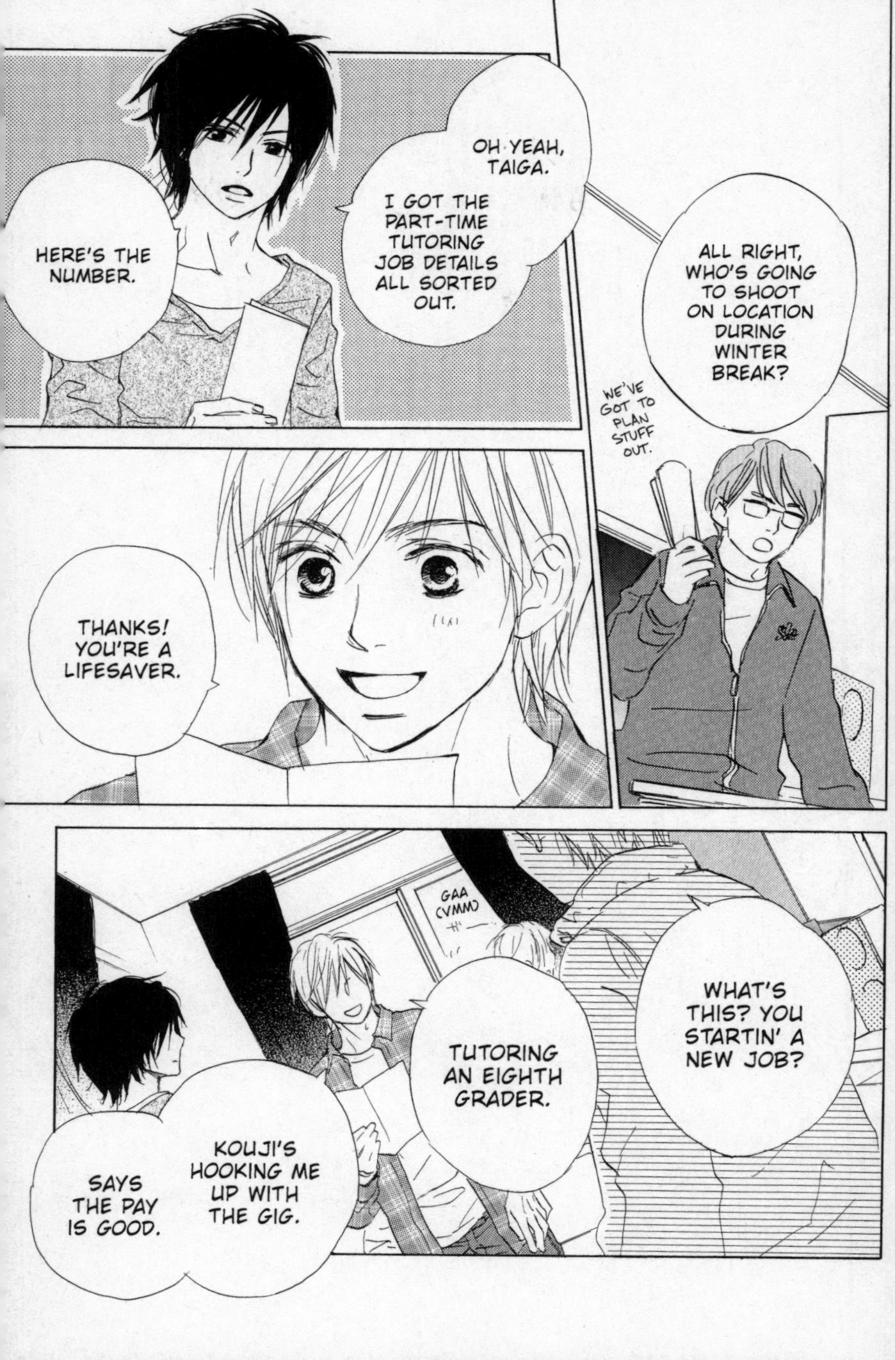
ALL RIGHT, WHO'S GOING TO SHOOT ON LOCATION DURING WINTER BREAK?
WE'VE GOT TO PLAN STUFF OUT.
OH YEAH, TAIGA.
I GOT THE PART-TIME TUTORING JOB DETAILS ALL SORTED OUT.
HERE'S THE NUMBER.
THANKS! YOU'RE A LIFESAVER.
GAA (VMM)
WHAT'S THIS? YOU STARTIN' A NEW JOB?
TUTORING AN EIGHTH GRADER.
KOUJI'S HOOKING ME UP WITH THE GIG.
SAYS THE PAY IS GOOD.

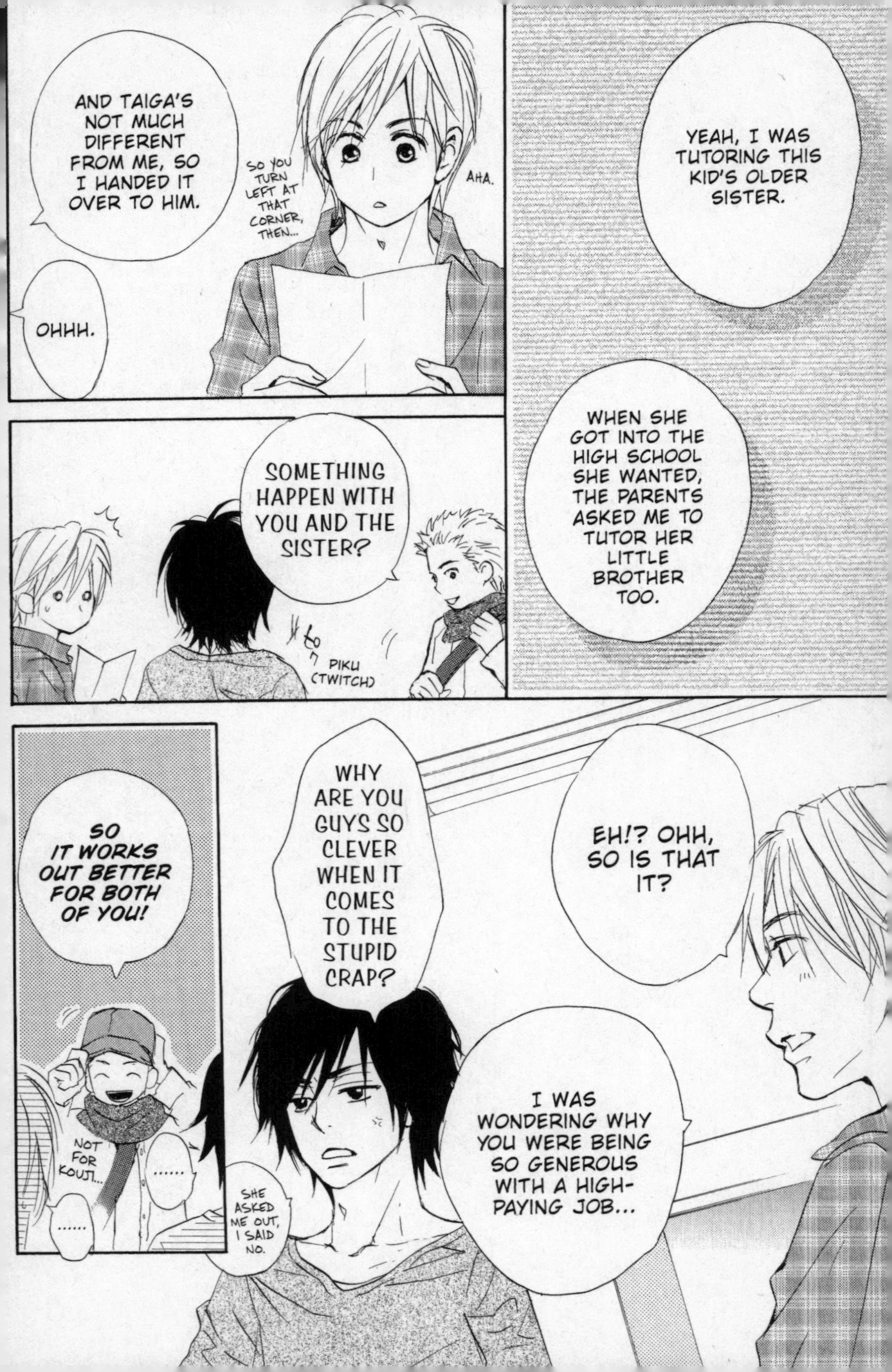
YEAH, I WAS TUTORING THIS KID'S OLDER SISTER.
WHEN SHE GOT INTO THE HIGH SCHOOL SHE WANTED, THE PARENTS ASKED ME TO TUTOR HER LITTLE BROTHER TOO.
AND TAIGA'S NOT MUCH DIFFERENT FROM ME, SO I HANDED IT OVER TO HIM.
OHHH.
SO YOU TURN LEFT AT THAT CORNER, THEN...
AHA.
SOMETHING HAPPEN WITH YOU AND THE SISTER?
PIKU (TWITCH)
EH!? OHH, SO IS THAT IT?
I WAS WONDERING WHY YOU WERE BEING SO GENEROUS WITH A HIGH-PAYING JOB...
WHY ARE YOU GUYS SO CLEVER WHEN IT COMES TO THE STUPID CRAP?
SHE ASKED ME OUT, I SAID NO.
SO IT WORKS OUT BETTER FOR BOTH OF YOU!
NOT FOR KOUJI...
......
......

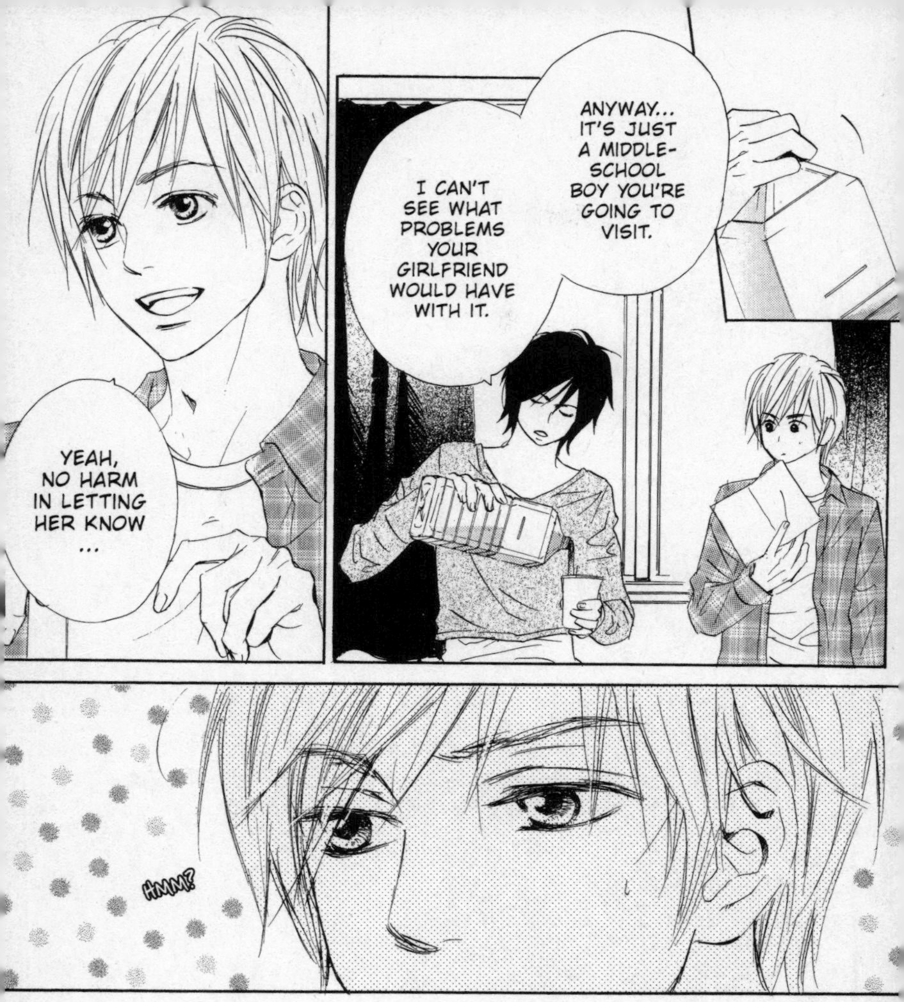
ANYWAY... IT'S JUST A MIDDLE-SCHOOL BOY YOU'RE GOING TO VISIT.
I CAN'T SEE WHAT PROBLEMS YOUR GIRLFRIEND WOULD HAVE WITH IT.
YEAH, NO HARM IN LETTING HER KNOW ...
HMM?

— *A MIDDLE SCHOOL* **"BOY."**

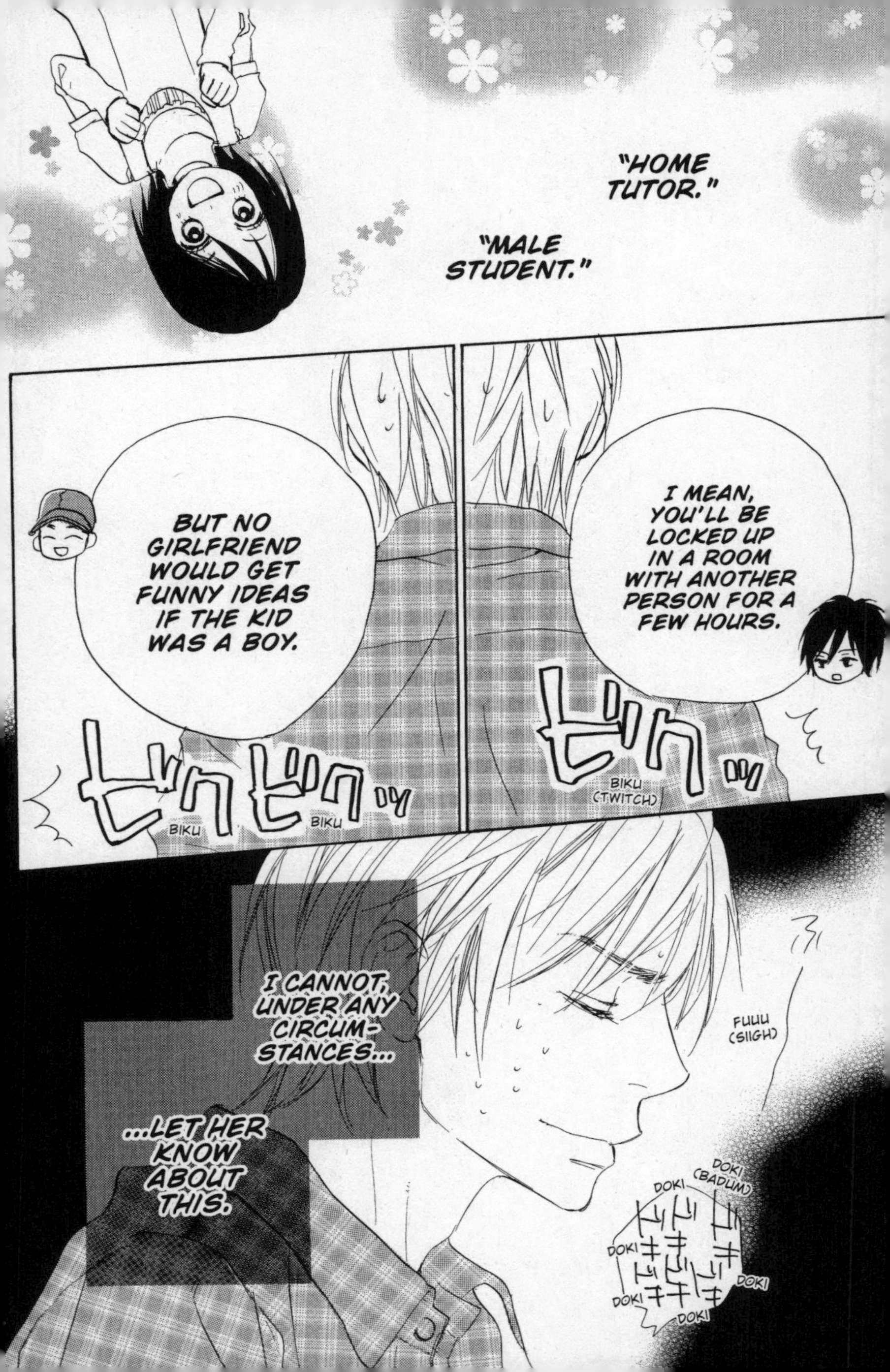
"HOME TUTOR."
"MALE STUDENT."
I MEAN, YOU'LL BE LOCKED UP IN A ROOM WITH ANOTHER PERSON FOR A FEW HOURS.
BIKU (TWITCH)
BUT NO GIRLFRIEND WOULD GET FUNNY IDEAS IF THE KID WAS A BOY.
BIKU BIKU
FUUU (SIIGH)
I CANNOT, UNDER ANY CIRCUM-STANCES...
...LET HER KNOW ABOUT THIS.
DOKI (BADUM) DOKI DOKI DOKI DOKI DOKI

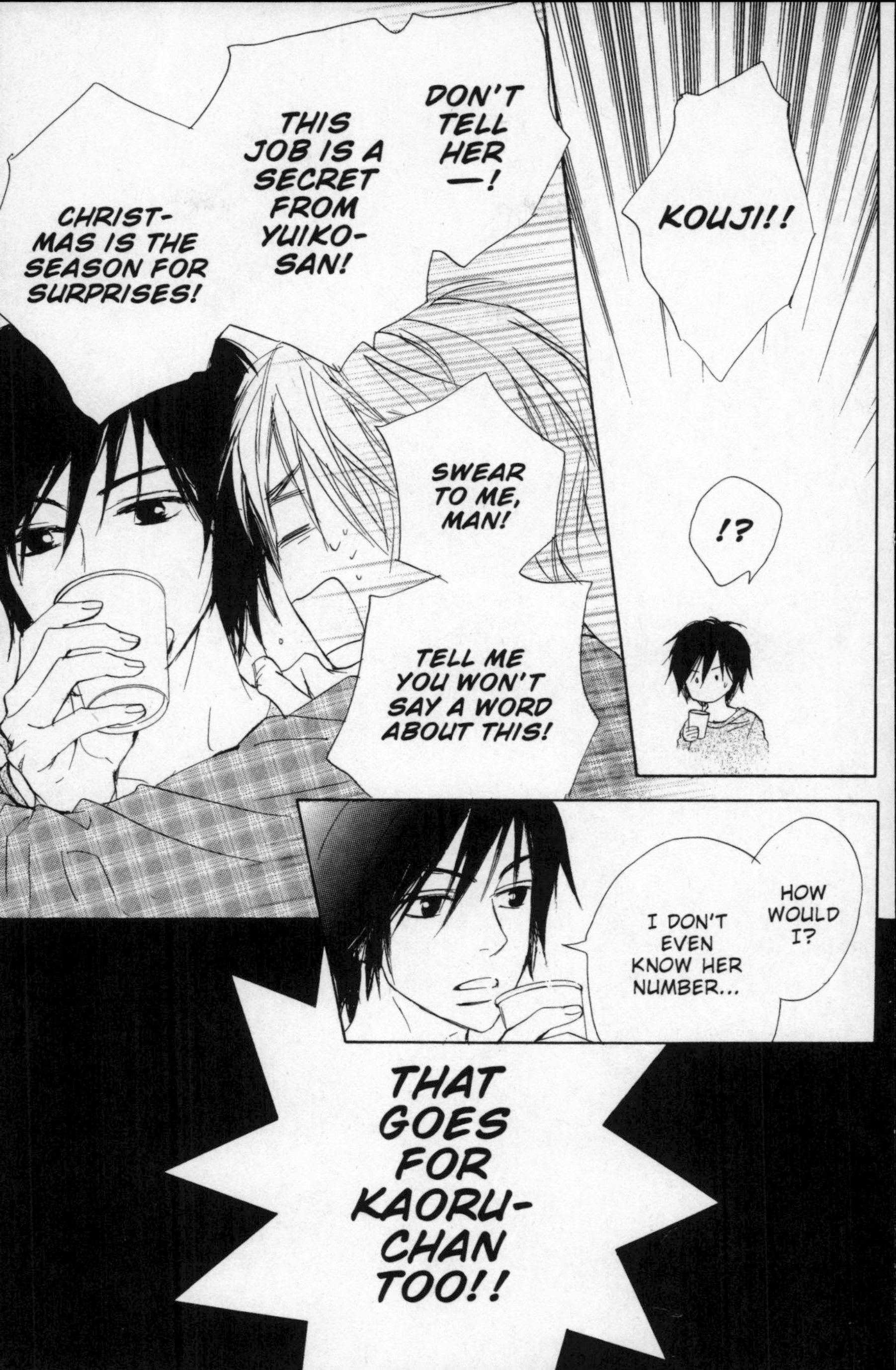
KOUJI!!
!?
DON'T TELL HER—!
THIS JOB IS A SECRET FROM YUIKO-SAN!
CHRISTMAS IS THE SEASON FOR SURPRISES!
SWEAR TO ME, MAN!
TELL ME YOU WON'T SAY A WORD ABOUT THIS!
HOW WOULD I?
I DON'T EVEN KNOW HER NUMBER...
THAT GOES FOR KAORU-CHAN TOO!!

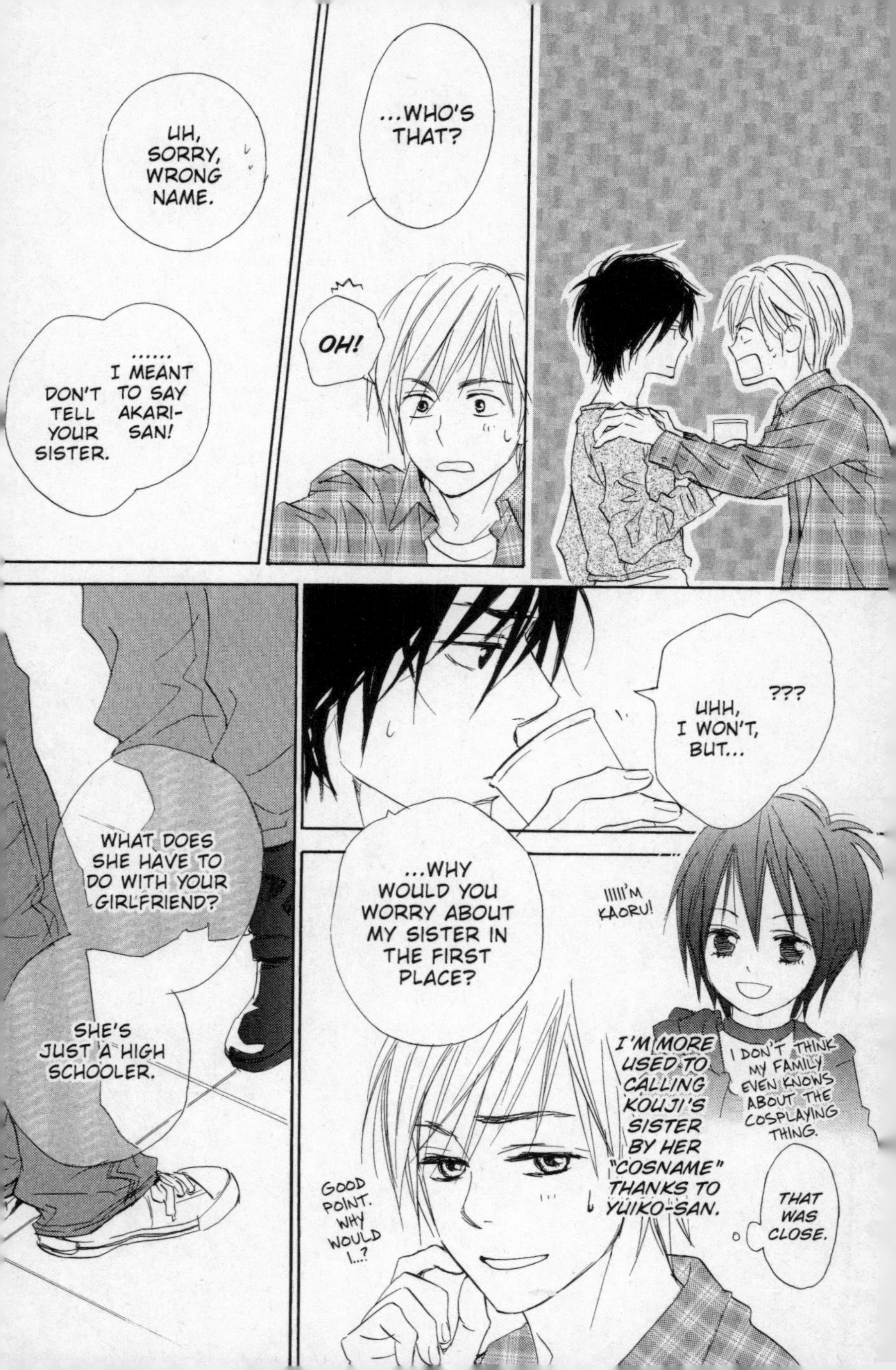
...WHO'S THAT?
OH!
UH, SORRY, WRONG NAME.
...... I MEANT TO SAY AKARI-SAN!
DON'T TELL YOUR SISTER.
???
UHH, I WON'T, BUT...
...WHY WOULD YOU WORRY ABOUT MY SISTER IN THE FIRST PLACE?
IIIII'M KAORU!
I DON'T THINK MY FAMILY EVEN KNOWS ABOUT THE COSPLAYING THING.
THAT WAS CLOSE.
I'M MORE USED TO CALLING KOUJI'S SISTER BY HER "COSNAME" THANKS TO YUIKO-SAN.
GOOD POINT. WHY WOULD I...?
WHAT DOES SHE HAVE TO DO WITH YOUR GIRLFRIEND?
SHE'S JUST A HIGH SCHOOLER.

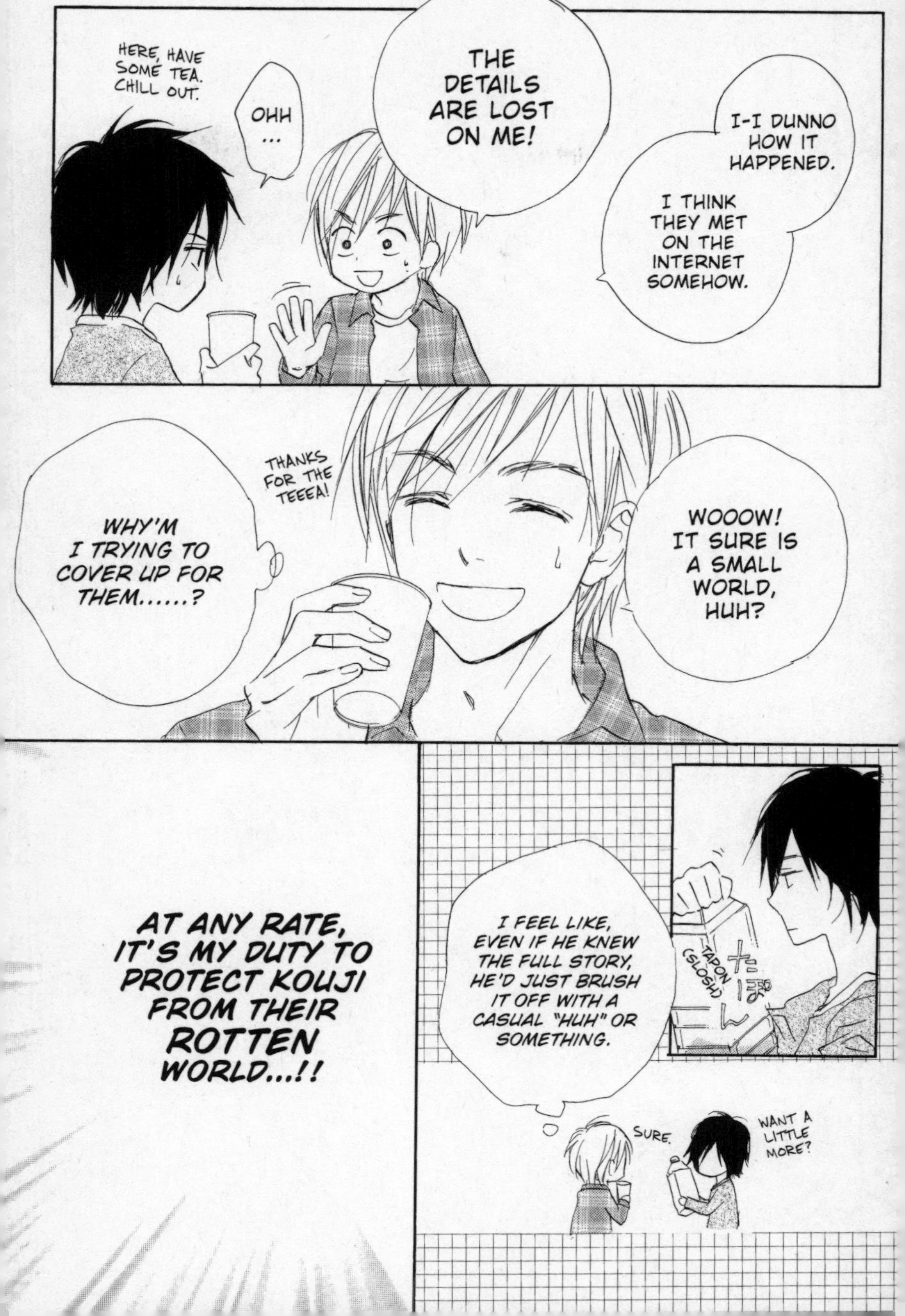
I-I DUNNO HOW IT HAPPENED.
I THINK THEY MET ON THE INTERNET SOMEHOW.
THE DETAILS ARE LOST ON ME!
OHH ...
HERE, HAVE SOME TEA. CHILL OUT.
WOOOW! IT SURE IS A SMALL WORLD, HUH?
THANKS FOR THE TEEEA!
WHY'M I TRYING TO COVER UP FOR THEM......?
TAPON (SLOSH)
I FEEL LIKE, EVEN IF HE KNEW THE FULL STORY, HE'D JUST BRUSH IT OFF WITH A CASUAL "HUH" OR SOMETHING.
WANT A LITTLE MORE?
SURE.
AT ANY RATE, IT'S MY DUTY TO PROTECT KOUJI FROM THEIR ROTTEN WORLD...!!

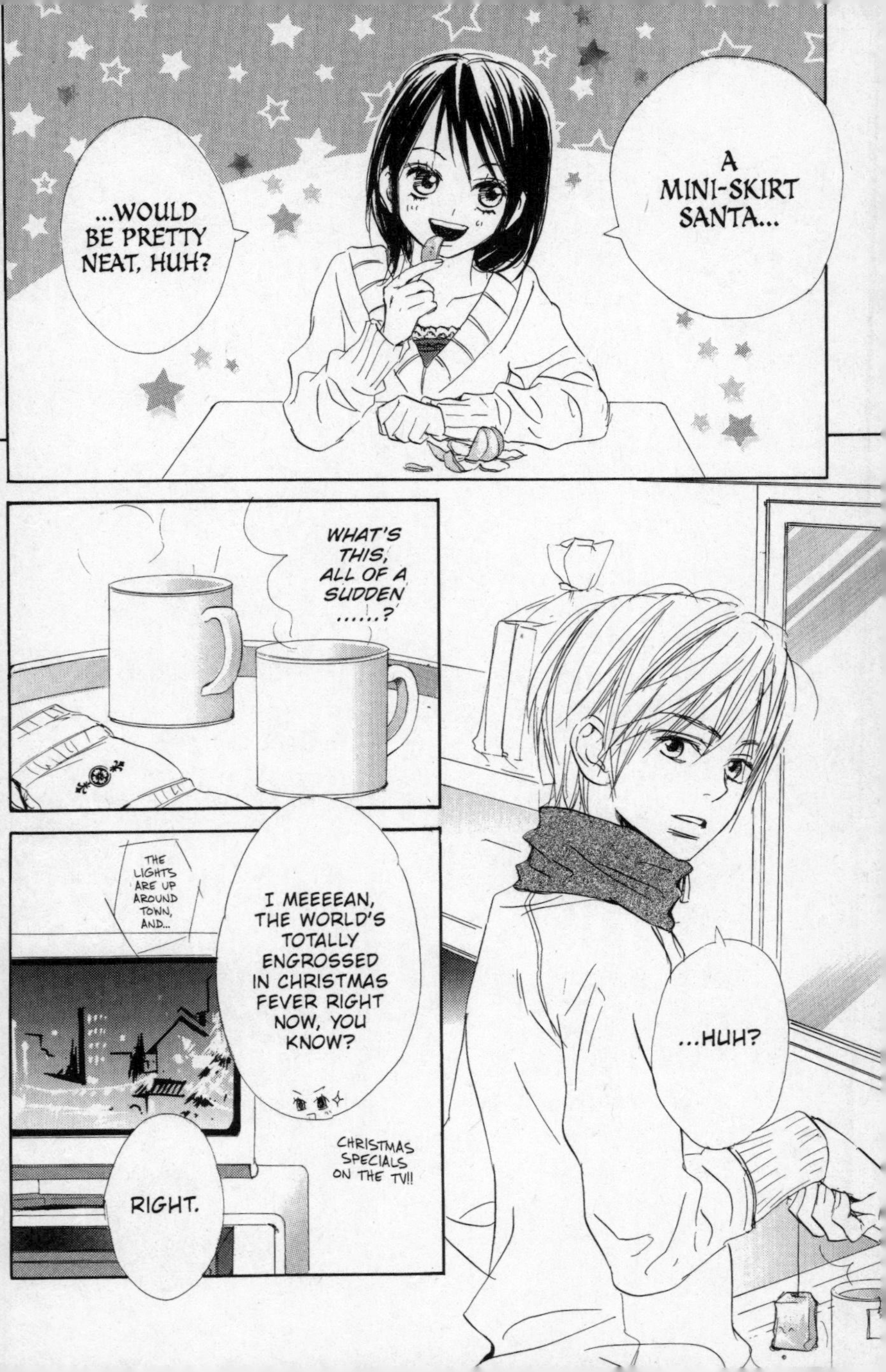
A MINI-SKIRT SANTA...
...WOULD BE PRETTY NEAT, HUH?
...HUH?
WHAT'S THIS, ALL OF A SUDDEN ......?
I MEEEEAN, THE WORLD'S TOTALLY ENGROSSED IN CHRISTMAS FEVER RIGHT NOW, YOU KNOW?
THE LIGHTS ARE UP AROUND TOWN, AND...
CHRISTMAS SPECIALS ON THE TV!!
RIGHT.

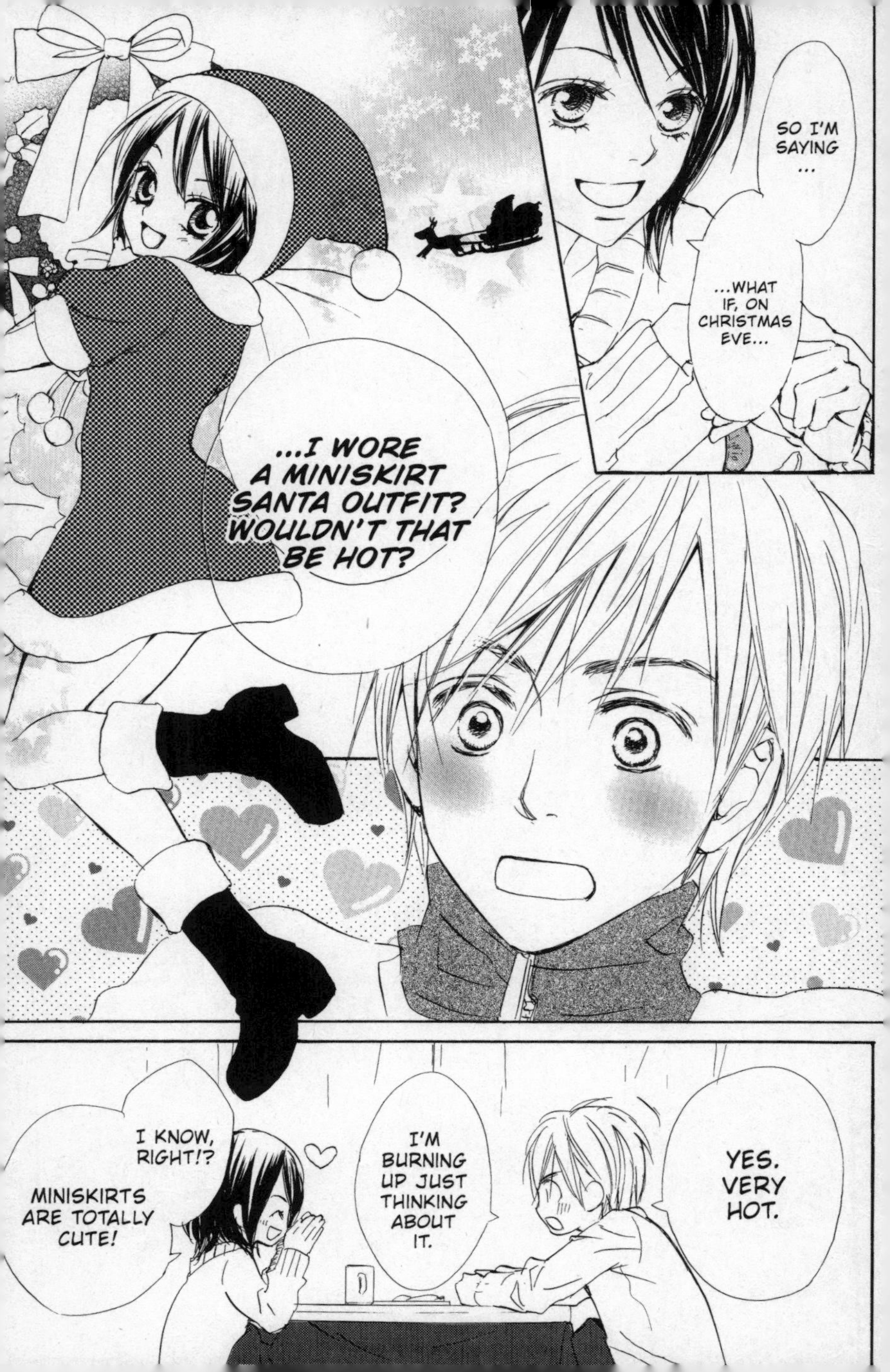
SO I'M SAYING ...
...WHAT IF, ON CHRISTMAS EVE...
...I WORE A MINISKIRT SANTA OUTFIT? WOULDN'T THAT BE HOT?
YES. VERY HOT.
I'M BURNING UP JUST THINKING ABOUT IT.
I KNOW, RIGHT!?
MINISKIRTS ARE TOTALLY CUTE!

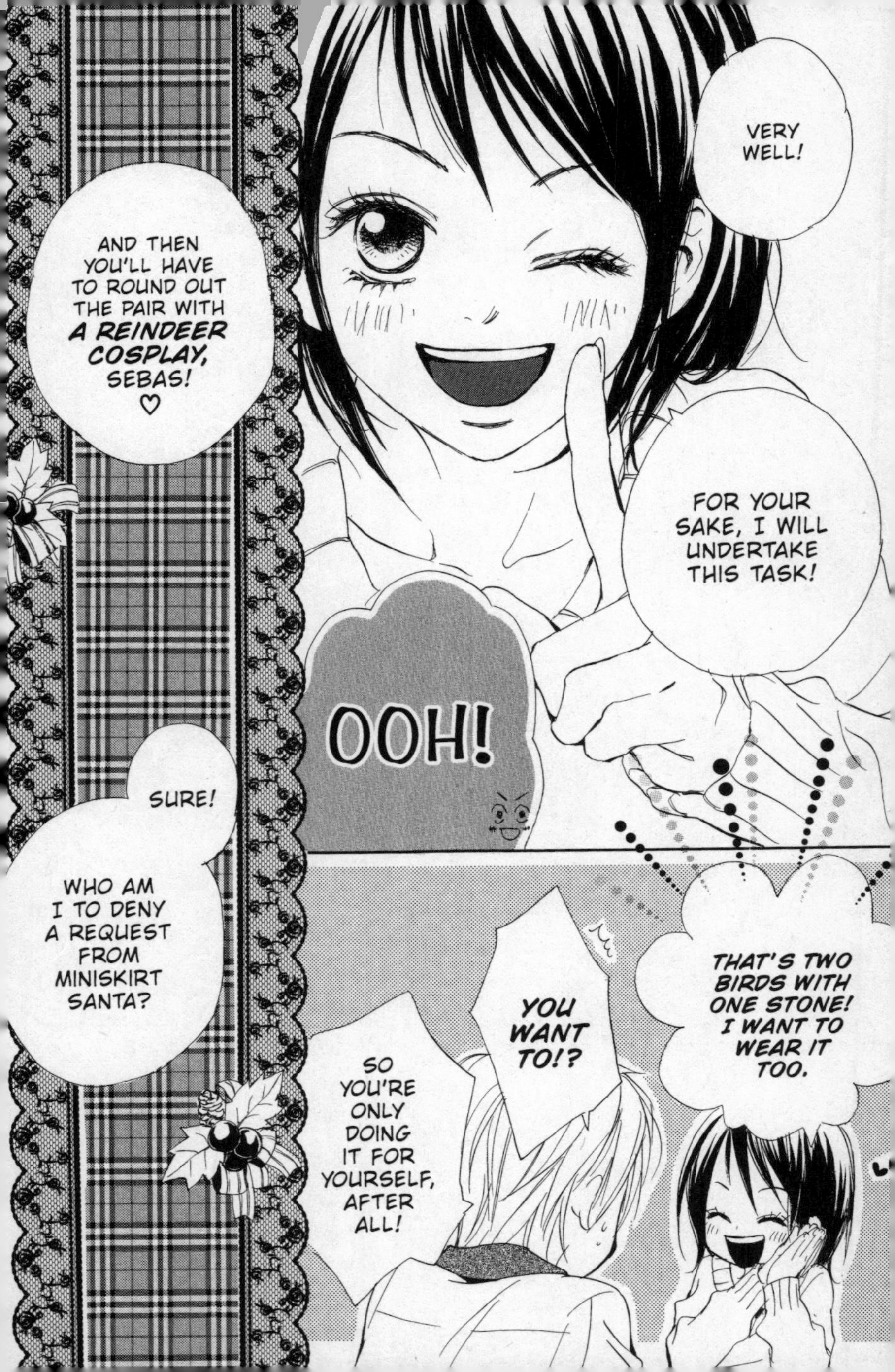

VERY WELL!
FOR YOUR SAKE, I WILL UNDERTAKE THIS TASK!
OOH!
THAT'S TWO BIRDS WITH ONE STONE! I WANT TO WEAR IT TOO.
YOU WANT TO!?
SO YOU'RE ONLY DOING IT FOR YOURSELF, AFTER ALL!
AND THEN YOU'LL HAVE TO ROUND OUT THE PAIR WITH A REINDEER COSPLAY, SEBAS! ♡
SURE!
WHO AM I TO DENY A REQUEST FROM MINISKIRT SANTA?

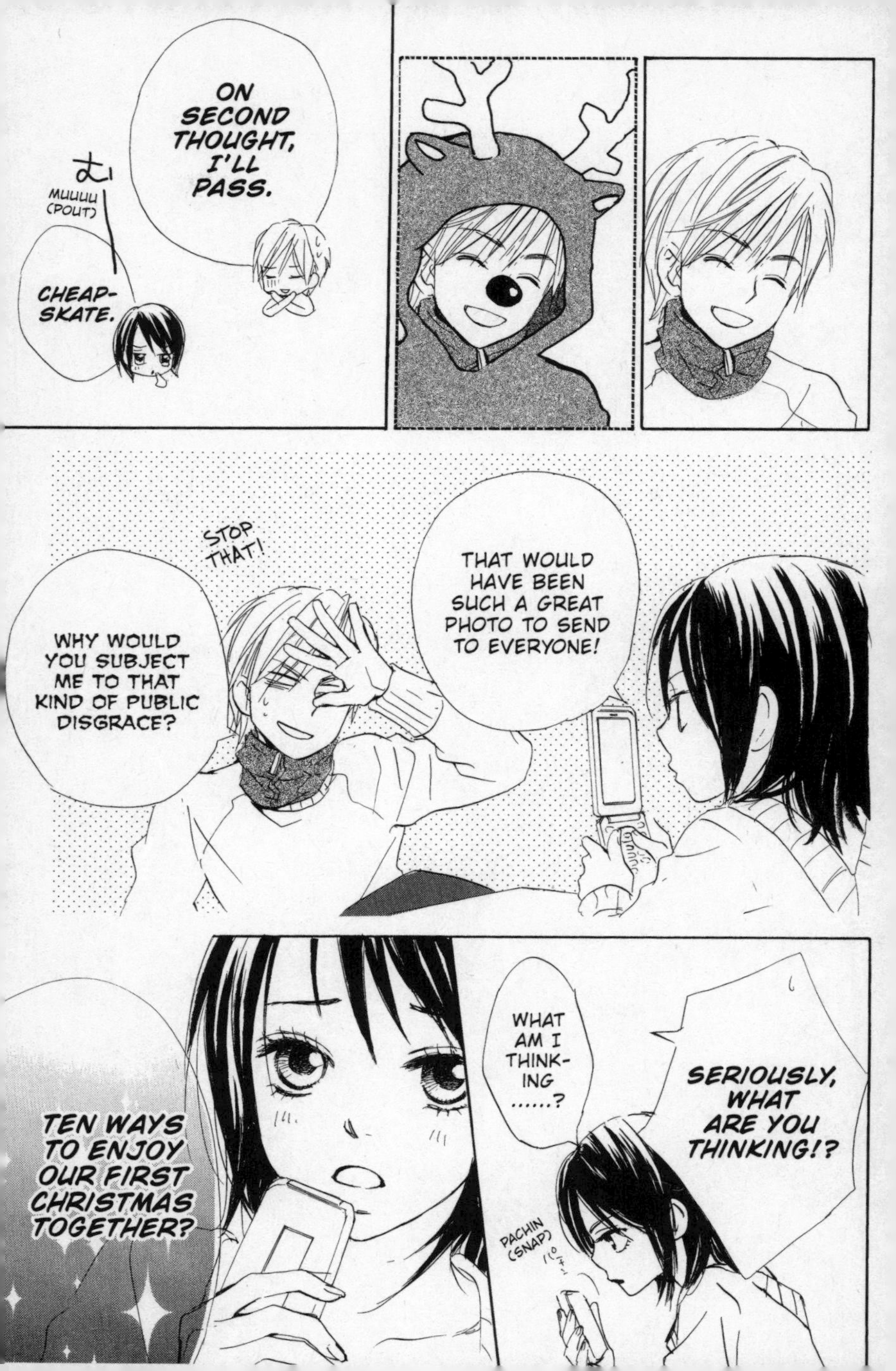
ON SECOND THOUGHT, I'LL PASS.
MUUUU (POUT)
CHEAP-SKATE.
THAT WOULD HAVE BEEN SUCH A GREAT PHOTO TO SEND TO EVERYONE!
STOP THAT!
WHY WOULD YOU SUBJECT ME TO THAT KIND OF PUBLIC DISGRACE?
SERIOUSLY, WHAT ARE YOU THINKING!?
WHAT AM I THINKING- ING ......?
PACHIN (SNAP)
TEN WAYS TO ENJOY OUR FIRST CHRISTMAS TOGETHER?

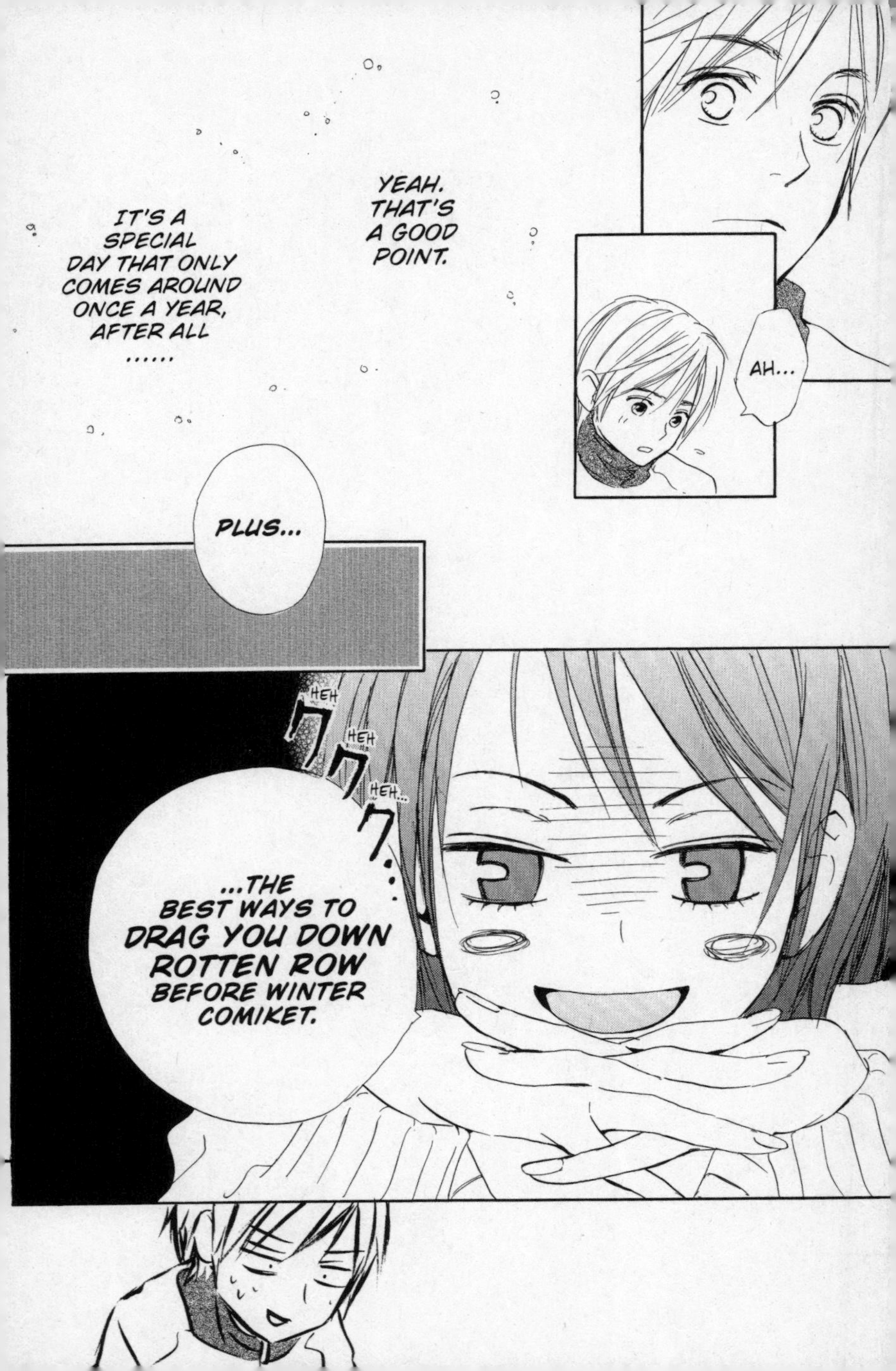
YEAH. THAT'S A GOOD POINT.
IT'S A SPECIAL DAY THAT ONLY COMES AROUND ONCE A YEAR, AFTER ALL ......
AH...
PLUS...
HEH HEH HEH...
...THE BEST WAYS TO DRAG YOU DOWN ROTTEN ROW BEFORE WINTER COMIKET.

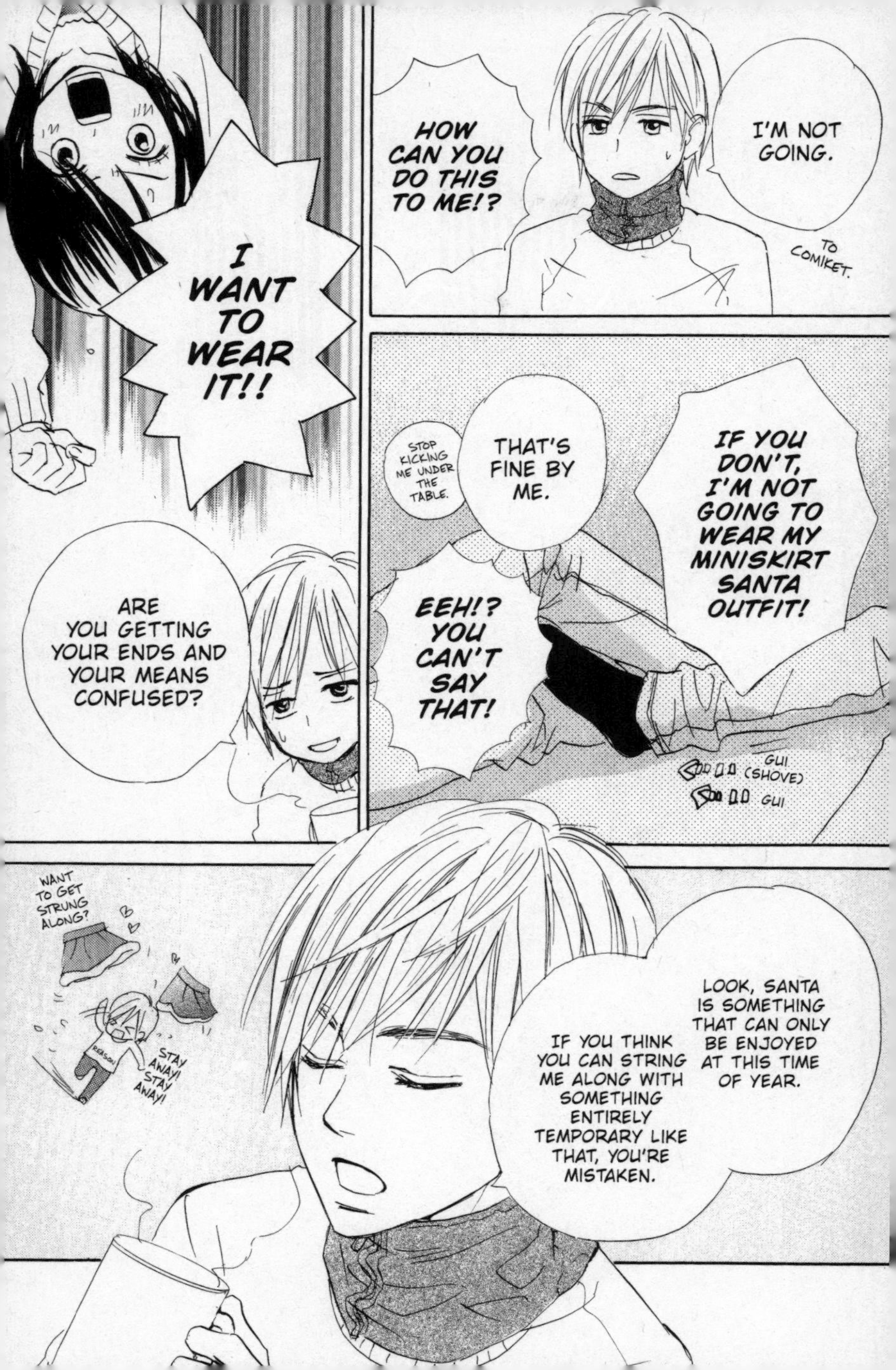
I'M NOT GOING.
TO COMIKET.
HOW CAN YOU DO THIS TO ME!?
I WANT TO WEAR IT!!
IF YOU DON'T, I'M NOT GOING TO WEAR MY MINISKIRT SANTA OUTFIT!
THAT'S FINE BY ME.
STOP KICKING ME UNDER THE TABLE.
EEH!? YOU CAN'T SAY THAT!
GUI (SHOVE)
GUI
ARE YOU GETTING YOUR ENDS AND YOUR MEANS CONFUSED?
LOOK, SANTA IS SOMETHING THAT CAN ONLY BE ENJOYED AT THIS TIME OF YEAR.
IF YOU THINK YOU CAN STRING ME ALONG WITH SOMETHING ENTIRELY TEMPORARY LIKE THAT, YOU'RE MISTAKEN.
WANT TO GET STRUNG ALONG?
STAY AWAY! STAY AWAY!
REASON

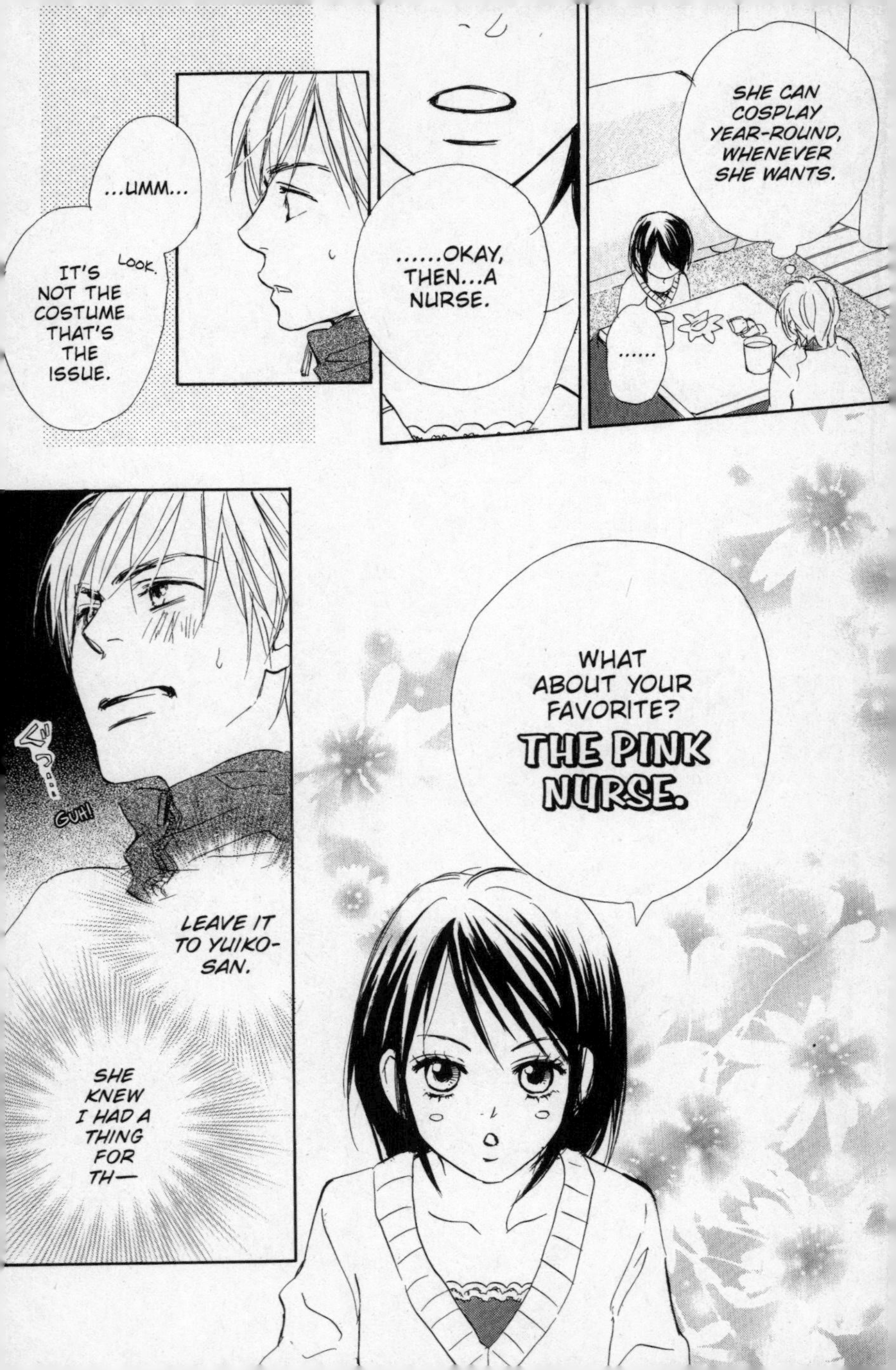

SHE CAN COSPLAY YEAR-ROUND, WHENEVER SHE WANTS.
......
......OKAY, THEN...A NURSE.
...UMM...
LOOK.
IT'S NOT THE COSTUME THAT'S THE ISSUE.
WHAT ABOUT YOUR FAVORITE? THE PINK NURSE.
GUH!
LEAVE IT TO YUIKO-SAN.
SHE KNEW I HAD A THING FOR TH—

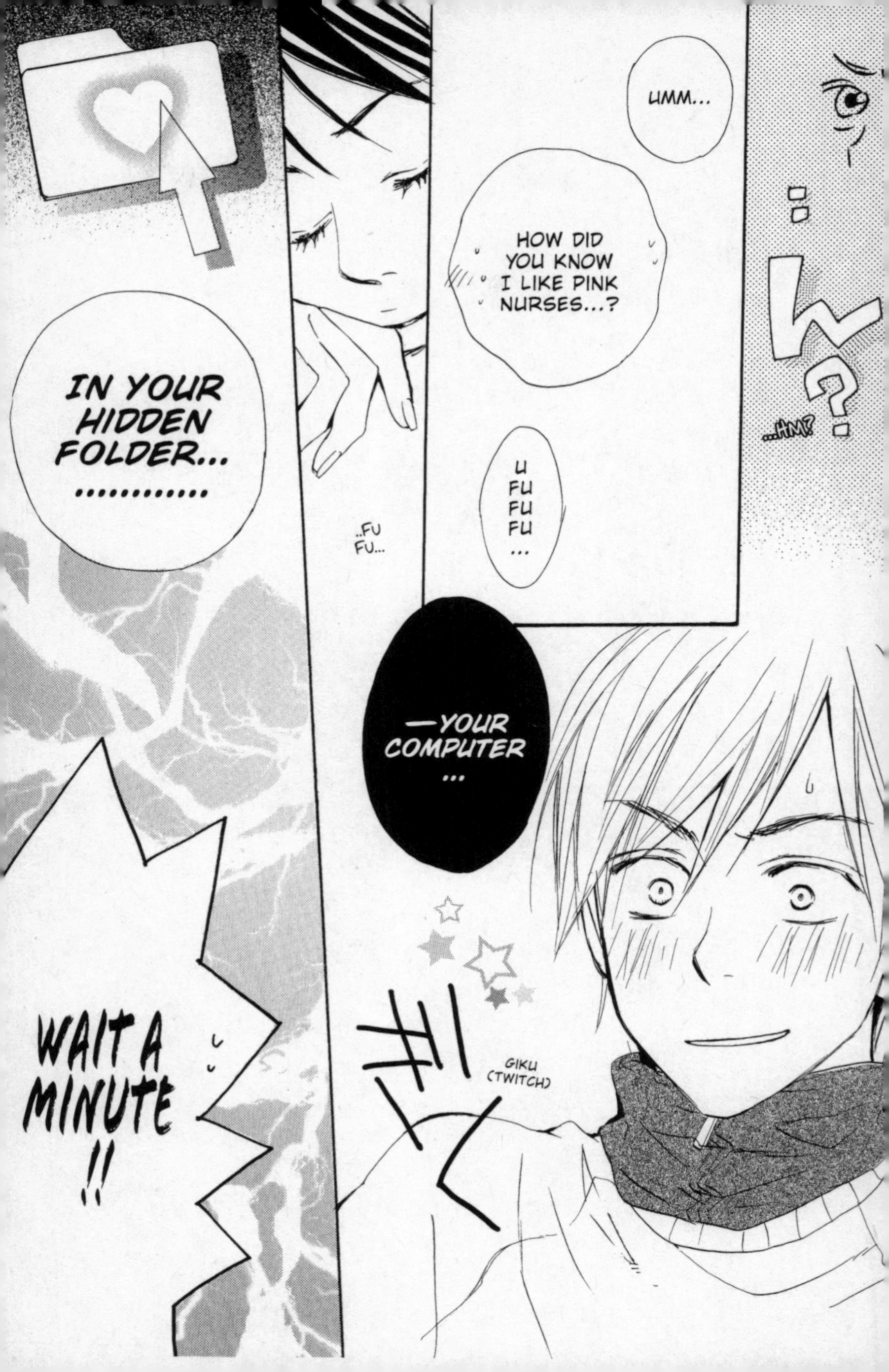
...HM?
UMM...
HOW DID YOU KNOW I LIKE PINK NURSES...?
U FU FU FU ...
..FU FU...
—YOUR COMPUTER ...
GIKU (TWITCH)
IN YOUR HIDDEN FOLDER... ....
WAIT A MINUTE !!

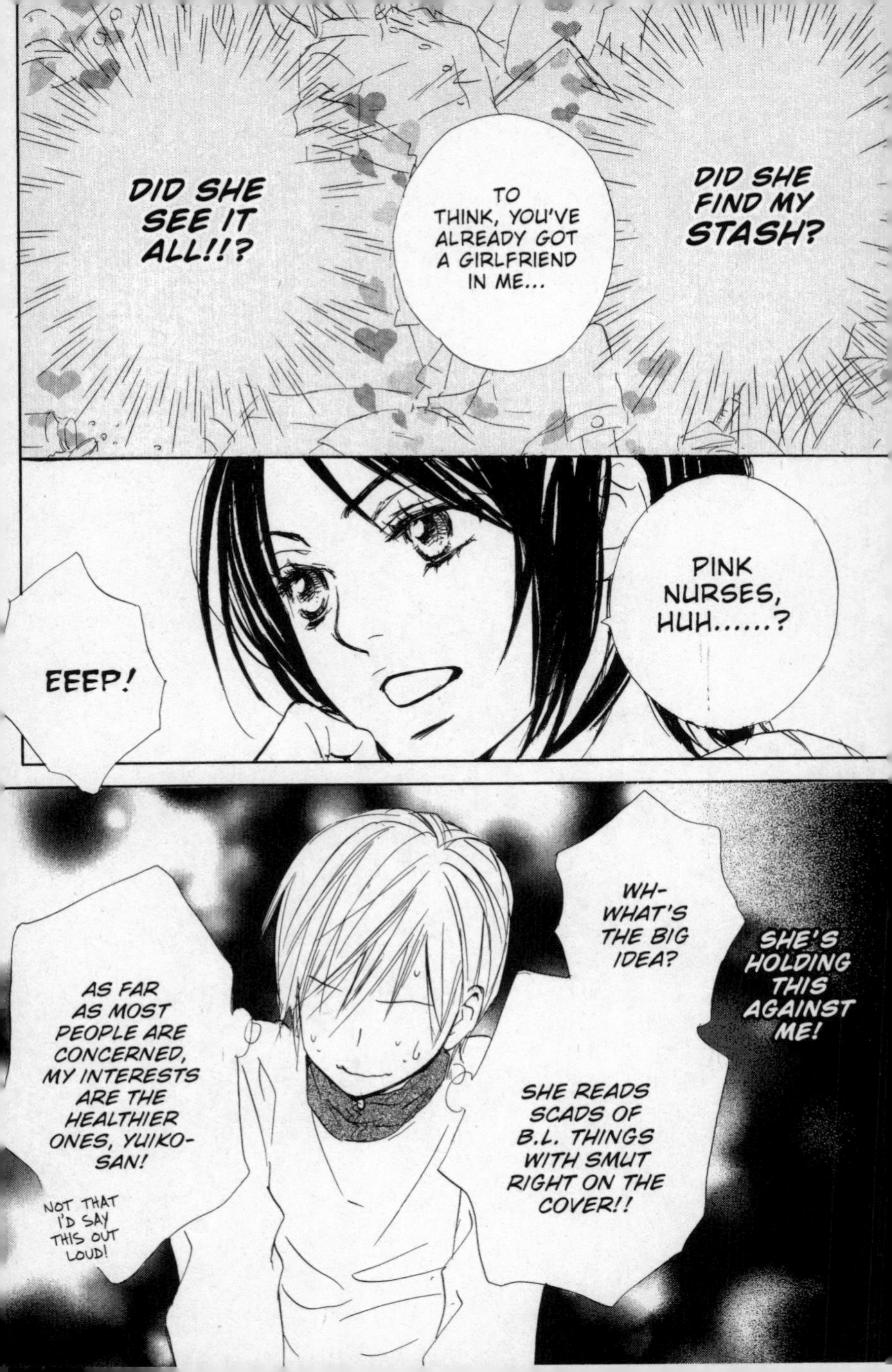
DID SHE FIND MY STASH?
TO THINK, YOU'VE ALREADY GOT A GIRLFRIEND IN ME...
DID SHE SEE IT ALL!!?
PINK NURSES, HUH......?
EEEP!
SHE'S HOLDING THIS AGAINST ME!
WH-WHAT'S THE BIG IDEA?
SHE READS SCADS OF B.L. THINGS WITH SMUT RIGHT ON THE COVER!!
AS FAR AS MOST PEOPLE ARE CONCERNED, MY INTERESTS ARE THE HEALTHIER ONES, YUIKO-SAN!
NOT THAT I'D SAY THIS OUT LOUD!

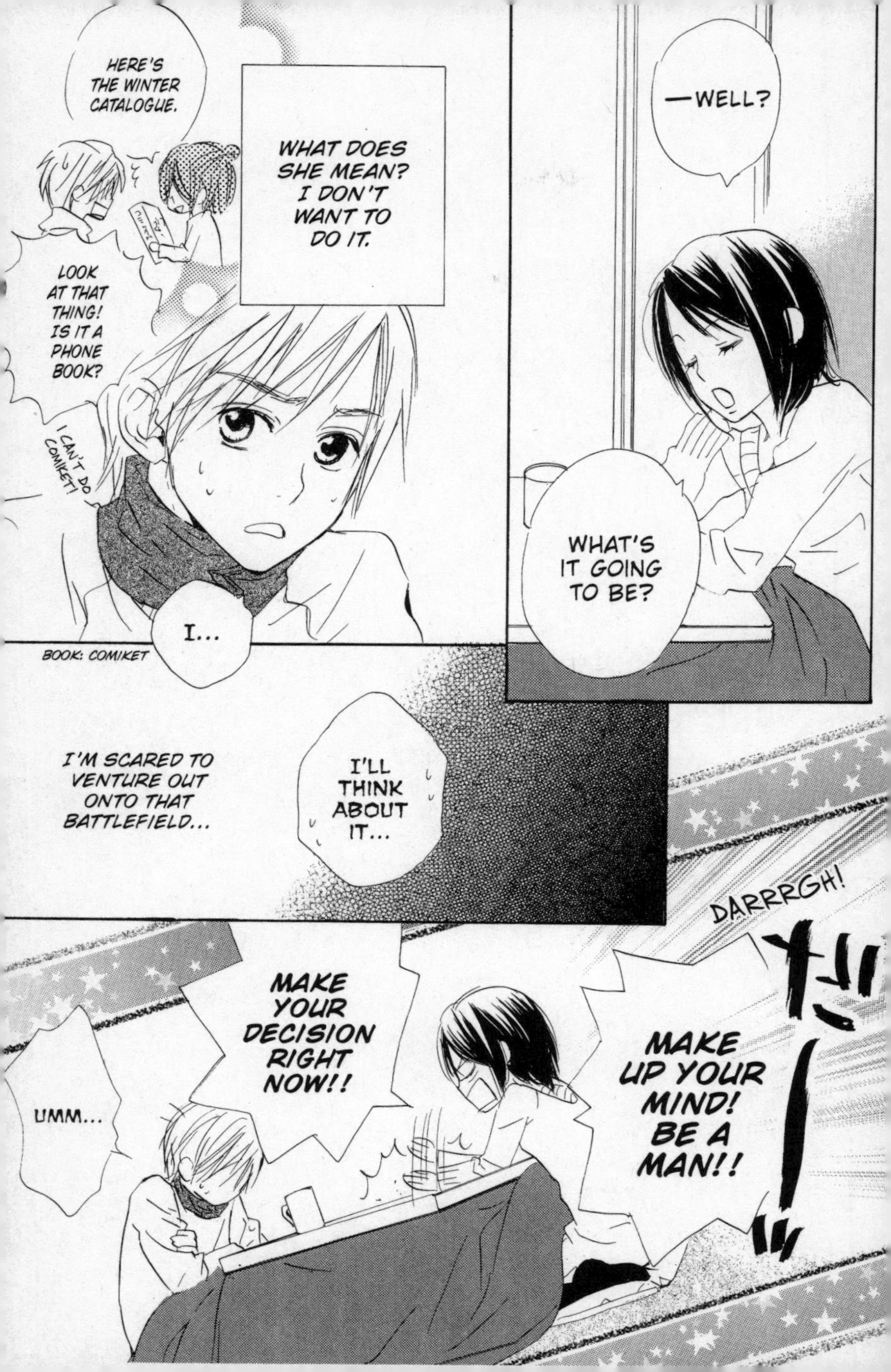
—WELL?
WHAT'S IT GOING TO BE?
WHAT DOES SHE MEAN? I DON'T WANT TO DO IT.
HERE'S THE WINTER CATALOGUE.
LOOK AT THAT THING! IS IT A PHONE BOOK?
I CAN'T DO COMIKET!
I...
BOOK: COMIKET
I'LL THINK ABOUT IT...
I'M SCARED TO VENTURE OUT ONTO THAT BATTLEFIELD...
DARRRGH!
MAKE UP YOUR MIND! BE A MAN!!
MAKE YOUR DECISION RIGHT NOW!!
UMM...

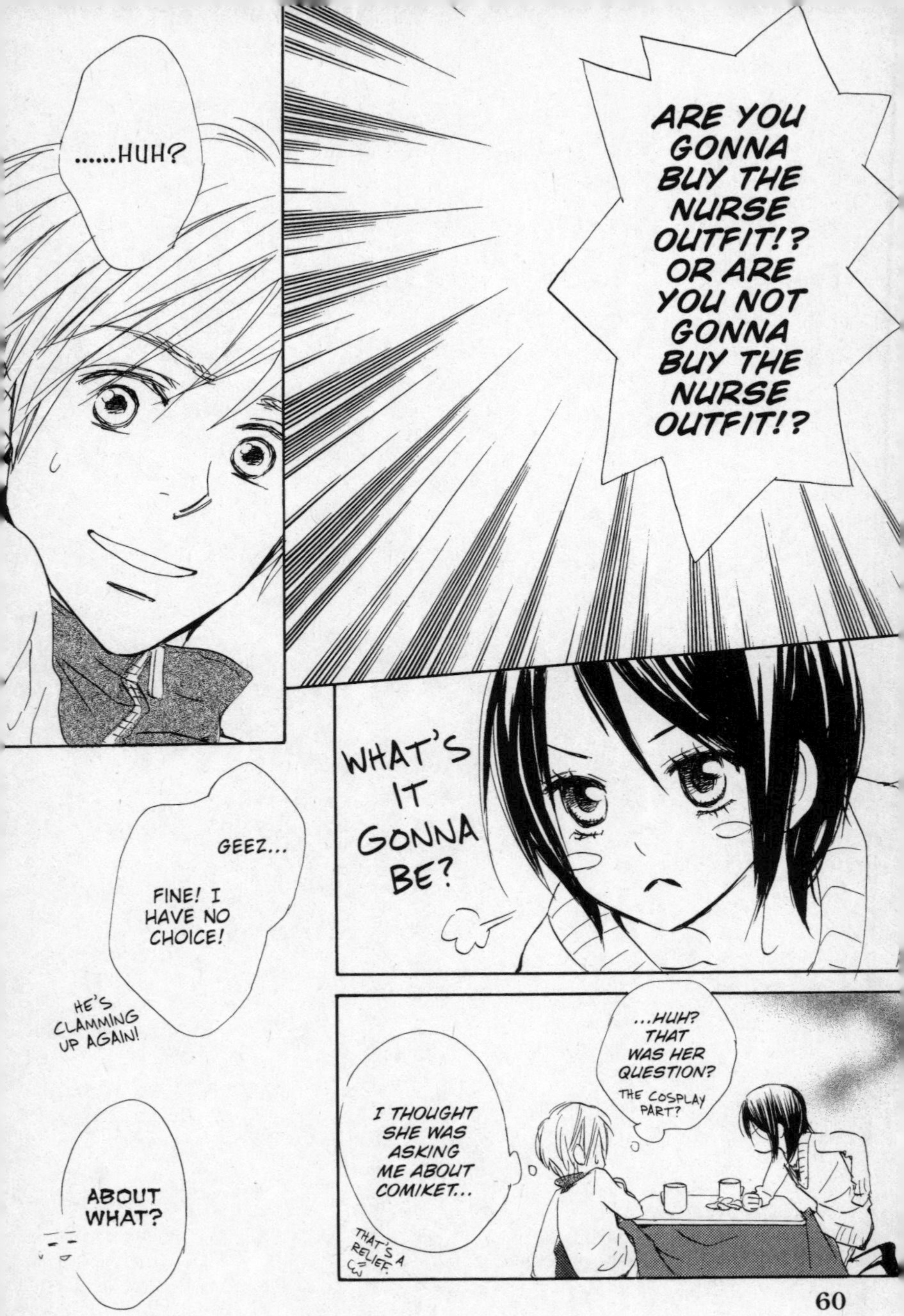
ARE YOU GONNA BUY THE NURSE OUTFIT!? OR ARE YOU NOT GONNA BUY THE NURSE OUTFIT!?
WHAT'S IT GONNA BE?
......HUH?
GEEZ...
FINE! I HAVE NO CHOICE!
HE'S CLAMMING UP AGAIN!
...HUH? THAT WAS HER QUESTION?
THE COSPLAY PART?
I THOUGHT SHE WAS ASKING ME ABOUT COMIKET...
THAT'S A RELIEF.
ABOUT WHAT?

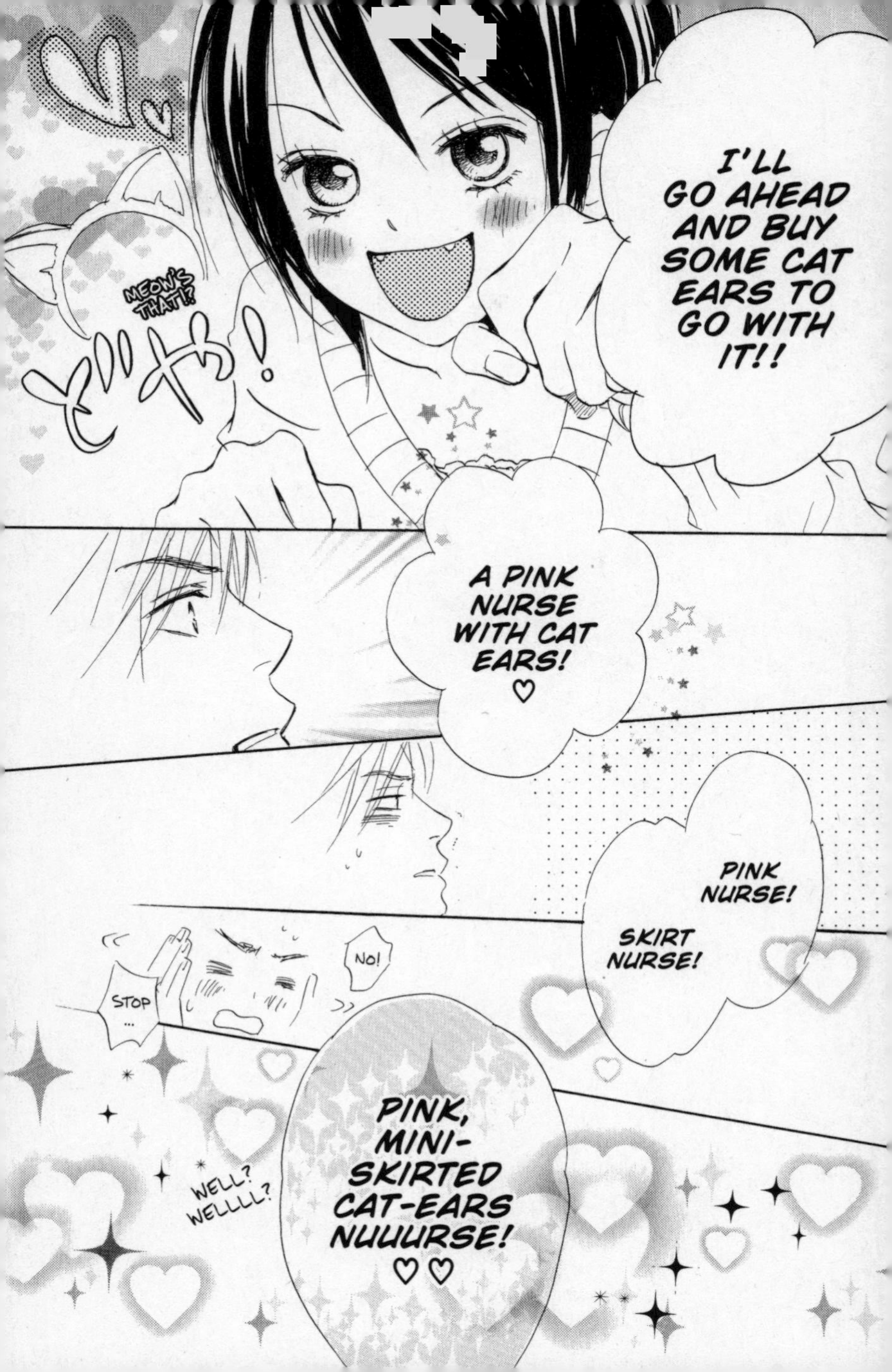
I'LL GO AHEAD AND BUY SOME CAT EARS TO GO WITH IT!!
MEOW'S THAT!?
A PINK NURSE WITH CAT EARS! ♡
PINK NURSE!
SKIRT NURSE!
NO!
STOP ...
PINK, MINI-SKIRTED CAT-EARS NUUURSE! ♡♡
WELL? WELLLL?

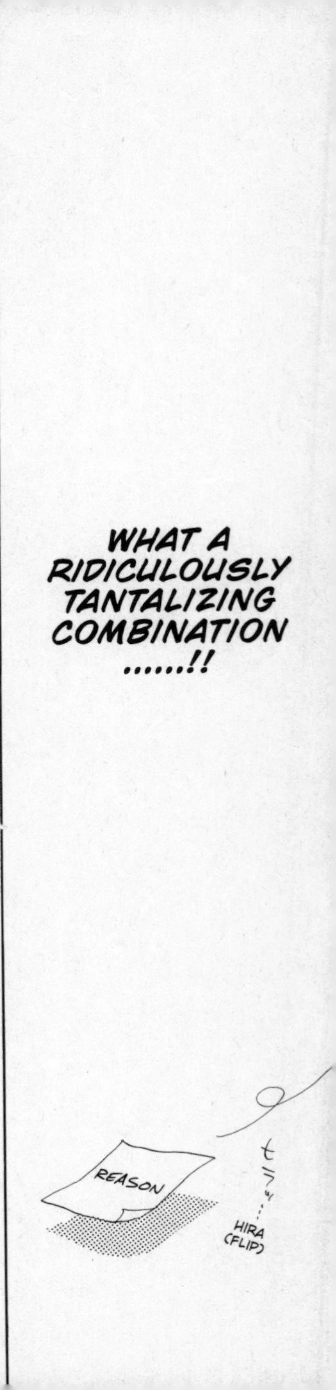
WHAT A RIDICULOUSLY TANTALIZING COMBINATION ......!!
ヒラッ…
HIRA (FLIP)
REASON

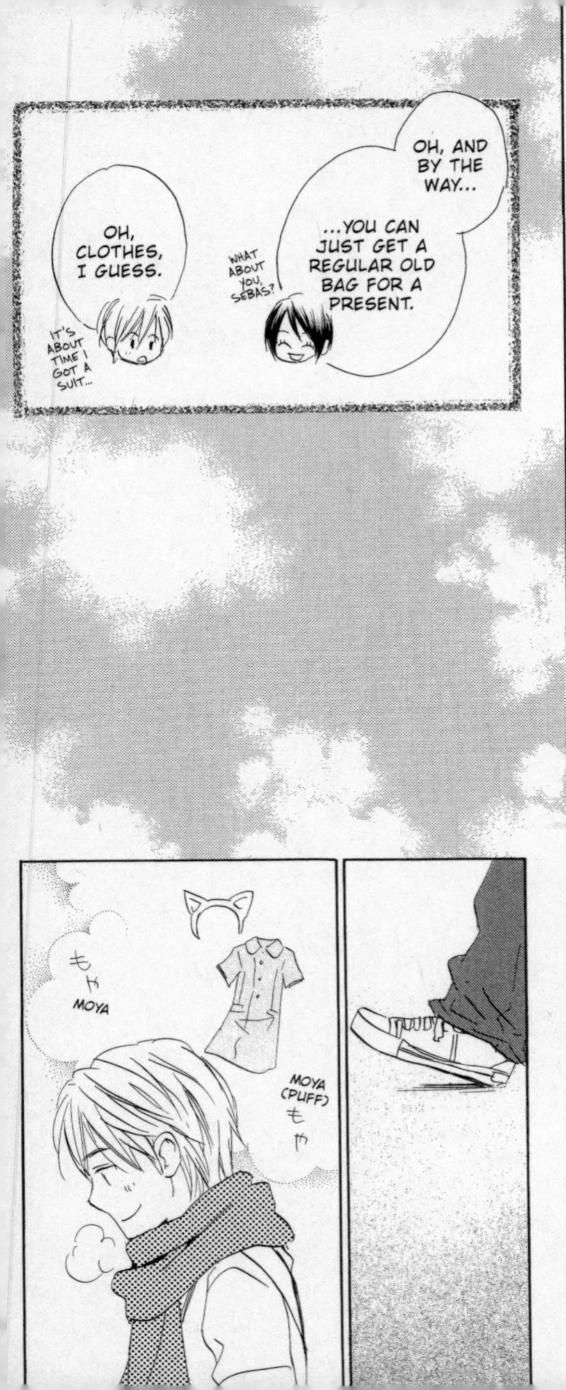
OH, AND BY THE WAY...
...YOU CAN JUST GET A REGULAR OLD BAG FOR A PRESENT.
WHAT ABOUT YOU, SEBAS?
OH, CLOTHES, I GUESS.
IT'S ABOUT TIME I GOT A SUIT...
もや
MOYA (PUFF)
もや
MOYA

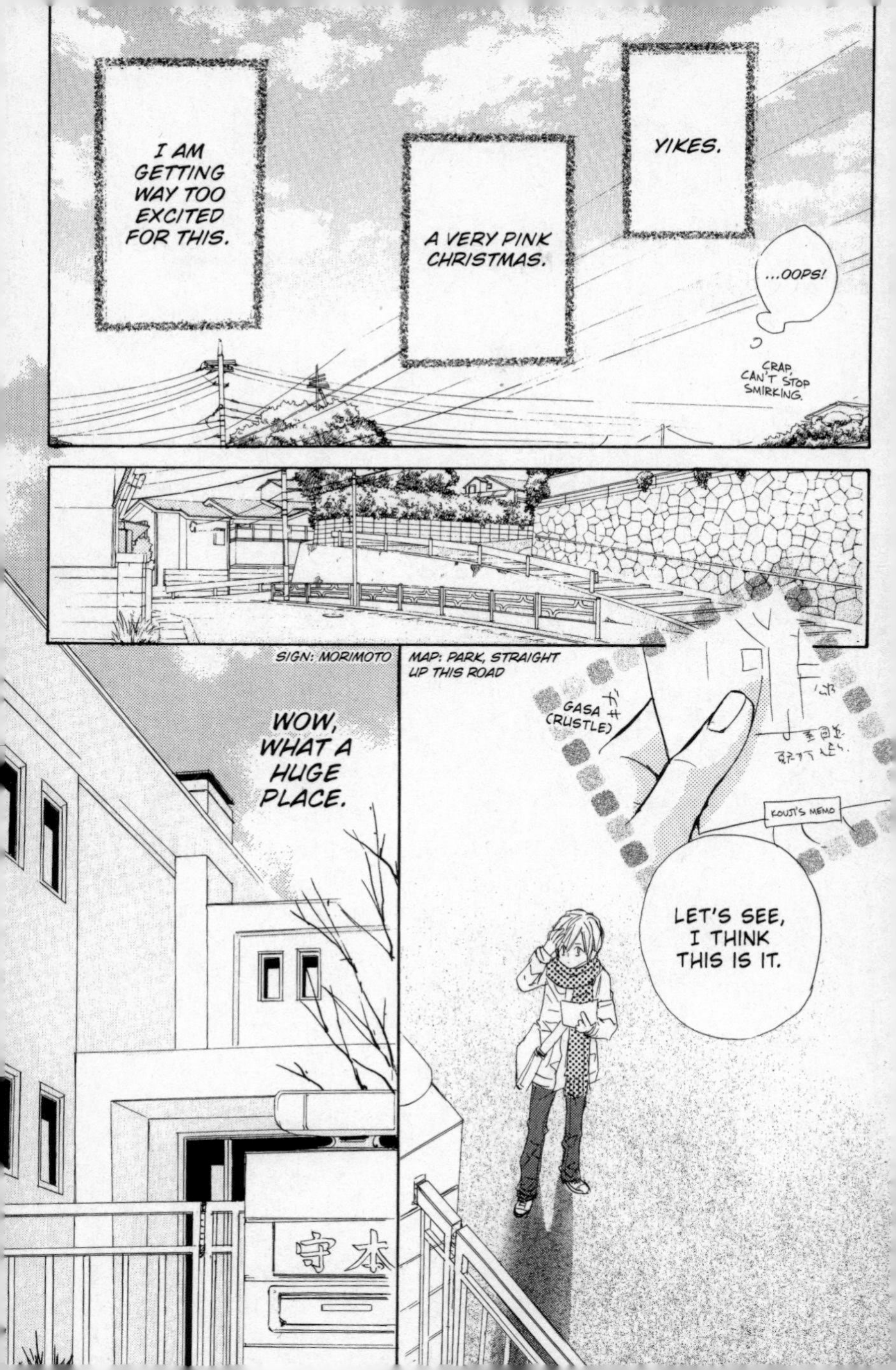
YIKES.
...OOPS!
CRAP, CAN'T STOP SMIRKING.
A VERY PINK CHRISTMAS.
I AM GETTING WAY TOO EXCITED FOR THIS.
MAP: PARK, STRAIGHT UP THIS ROAD
GASA (RUSTLE)
KOUJI'S MEMO
LET'S SEE, I THINK THIS IS IT.
SIGN: MORIMOTO
WOW, WHAT A HUGE PLACE.
守本

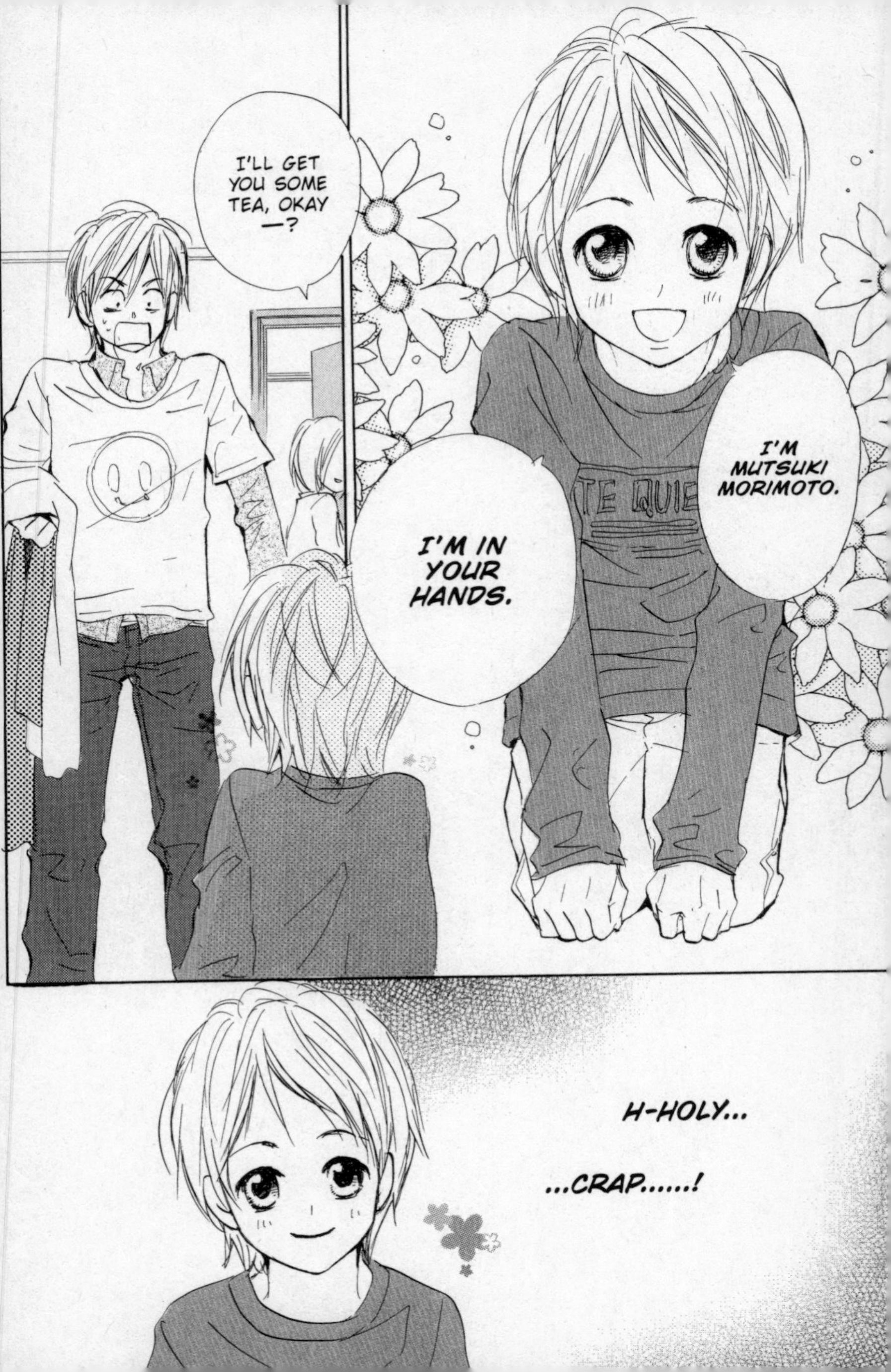
I'M MUTSUKI MORIMOTO.
I'M IN YOUR HANDS.
I'LL GET YOU SOME TEA, OKAY —?
H-HOLY...
...CRAP......!

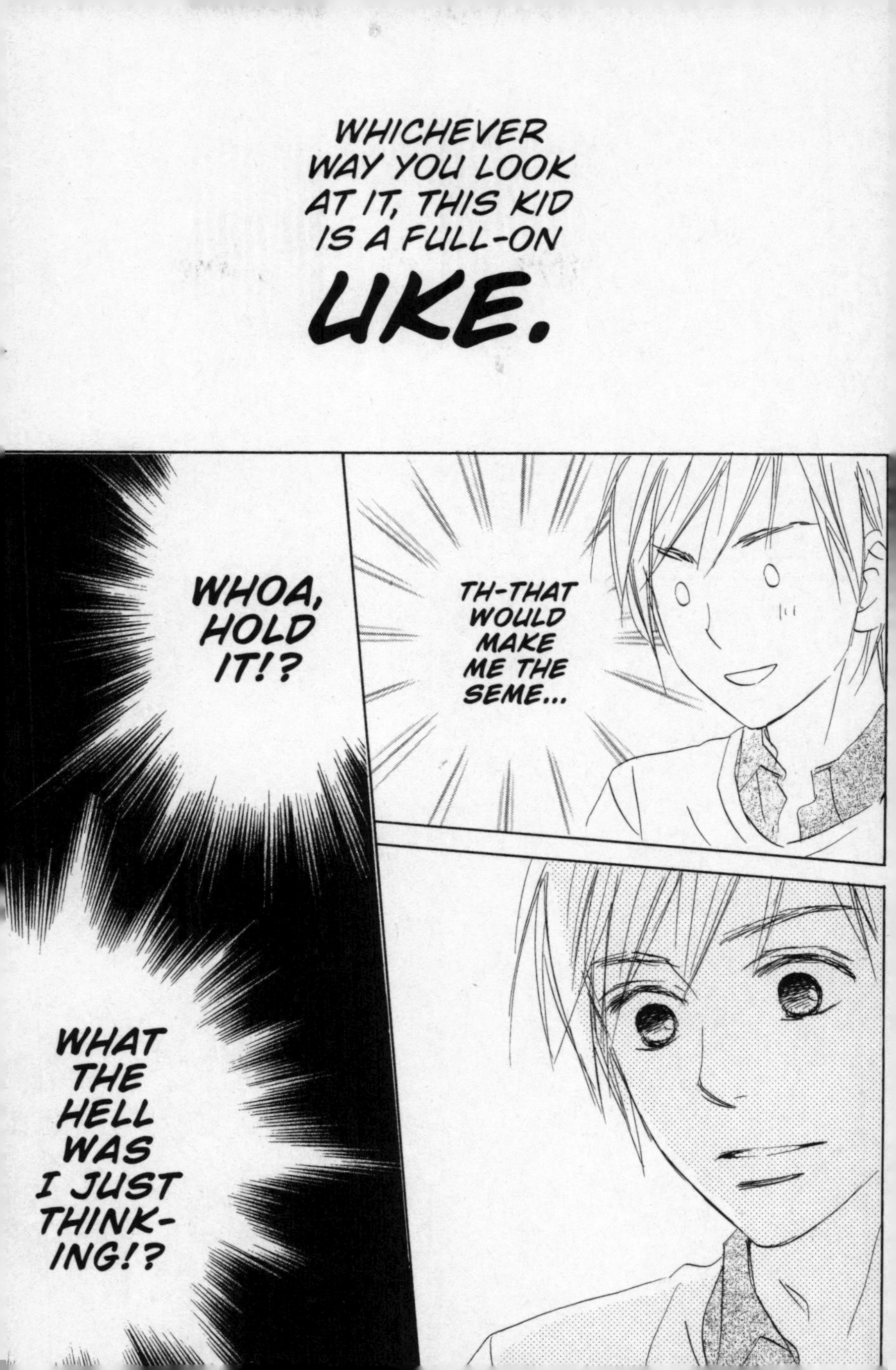

WHICHEVER WAY YOU LOOK AT IT, THIS KID IS A FULL-ON
UKE.
TH-THAT WOULD MAKE ME THE SEME...
WHOA, HOLD IT!?
WHAT THE HELL WAS I JUST THINKING!?

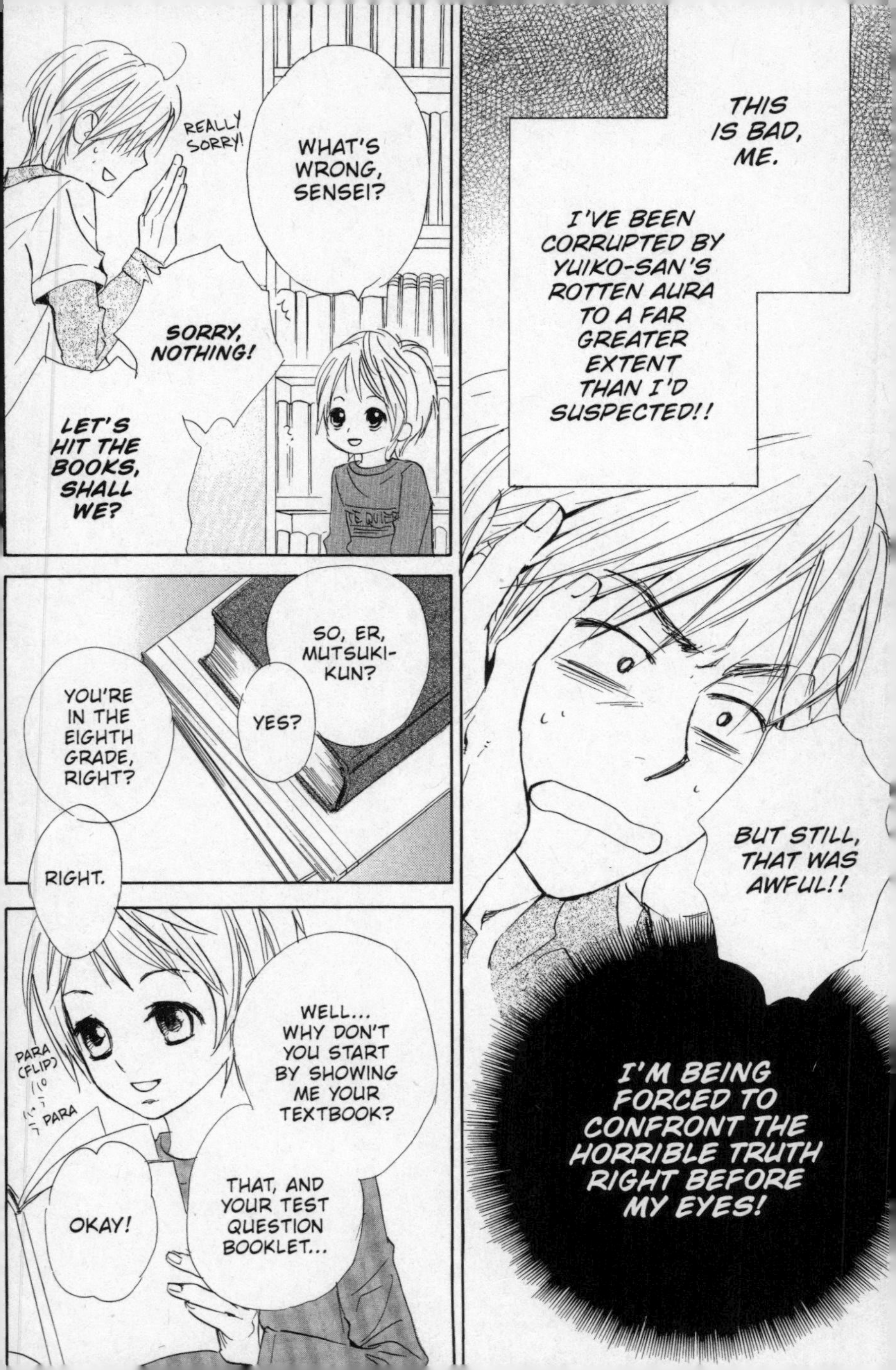
THIS IS BAD, ME.
I'VE BEEN CORRUPTED BY YUIKO-SAN'S ROTTEN AURA TO A FAR GREATER EXTENT THAN I'D SUSPECTED!!
BUT STILL, THAT WAS AWFUL!!
I'M BEING FORCED TO CONFRONT THE HORRIBLE TRUTH RIGHT BEFORE MY EYES!
WHAT'S WRONG, SENSEI?
REALLY SORRY!
SORRY, NOTHING!
LET'S HIT THE BOOKS, SHALL WE?
SO, ER, MUTSUKI-KUN?
YES?
YOU'RE IN THE EIGHTH GRADE, RIGHT?
RIGHT.
WELL... WHY DON'T YOU START BY SHOWING ME YOUR TEXTBOOK?
THAT, AND YOUR TEST QUESTION BOOKLET...
PARA (FLIP) PARA
OKAY!

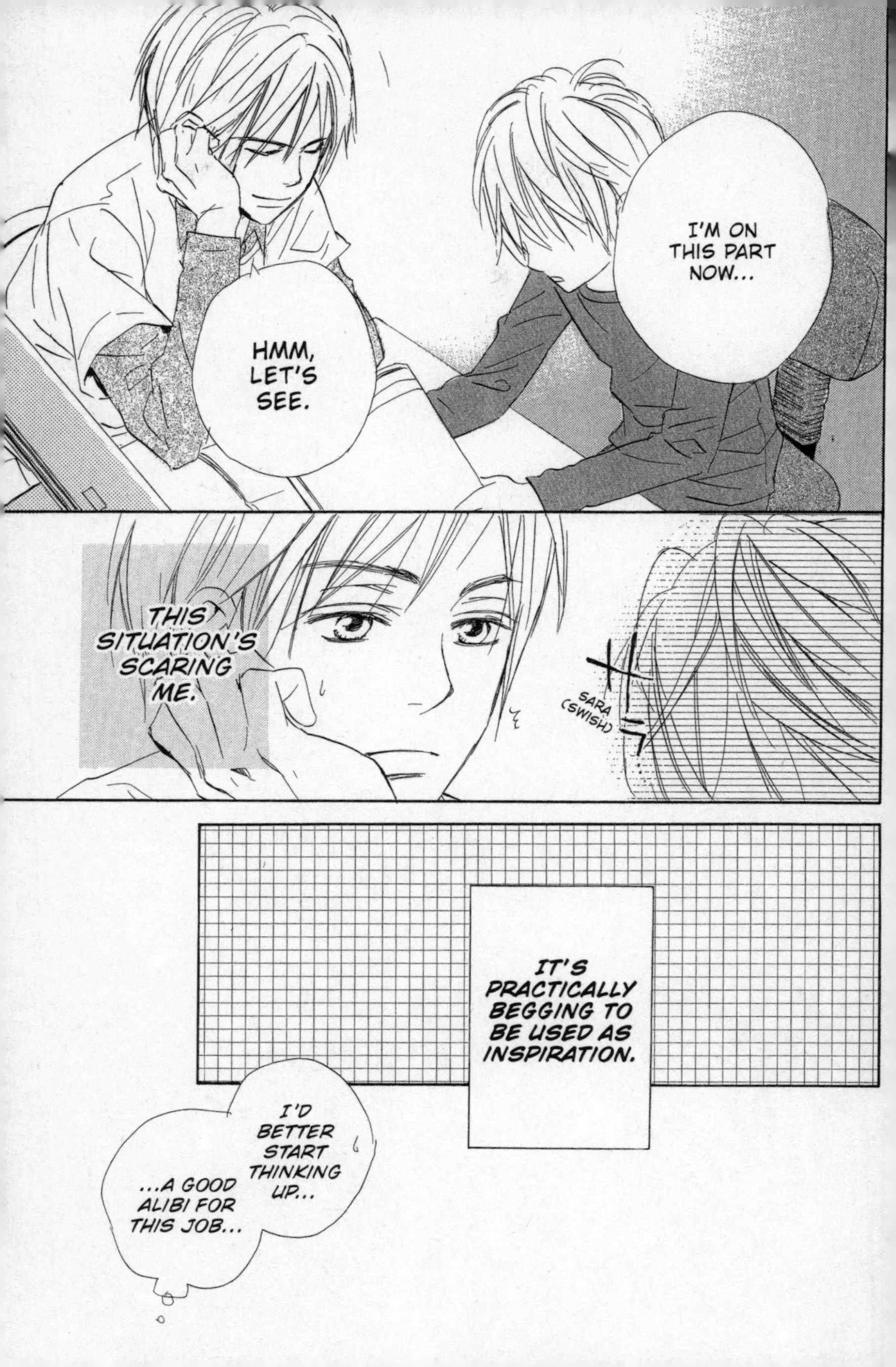
I'M ON THIS PART NOW...
HMM, LET'S SEE.
SARA (SWISH)
THIS SITUATION'S SCARING ME.
IT'S PRACTICALLY BEGGING TO BE USED AS INSPIRATION.
I'D BETTER START THINKING UP...
...A GOOD ALIBI FOR THIS JOB...

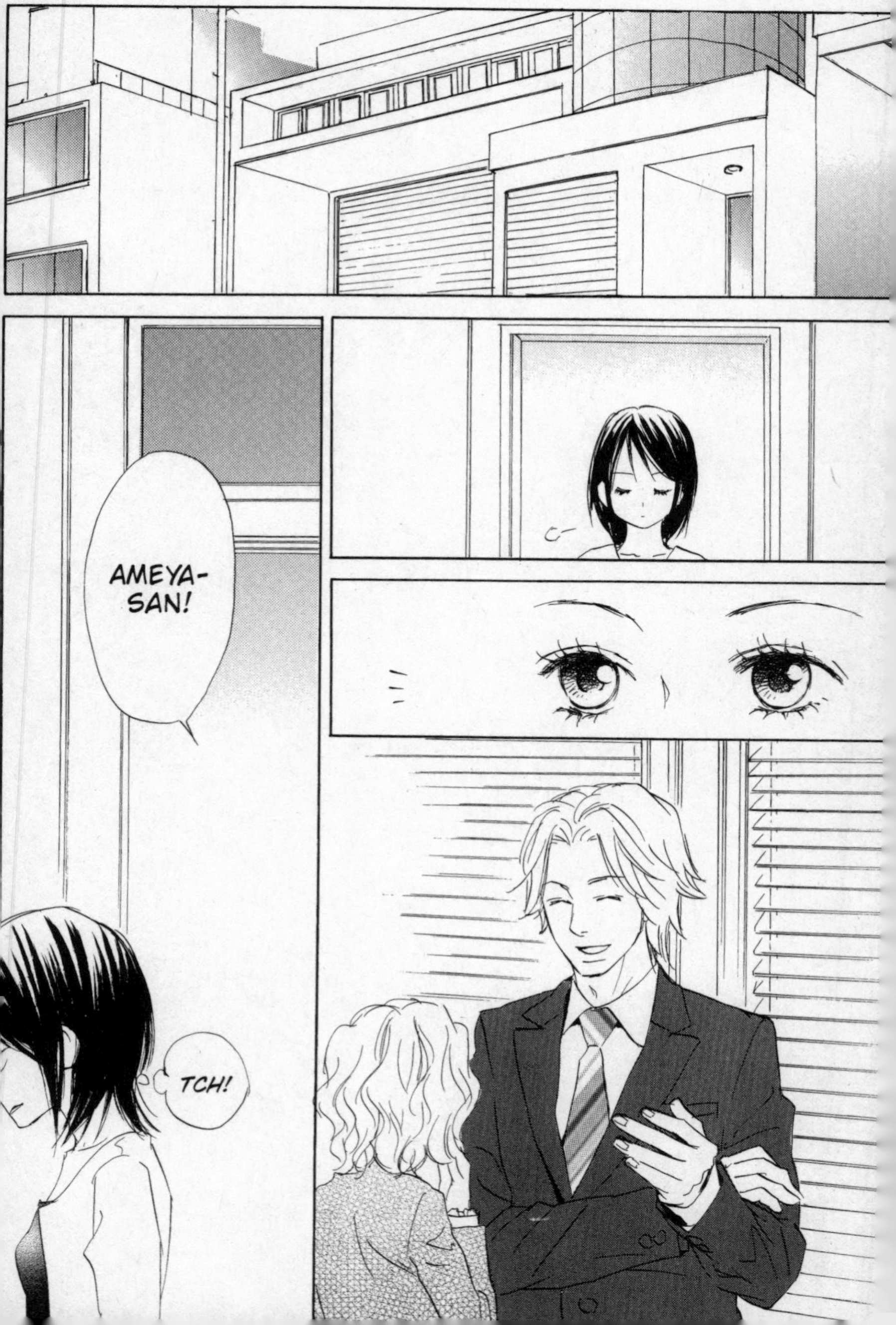
AMEYA-SAN!
TCH!

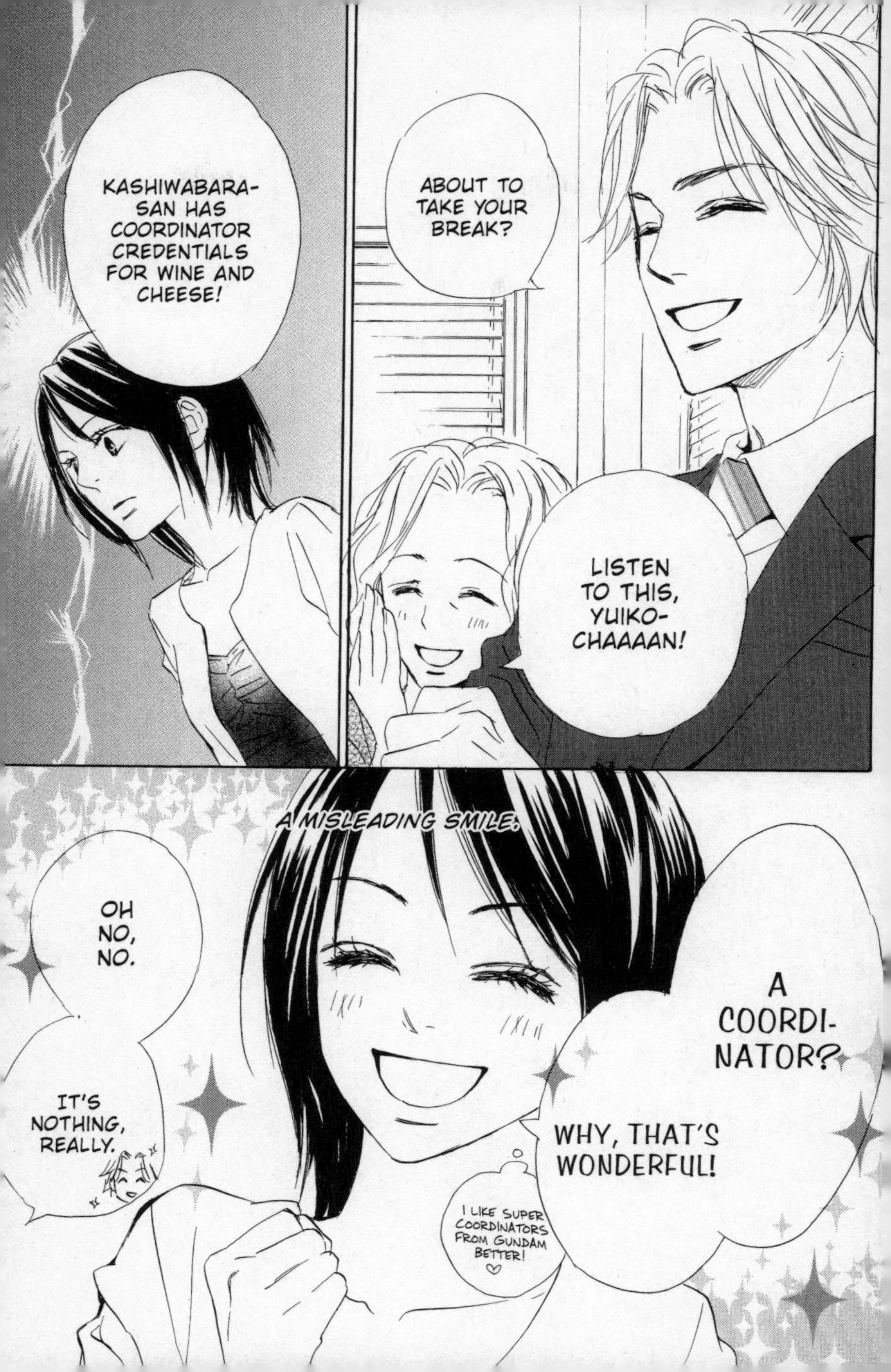
ABOUT TO TAKE YOUR BREAK?
LISTEN TO THIS, YUIKO-CHAAAAN!
KASHIWABARA-SAN HAS COORDINATOR CREDENTIALS FOR WINE AND CHEESE!
A MISLEADING SMILE.
A COORDINATOR?
WHY, THAT'S WONDERFUL!
I LIKE SUPER COORDINATORS FROM GUNDAM BETTER! ♡
OH NO, NO.
IT'S NOTHING, REALLY.

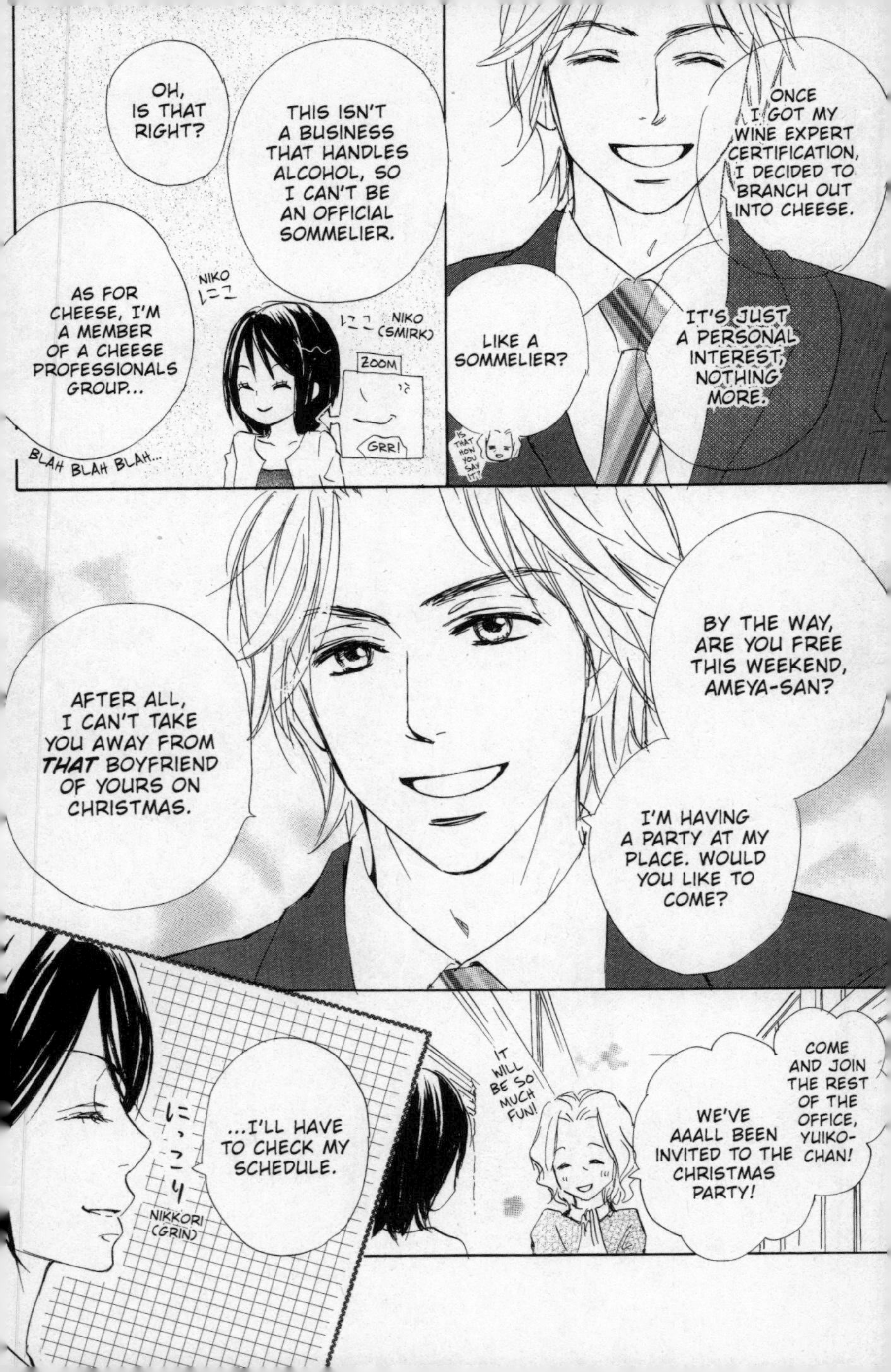
ONCE I GOT MY WINE EXPERT CERTIFICATION, I DECIDED TO BRANCH OUT INTO CHEESE.
IT'S JUST A PERSONAL INTEREST, NOTHING MORE.
LIKE A SOMMELIER?
IS THAT HOW YOU SAY IT?
THIS ISN'T A BUSINESS THAT HANDLES ALCOHOL, SO I CAN'T BE AN OFFICIAL SOMMELIER.
OH, IS THAT RIGHT?
にこ NIKO
にこ NIKO (SMIRK)
AS FOR CHEESE, I'M A MEMBER OF A CHEESE PROFESSIONALS GROUP...
ZOOM
GRR!
BLAH BLAH BLAH...
BY THE WAY, ARE YOU FREE THIS WEEKEND, AMEYA-SAN?
I'M HAVING A PARTY AT MY PLACE. WOULD YOU LIKE TO COME?
AFTER ALL, I CAN'T TAKE YOU AWAY FROM *THAT* BOYFRIEND OF YOURS ON CHRISTMAS.
COME AND JOIN THE REST OF THE OFFICE, YUIKO-CHAN!
WE'VE AAALL BEEN INVITED TO THE CHRISTMAS PARTY!
IT WILL BE SO MUCH FUN!
...I'LL HAVE TO CHECK MY SCHEDULE.
にっこり NIKKORI (GRIN)

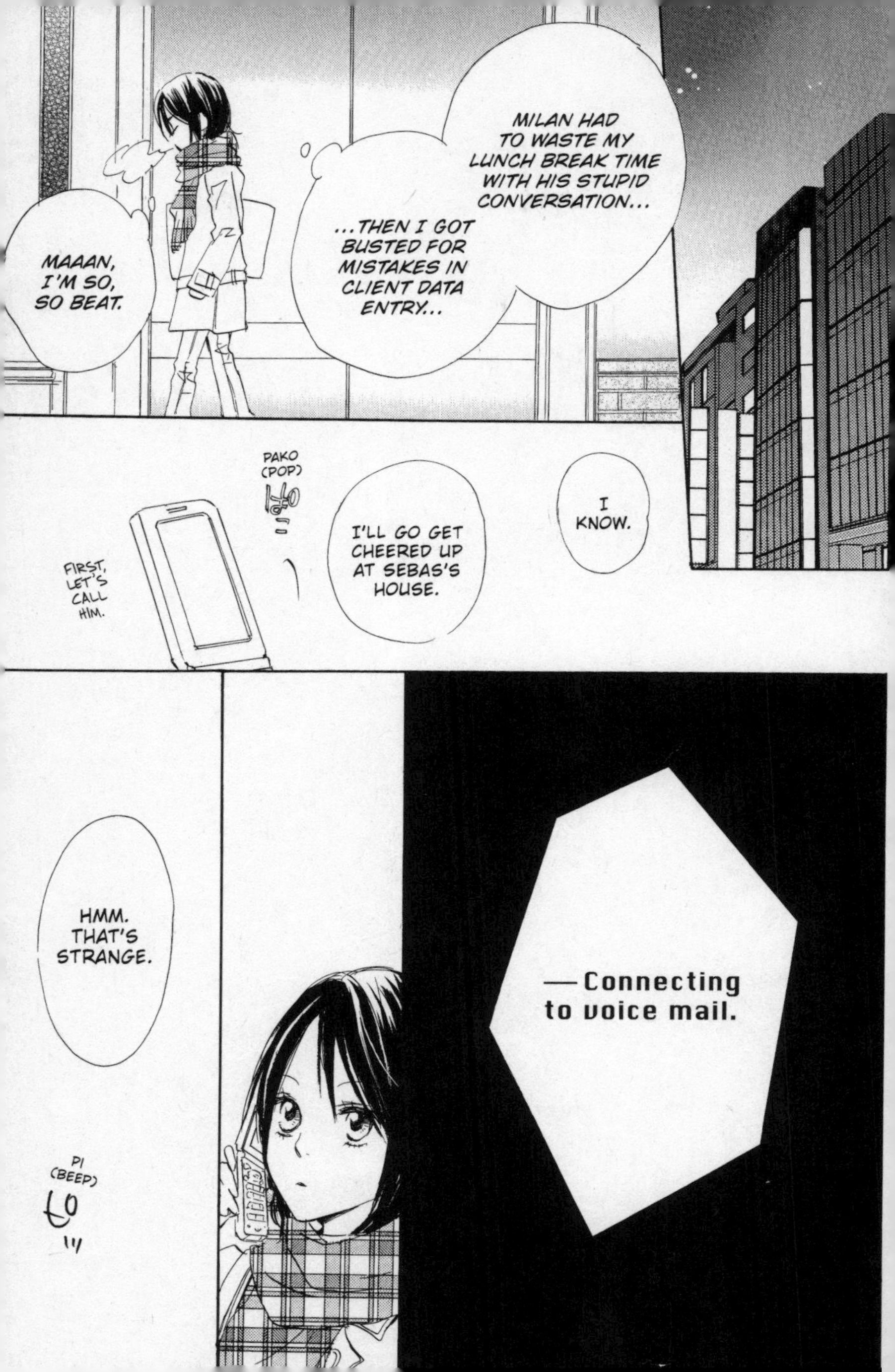
MILAN HAD TO WASTE MY LUNCH BREAK TIME WITH HIS STUPID CONVERSATION...
...THEN I GOT BUSTED FOR MISTAKES IN CLIENT DATA ENTRY...
MAAAN, I'M SO, SO BEAT.
I KNOW.
I'LL GO GET CHEERED UP AT SEBAS'S HOUSE.
PAKO (POP)
FIRST, LET'S CALL HIM.
—Connecting to voice mail.
PI (BEEP)
HMM. THAT'S STRANGE.

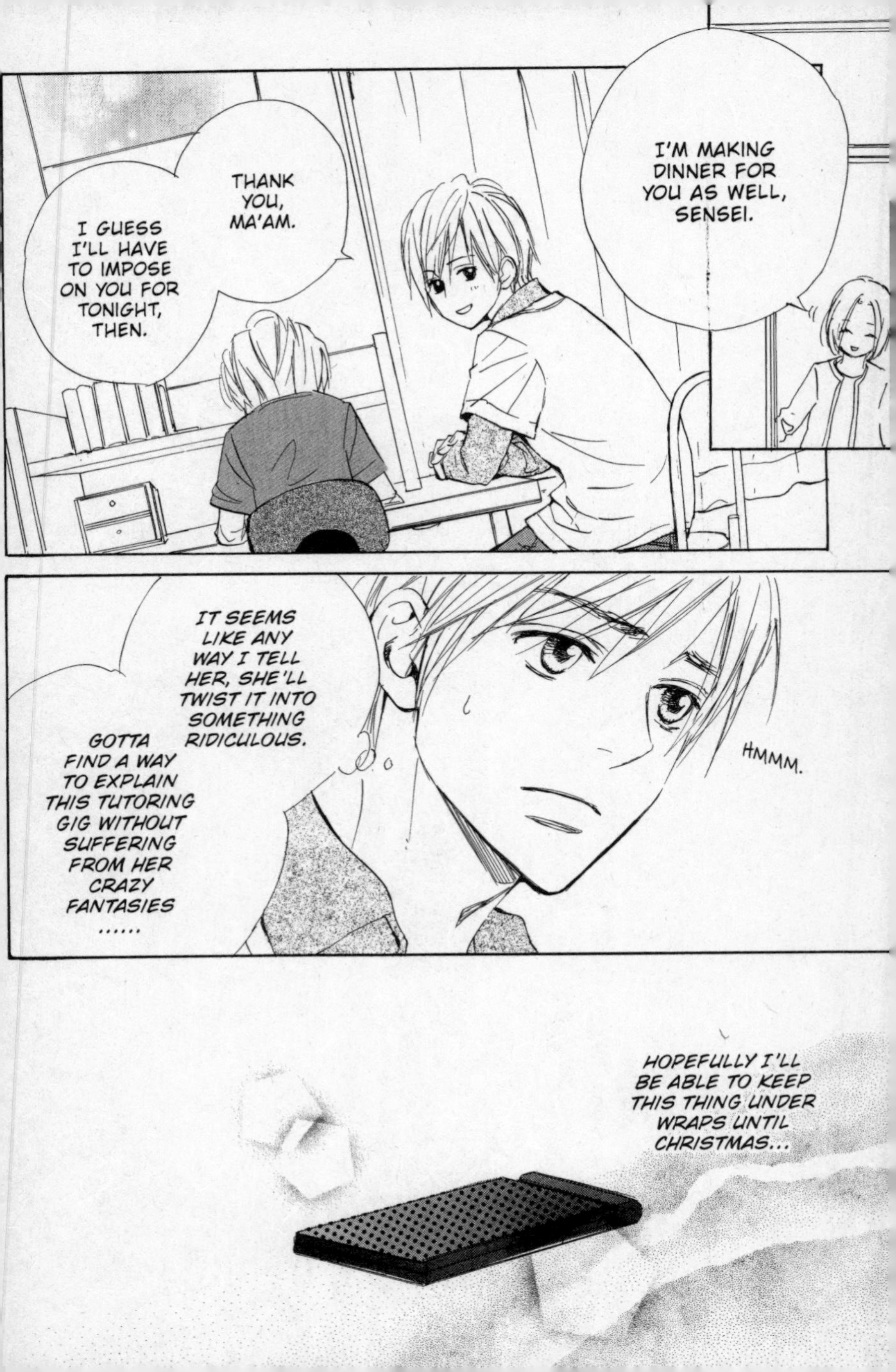
I'M MAKING DINNER FOR YOU AS WELL, SENSEI.
THANK YOU, MA'AM.
I GUESS I'LL HAVE TO IMPOSE ON YOU FOR TONIGHT, THEN.
HMMM.
IT SEEMS LIKE ANY WAY I TELL HER, SHE'LL TWIST IT INTO SOMETHING RIDICULOUS.
GOTTA FIND A WAY TO EXPLAIN THIS TUTORING GIG WITHOUT SUFFERING FROM HER CRAZY FANTASIES ......
HOPEFULLY I'LL BE ABLE TO KEEP THIS THING UNDER WRAPS UNTIL CHRISTMAS...

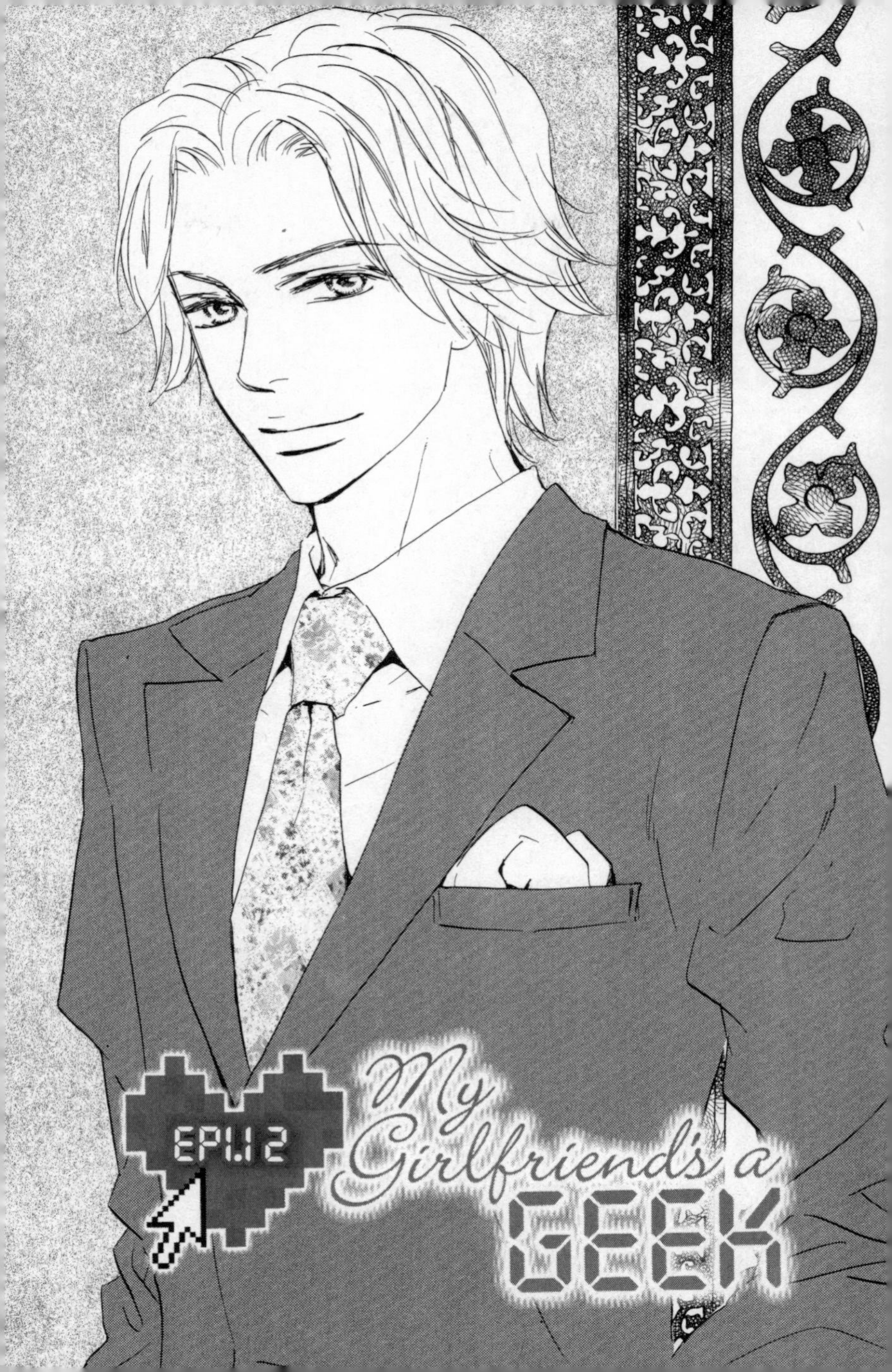
EPI.I 2
My Girlfriend's a
GEEK

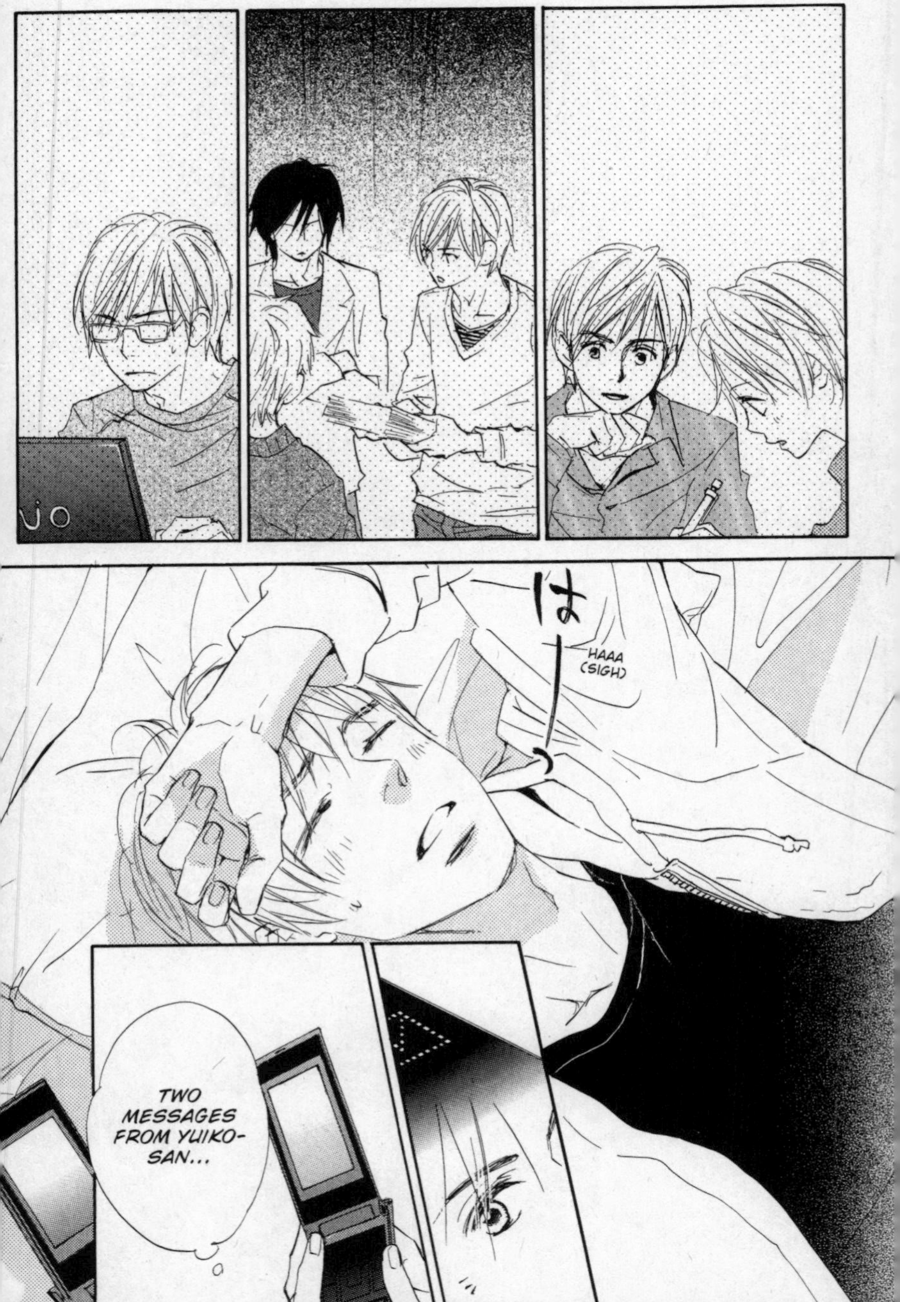
はー
HAAA (SIGH)
TWO MESSAGES FROM YUIKO-SAN...

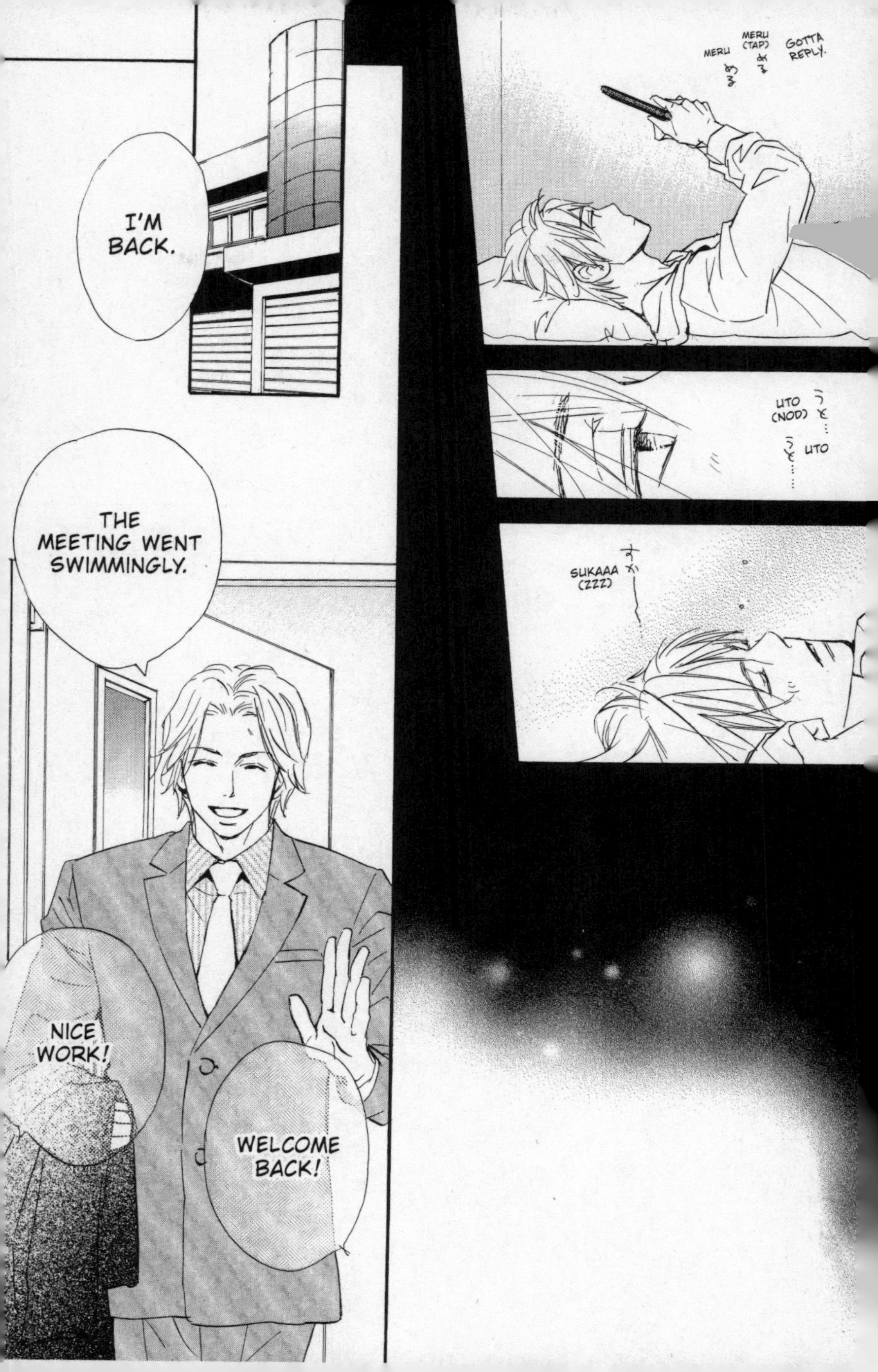
GOTTA REPLY.
MERU (TAP)
める
MERU
める
UTO (NOD)
うと…
UTO
うと…
SUKAAA (ZZZ)
すかー
I'M BACK.
THE MEETING WENT SWIMMINGLY.
WELCOME BACK!
NICE WORK!

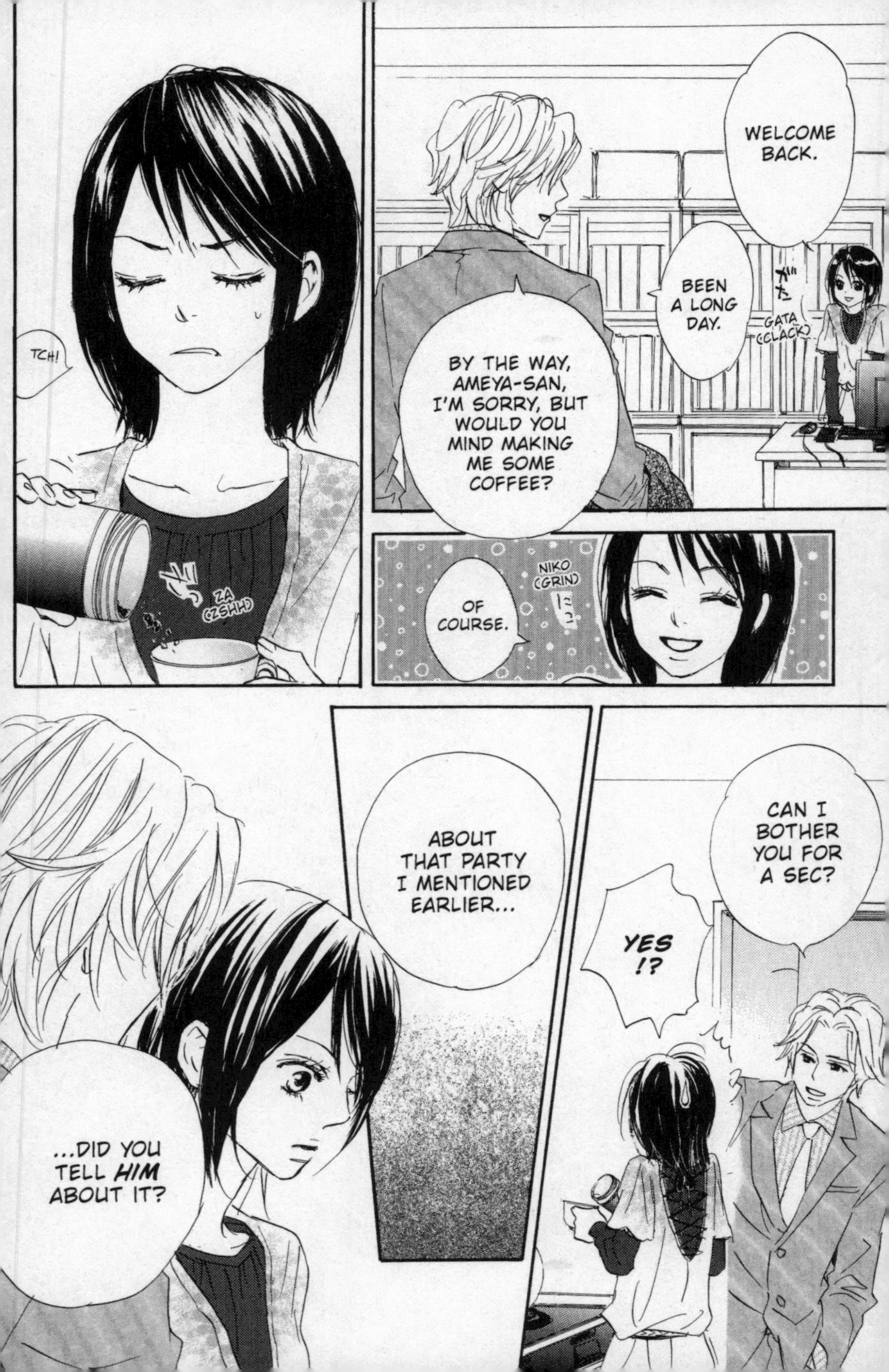
WELCOME BACK.
BEEN A LONG DAY.
GATA (CLACK)
BY THE WAY, AMEYA-SAN, I'M SORRY, BUT WOULD YOU MIND MAKING ME SOME COFFEE?
NIKO (GRIN)
OF COURSE.
TCH!
ZA (ZSHHH)
CAN I BOTHER YOU FOR A SEC?
YES !?
ABOUT THAT PARTY I MENTIONED EARLIER...
...DID YOU TELL *HIM* ABOUT IT?

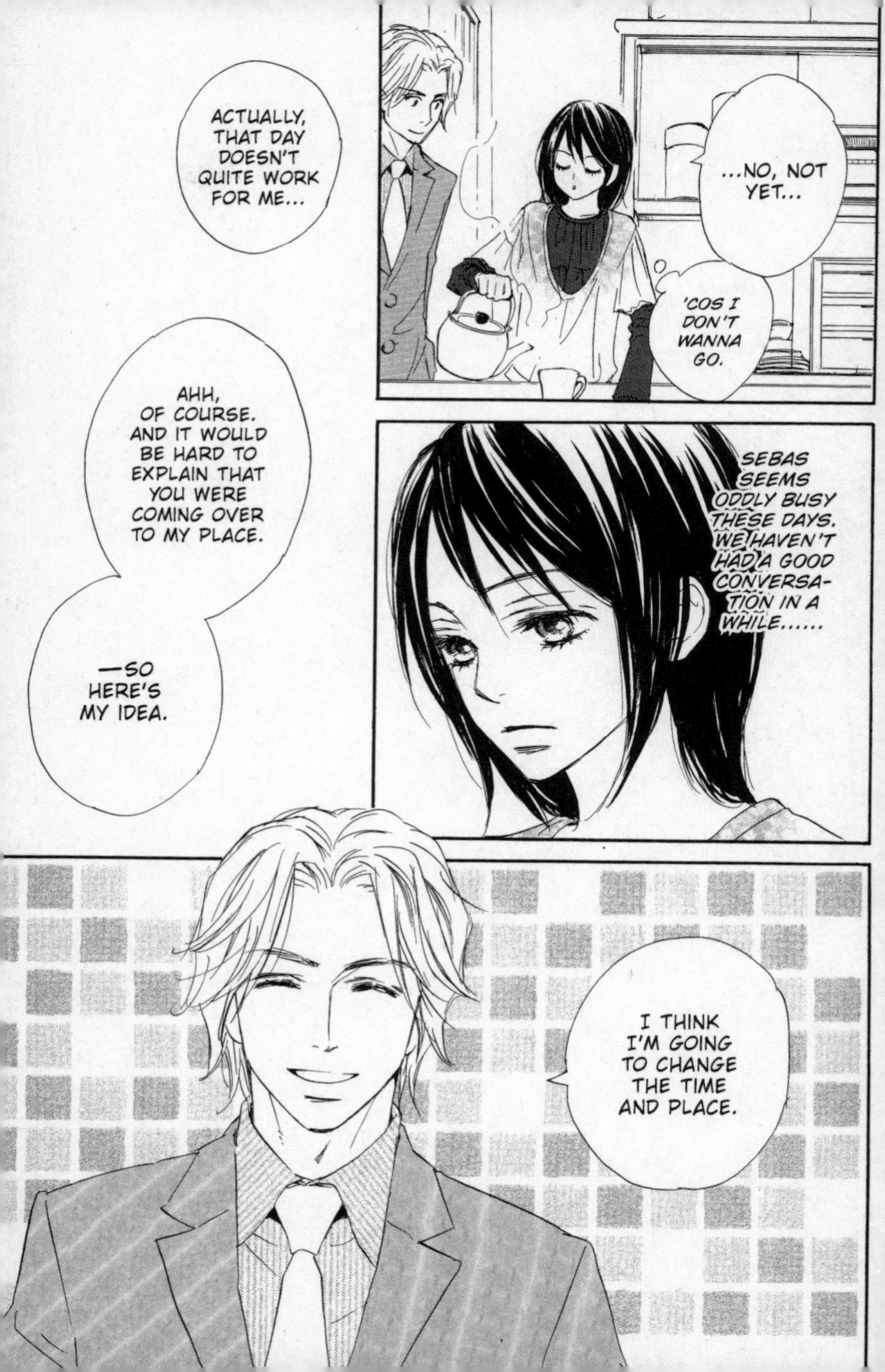
...NO, NOT YET...
'COS I DON'T WANNA GO.
ACTUALLY, THAT DAY DOESN'T QUITE WORK FOR ME...
SEBAS SEEMS ODDLY BUSY THESE DAYS. WE HAVEN'T HAD A GOOD CONVERSA-TION IN A WHILE......
AHH, OF COURSE. AND IT WOULD BE HARD TO EXPLAIN THAT YOU WERE COMING OVER TO MY PLACE.
—SO HERE'S MY IDEA.
I THINK I'M GOING TO CHANGE THE TIME AND PLACE.

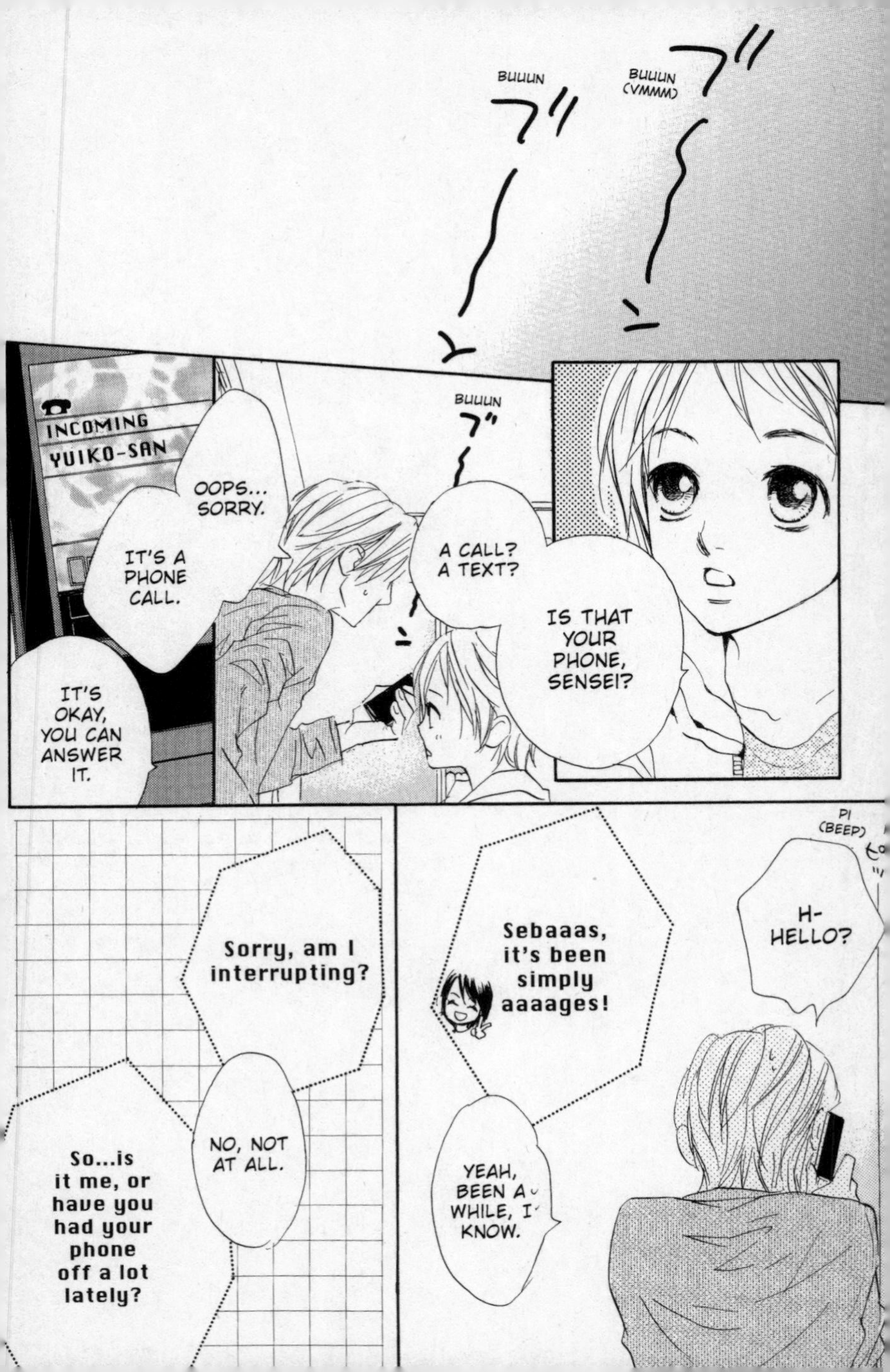
BUUUN (VMMM)
BUUUN
IS THAT YOUR PHONE, SENSEI?
BUUUN
A CALL? A TEXT?
OOPS... SORRY.
IT'S A PHONE CALL.
INCOMING
YUIKO-SAN
IT'S OKAY, YOU CAN ANSWER IT.
PI (BEEP)
H-HELLO?
Sebaaas, it's been simply aaaages!
YEAH, BEEN A WHILE, I KNOW.
Sorry, am I interrupting?
NO, NOT AT ALL.
So...is it me, or have you had your phone off a lot lately?

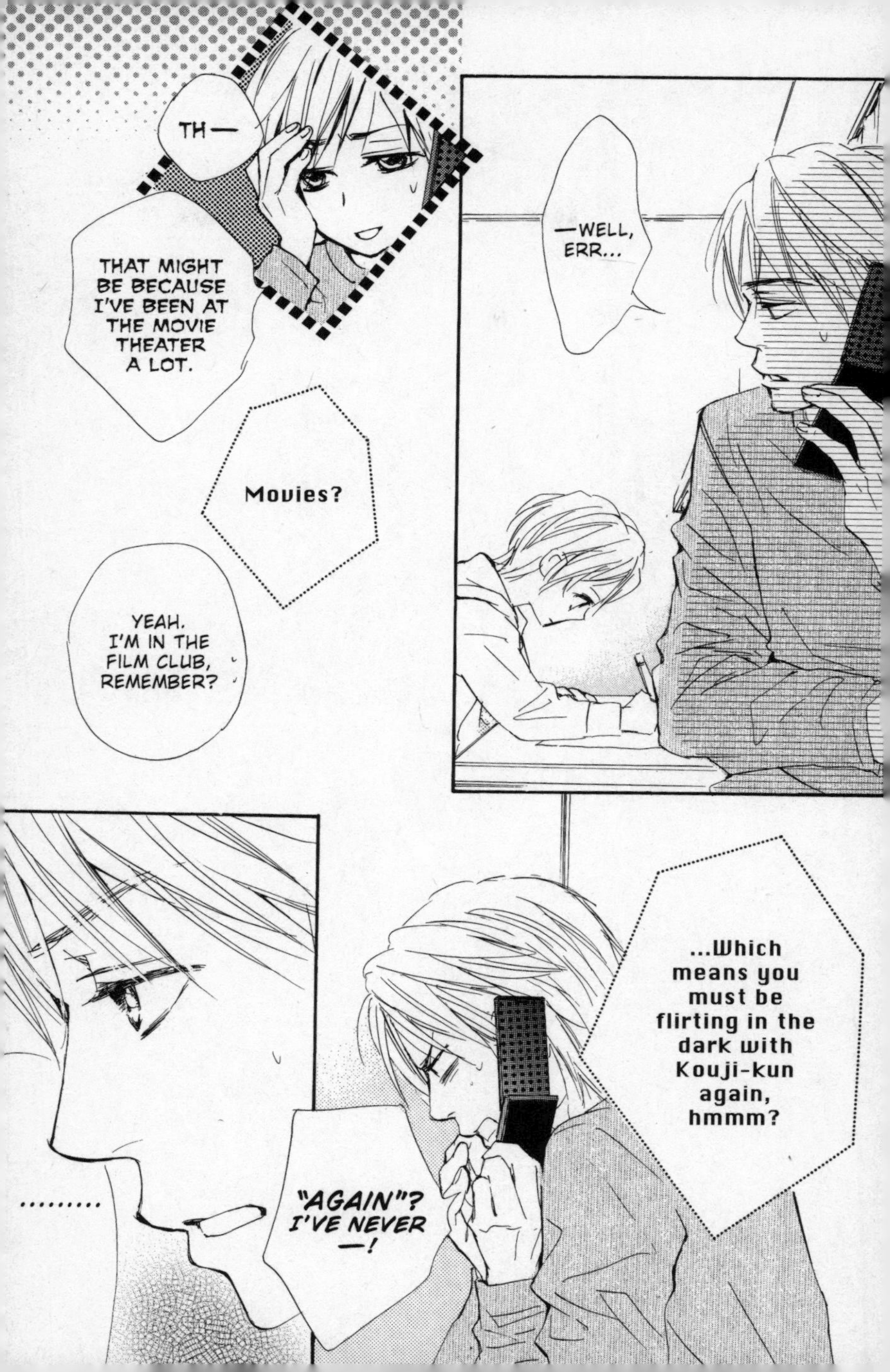
—WELL, ERR...
TH—
THAT MIGHT BE BECAUSE I'VE BEEN AT THE MOVIE THEATER A LOT.
Movies?
YEAH. I'M IN THE FILM CLUB, REMEMBER?
...Which means you must be flirting in the dark with Kouji-kun again, hmmm?
"AGAIN"? I'VE NEVER —!
....

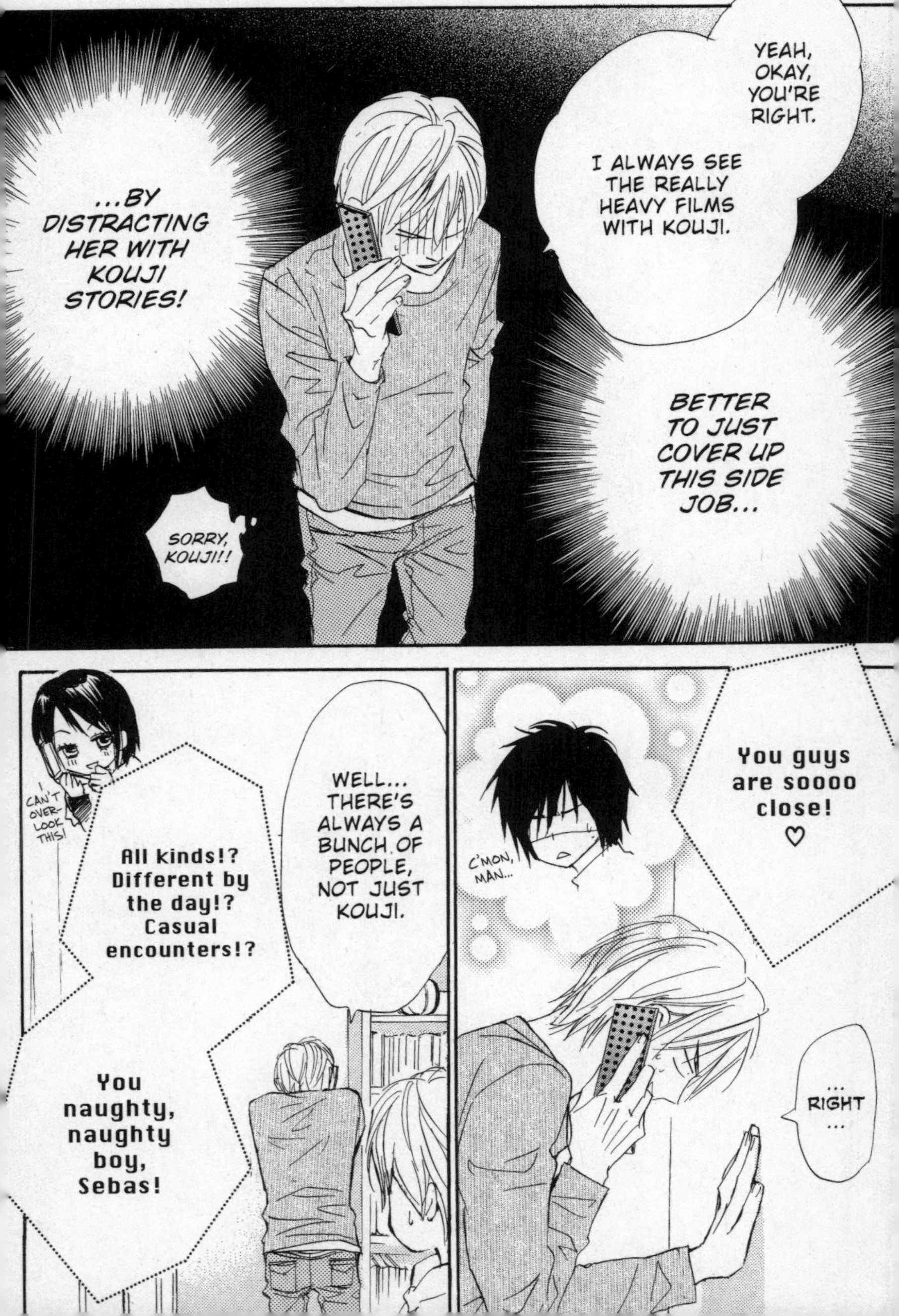
YEAH, OKAY, YOU'RE RIGHT.
I ALWAYS SEE THE REALLY HEAVY FILMS WITH KOUJI.
BETTER TO JUST COVER UP THIS SIDE JOB...
...BY DISTRACTING HER WITH KOUJI STORIES!
SORRY, KOUJI!!
You guys are soooo close! ♡
C'MON, MAN...
...RIGHT...
WELL... THERE'S ALWAYS A BUNCH OF PEOPLE, NOT JUST KOUJI.
I CAN'T OVER-LOOK THIS!
All kinds!? Different by the day!? Casual encounters!?
You naughty, naughty boy, Sebas!

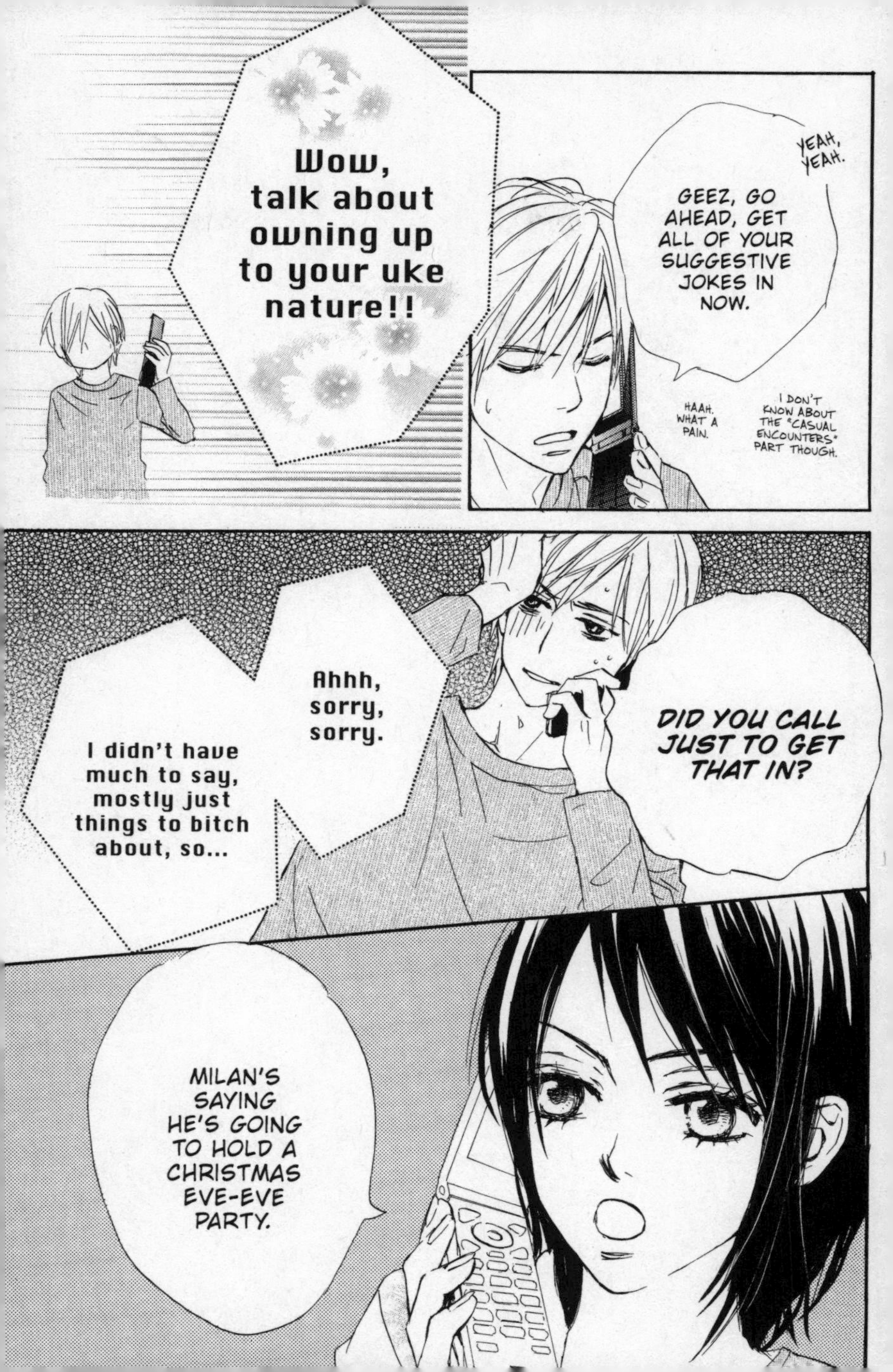
YEAH, YEAH.
GEEZ, GO AHEAD, GET ALL OF YOUR SUGGESTIVE JOKES IN NOW.
I DON'T KNOW ABOUT THE "CASUAL ENCOUNTERS" PART THOUGH.
HAAH. WHAT A PAIN.
Wow, talk about owning up to your uke nature!!
DID YOU CALL JUST TO GET THAT IN?
Ahhh, sorry, sorry.
I didn't have much to say, mostly just things to bitch about, so...
MILAN'S SAYING HE'S GOING TO HOLD A CHRISTMAS EVE-EVE PARTY.

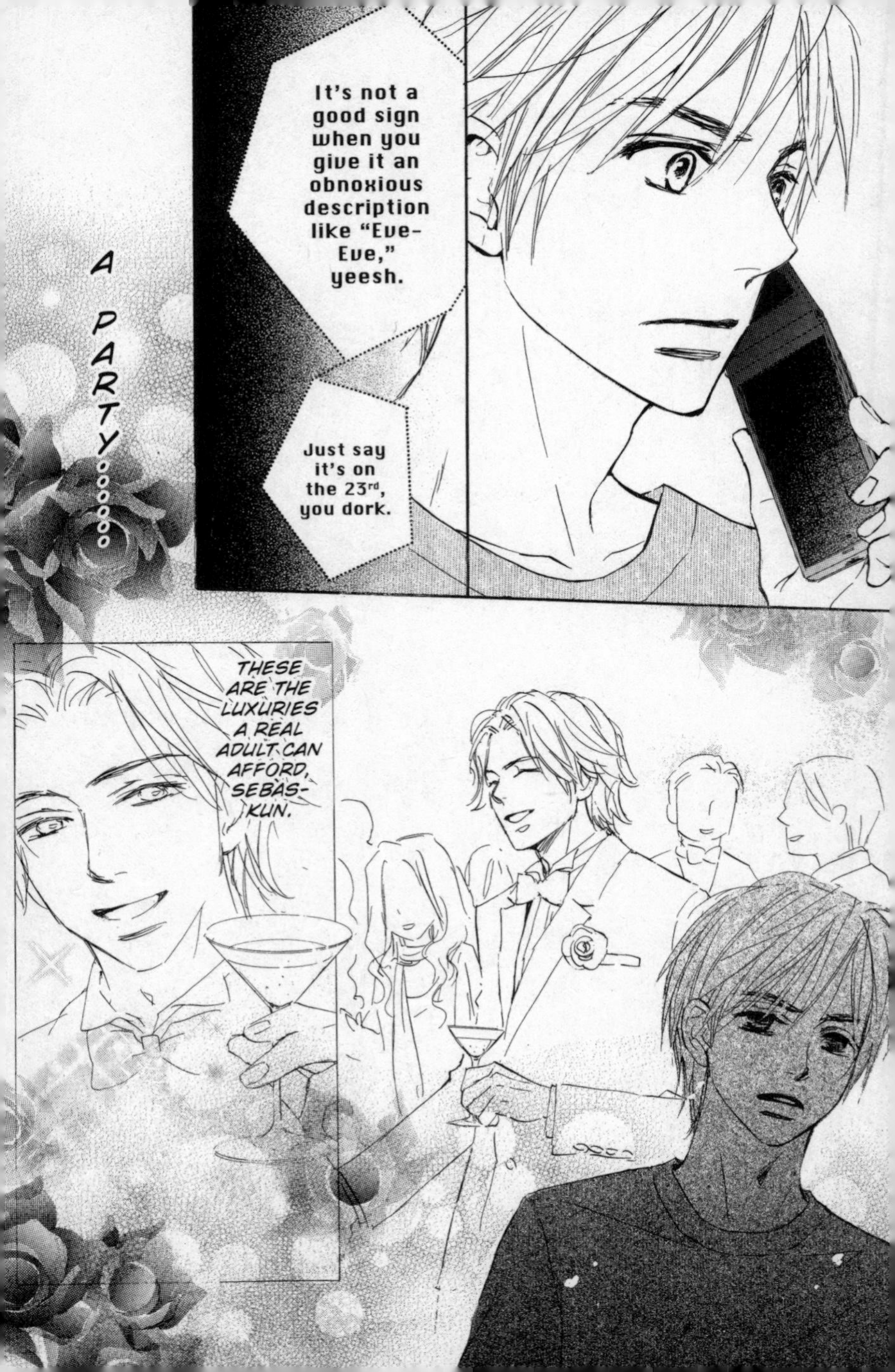

It's not a good sign when you give it an obnoxious description like "Eve-Eve," yeesh.
Just say it's on the 23rd, you dork.
A PARTYoooooo
THESE ARE THE LUXURIES A REAL ADULT CAN AFFORD, SEBAS-KUN.

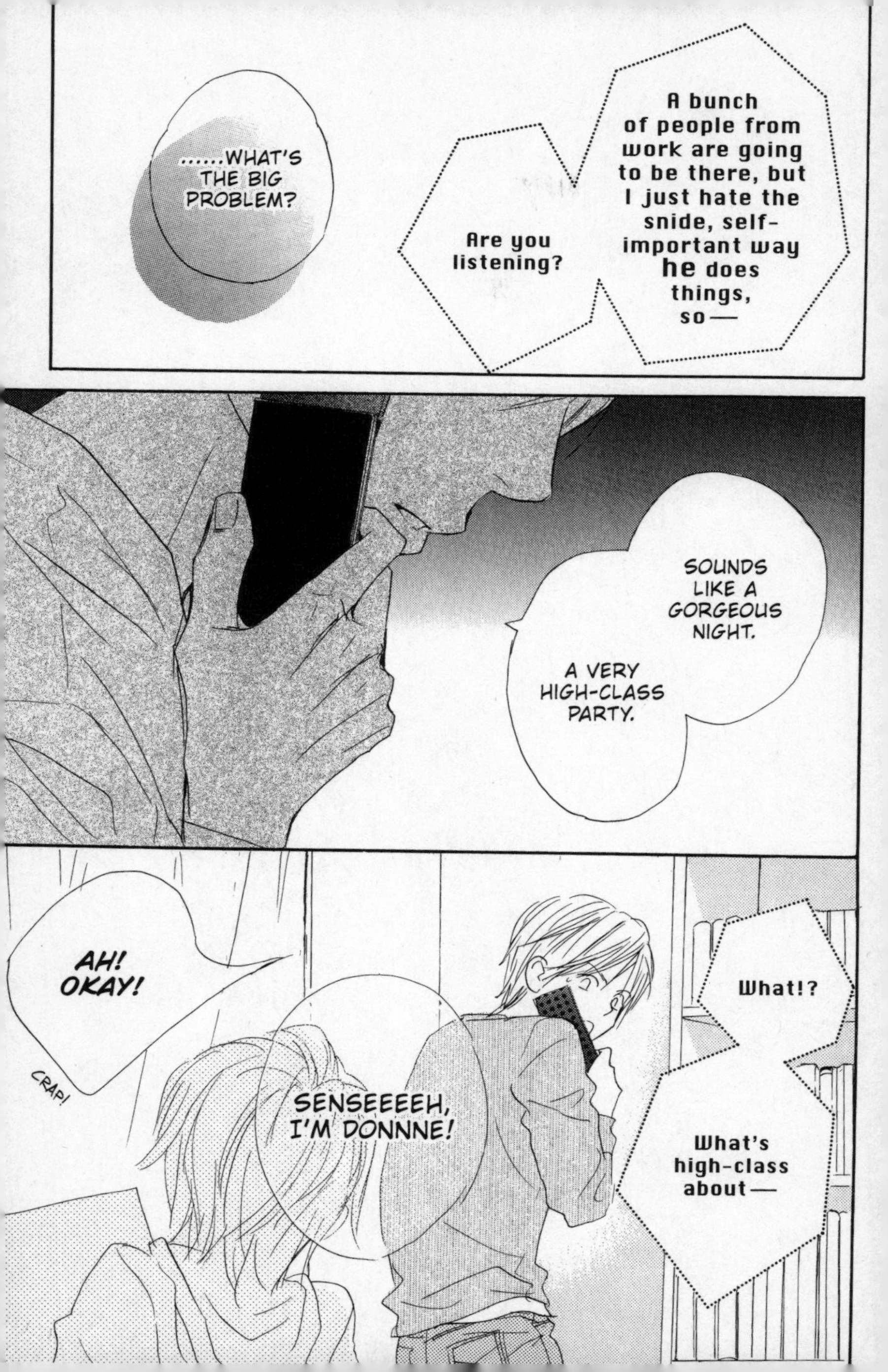
A bunch of people from work are going to be there, but I just hate the snide, self-important way he does things, so—
Are you listening?
......WHAT'S THE BIG PROBLEM?
SOUNDS LIKE A GORGEOUS NIGHT.
A VERY HIGH-CLASS PARTY.
What!?
What's high-class about—
SENSEEEEH, I'M DONNNE!
AH! OKAY!
CRAP!

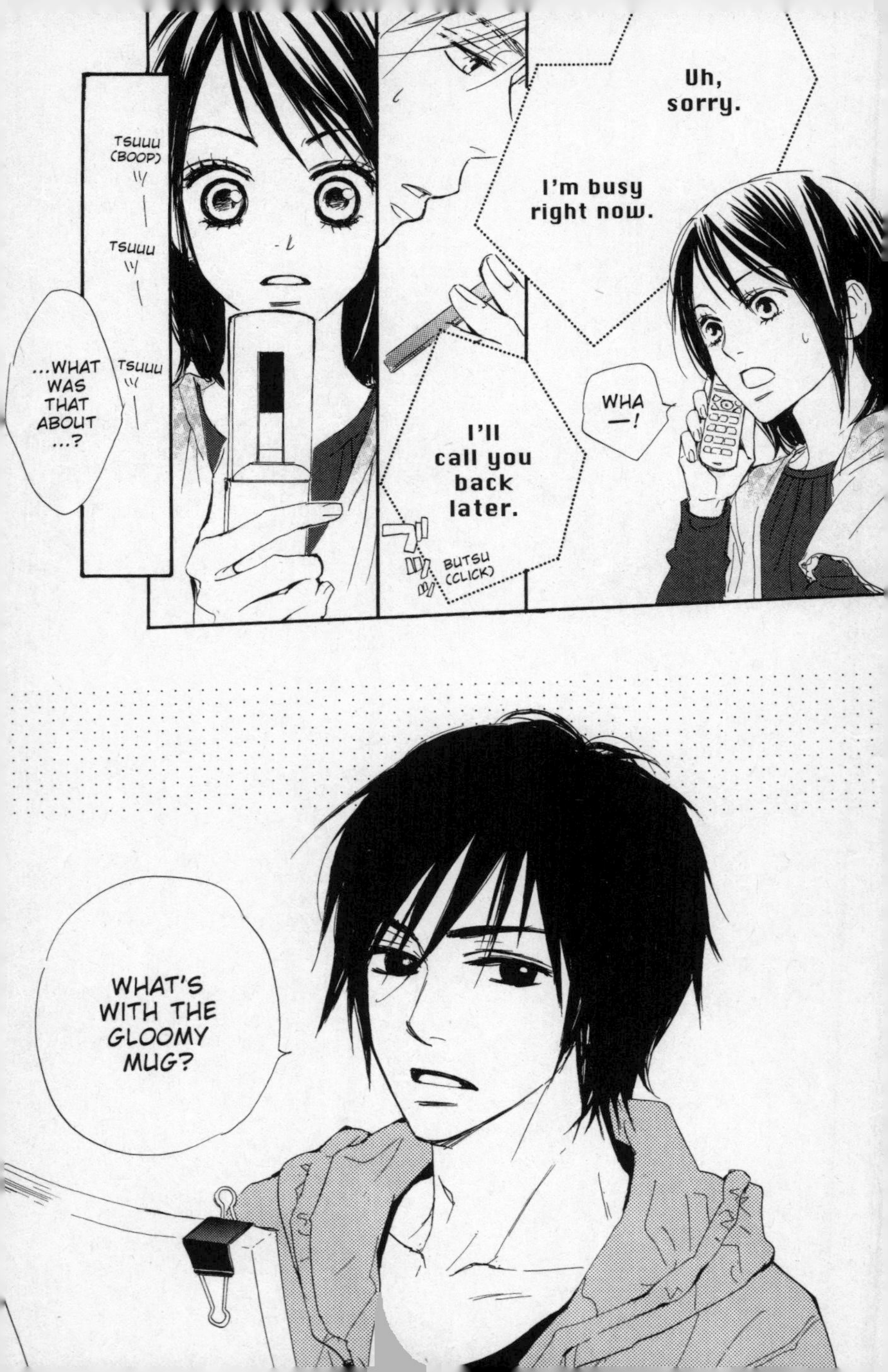
Uh, sorry.
I'm busy right now.
WHA—!
I'll call you back later.
BUTSU (CLICK)
TSUUU (BOOP)
TSUUU
TSUUU
...WHAT WAS THAT ABOUT...?
WHAT'S WITH THE GLOOMY MUG?

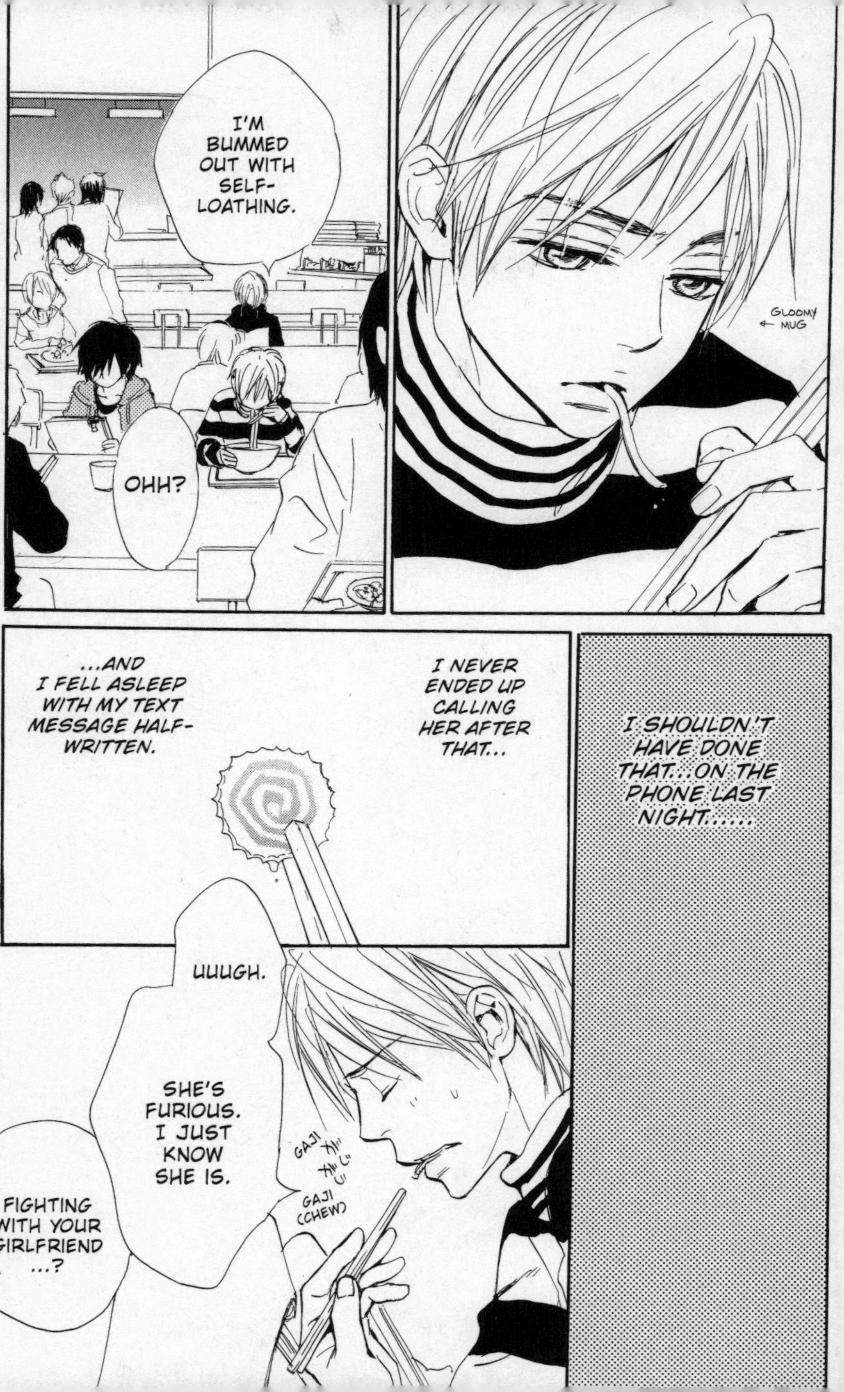
GLOOMY MUG
I'M BUMMED OUT WITH SELF-LOATHING.
OHH?
I SHOULDN'T HAVE DONE THAT...ON THE PHONE LAST NIGHT......
I NEVER ENDED UP CALLING HER AFTER THAT...
...AND I FELL ASLEEP WITH MY TEXT MESSAGE HALF-WRITTEN.
UUUGH.
SHE'S FURIOUS. I JUST KNOW SHE IS.
GAJI
GAJI (CHEW)
FIGHTING WITH YOUR GIRLFRIEND ...?

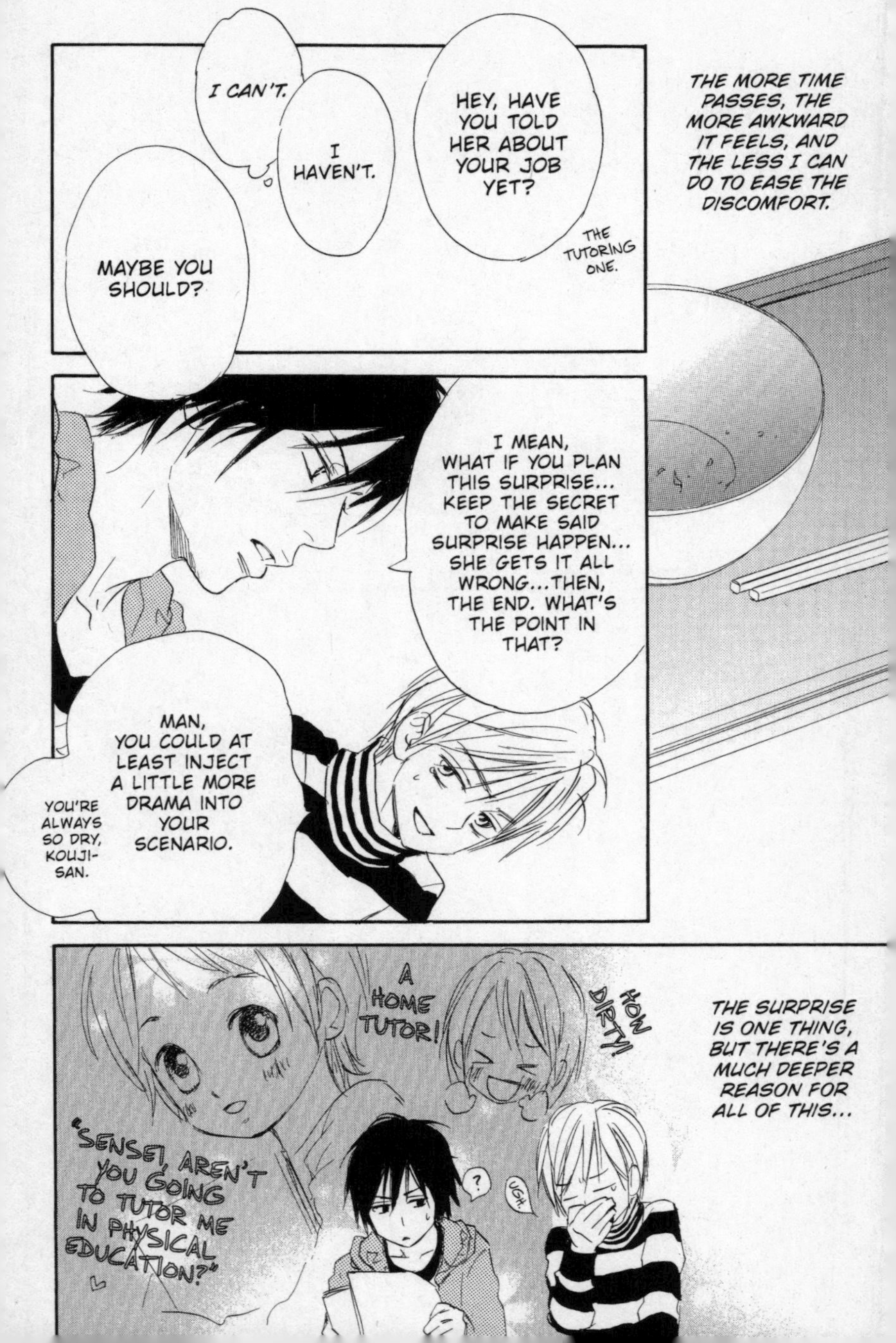
THE MORE TIME PASSES, THE MORE AWKWARD IT FEELS, AND THE LESS I CAN DO TO EASE THE DISCOMFORT.
HEY, HAVE YOU TOLD HER ABOUT YOUR JOB YET?
THE TUTORING ONE.
I HAVEN'T.
I CAN'T.
MAYBE YOU SHOULD?
I MEAN, WHAT IF YOU PLAN THIS SURPRISE... KEEP THE SECRET TO MAKE SAID SURPRISE HAPPEN... SHE GETS IT ALL WRONG...THEN, THE END. WHAT'S THE POINT IN THAT?
MAN, YOU COULD AT LEAST INJECT A LITTLE MORE DRAMA INTO YOUR SCENARIO.
YOU'RE ALWAYS SO DRY, KOUJI-SAN.
THE SURPRISE IS ONE THING, BUT THERE'S A MUCH DEEPER REASON FOR ALL OF THIS...
HOW DIRTY!
A HOME TUTOR!
"SENSEI, AREN'T YOU GOING TO TUTOR ME IN PHYSICAL EDUCATION?"
?
UGH.

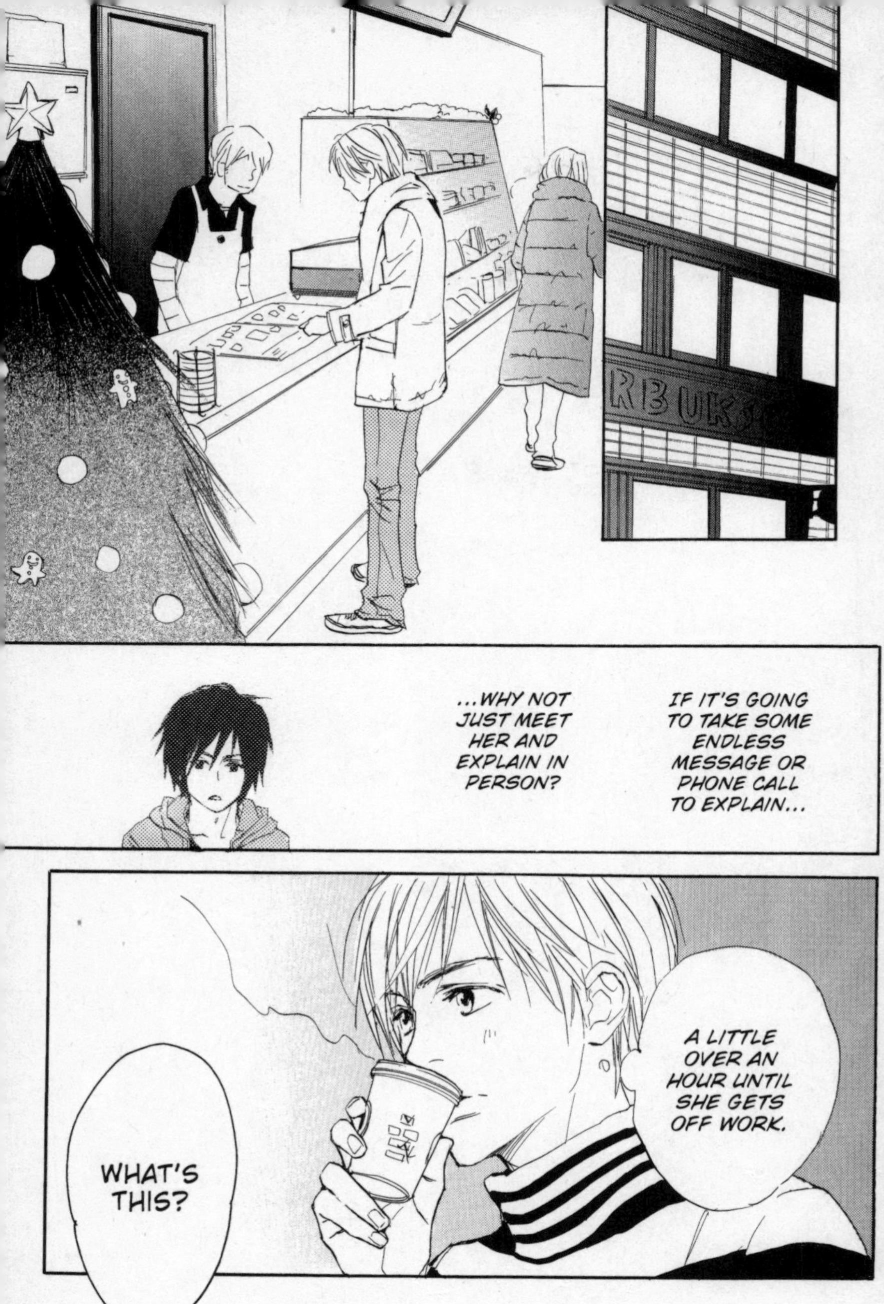
IF IT'S GOING TO TAKE SOME ENDLESS MESSAGE OR PHONE CALL TO EXPLAIN...
...WHY NOT JUST MEET HER AND EXPLAIN IN PERSON?
A LITTLE OVER AN HOUR UNTIL SHE GETS OFF WORK.
WHAT'S THIS?

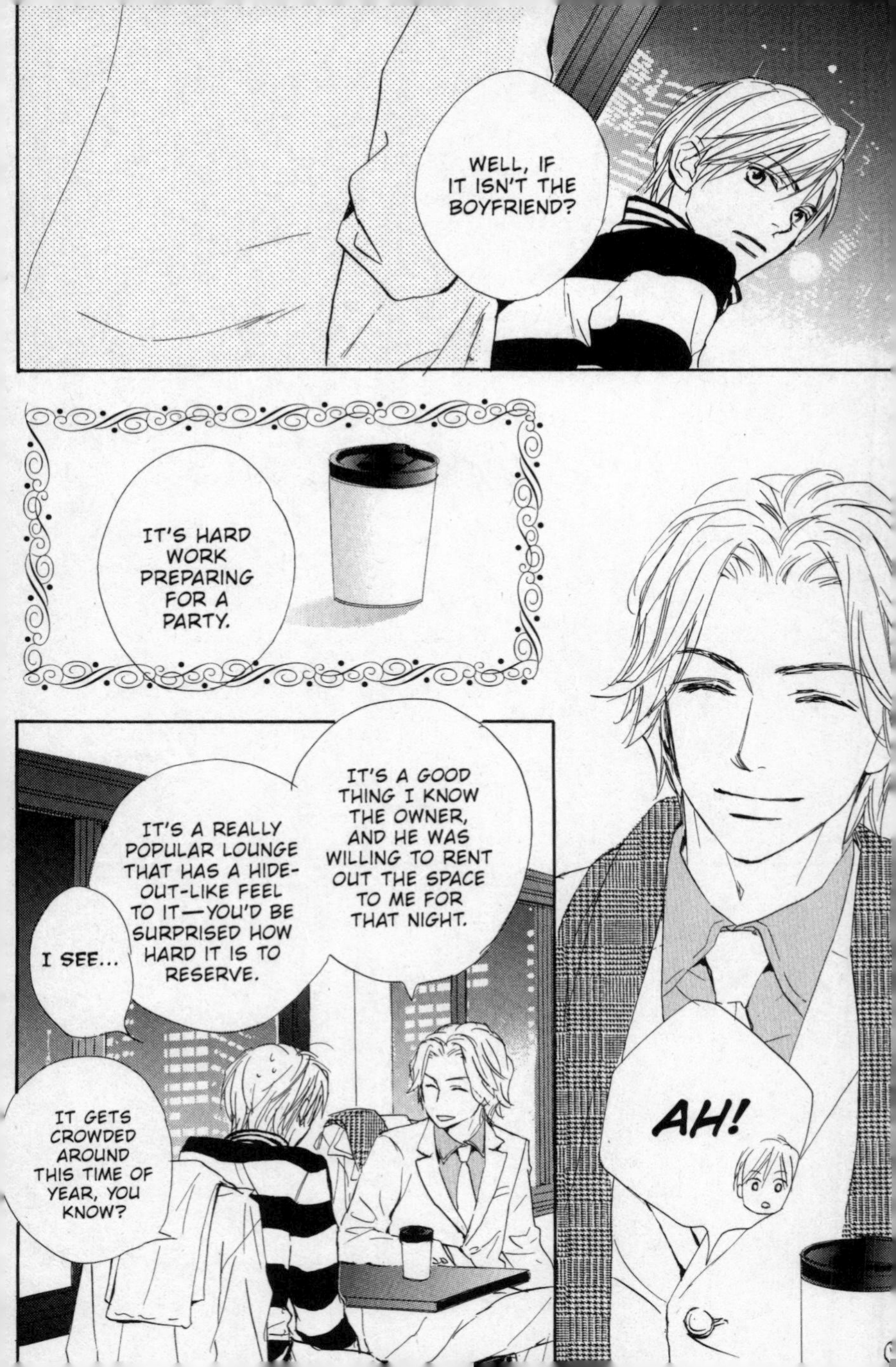
WELL, IF IT ISN'T THE BOYFRIEND?
AH!
IT'S HARD WORK PREPARING FOR A PARTY.
IT'S A GOOD THING I KNOW THE OWNER, AND HE WAS WILLING TO RENT OUT THE SPACE TO ME FOR THAT NIGHT.
IT'S A REALLY POPULAR LOUNGE THAT HAS A HIDE-OUT-LIKE FEEL TO IT—YOU'D BE SURPRISED HOW HARD IT IS TO RESERVE.
I SEE...
IT GETS CROWDED AROUND THIS TIME OF YEAR, YOU KNOW?

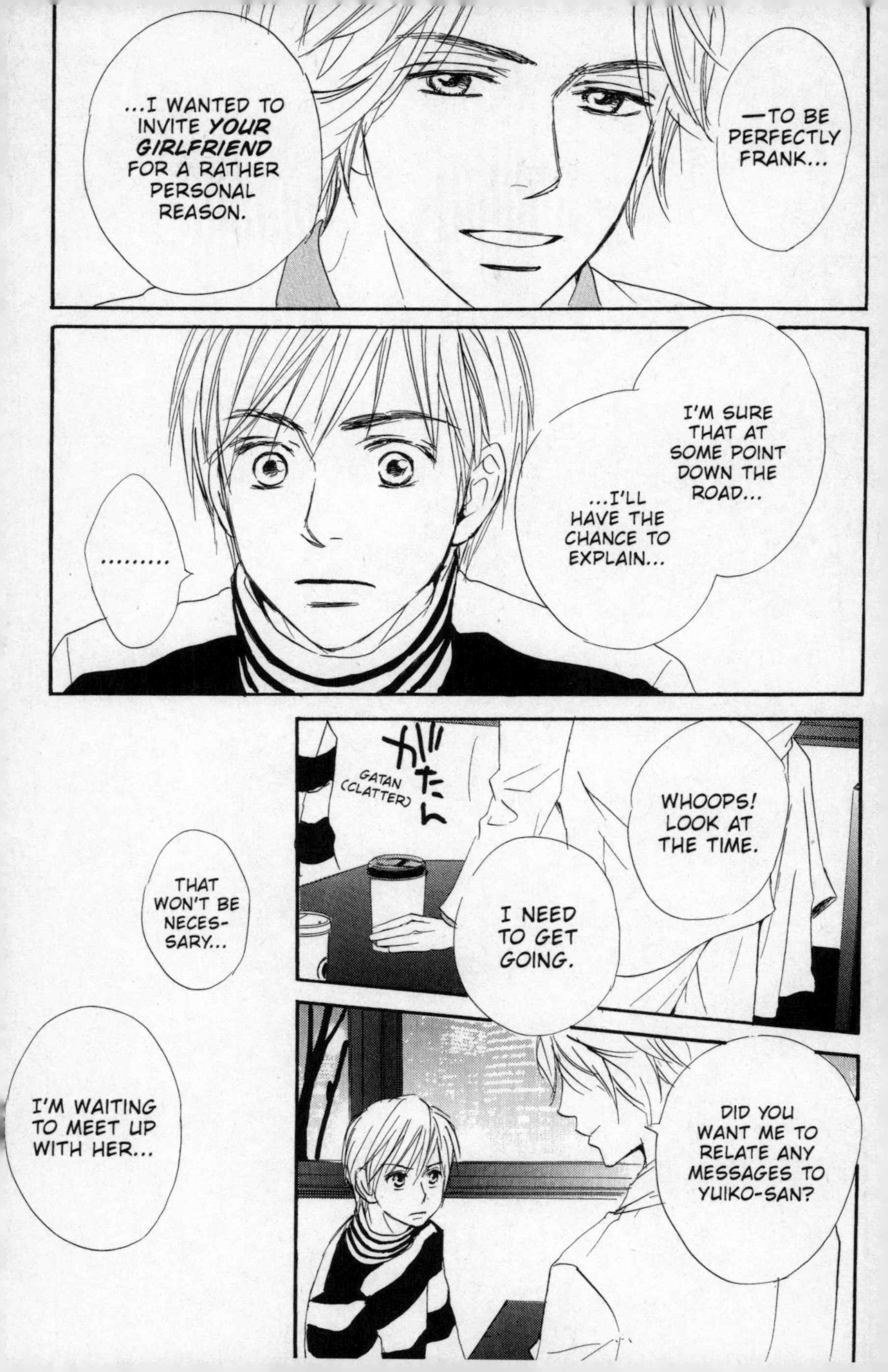
—TO BE PERFECTLY FRANK...
...I WANTED TO INVITE ***YOUR GIRLFRIEND*** FOR A RATHER PERSONAL REASON.
I'M SURE THAT AT SOME POINT DOWN THE ROAD...
...I'LL HAVE THE CHANCE TO EXPLAIN...
....
がたん
GATAN (CLATTER)
WHOOPS! LOOK AT THE TIME.
I NEED TO GET GOING.
THAT WON'T BE NECES-SARY...
DID YOU WANT ME TO RELATE ANY MESSAGES TO YUIKO-SAN?
I'M WAITING TO MEET UP WITH HER...

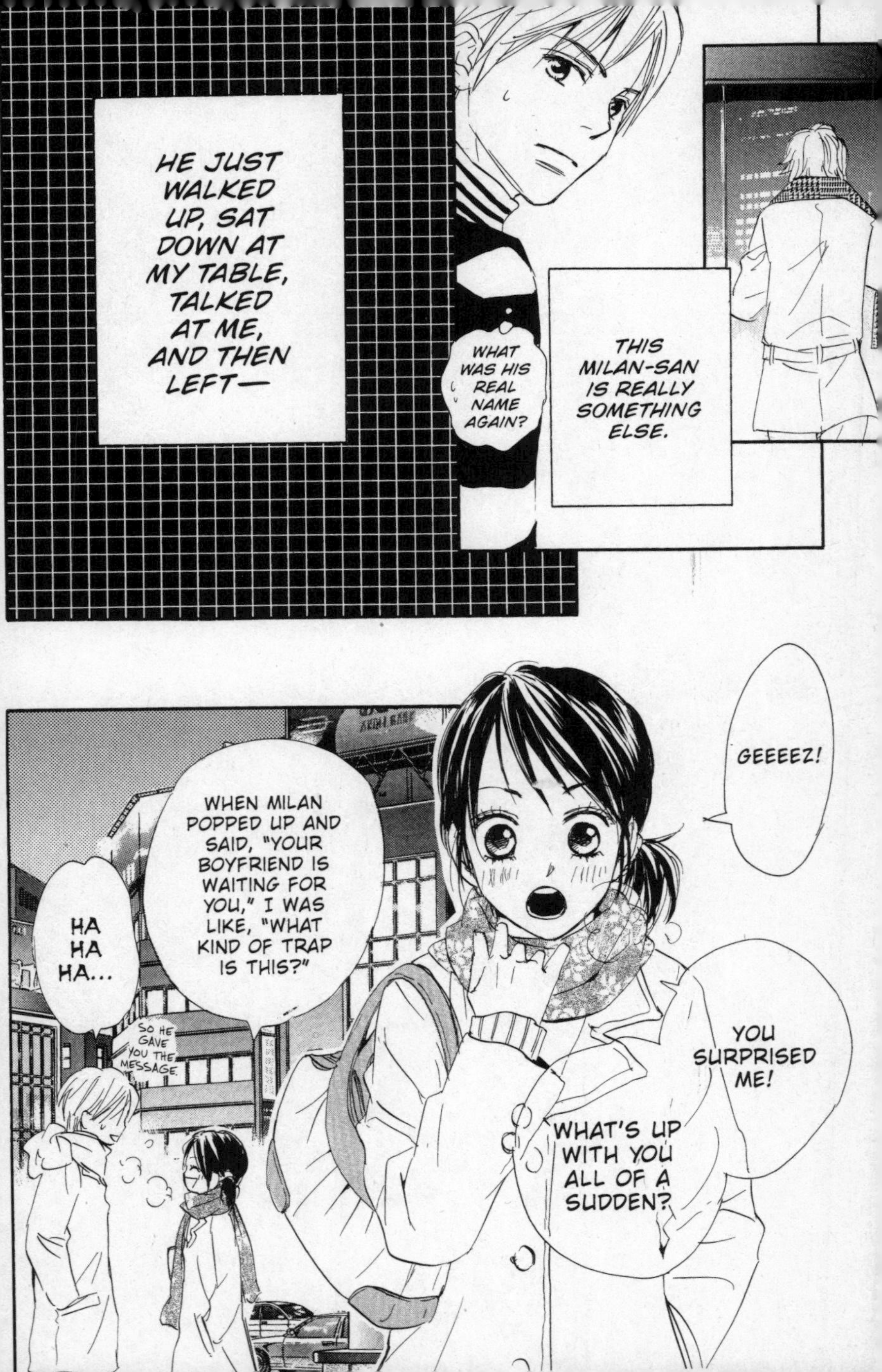
THIS MILAN-SAN IS REALLY SOMETHING ELSE.
WHAT WAS HIS REAL NAME AGAIN?
HE JUST WALKED UP, SAT DOWN AT MY TABLE, TALKED AT ME, AND THEN LEFT—
GEEEEZ!
YOU SURPRISED ME!
WHAT'S UP WITH YOU ALL OF A SUDDEN?
WHEN MILAN POPPED UP AND SAID, "YOUR BOYFRIEND IS WAITING FOR YOU," I WAS LIKE, "WHAT KIND OF TRAP IS THIS?"
HA HA HA...
SO HE GAVE YOU THE MESSAGE.

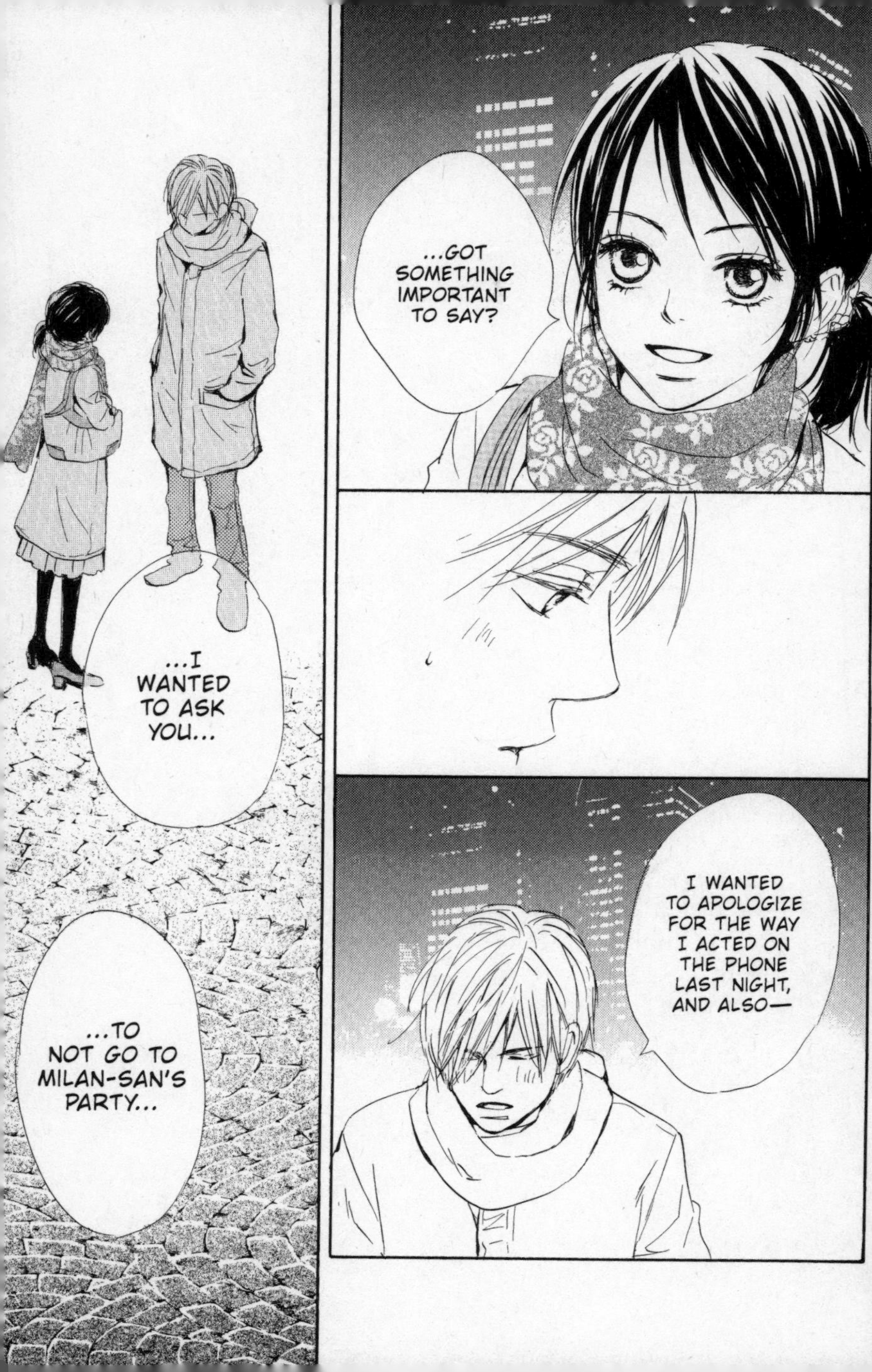
...GOT SOMETHING IMPORTANT TO SAY?
I WANTED TO APOLOGIZE FOR THE WAY I ACTED ON THE PHONE LAST NIGHT, AND ALSO—
...I WANTED TO ASK YOU...
...TO NOT GO TO MILAN-SAN'S PARTY...

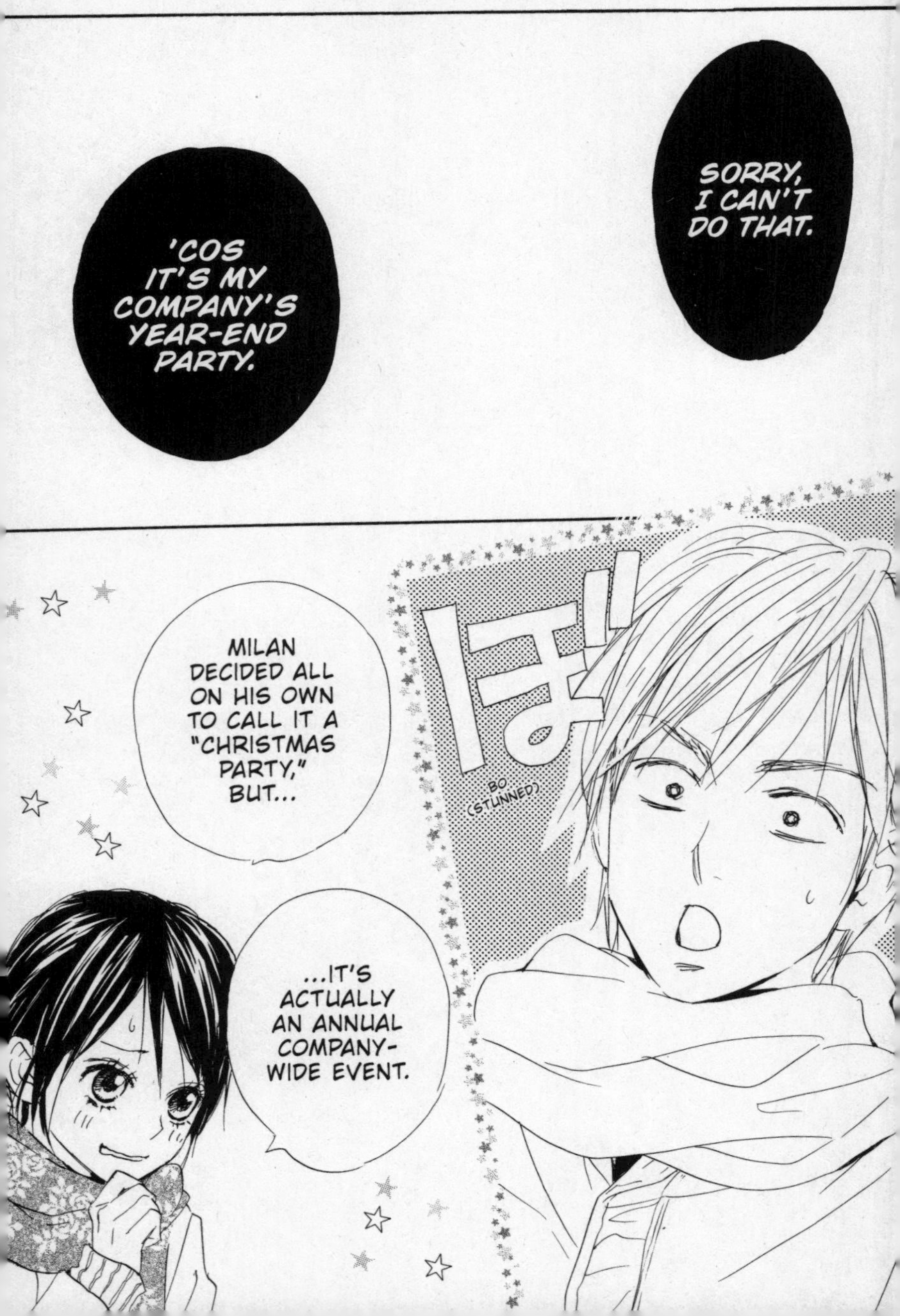
SORRY, I CAN'T DO THAT.
'COS IT'S MY COMPANY'S YEAR-END PARTY.
ぼ
BO (STUNNED)
MILAN DECIDED ALL ON HIS OWN TO CALL IT A "CHRISTMAS PARTY," BUT...
...IT'S ACTUALLY AN ANNUAL COMPANY-WIDE EVENT.

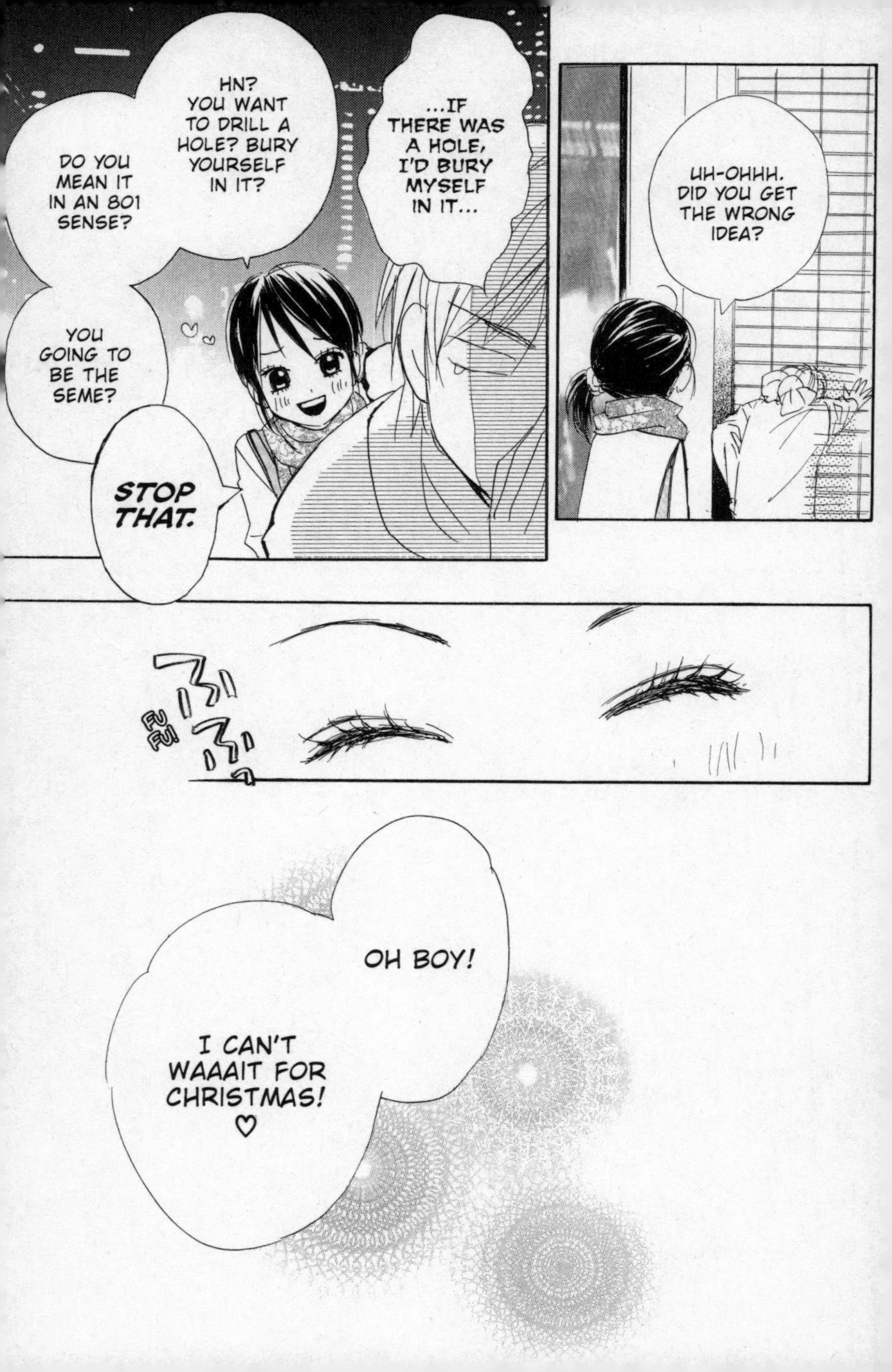
UH-OHHH. DID YOU GET THE WRONG IDEA?
...IF THERE WAS A HOLE, I'D BURY MYSELF IN IT...
HN? YOU WANT TO DRILL A HOLE? BURY YOURSELF IN IT?
DO YOU MEAN IT IN AN 801 SENSE?
YOU GOING TO BE THE SEME?
STOP THAT.
FU FU!
OH BOY!
I CAN'T WAAAIT FOR CHRISTMAS! ♡

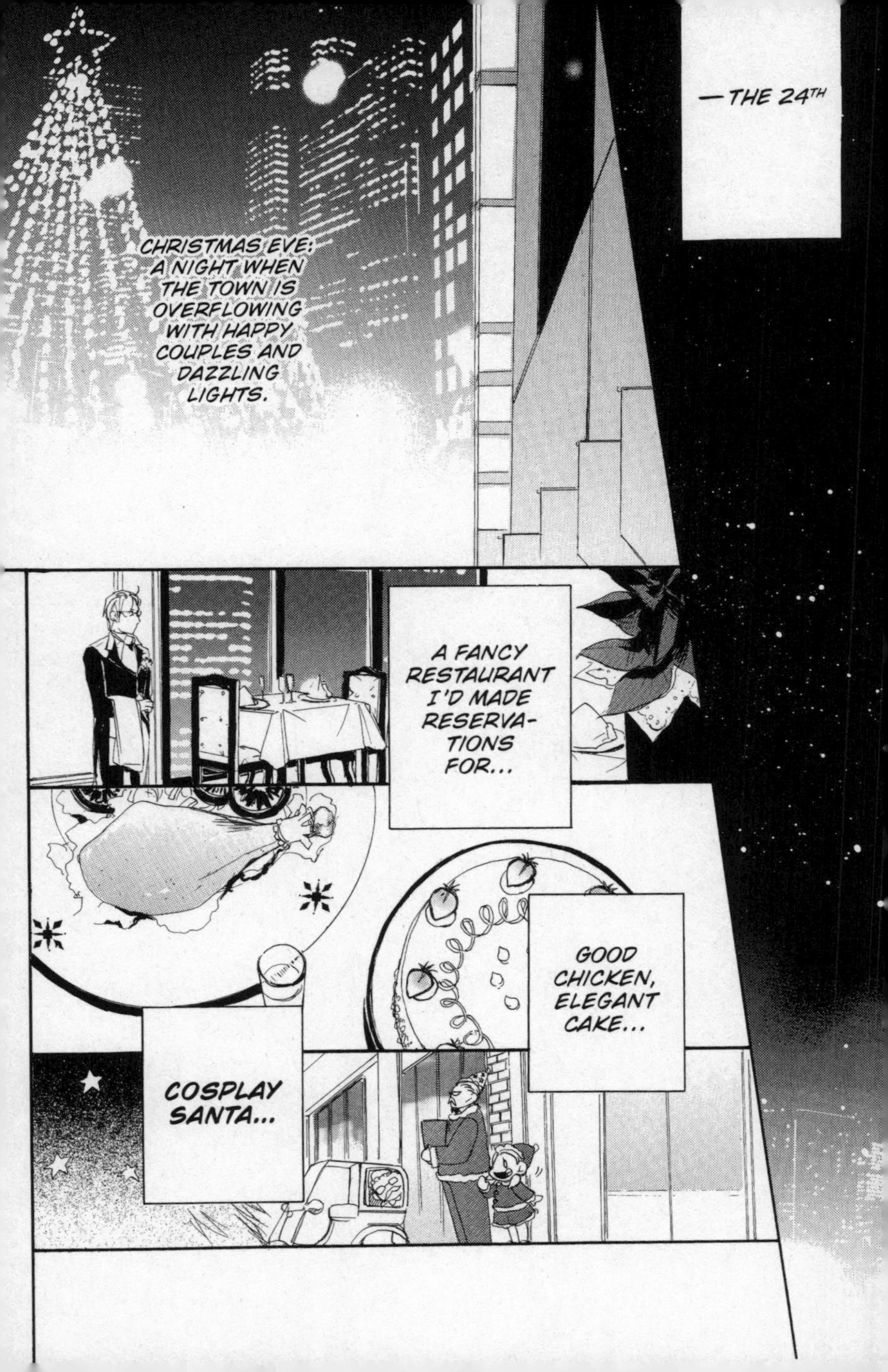
—THE 24TH
CHRISTMAS EVE: A NIGHT WHEN THE TOWN IS OVERFLOWING WITH HAPPY COUPLES AND DAZZLING LIGHTS.
A FANCY RESTAURANT I'D MADE RESERVATIONS FOR...
GOOD CHICKEN, ELEGANT CAKE...
COSPLAY SANTA...

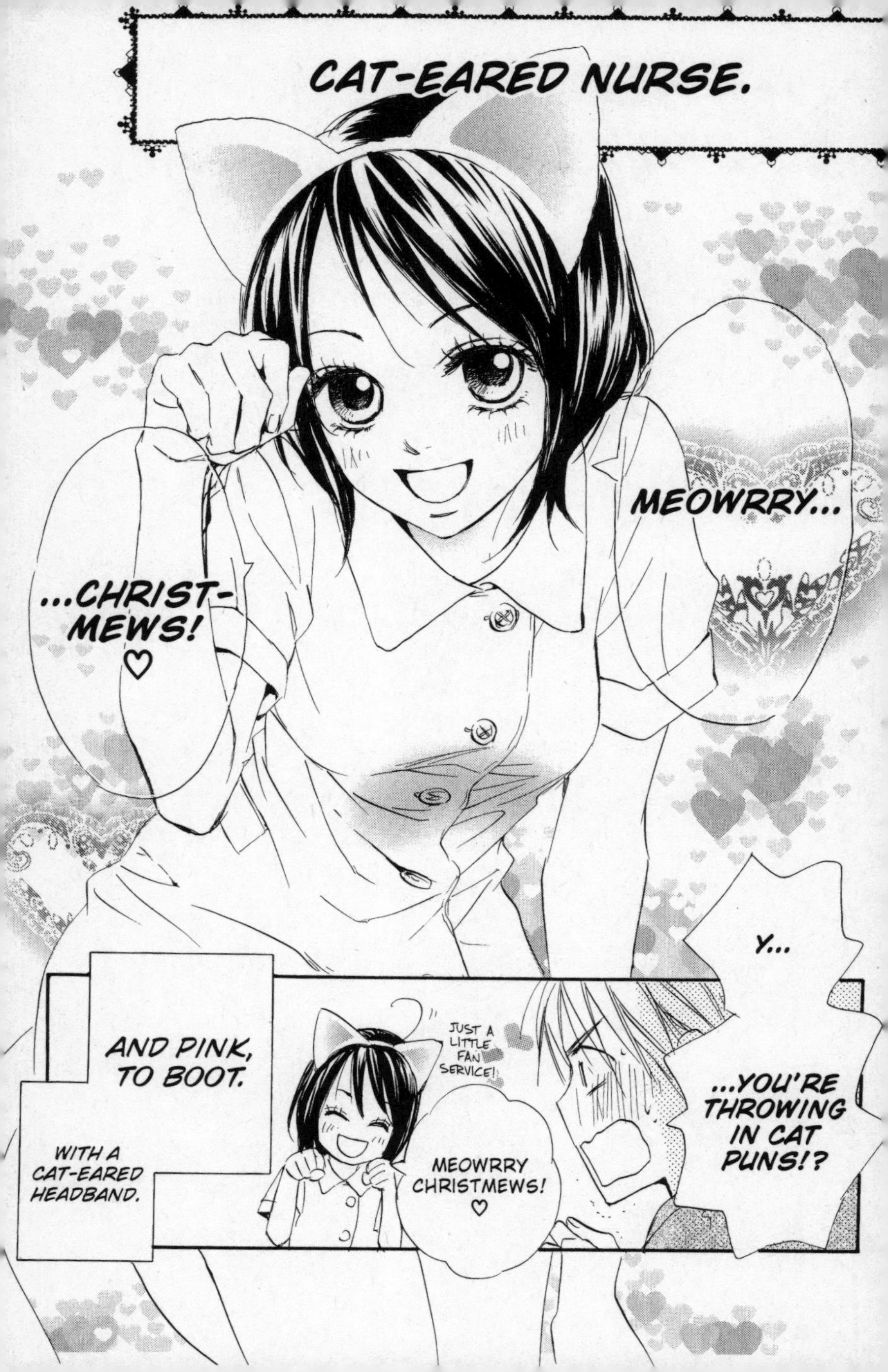
CAT-EARED NURSE.
MEOWRRY...
...CHRIST-MEWS! ♡
Y...
...YOU'RE THROWING IN CAT PUNS!?
JUST A LITTLE FAN SERVICE!
MEOWRRY CHRISTMEWS! ♡
AND PINK, TO BOOT.
WITH A CAT-EARED HEADBAND.

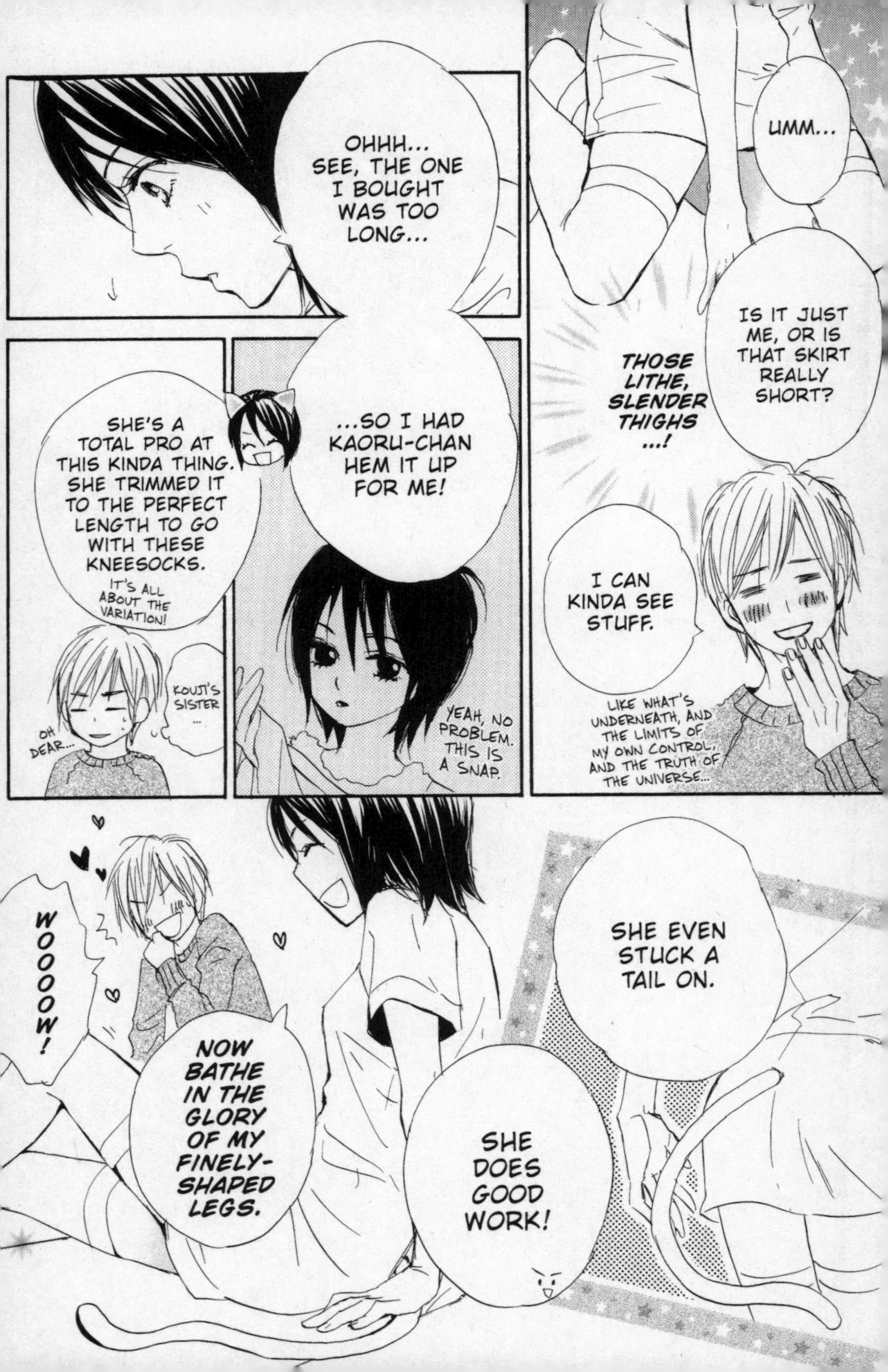
UMM...
IS IT JUST ME, OR IS THAT SKIRT REALLY SHORT?
THOSE LITHE, SLENDER THIGHS ...!
I CAN KINDA SEE STUFF.
LIKE WHAT'S UNDERNEATH, AND THE LIMITS OF MY OWN CONTROL, AND THE TRUTH OF THE UNIVERSE...
OHHH... SEE, THE ONE I BOUGHT WAS TOO LONG...
...SO I HAD KAORU-CHAN HEM IT UP FOR ME!
YEAH, NO PROBLEM. THIS IS A SNAP.
SHE'S A TOTAL PRO AT THIS KINDA THING. SHE TRIMMED IT TO THE PERFECT LENGTH TO GO WITH THESE KNEESOCKS.
IT'S ALL ABOUT THE VARIATION!
KOUJI'S SISTER ...
OH DEAR...
SHE EVEN STUCK A TAIL ON.
SHE DOES GOOD WORK!
NOW BATHE IN THE GLORY OF MY FINELY-SHAPED LEGS.
WOOOOOW!

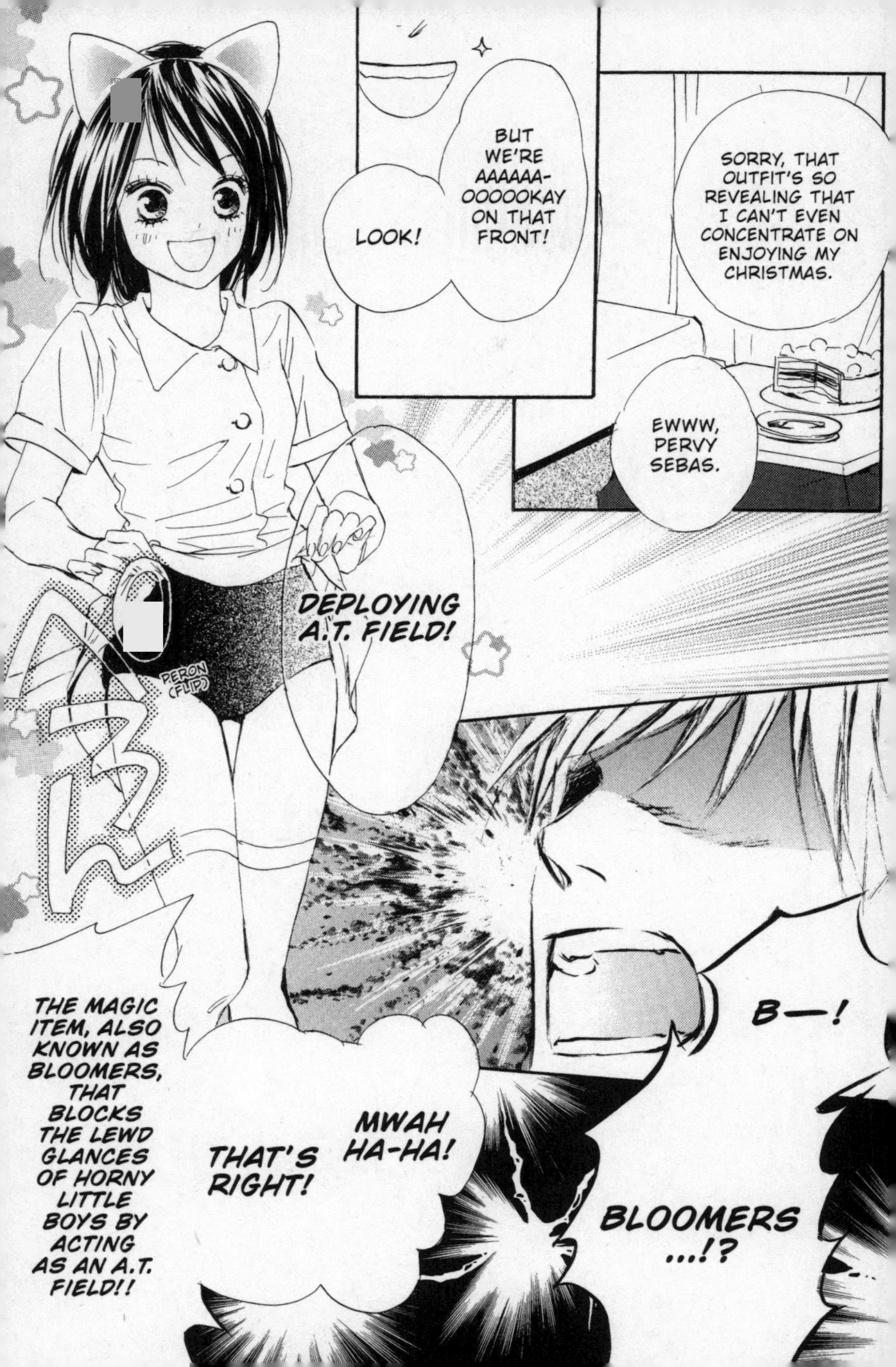

SORRY, THAT OUTFIT'S SO REVEALING THAT I CAN'T EVEN CONCENTRATE ON ENJOYING MY CHRISTMAS.
EWWW, PERVY SEBAS.
BUT WE'RE AAAAAA-OOOOOKAY ON THAT FRONT!
LOOK!
DEPLOYING A.T. FIELD!
PERON (FLIP)
B—!
BLOOMERS ...!?
MWAH HA-HA!
THAT'S RIGHT!
THE MAGIC ITEM, ALSO KNOWN AS BLOOMERS, THAT BLOCKS THE LEWD GLANCES OF HORNY LITTLE BOYS BY ACTING AS AN A.T. FIELD!!

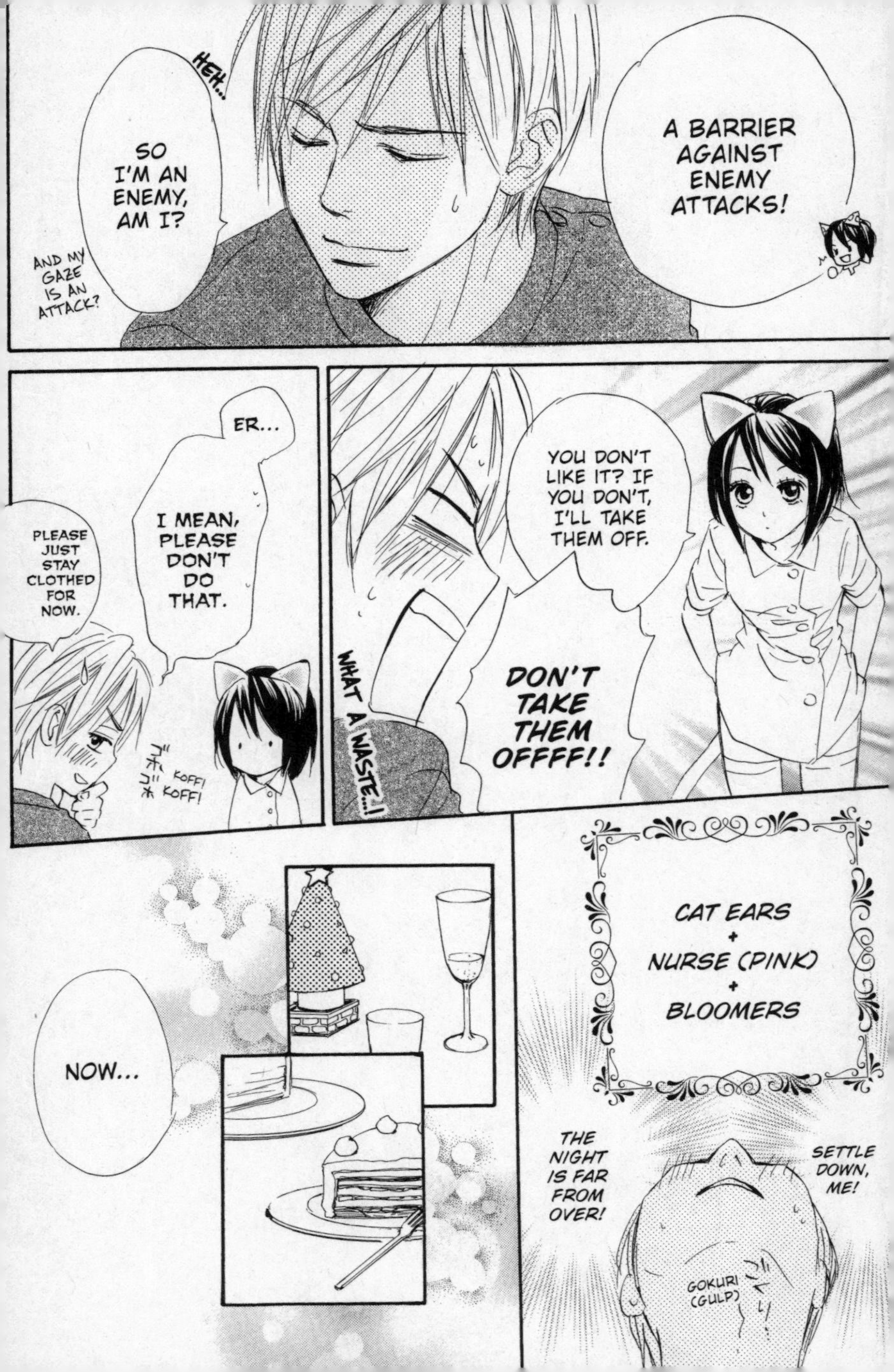
A BARRIER AGAINST ENEMY ATTACKS!
HEH...
SO I'M AN ENEMY, AM I?
AND MY GAZE IS AN ATTACK?
YOU DON'T LIKE IT? IF YOU DON'T, I'LL TAKE THEM OFF.
DON'T TAKE THEM OFFFF!!
WHAT A WASTE...!
ER...
I MEAN, PLEASE DON'T DO THAT.
PLEASE JUST STAY CLOTHED FOR NOW.
KOFF! KOFF!
CAT EARS + NURSE (PINK) + BLOOMERS
SETTLE DOWN, ME!
THE NIGHT IS FAR FROM OVER!
GOKURI (GULP)
NOW...

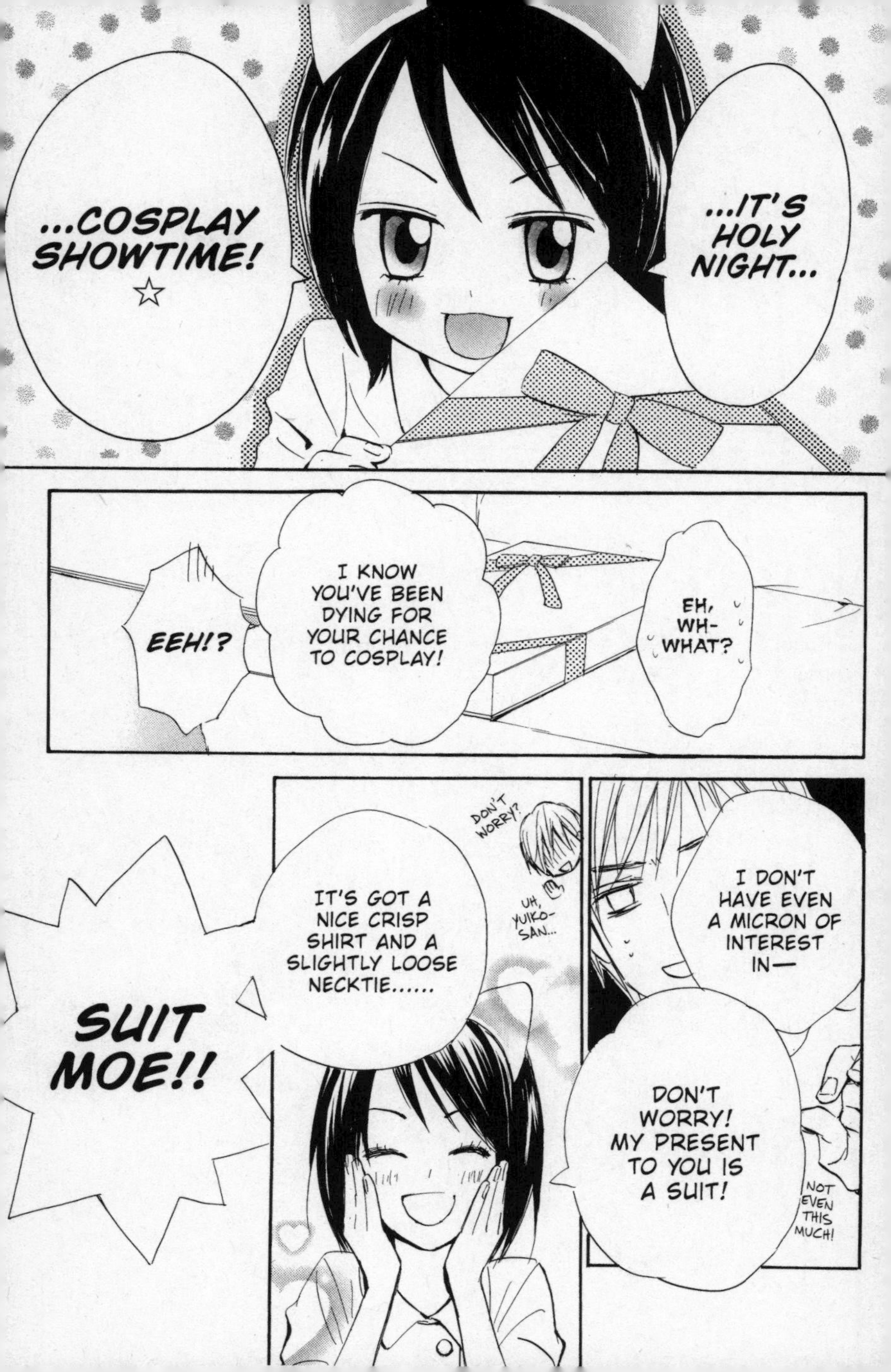
...IT'S HOLY NIGHT...
...COSPLAY SHOWTIME! ☆
EH, WH-WHAT?
I KNOW YOU'VE BEEN DYING FOR YOUR CHANCE TO COSPLAY!
EEH!?
I DON'T HAVE EVEN A MICRON OF INTEREST IN—
DON'T WORRY! MY PRESENT TO YOU IS A SUIT!
NOT EVEN THIS MUCH!
DON'T WORRY?
UH, YUIKO-SAN...
IT'S GOT A NICE CRISP SHIRT AND A SLIGHTLY LOOSE NECKTIE......
SUIT MOE!!

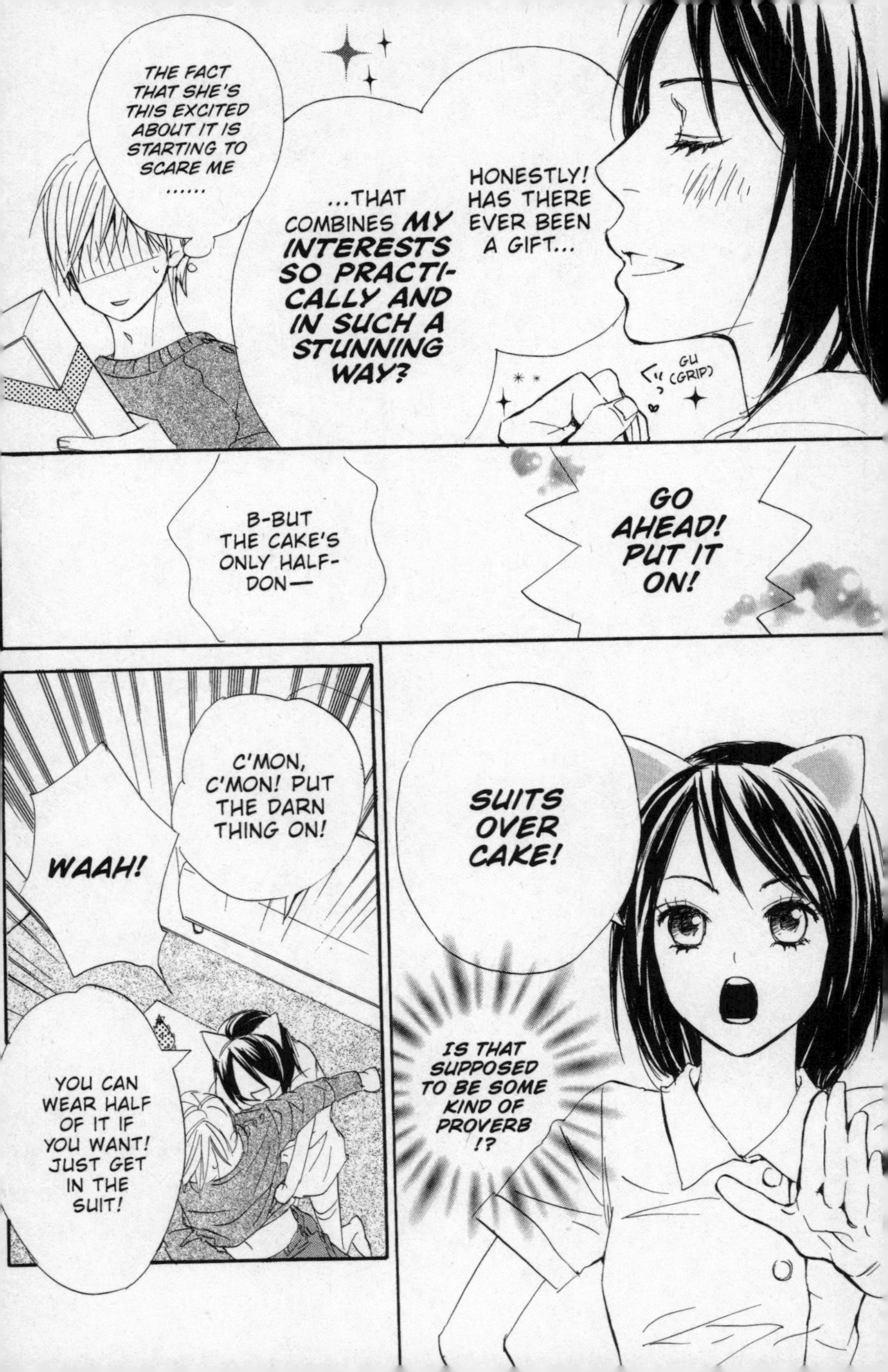
HONESTLY! HAS THERE EVER BEEN A GIFT...
...THAT COMBINES MY INTERESTS SO PRACTICALLY AND IN SUCH A STUNNING WAY?
GU (GRIP)
THE FACT THAT SHE'S THIS EXCITED ABOUT IT IS STARTING TO SCARE ME ......
GO AHEAD! PUT IT ON!
B-BUT THE CAKE'S ONLY HALF-DON—
SUITS OVER CAKE!
IS THAT SUPPOSED TO BE SOME KIND OF PROVERB !?
C'MON, C'MON! PUT THE DARN THING ON!
WAAH!
YOU CAN WEAR HALF OF IT IF YOU WANT! JUST GET IN THE SUIT!

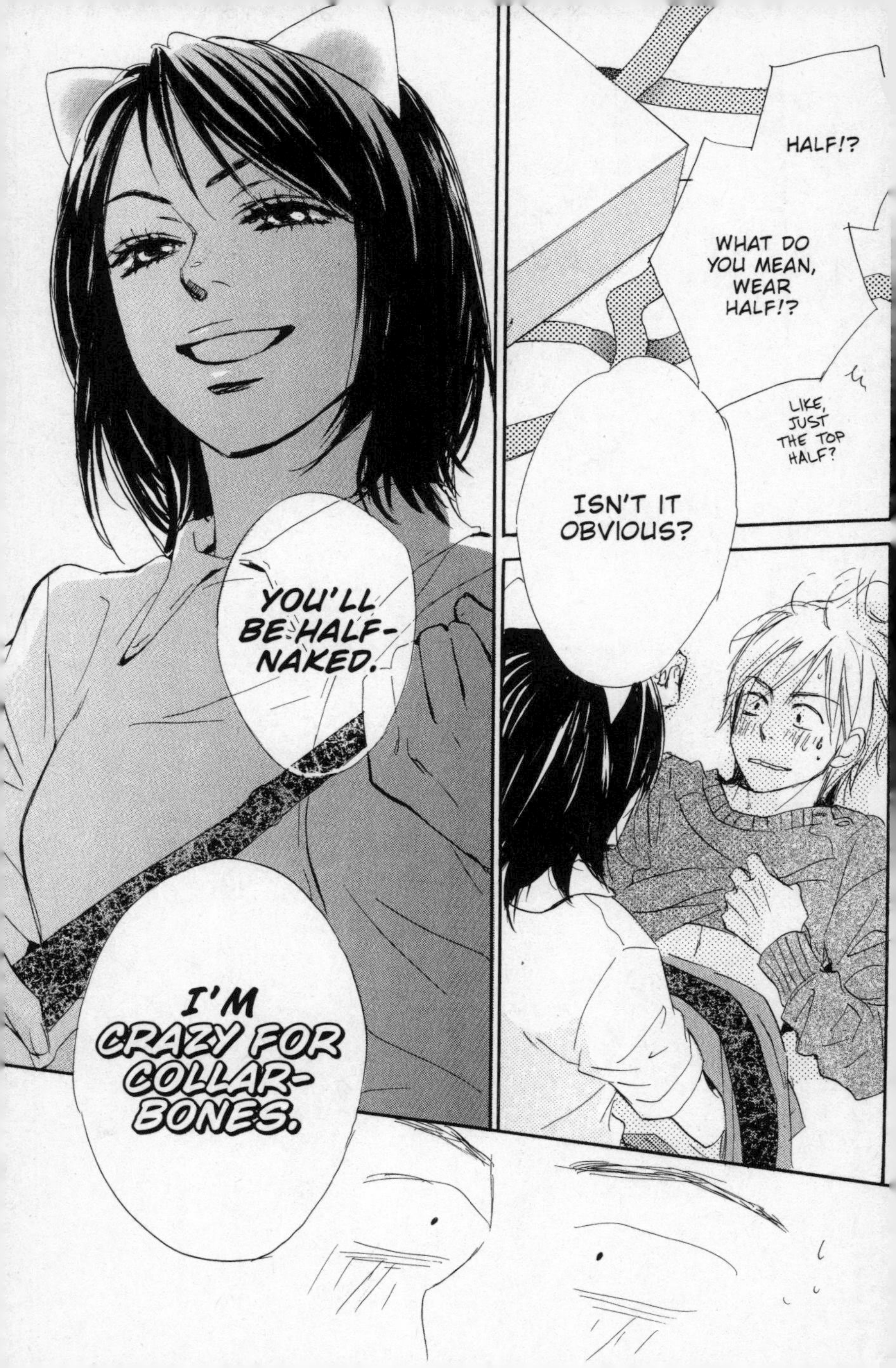
HALF!?
WHAT DO YOU MEAN, WEAR HALF!?
LIKE, JUST THE TOP HALF?
ISN'T IT OBVIOUS?
YOU'LL BE HALF-NAKED.
I'M CRAZY FOR COLLAR-BONES.

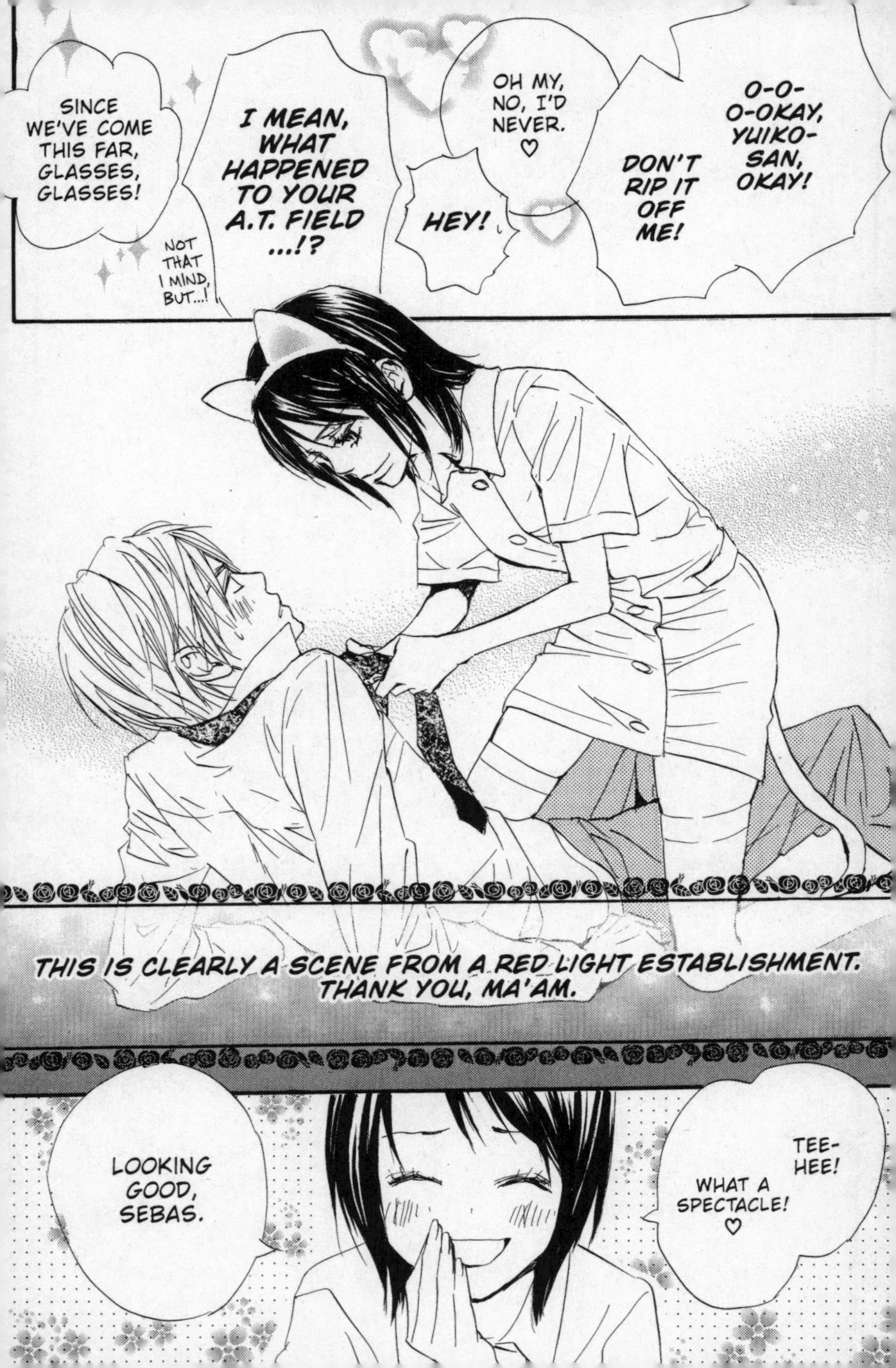
O-O-O-OKAY, YUIKO-SAN, OKAY!
OH MY, NO, I'D NEVER. ♡
DON'T RIP IT OFF ME!
HEY!
I MEAN, WHAT HAPPENED TO YOUR A.T. FIELD ...!?
SINCE WE'VE COME THIS FAR, GLASSES, GLASSES!
NOT THAT I MIND, BUT...!
THIS IS CLEARLY A SCENE FROM A RED LIGHT ESTABLISHMENT. THANK YOU, MA'AM.
TEE-HEE!
WHAT A SPECTACLE! ♡
LOOKING GOOD, SEBAS.

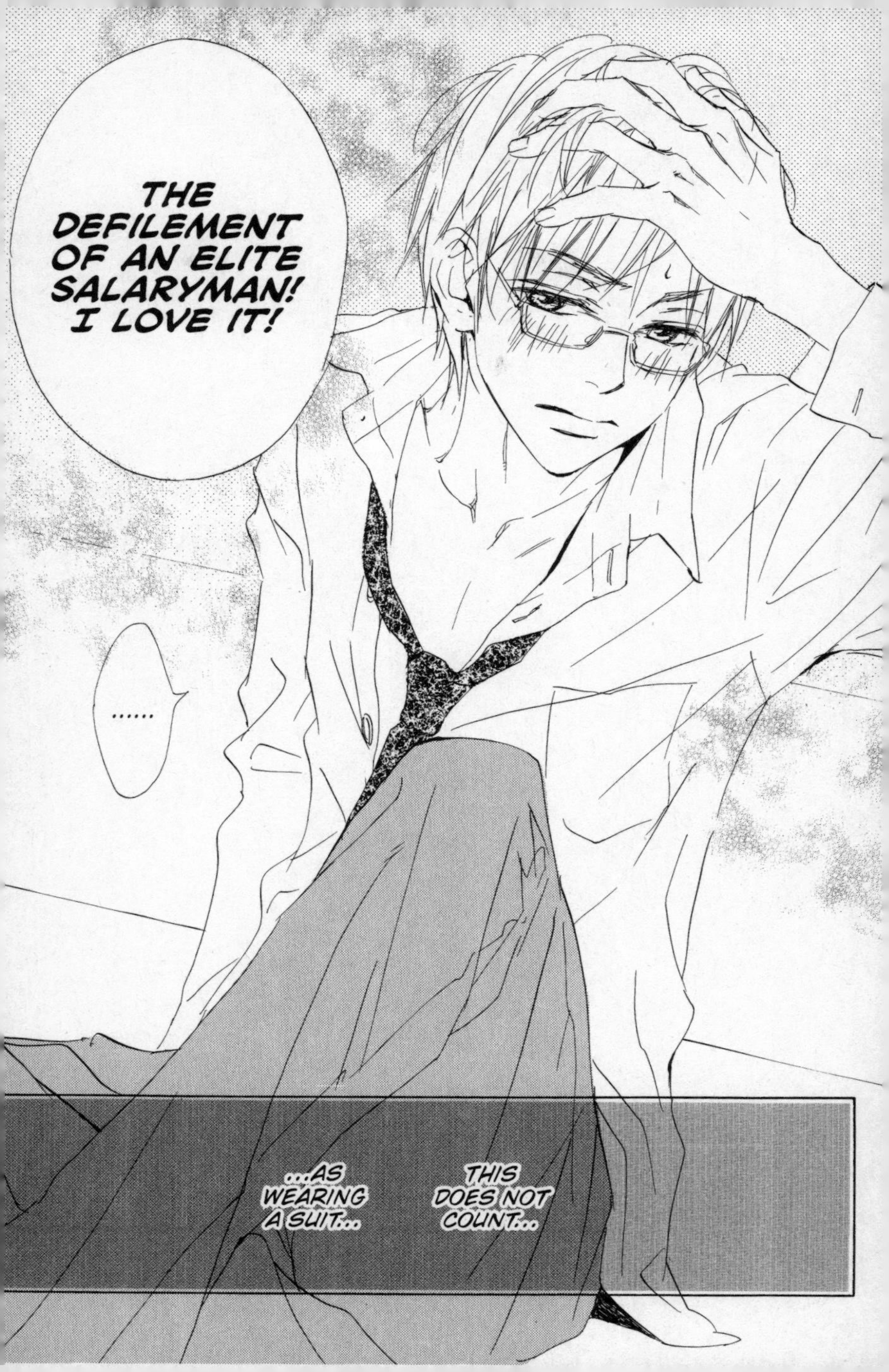
THE DEFILEMENT OF AN ELITE SALARYMAN! I LOVE IT!
......
THIS DOES NOT COUNT...
...AS WEARING A SUIT...

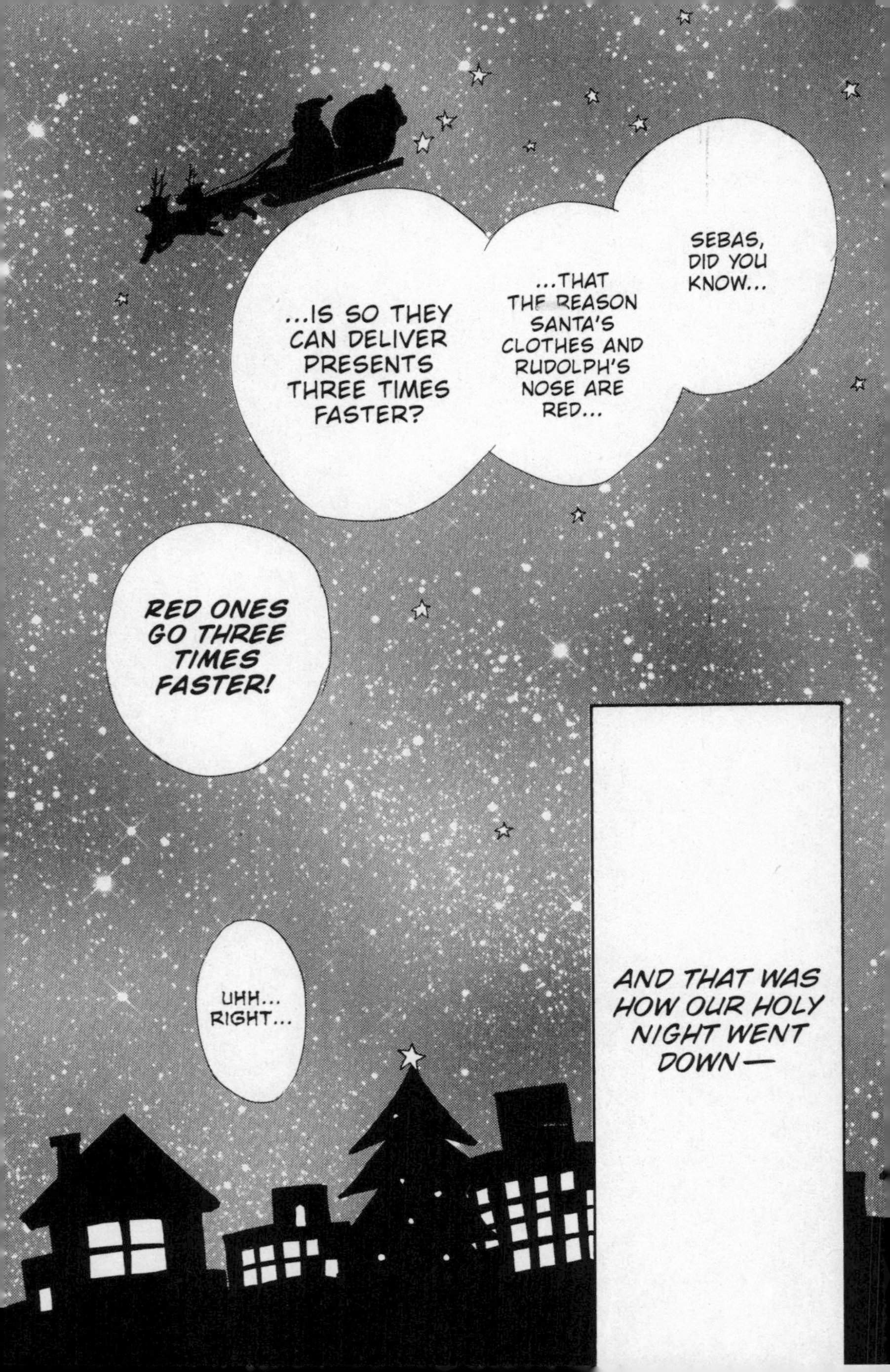
SEBAS, DID YOU KNOW...
...THAT THE REASON SANTA'S CLOTHES AND RUDOLPH'S NOSE ARE RED...
...IS SO THEY CAN DELIVER PRESENTS THREE TIMES FASTER?
RED ONES GO THREE TIMES FASTER!
UHH... RIGHT...
AND THAT WAS HOW OUR HOLY NIGHT WENT DOWN—

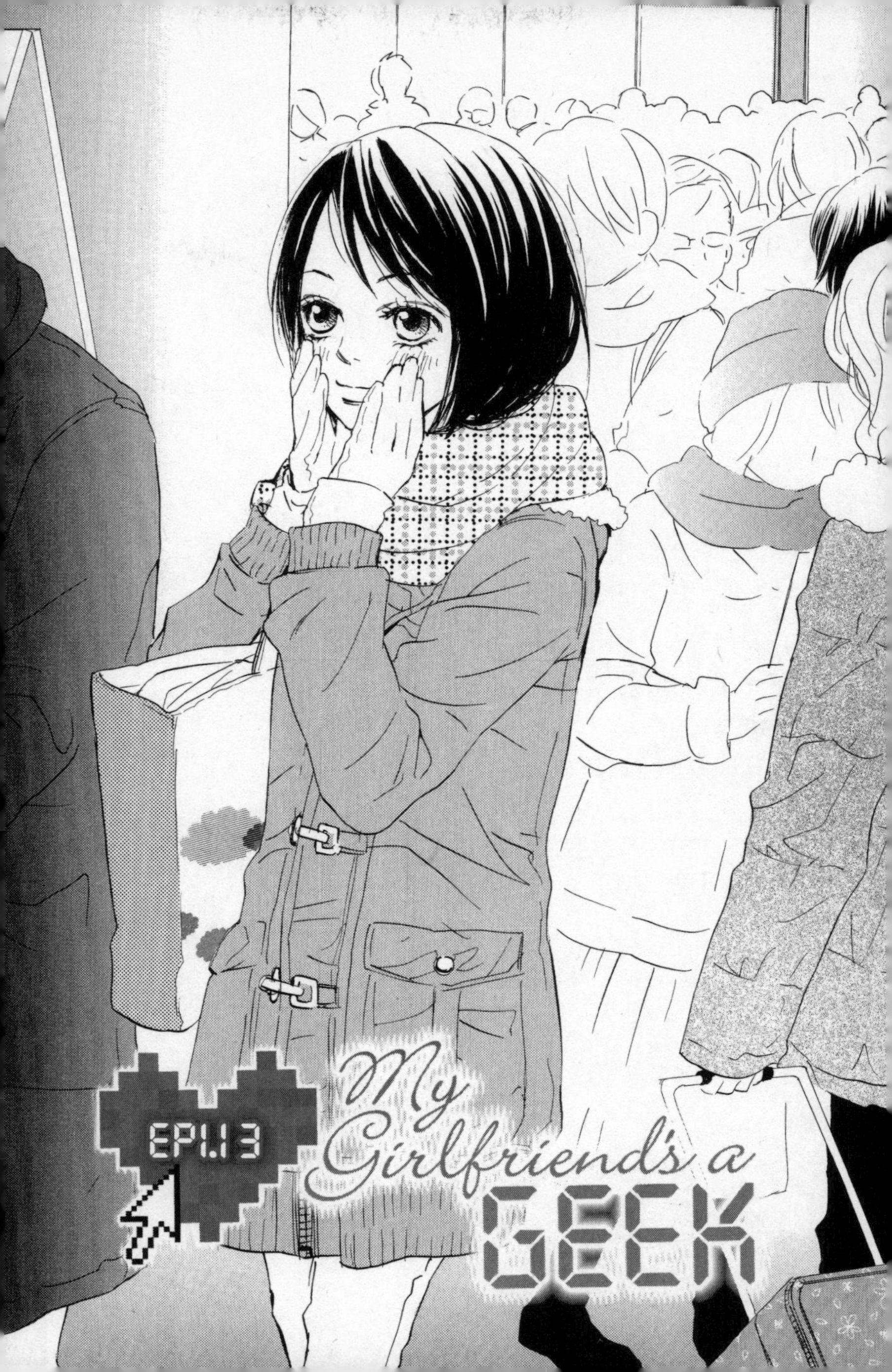
EPI.13
My Girlfriend's a
GEEK

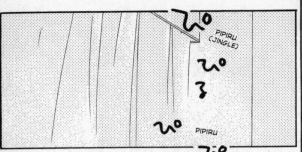

PIPIRU
(JINGLE)

PIPIRU

DECEMBER 29TH

MORNING ALREADY ......?

SO COLD.

PIPIRU

From Yuiko-san

Perfect Comiket weather!

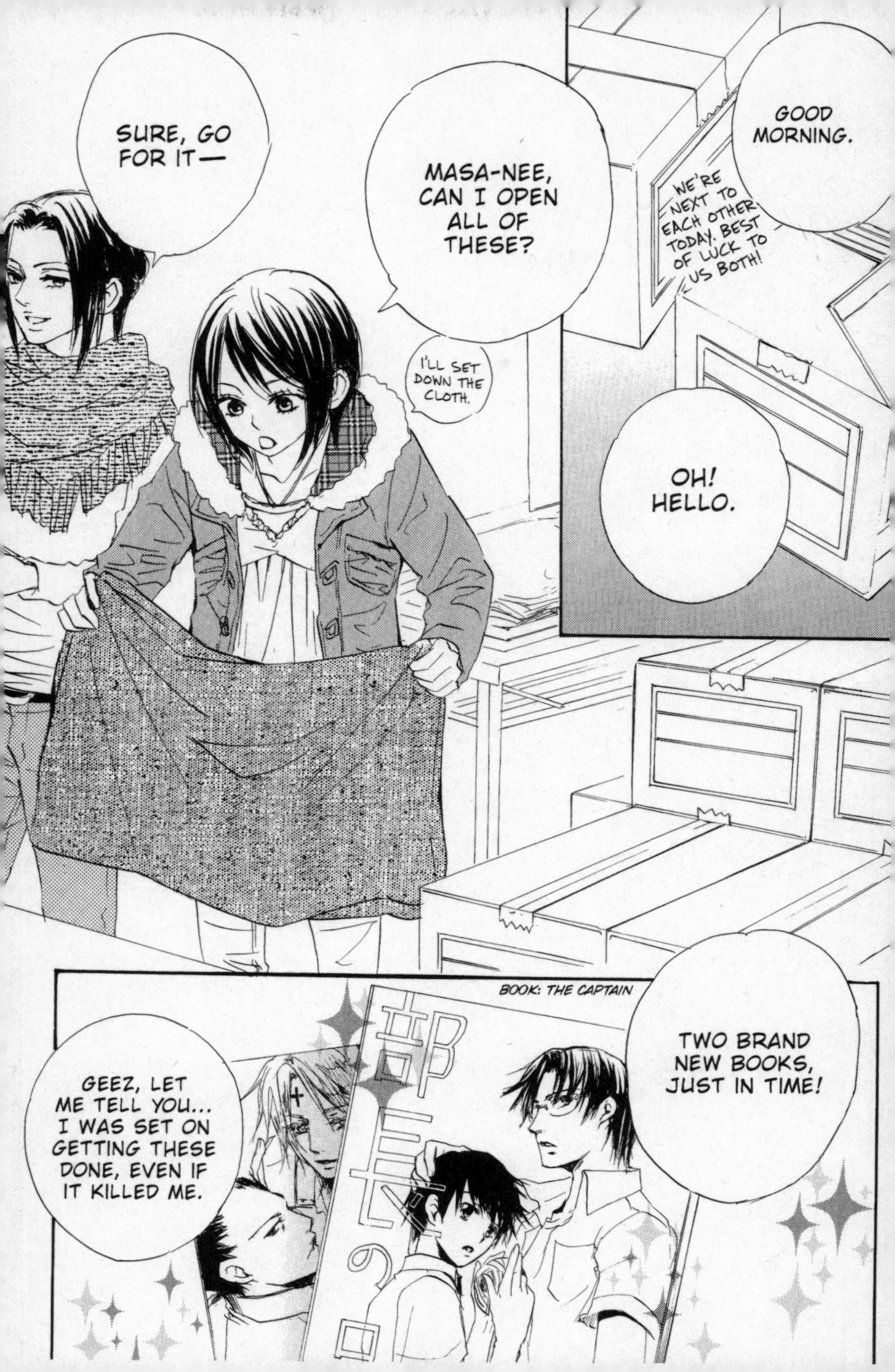
GOOD MORNING.
WE'RE NEXT TO EACH OTHER TODAY. BEST OF LUCK TO US BOTH!
OH! HELLO.
MASA-NEE, CAN I OPEN ALL OF THESE?
SURE, GO FOR IT—
I'LL SET DOWN THE CLOTH.
BOOK: THE CAPTAIN
TWO BRAND NEW BOOKS, JUST IN TIME!
GEEZ, LET ME TELL YOU... I WAS SET ON GETTING THESE DONE, EVEN IF IT KILLED ME.

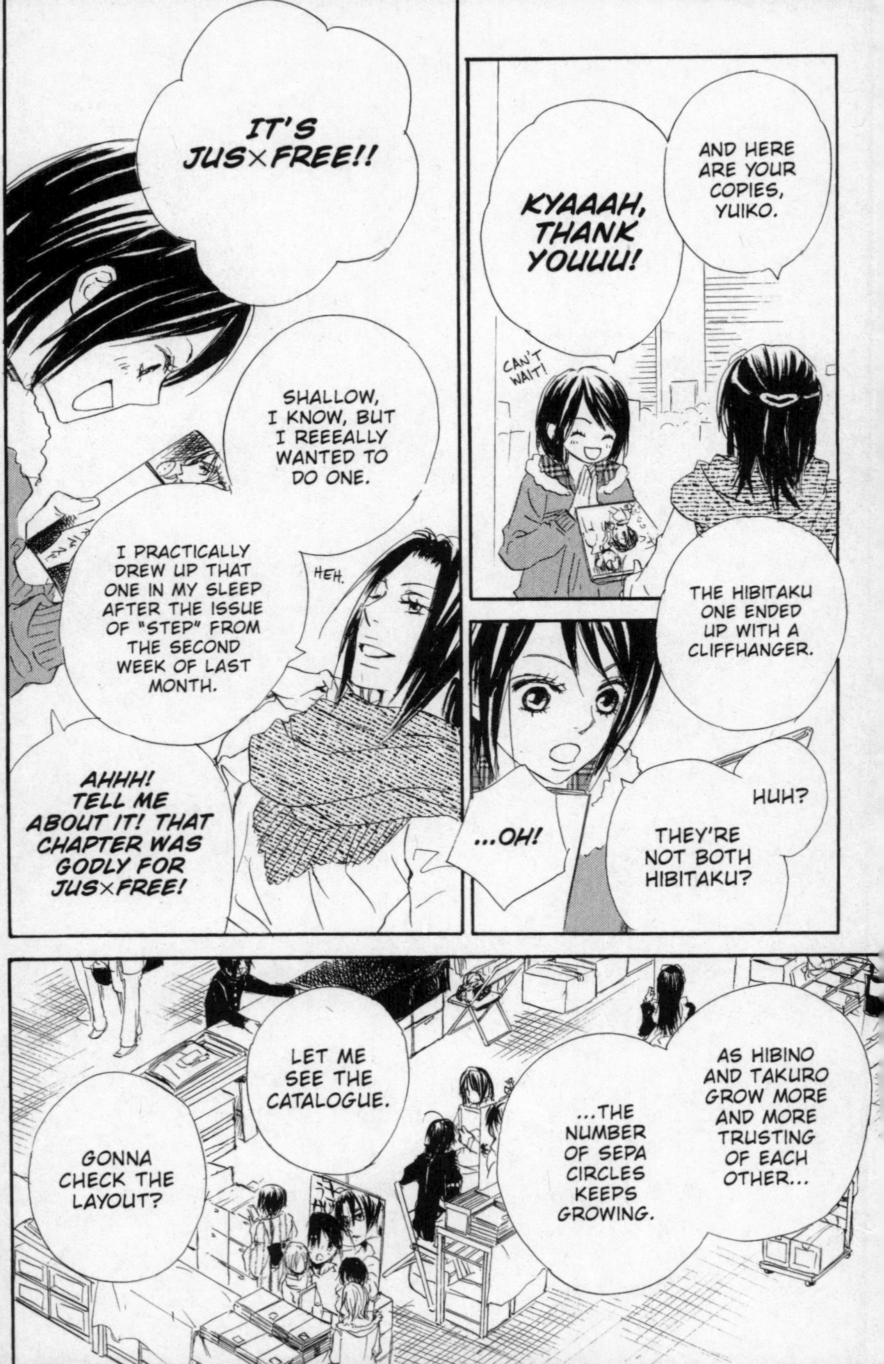
AND HERE ARE YOUR COPIES, YUIKO.
KYAAAH, THANK YOUUU!
CAN'T WAIT!
THE HIBITAKU ONE ENDED UP WITH A CLIFFHANGER.
HUH?
THEY'RE NOT BOTH HIBITAKU?
...OH!
IT'S JUS×FREE!!
SHALLOW, I KNOW, BUT I REEEALLY WANTED TO DO ONE.
I PRACTICALLY DREW UP THAT ONE IN MY SLEEP AFTER THE ISSUE OF "STEP" FROM THE SECOND WEEK OF LAST MONTH.
HEH.
AHHH! TELL ME ABOUT IT! THAT CHAPTER WAS GODLY FOR JUS×FREE!
AS HIBINO AND TAKURO GROW MORE AND MORE TRUSTING OF EACH OTHER...
...THE NUMBER OF SEPA CIRCLES KEEPS GROWING.
LET ME SEE THE CATALOGUE.
GONNA CHECK THE LAYOUT?

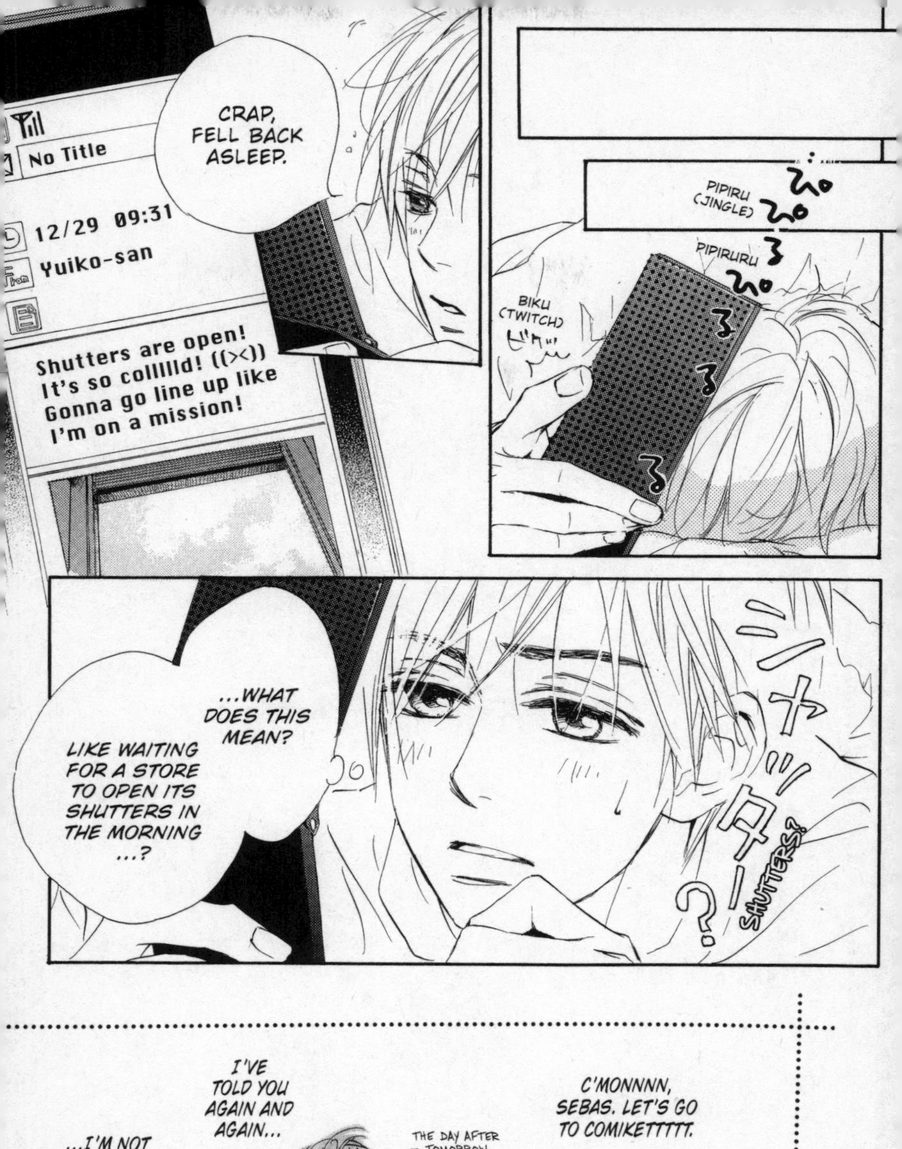
PIPIRU (JINGLE)
PIPIRURU
BIKU (TWITCH)
CRAP, FELL BACK ASLEEP.
No Title
12/29 09:31
Yuiko-san
Shutters are open!
It's so collllld! ((><))
Gonna go line up like
I'm on a mission!
...WHAT DOES THIS MEAN?
LIKE WAITING FOR A STORE TO OPEN ITS SHUTTERS IN THE MORNING ...?
SHUTTERS?
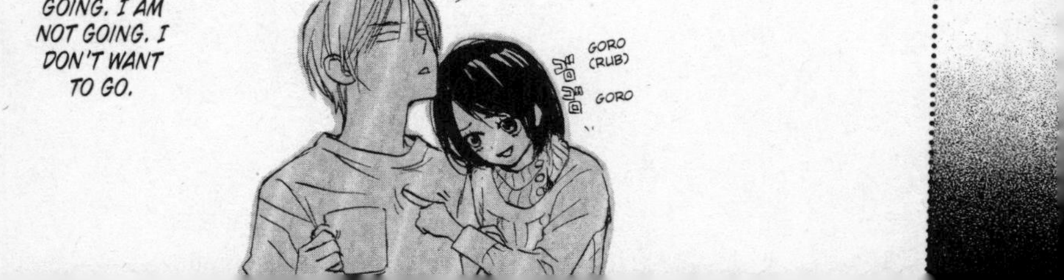
C'MONNNN, SEBAS. LET'S GO TO COMIKETTTTTT.
THE DAY AFTER TOMORROW
GORO (RUB)
GORO
I'VE TOLD YOU AGAIN AND AGAIN...
...I'M NOT GOING. I AM NOT GOING. I DON'T WANT TO GO.

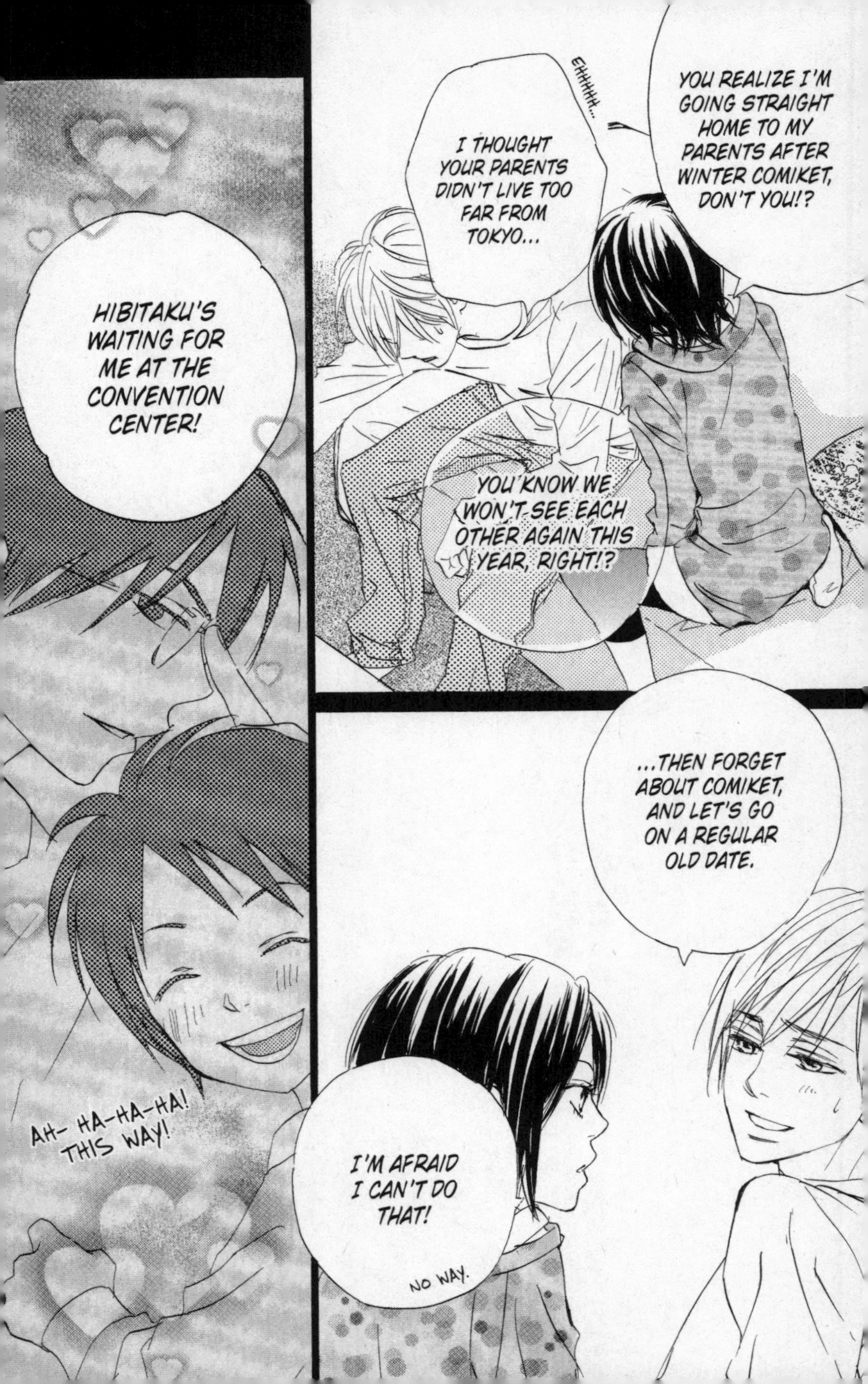
YOU REALIZE I'M GOING STRAIGHT HOME TO MY PARENTS AFTER WINTER COMIKET, DON'T YOU!?
EHHHHH...
I THOUGHT YOUR PARENTS DIDN'T LIVE TOO FAR FROM TOKYO...
YOU KNOW WE WON'T SEE EACH OTHER AGAIN THIS YEAR, RIGHT!?
...THEN FORGET ABOUT COMIKET, AND LET'S GO ON A REGULAR OLD DATE.
I'M AFRAID I CAN'T DO THAT!
NO WAY.
HIBITAKU'S WAITING FOR ME AT THE CONVENTION CENTER!
AH- HA-HA-HA! THIS WAY!

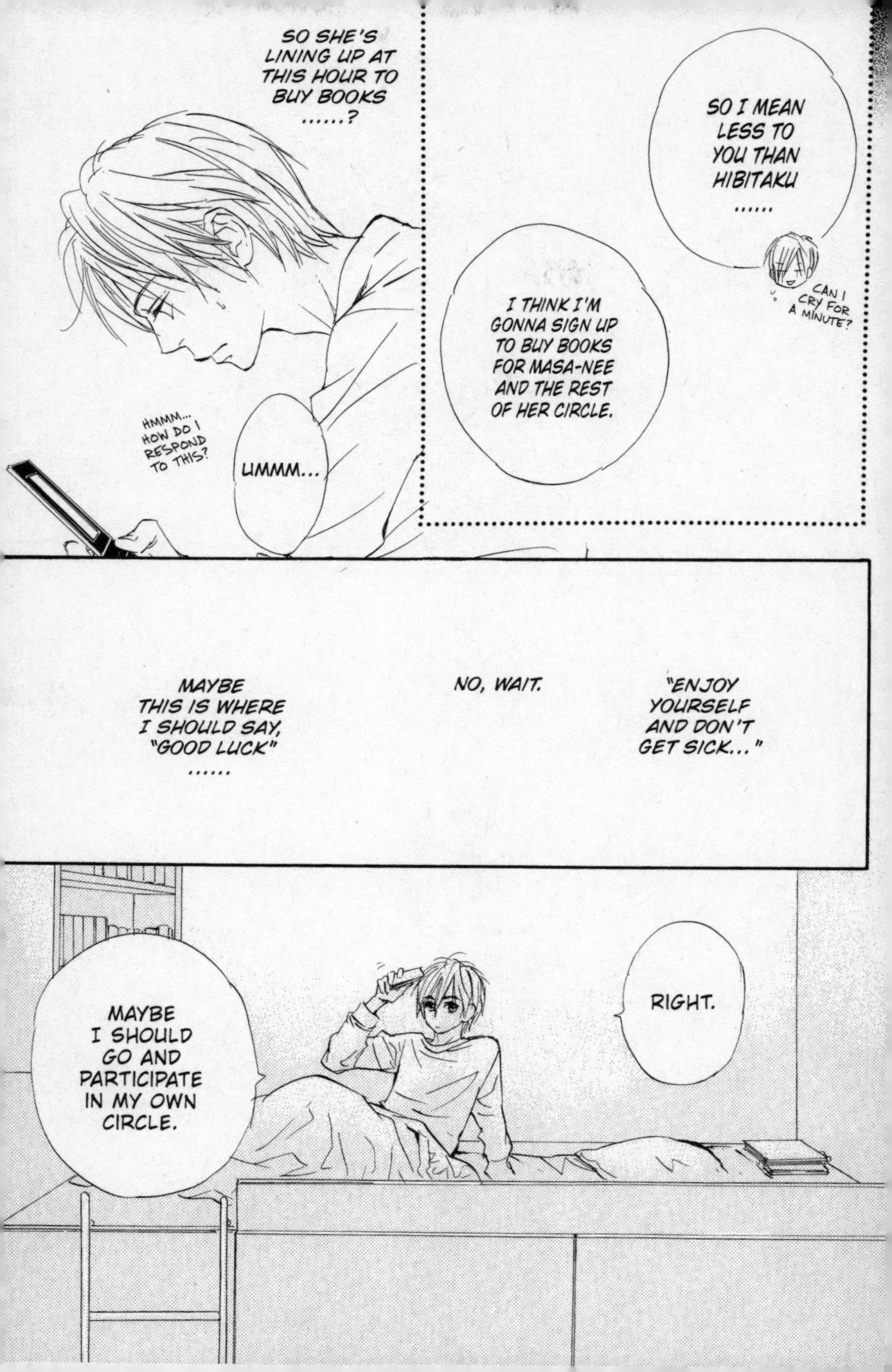
SO I MEAN LESS TO YOU THAN HIBITAKU ......
CAN I CRY FOR A MINUTE?
I THINK I'M GONNA SIGN UP TO BUY BOOKS FOR MASA-NEE AND THE REST OF HER CIRCLE.
SO SHE'S LINING UP AT THIS HOUR TO BUY BOOKS ......?
UMMM...
HMMM... HOW DO I RESPOND TO THIS?
"ENJOY YOURSELF AND DON'T GET SICK..."
NO, WAIT.
MAYBE THIS IS WHERE I SHOULD SAY, "GOOD LUCK" ......
RIGHT.
MAYBE I SHOULD GO AND PARTICIPATE IN MY OWN CIRCLE.

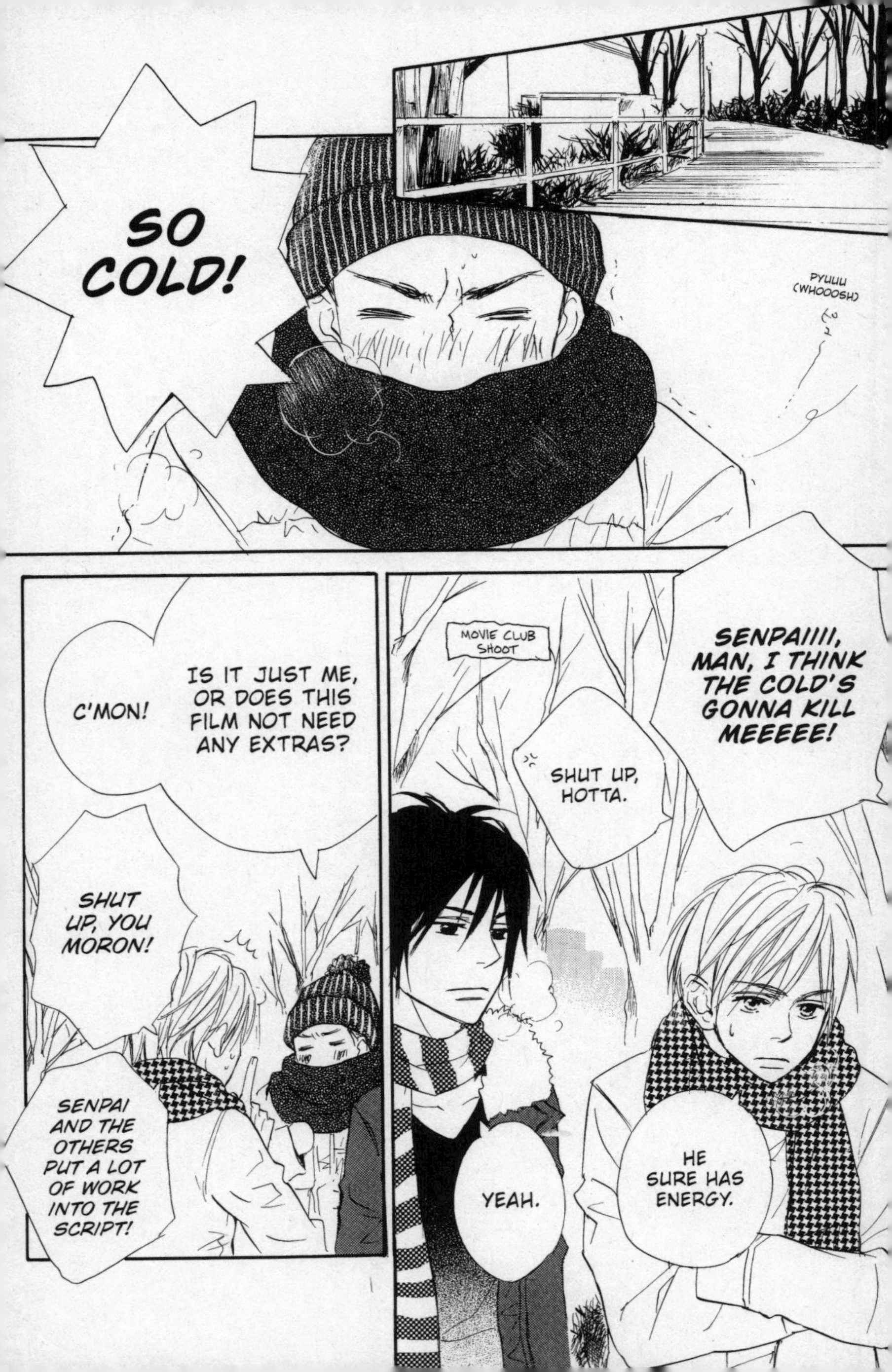
SO COLD!
PYUUU (WHOOOSH)
SENPAIIII, MAN, I THINK THE COLD'S GONNA KILL MEEEEE!
MOVIE CLUB SHOOT
SHUT UP, HOTTA.
HE SURE HAS ENERGY.
YEAH.
IS IT JUST ME, OR DOES THIS FILM NOT NEED ANY EXTRAS?
C'MON!
SHUT UP, YOU MORON!
SENPAI AND THE OTHERS PUT A LOT OF WORK INTO THE SCRIPT!

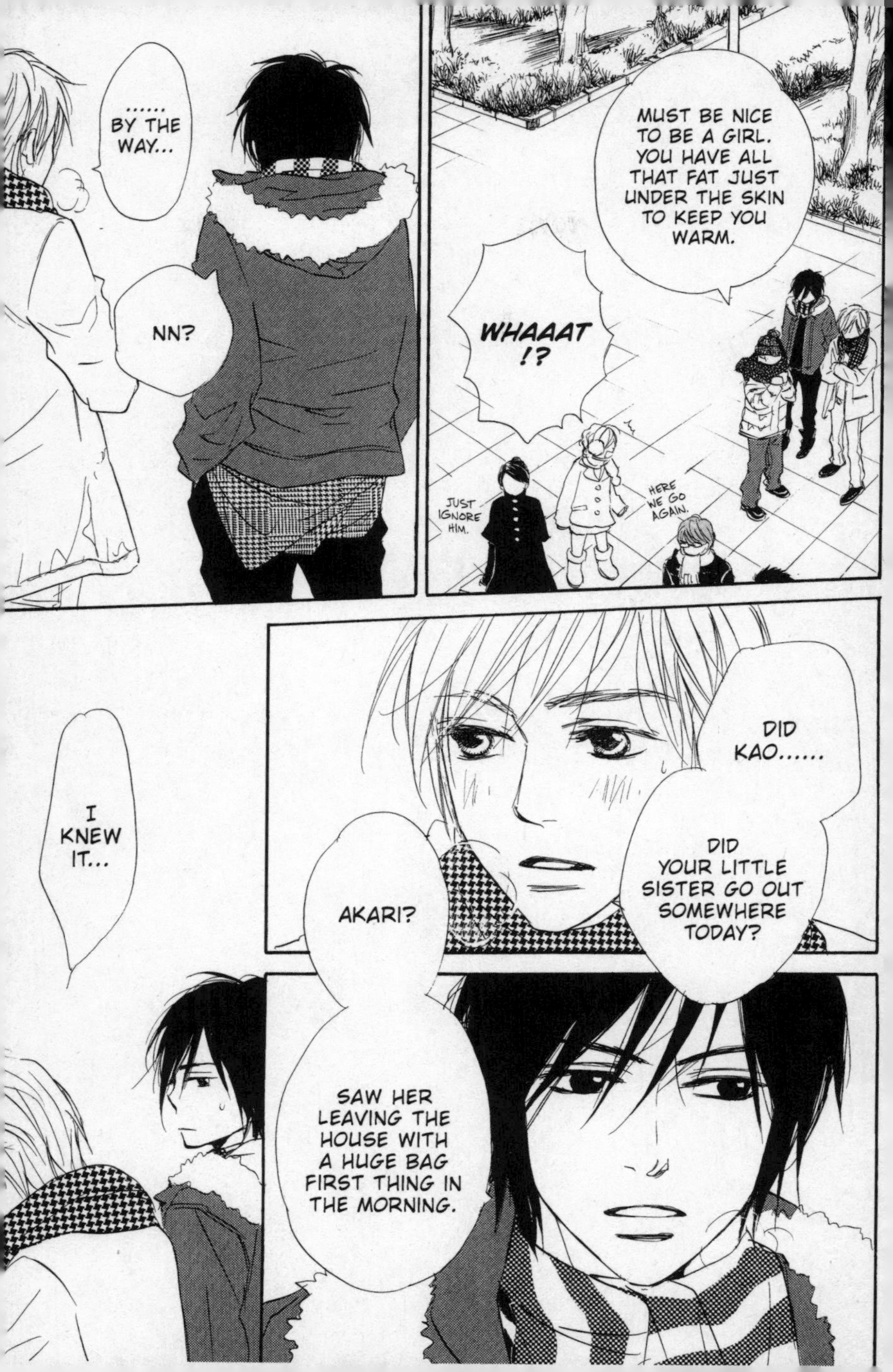
MUST BE NICE TO BE A GIRL. YOU HAVE ALL THAT FAT JUST UNDER THE SKIN TO KEEP YOU WARM.
WHAAAT !?
HERE WE GO AGAIN.
JUST IGNORE HIM.
...... BY THE WAY...
NN?
DID KAO......
DID YOUR LITTLE SISTER GO OUT SOMEWHERE TODAY?
AKARI?
SAW HER LEAVING THE HOUSE WITH A HUGE BAG FIRST THING IN THE MORNING.
I KNEW IT...

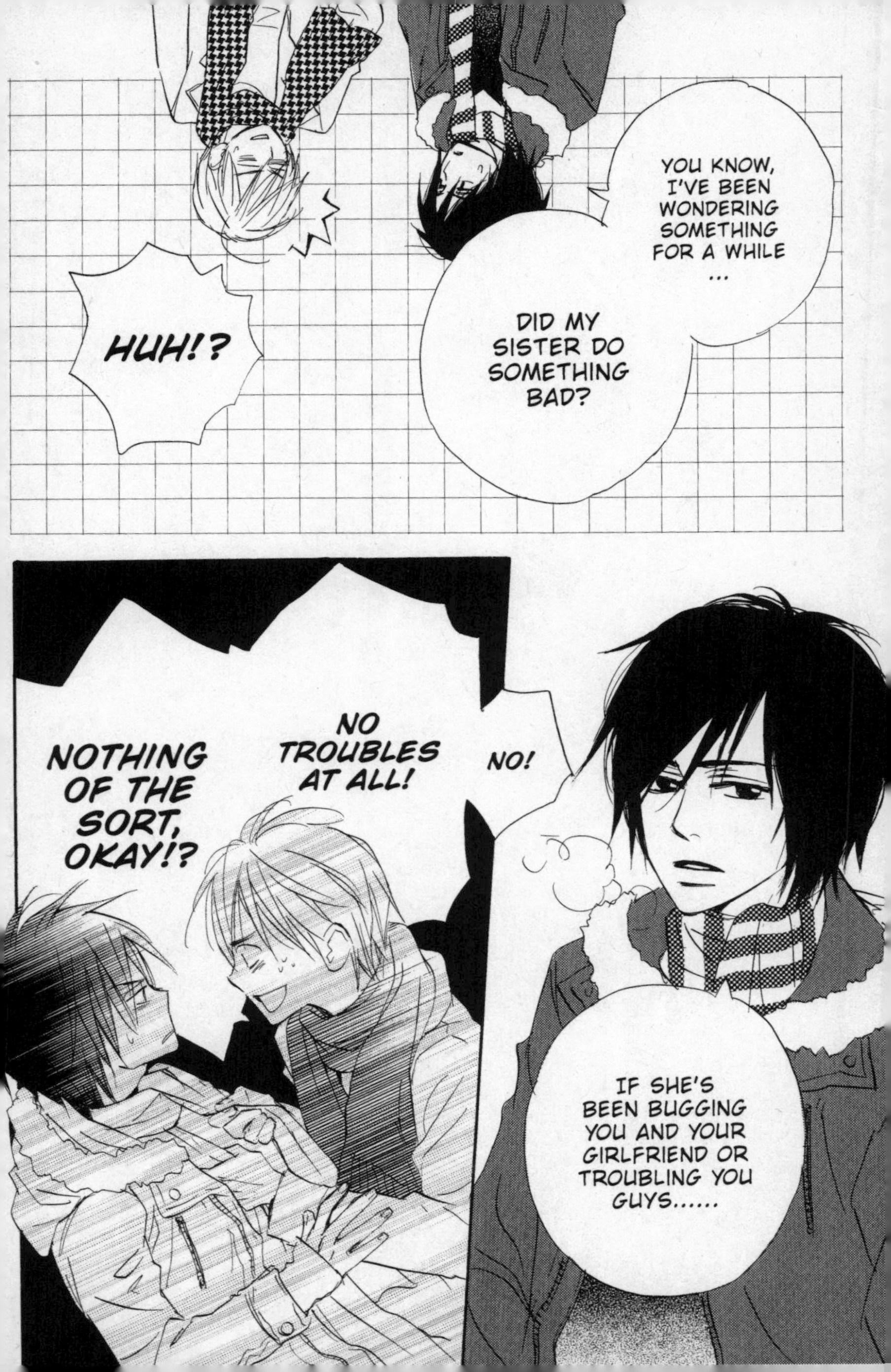
YOU KNOW, I'VE BEEN WONDERING SOMETHING FOR A WHILE ...
DID MY SISTER DO SOMETHING BAD?
HUH!?
IF SHE'S BEEN BUGGING YOU AND YOUR GIRLFRIEND OR TROUBLING YOU GUYS......
NO!
NO TROUBLES AT ALL!
NOTHING OF THE SORT, OKAY!?

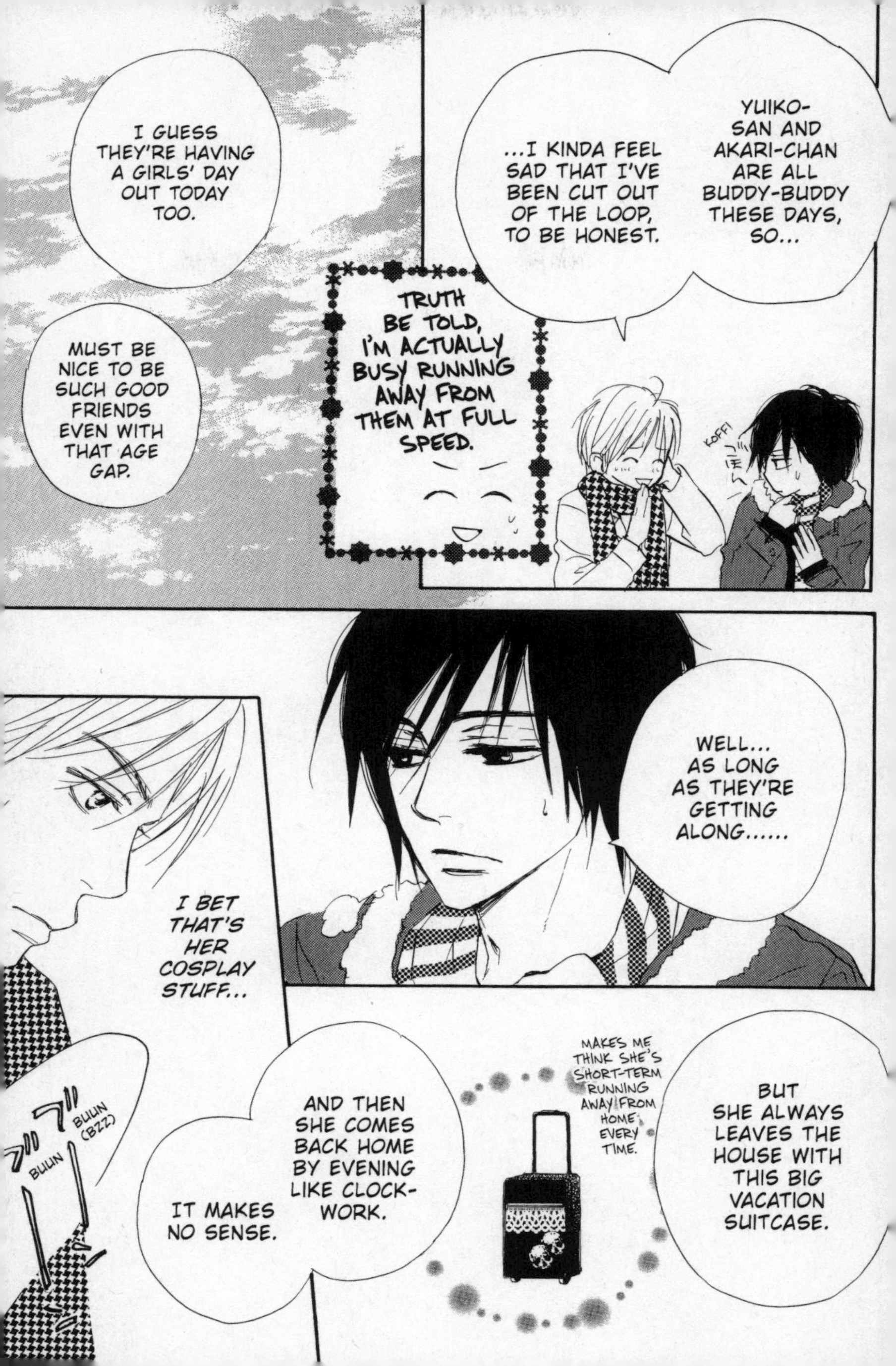
YUIKO-SAN AND AKARI-CHAN ARE ALL BUDDY-BUDDY THESE DAYS, SO...
...I KINDA FEEL SAD THAT I'VE BEEN CUT OUT OF THE LOOP, TO BE HONEST.
TRUTH BE TOLD, I'M ACTUALLY BUSY RUNNING AWAY FROM THEM AT FULL SPEED.
KOFF!
I GUESS THEY'RE HAVING A GIRLS' DAY OUT TODAY TOO.
MUST BE NICE TO BE SUCH GOOD FRIENDS EVEN WITH THAT AGE GAP.
WELL... AS LONG AS THEY'RE GETTING ALONG......
I BET THAT'S HER COSPLAY STUFF...
BUT SHE ALWAYS LEAVES THE HOUSE WITH THIS BIG VACATION SUITCASE.
MAKES ME THINK SHE'S SHORT-TERM RUNNING AWAY FROM HOME EVERY TIME.
AND THEN SHE COMES BACK HOME BY EVENING LIKE CLOCK-WORK.
IT MAKES NO SENSE.
BUUN (BZZ)
BUUN

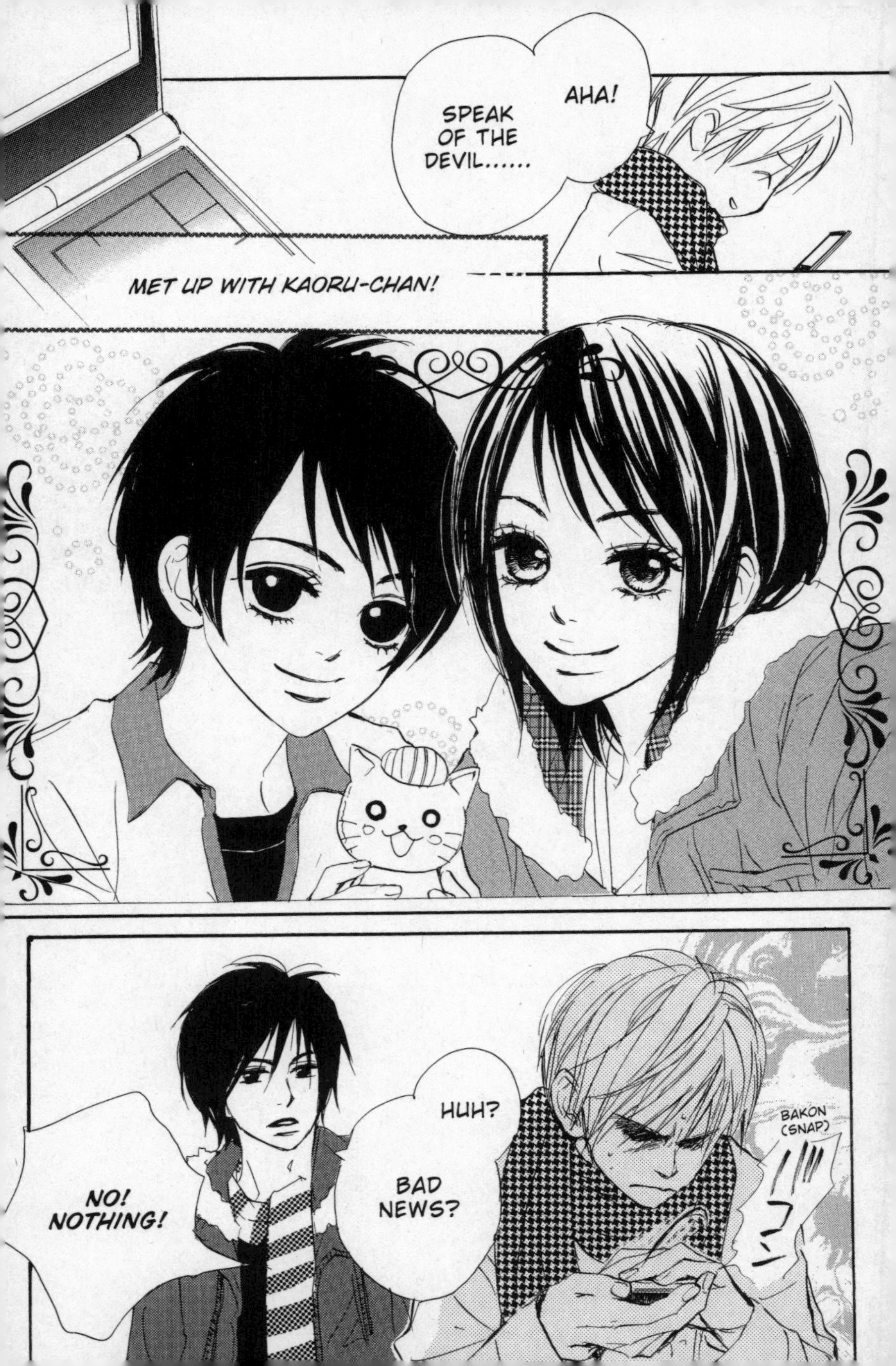
AHA!
SPEAK OF THE DEVIL......
MET UP WITH KAORU-CHAN!
BAKON (SNAP)
HUH?
BAD NEWS?
NO! NOTHING!

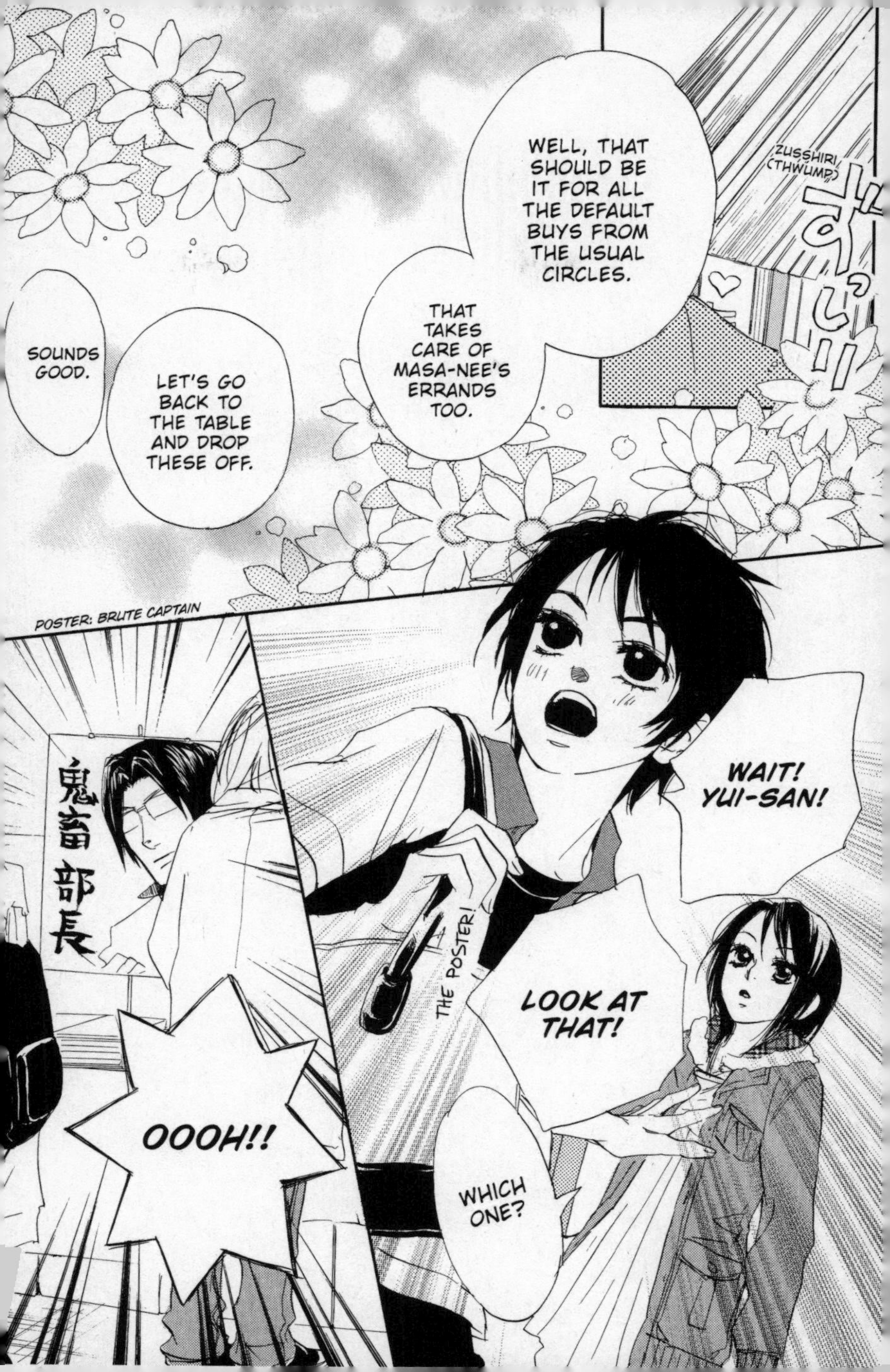

ZUSSHIRI (THWUMP)
WELL, THAT SHOULD BE IT FOR ALL THE DEFAULT BUYS FROM THE USUAL CIRCLES.
THAT TAKES CARE OF MASA-NEE'S ERRANDS TOO.
LET'S GO BACK TO THE TABLE AND DROP THESE OFF.
SOUNDS GOOD.
WAIT! YUI-SAN!
THE POSTER!
LOOK AT THAT!
WHICH ONE?
POSTER: BRUTE CAPTAIN
鬼畜部長
OOOH!!

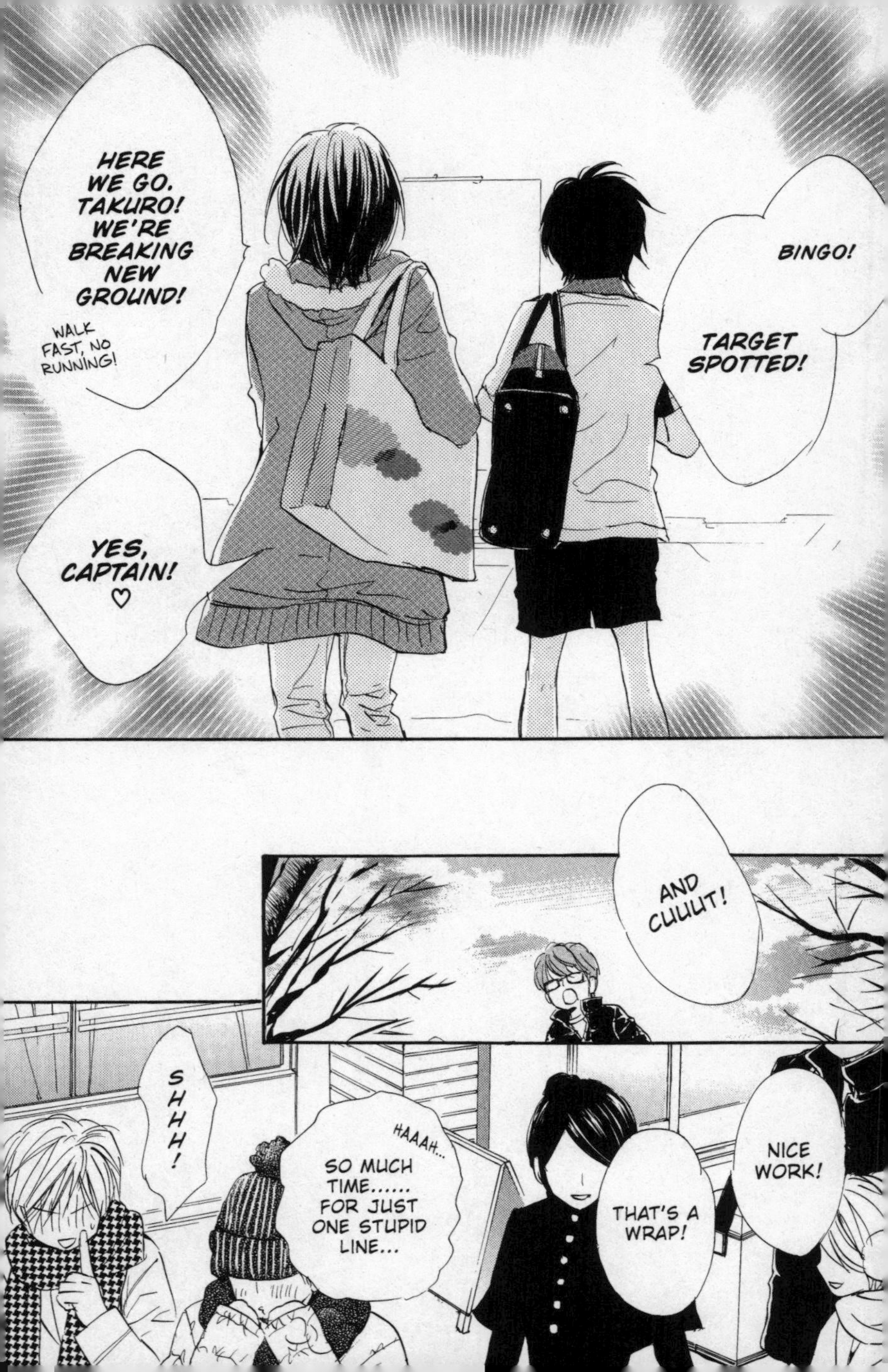
BINGO!
TARGET SPOTTED!
HERE WE GO. TAKURO! WE'RE BREAKING NEW GROUND!
WALK FAST, NO RUNNING!
YES, CAPTAIN! ♡
AND CUUUT!
NICE WORK!
THAT'S A WRAP!
HAAAH...
SO MUCH TIME...... FOR JUST ONE STUPID LINE...
SHHH!

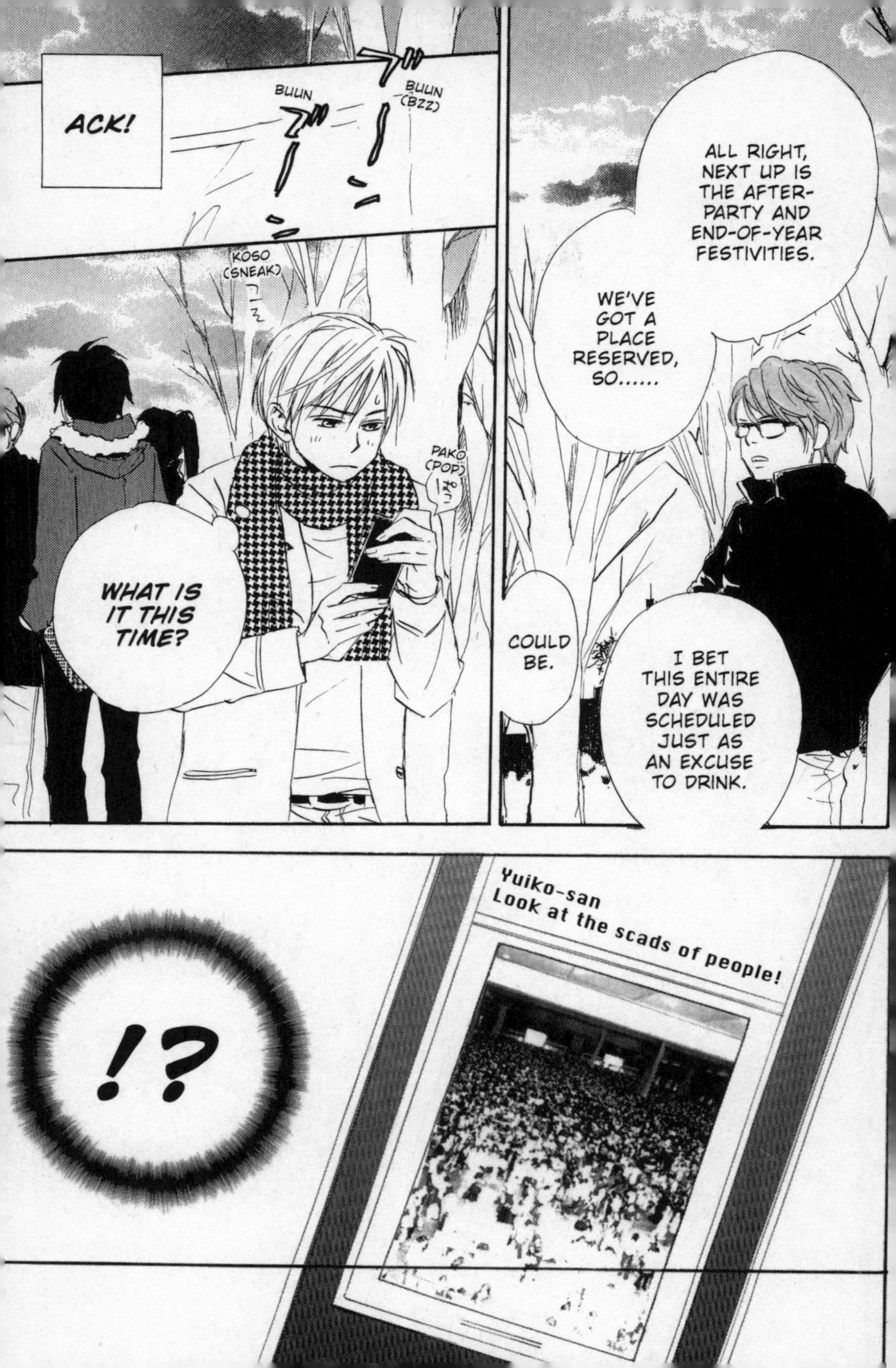
ALL RIGHT, NEXT UP IS THE AFTER-PARTY AND END-OF-YEAR FESTIVITIES.
WE'VE GOT A PLACE RESERVED, SO......
I BET THIS ENTIRE DAY WAS SCHEDULED JUST AS AN EXCUSE TO DRINK.
COULD BE.
BUUN (BZZ)
BUUN
ACK!
KOSO (SNEAK)
PAKO (POP)
WHAT IS IT THIS TIME?
Yuiko-san
Look at the scads of people!
!?

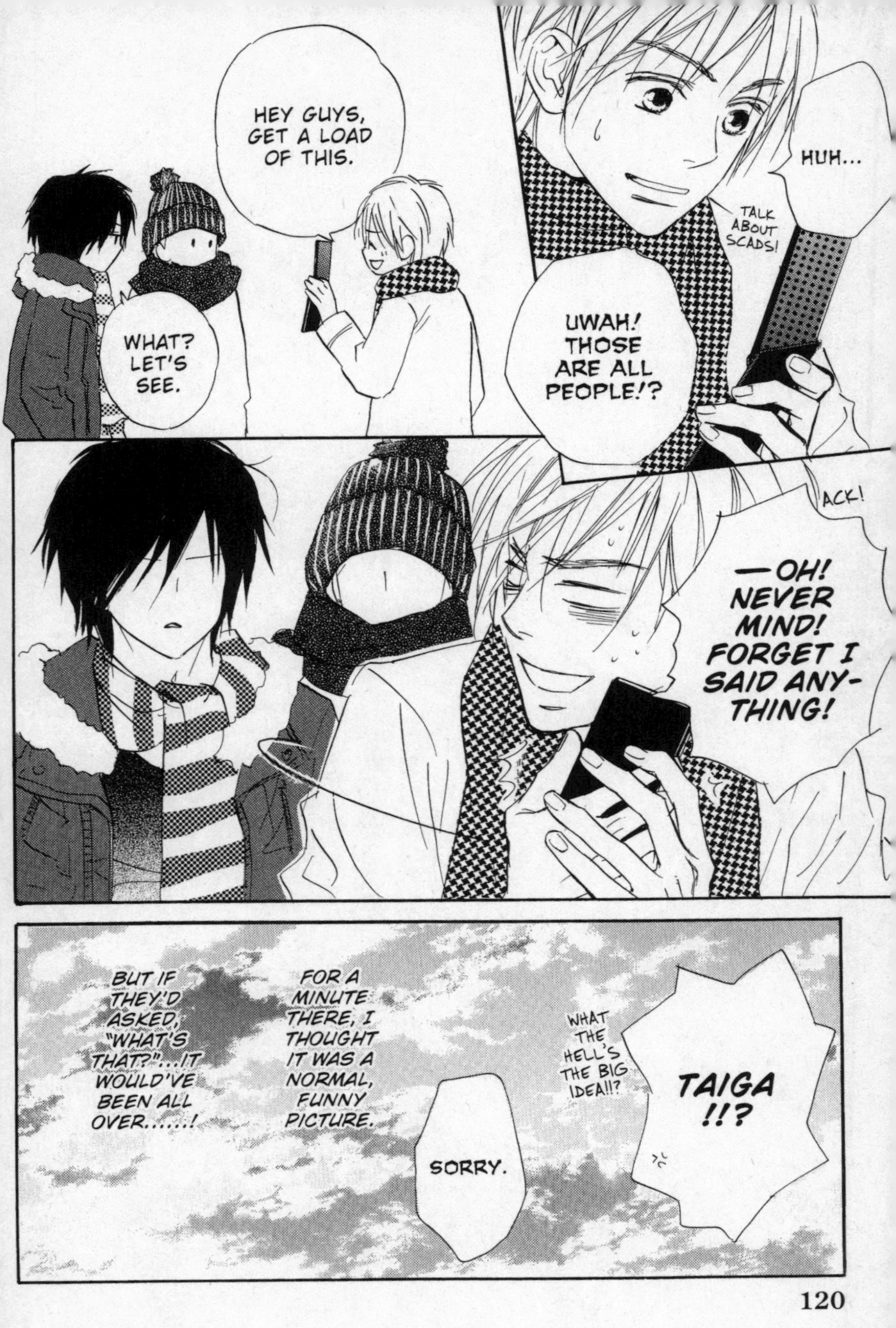
HUH...
TALK ABOUT SCADS!
UWAH! THOSE ARE ALL PEOPLE!?
HEY GUYS, GET A LOAD OF THIS.
WHAT? LET'S SEE.
ACK!
—OH! NEVER MIND! FORGET I SAID ANY-THING!
TAIGA!!?
WHAT THE HELL'S THE BIG IDEA!!?
SORRY.
FOR A MINUTE THERE, I THOUGHT IT WAS A NORMAL, FUNNY PICTURE.
BUT IF THEY'D ASKED, "WHAT'S THAT?"...IT WOULD'VE BEEN ALL OVER......!

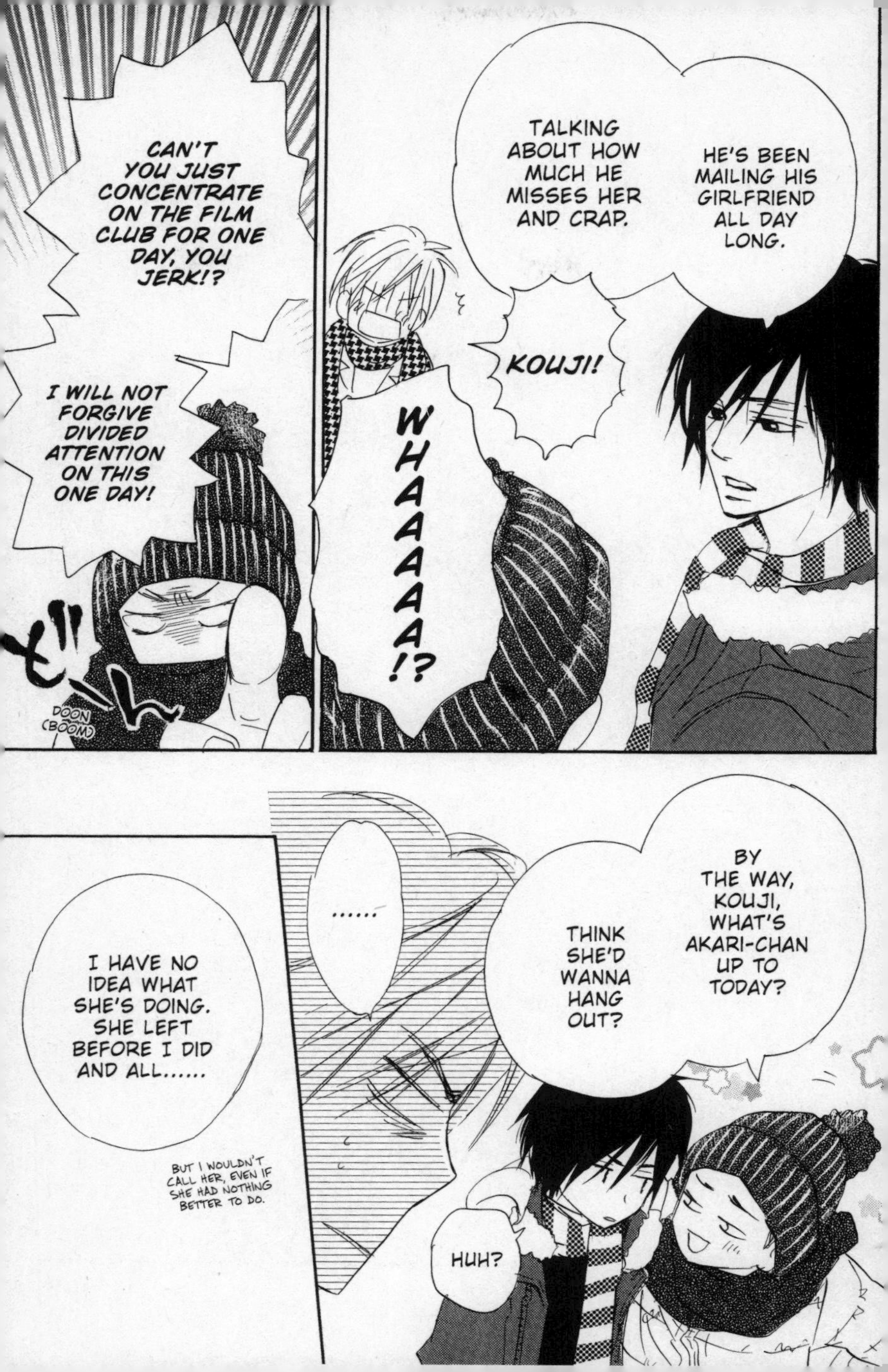
HE'S BEEN MAILING HIS GIRLFRIEND ALL DAY LONG.
TALKING ABOUT HOW MUCH HE MISSES HER AND CRAP.
KOUJI!
WHAAAAAA!?
CAN'T YOU JUST CONCENTRATE ON THE FILM CLUB FOR ONE DAY, YOU JERK!?
I WILL NOT FORGIVE DIVIDED ATTENTION ON THIS ONE DAY!
DOON (BOOM)
BY THE WAY, KOUJI, WHAT'S AKARI-CHAN UP TO TODAY?
THINK SHE'D WANNA HANG OUT?
HUH?
......
I HAVE NO IDEA WHAT SHE'S DOING. SHE LEFT BEFORE I DID AND ALL......
BUT I WOULDN'T CALL HER, EVEN IF SHE HAD NOTHING BETTER TO DO.

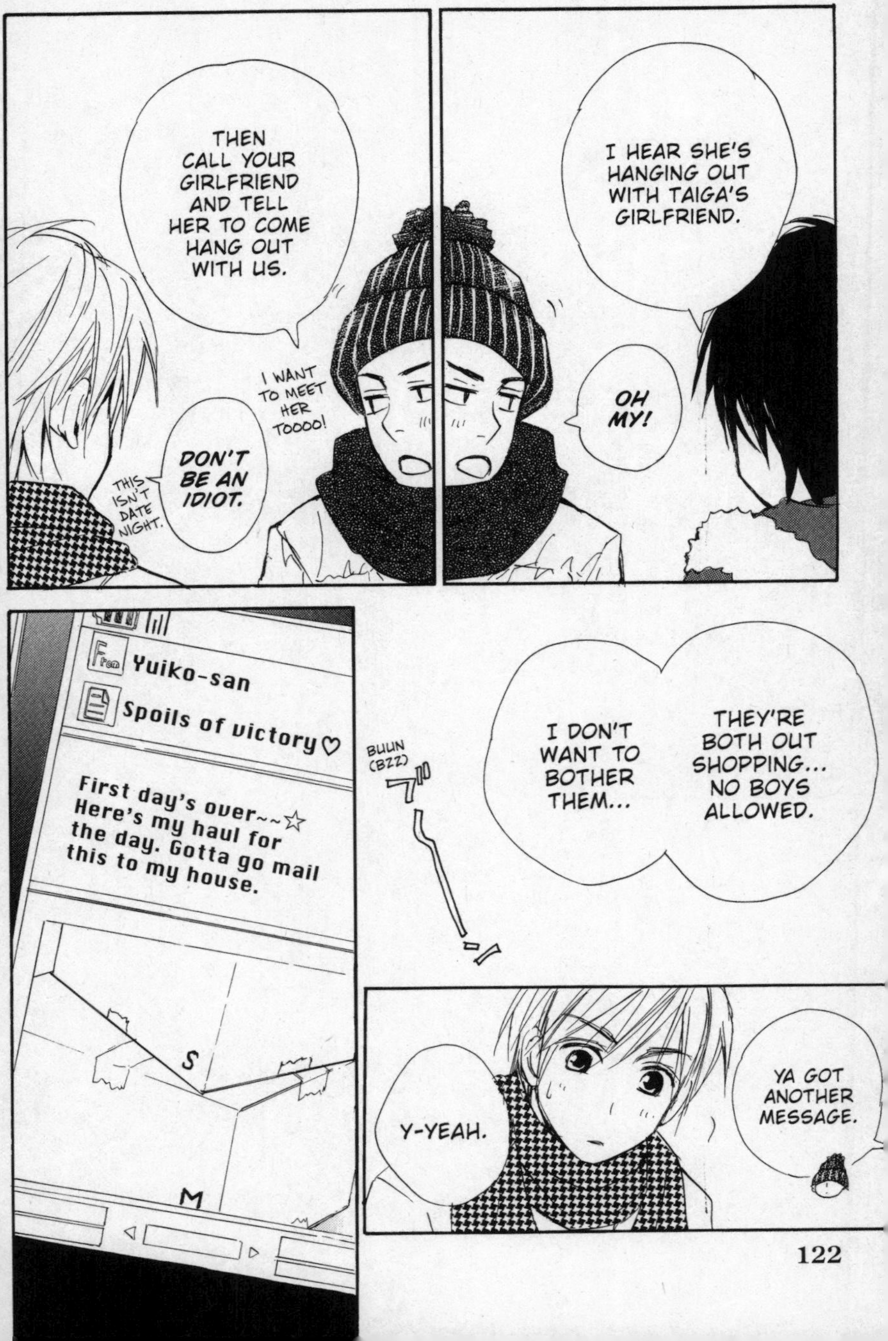
I HEAR SHE'S HANGING OUT WITH TAIGA'S GIRLFRIEND.
OH MY!
THEN CALL YOUR GIRLFRIEND AND TELL HER TO COME HANG OUT WITH US.
I WANT TO MEET HER TOOOO!
DON'T BE AN IDIOT.
THIS ISN'T DATE NIGHT.
THEY'RE BOTH OUT SHOPPING... NO BOYS ALLOWED.
I DON'T WANT TO BOTHER THEM...
BUUN (BZZ)
YA GOT ANOTHER MESSAGE.
Y-YEAH.
From
Yuiko-san
Spoils of victory♡
First day's over~~☆ Here's my haul for the day. Gotta go mail this to my house.
S
M

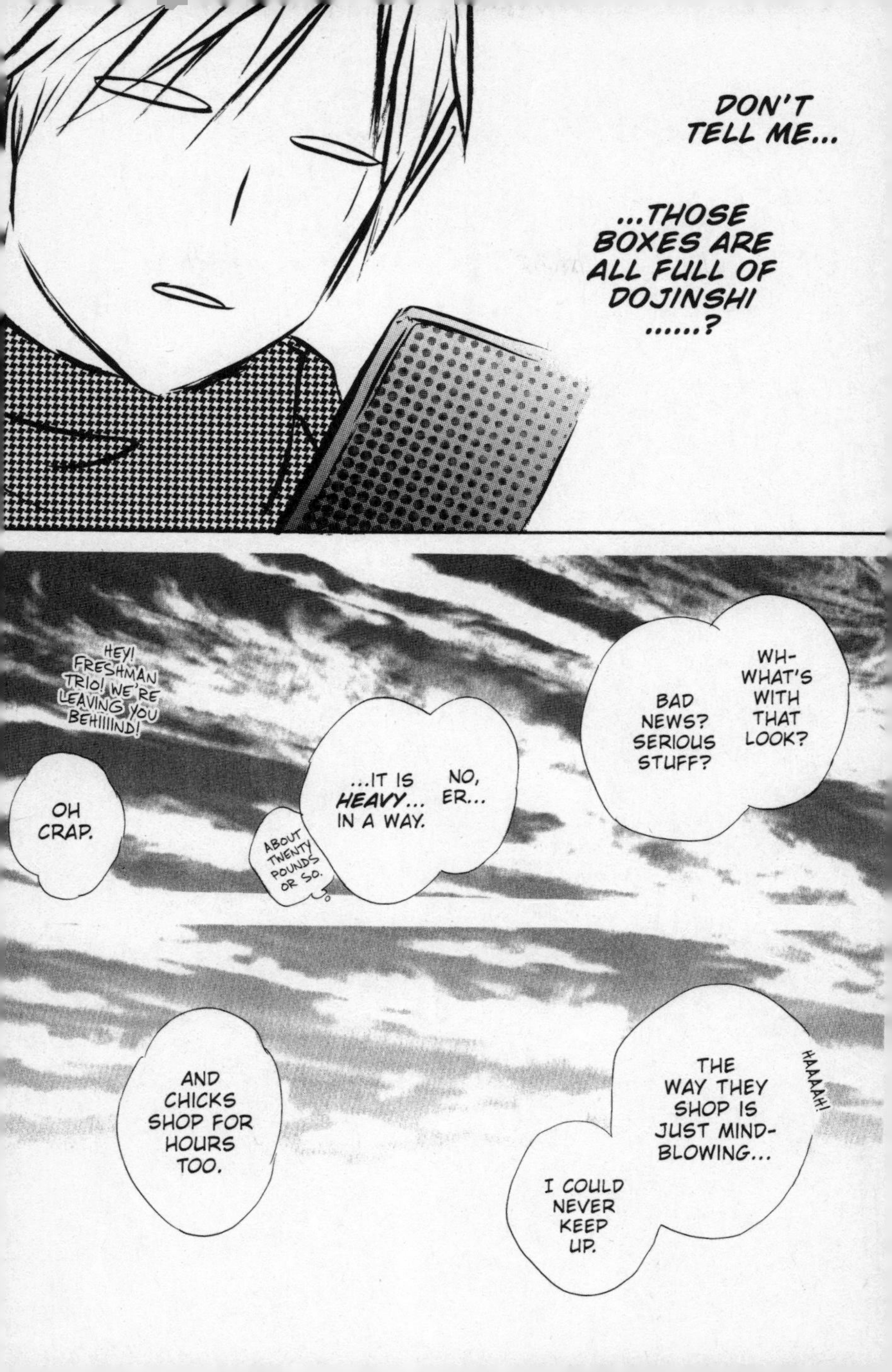
DON'T TELL ME...
...THOSE BOXES ARE ALL FULL OF DOJINSHI ......?
WH-WHAT'S WITH THAT LOOK?
BAD NEWS? SERIOUS STUFF?
NO, ER...
...IT IS *HEAVY*... IN A WAY.
ABOUT TWENTY POUNDS OR SO.
HEY! FRESHMAN TRIO! WE'RE LEAVING YOU BEHIIIIND!
OH CRAP.
HAAAAH!
THE WAY THEY SHOP IS JUST MIND-BLOWING...
I COULD NEVER KEEP UP.
AND CHICKS SHOP FOR HOURS TOO.

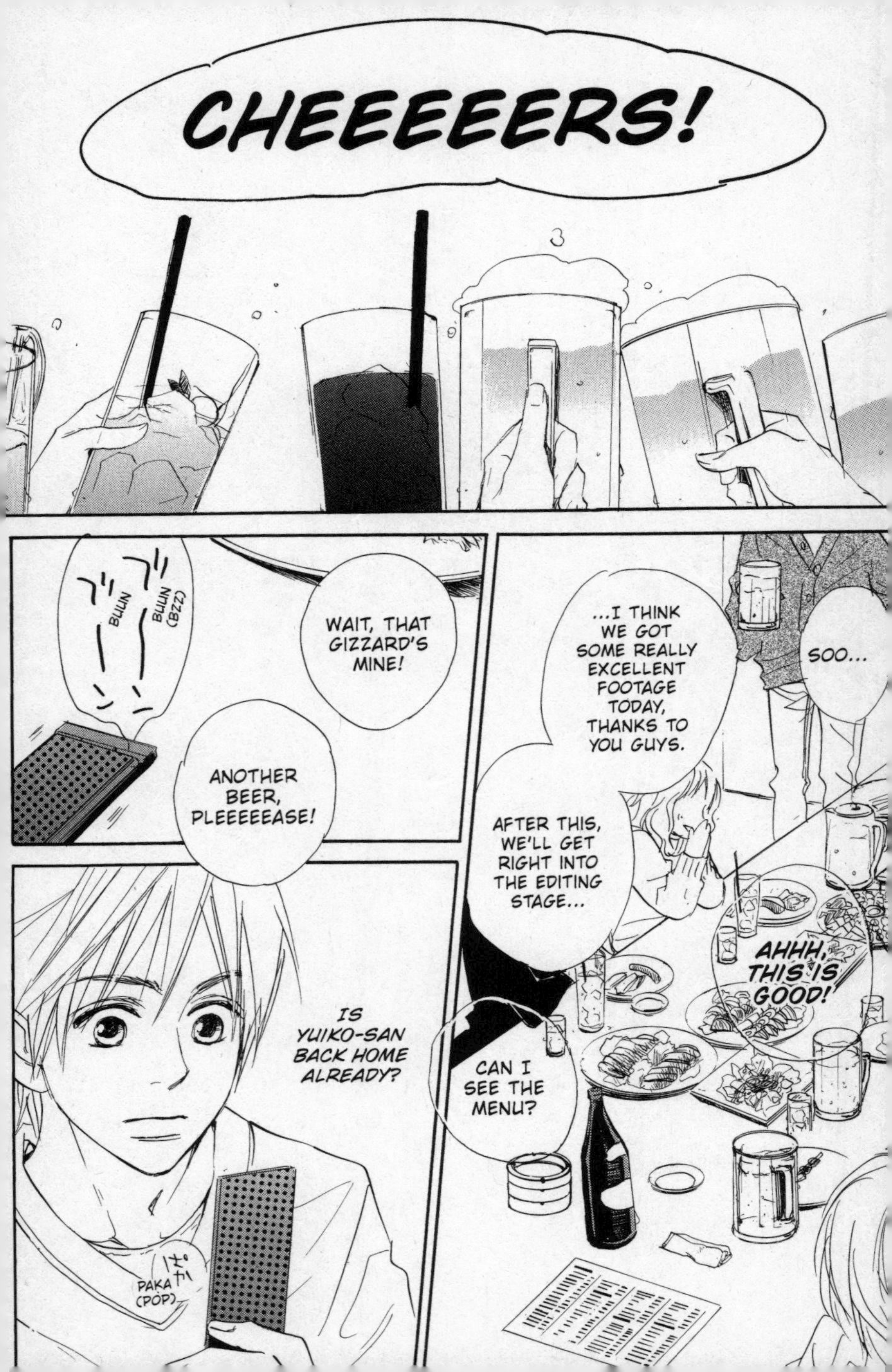
CHEEEEERS!
SOO...
...I THINK WE GOT SOME REALLY EXCELLENT FOOTAGE TODAY, THANKS TO YOU GUYS.
AFTER THIS, WE'LL GET RIGHT INTO THE EDITING STAGE...
AHHH, THIS IS GOOD!
CAN I SEE THE MENU?
WAIT, THAT GIZZARD'S MINE!
BULIN BULIN (BZZ)
ANOTHER BEER, PLEEEEEASE!
IS YUIKO-SAN BACK HOME ALREADY?
PAKA (POP)

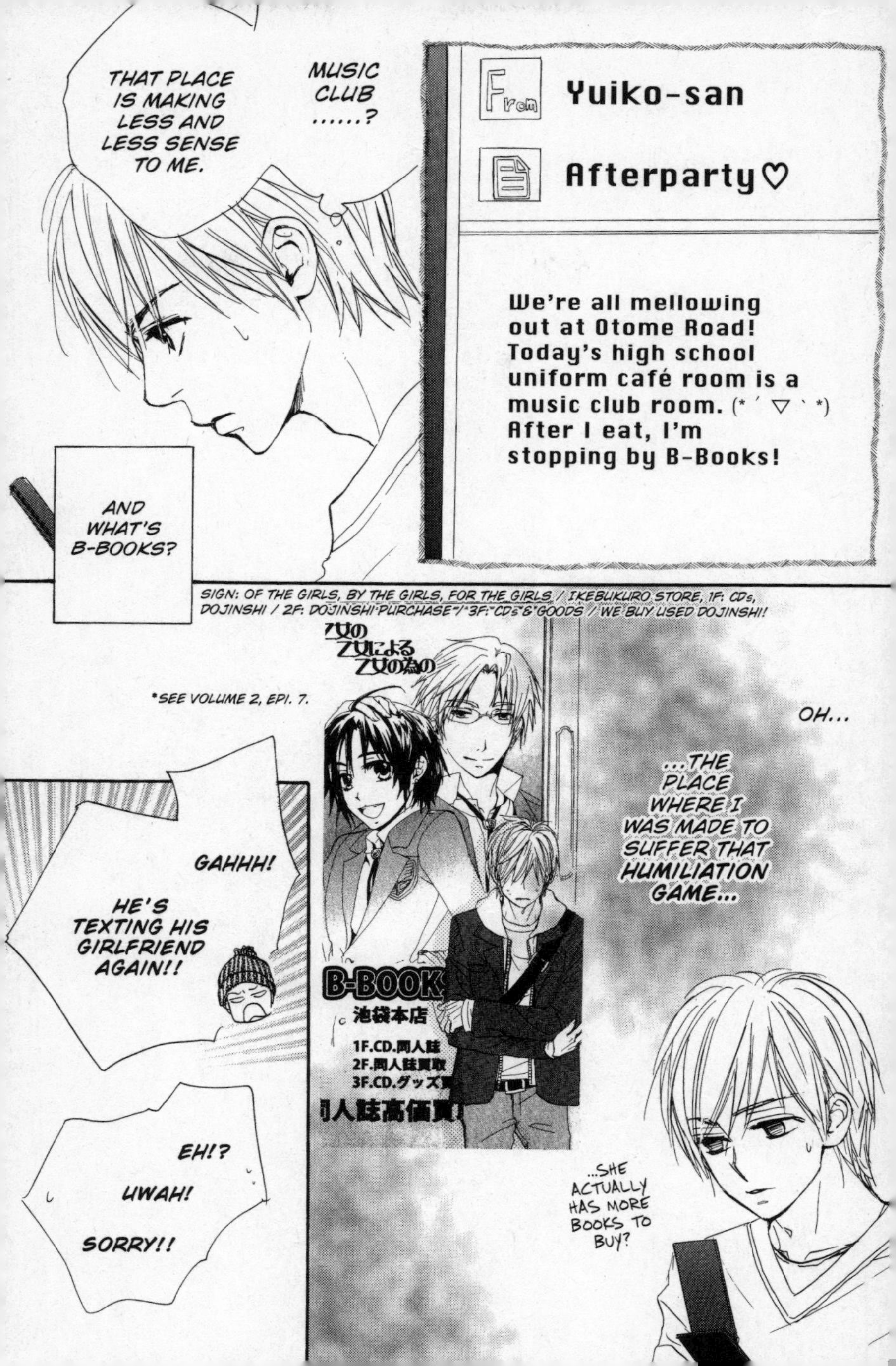
From
Yuiko-san
Afterparty♡
We're all mellowing out at Otome Road! Today's high school uniform café room is a music club room. (*´▽`*) After I eat, I'm stopping by B-Books!
MUSIC CLUB ......?
THAT PLACE IS MAKING LESS AND LESS SENSE TO ME.
AND WHAT'S B-BOOKS?
SIGN: OF THE GIRLS, BY THE GIRLS, FOR THE GIRLS / IKEBUKURO STORE, 1F: CDs, DOJINSHI / 2F: DOJINSHI PURCHASE / 3F: CDs & GOODS / WE BUY USED DOJINSHI!
乙女の
乙女による
乙女の為の
池袋本店
1F.CD.同人誌
2F.同人誌買取
OH...
...THE PLACE WHERE I WAS MADE TO SUFFER THAT HUMILIATION GAME...
*SEE VOLUME 2, EPI. 7.
...SHE ACTUALLY HAS MORE BOOKS TO BUY?
GAHHH!
HE'S TEXTING HIS GIRLFRIEND AGAIN!!
EH!?
UWAH!
SORRY!!

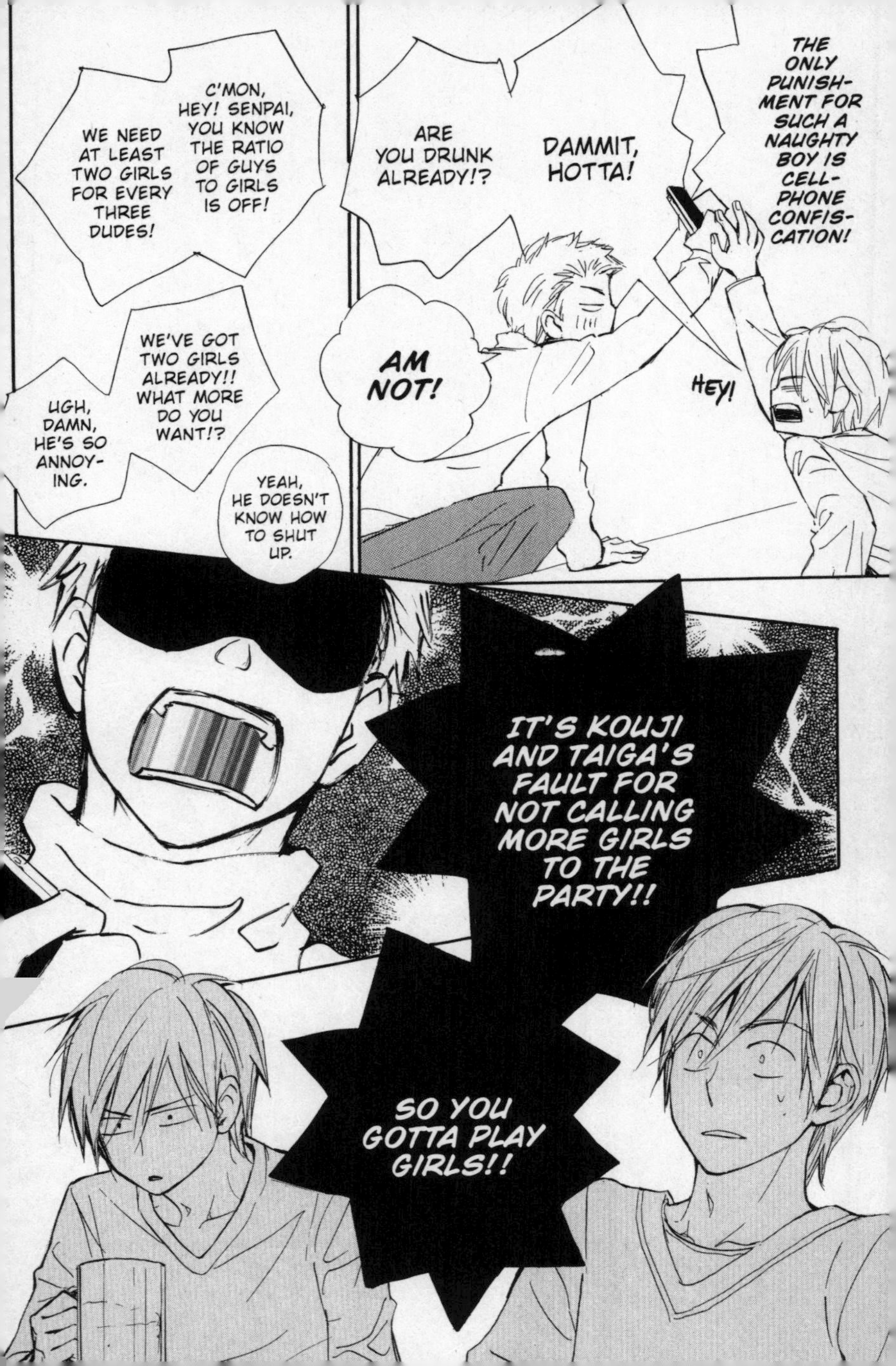
THE ONLY PUNISHMENT FOR SUCH A NAUGHTY BOY IS CELLPHONE CONFISCATION!
DAMMIT, HOTTA!
ARE YOU DRUNK ALREADY!?
HEY!
AM NOT!
C'MON, HEY! SENPAI, YOU KNOW THE RATIO OF GUYS TO GIRLS IS OFF!
WE NEED AT LEAST TWO GIRLS FOR EVERY THREE DUDES!
WE'VE GOT TWO GIRLS ALREADY!! WHAT MORE DO YOU WANT!?
UGH, DAMN, HE'S SO ANNOYING.
YEAH, HE DOESN'T KNOW HOW TO SHUT UP.
IT'S KOUJI AND TAIGA'S FAULT FOR NOT CALLING MORE GIRLS TO THE PARTY!!
SO YOU GOTTA PLAY GIRLS!!

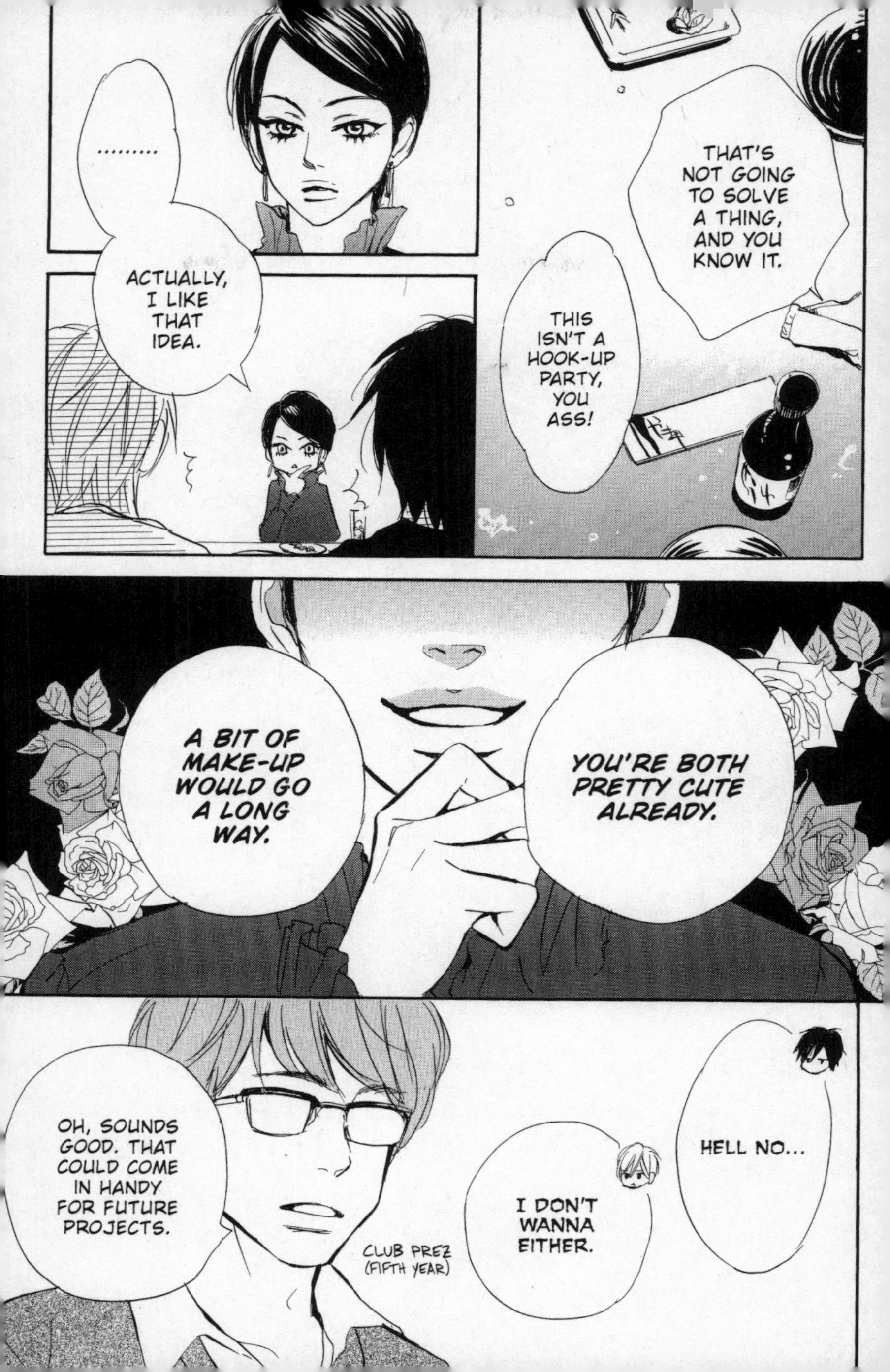
THAT'S NOT GOING TO SOLVE A THING, AND YOU KNOW IT.
THIS ISN'T A HOOK-UP PARTY, YOU ASS!
....
ACTUALLY, I LIKE THAT IDEA.
YOU'RE BOTH PRETTY CUTE ALREADY.
A BIT OF MAKE-UP WOULD GO A LONG WAY.
HELL NO...
I DON'T WANNA EITHER.
CLUB PREZ (FIFTH YEAR)
OH, SOUNDS GOOD. THAT COULD COME IN HANDY FOR FUTURE PROJECTS.

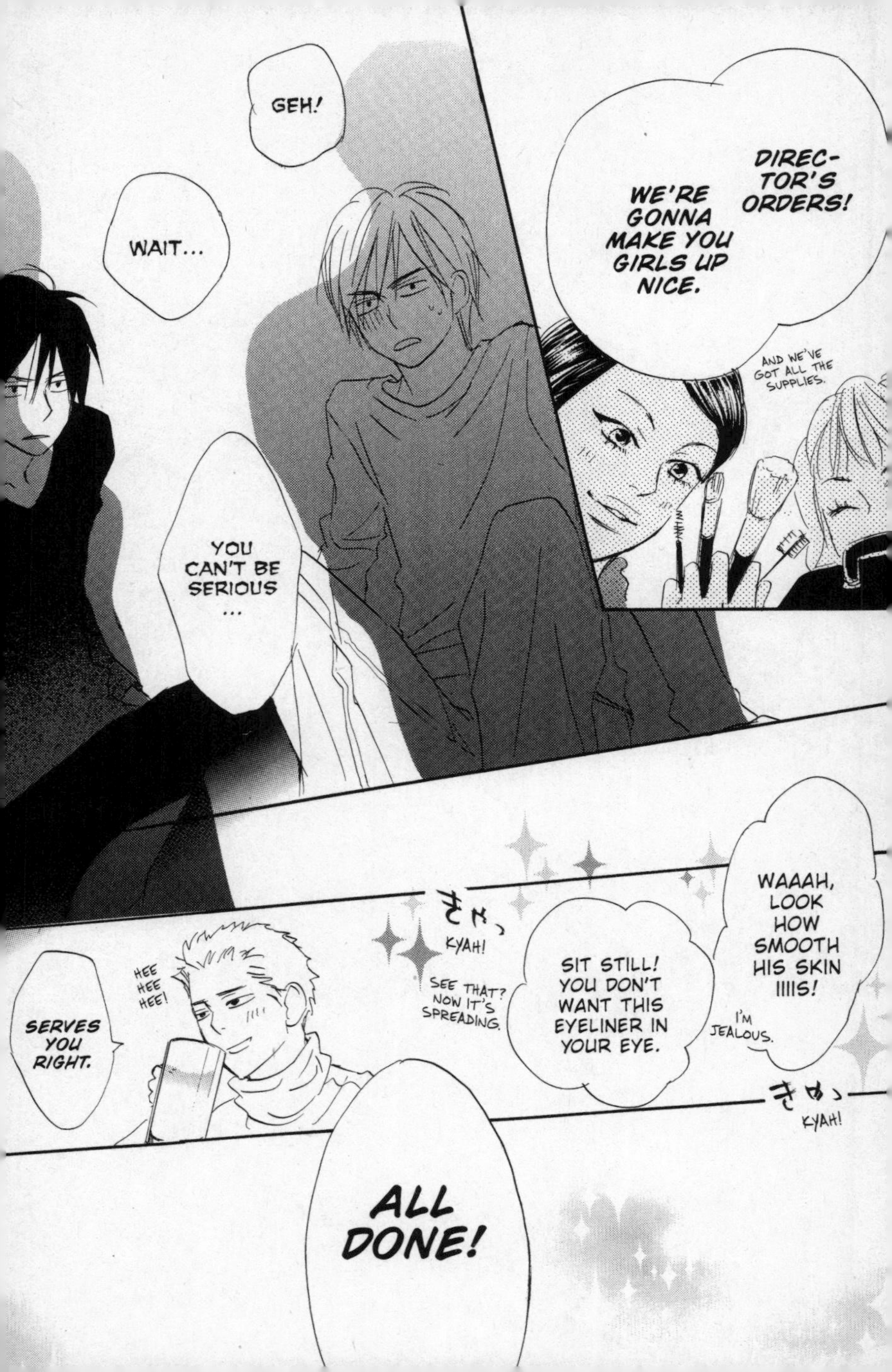
DIRECTOR'S ORDERS!
WE'RE GONNA MAKE YOU GIRLS UP NICE.
AND WE'VE GOT ALL THE SUPPLIES.
GEH!
WAIT...
YOU CAN'T BE SERIOUS...
WAAAH, LOOK HOW SMOOTH HIS SKIN IIIIS!
I'M JEALOUS.
きゃっ KYAH!
SIT STILL! YOU DON'T WANT THIS EYELINER IN YOUR EYE.
きゃっ KYAH!
SEE THAT? NOW IT'S SPREADING.
HEE HEE HEE!
SERVES YOU RIGHT.
ALL DONE!

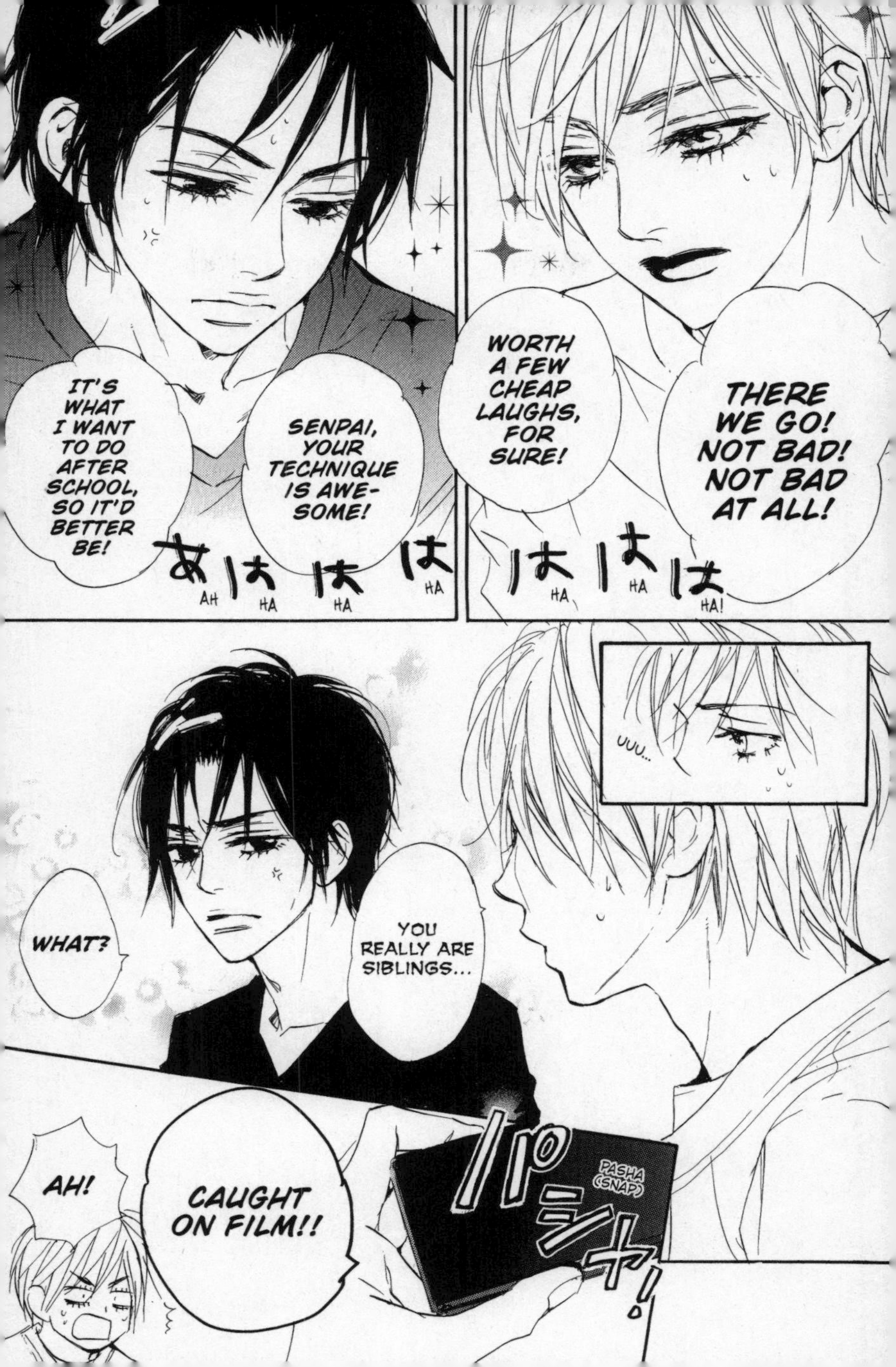
THERE WE GO! NOT BAD! NOT BAD AT ALL!
WORTH A FEW CHEAP LAUGHS, FOR SURE!
ははは
HA HA HA!
SENPAI, YOUR TECHNIQUE IS AWE-SOME!
IT'S WHAT I WANT TO DO AFTER SCHOOL, SO IT'D BETTER BE!
あははは
AH HA HA HA
UUU...
YOU REALLY ARE SIBLINGS...
WHAT?
パシャ!
PASHA (SNAP)
CAUGHT ON FILM!!
AH!

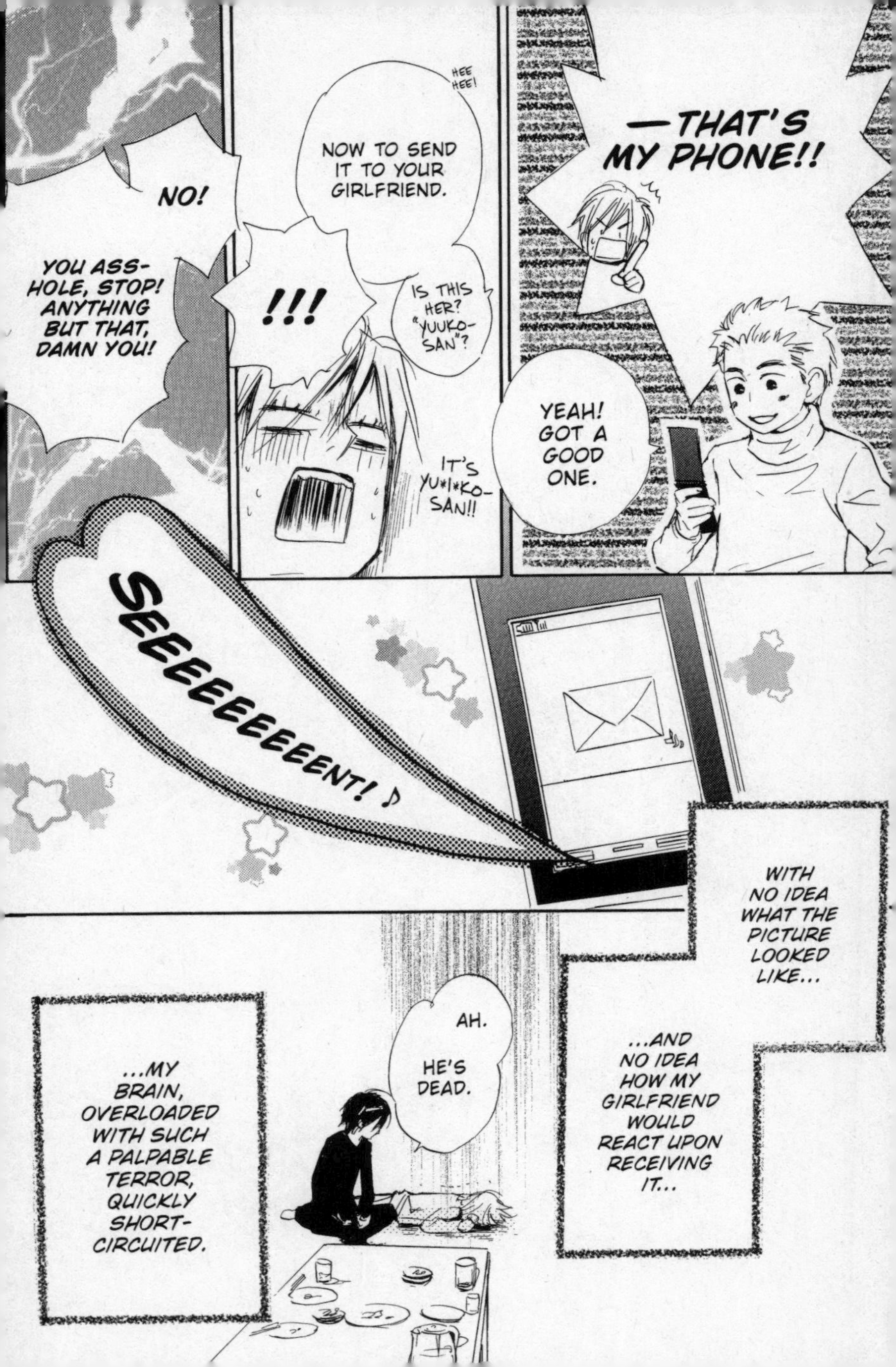
—THAT'S MY PHONE!!
YEAH! GOT A GOOD ONE.
HEE HEE!
NOW TO SEND IT TO YOUR GIRLFRIEND.
IS THIS HER? "YUUKO-SAN"?
!!!
IT'S YU*I*KO-SAN!!
NO!
YOU ASS-HOLE, STOP! ANYTHING BUT THAT, DAMN YOU!
SEEEEEEEEEENT! ♪
WITH NO IDEA WHAT THE PICTURE LOOKED LIKE...
...AND NO IDEA HOW MY GIRLFRIEND WOULD REACT UPON RECEIVING IT...
AH.
HE'S DEAD.
...MY BRAIN, OVERLOADED WITH SUCH A PALPABLE TERROR, QUICKLY SHORT-CIRCUITED.

FUJOSHI NEWS

vol.08

YUIKO-SAN GLOSSARY

P.13
ONLY - A DOJINSHI EVENT DEDICATED TO A PARTICULAR CHARACTER OR COUPLING. ONLY PEOPLE WITH THE SAME TASTE WILL CONVENE HERE. WINTER COMIKET IS AN ALL-GENRE EVENT.

P.14
YANDERE - A TERM DESCRIBING A CHARACTER ARCHETYPE. COMBINING YANDEIRU ("SICK") WITH DERE ("SAPPY"). WHEN ONE IS SO SICK WITH LOVE FOR ANOTHER THAT HIS OR HER WORDS AND ACTIONS GO OFF THE DEEP END, LEADING TO DARK FANATICISM AND OBSESSION.

P.22
ANIME BOX SET - A MAGICAL TREASURE CHEST SOLD AFTER A TELEVISION SERIES HAS ENDED, CONTAINING DVDs OF THE ENTIRE SERIES RUN. THEY OFTEN COME IN DELUXE PACKAGING OR CONTAIN FIGURINES.

P.23
TSUNDERE - A CHARACTER WHO IS NORMALLY BLUNT AND COLD, BUT CAN TURN ABRUPTLY SOFT AND CUTE AT CERTAIN VULNERABLE MOMENTS. BOTH OF THESE FEATURES ARE SIGNS OF AFFECTION.

P.27
WINTER COMIKET - A LARGE-SCALE DOJINSHI RETAIL EVENT HELD AT THE END OF THE YEAR. THE ENTHUSIASM OF THE ATTENDEES FOR THEIR FAVORITE SERIES HELPS TO WARM JAPAN IN THE FRIGID WINTER MONTHS.

P.31
MANNING THE CIRCLE TABLE - TO ATTEND A DOJINSHI EVENT AS A CIRCLE SELLING BOOKS, RATHER THAN BUYING. THESE ARE THE FOLKS WHO CREATE LOVE WITH THEIR PENS AND KEYBOARDS. THIS CARRIES ITS OWN PLEASURES, SUCH AS DESIGNING A "STOREFRONT" WITH THE PERFECT COVER ART AND ARRANGEMENT.

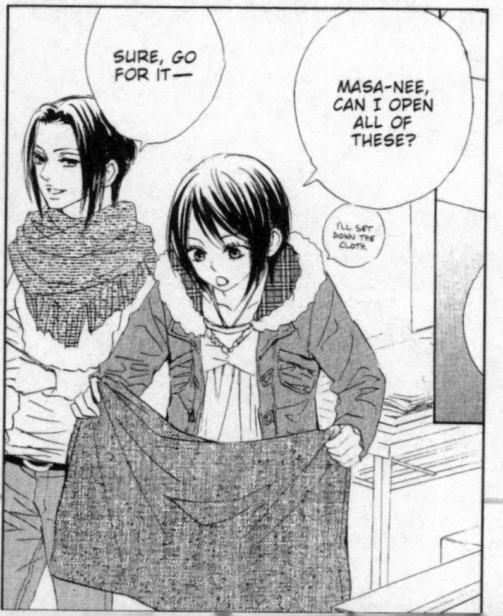
MASA-NEE, CAN I OPEN ALL OF THESE?
SURE, GO FOR IT—
I'LL SET DOWN THE CLOTH.

P.40
COSNAME - A NAME ONE USES WHEN COSPLAYING, MUCH LIKE A PEN NAME. THE COSNAME "KAORU SETO" IS RATHER ELEGANT TO WRITE IN JAPANESE.

P.57
HIDDEN FOLDER - WHEN A COMPUTER FOLDER IS SET TO NOT DISPLAY BY DEFAULT.

P.67
INSPIRATION - A FRESH-FACED YOUNG BOY AND HIS COLLEGE-AGE TUTOR MEETING ALONE IN A BEDROOM... WHO KNOWS WHAT KIND OF "LESSONS" HE COULD BE TEACHING HIS STUDENT IN THERE? AN IRRESISTIBLE SITUATION FOR ANY FUJOSHI.

P.96
KNEESOCKS - SOCKS THAT COME UP JUST HIGH ENOUGH TO COVER THE KNEE. SOME CALL THE STRIP OF SKIN BETWEEN THE TOP OF THE SOCKS AND THE BOTTOM OF THE SHORTS OR SKIRT THE "ABSOLUTE TERRITORY."

P.107
NEW BOOK - THE NEWEST PUBLICATION OF A DOJINSHI CIRCLE. MANY FANS COME TO AN EVENT SEEKING THESE.

P.108
CATALOGUE - A BOOK LISTING ALL OF THE CIRCLES AND ARTISTS PARTICIPATING IN AN EVENT. THE WINTER COMIKET CATALOGUE HAS SO MANY ENTRIES IN IT THAT IT'S THE SIZE OF A PHONE BOOK.

LAYOUT - THE MAP OF THE CONVENTION CENTER. EACH CIRCLE HAS A MARKED LOCATION SUCH AS "A-12A" THAT HELPS ATTENDEES FIND THEM. WHEN YOUR FINGERS ARE BLACK FROM BRUSHING AGAINST THE CATALOGUE, YOU WILL BE READY TO SEIZE YOUR HOPES AND DREAMS!

P.109
SHUTTERS - THE MOST POPULAR CIRCLES THAT ATTRACT THE LONGEST LINES ARE PLACED BEHIND LARGE SHUTTERS. WHEN THESE ARE OPENED, MORE LINES OF VISITORS CAN FORM TO EASE TRAFFIC.

P.115
VACATION SUITCASE - A CARRY-ON BAG, USEFUL FOR TRANSPORTING HEAVY AND BULKY ITEMS. KAORU-CHAN'S BAG IS FULL OF HER COSPLAY MATERIALS, PLUSHIES OF THE SPIRIT OF SEPA, DOJINSHI, DREAMS, AND SO ON.

P.117
DEFAULT BUY - SOMETHING YOU BUY AUTOMATICALLY—THE BOOK YOU CAME TO GET. IT CAN BE DIFFICULT TO OVERCOME ONE'S DESIRE TO GET EVERY SINGLE GENRE, CIRCLE, AND COUPLING OF INTEREST IN THE COURSE OF AN EVENT.

SEPATTE TAKURO

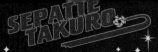

FINALLY PUT INTO COMIC FORM!!

YUIKO-SAN'S MANGA BIBLE, *SEPATTE TAKURO*, IS HERE! HAVE SOME OF YOU WONDERED WHAT THIS STORY MIGHT BE LIKE, BASED ON ALL THE REFERENCES TO GLOOMY TAKURO, THE COOL TEAM CAPTAIN, THE SCATTERBRAINED HIKARU, AND SO ON? WELL, YOUR PRAYERS ARE ANSWERED! IT'S A MANGA NOW! AND DRAWN BY NONE OTHER THAN HIROMI NAMIKI-SENSEI, WHO HAS HAD ACTUAL EXPERIENCE BEING PUBLISHED IN SHOUNEN MANGA MAGAZINES! ♥

WHAT SORT OF MANGA WILL COME OUT OF THESE THREE CHARACTERS......!?

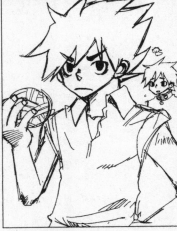

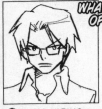

YUMA HIBINO

CLASS PRESIDENT AND SEPAK TAKRAW TEAM CAPTAIN OF MAREI MIDDLE SCHOOL. VERY SERIOUS AND FUSSY. HAS BEEN PLAYING SEPAK TAKRAW SINCE CHILDHOOD.

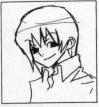

HIKARU HOSHIKAGE

THE LAID BACK AND CAREFREE ACE OF THE SEPAK TAKRAW TEAM. HE IS A GENIUS AT THE GAME AND OFTEN "BREAKS THE MOLD" WITH BRILLIANT SPONTANEOUS PLAYS.

TAKURO SEBA

NORMALLY INTROVERTED AND DEPRESSED, HE BECOMES FIERCE AND COMPETITIVE WHEN THE SEPA SPIRIT POSSESSES HIM. HE HAS NEVER PLAYED SEPAK TAKRAW BEFORE, BUT HARBORS AN INCREDIBLE NATURAL TALENT FOR THE GAME.

■ AUTHOR:

FIGHT OHYAMA-SENSEI

■ SERIALIZED IN:

WEEKLY SHOUNEN STEP

※ THIS IS A FICTIONAL MAGAZINE. ♥

[THE STORY] ———

DARK AND BROODING TAKURO SEBA HAS JUST STARTED HIS FIRST YEAR AT MAREI PRIVATE MIDDLE SCHOOL. HE WANTS TO JOIN AN ATHLETICS CLUB IN ORDER TO FIND A NEW INTEREST AND CHANGE HIS INTROVERTED WAYS, BUT HE FINDS HIMSELF AFRAID TO CHOOSE ONE. ONE DAY, TAKURO PICKS UP A MYSTERIOUS BALL. WHEN THE MYSTERIOUS "SEPA SPIRIT" EMERGES FROM THAT BALL, IT CLAIMS THAT TAKURO HAS BEEN CURSED AND MUST RISE TO VICTORY AT SEPAK TAKRAW IN ORDER TO UNDO THE EVIL SPELL! THE NEXT DAY, TAKURO FINDS HIMSELF UNCONSCIOUSLY WALKING TO THE GYM. THERE, HE SEES THE SEPAK TAKRAW TEAM CAPTAIN, HIBINO, TRADING FIERCE VOLLEYS WITH THE TEAM ACE, HIKARU......!!

AND THE SPECIAL GUEST ARTIST IN ♥ CHARGE OF TURNING THIS INTO A REAL MANGA IS......

HIROMI NAMIKI-SENSEI!!

BORN IN MIYAGI PREFECTURE IN 1977, RAISED IN TOKYO. DEBUTED IN THE SHOUNEN MAGAZINE, *SUNDAY SUPER* (SHOGAKUKAN). AFTER MANY TWISTS AND TURNS, HER *GENZAI KANRYOKEI MOFU* RAN FOR EIGHT VOLUMES IN THE PAGES OF *WEEKLY BIG COMIC SPIRITS*. IN DECEMBER 2008, SHE BEGAN A NEW ICE HOCKEY SERIES, "88," IN *MONTHLY SHOUNEN MAGAZINE*. SHE HAS ONE PET TURTLE.

AND EVEN MORE COLLABORATORS!!

SEPATAKU SHOE DESIGN: SPINGLE COMPANY - HTTP://WWW.SPINGLE.JP THE SHOES BEING WORN BY THE CHARACTER IN *SEPATAKU* ARE BASED ON REAL DESIGNS BY SPINGLE COMPANY, THE ONLY BUSINESS IN JAPAN DEVELOPING AND SELLING AUTHENTIC SEPAK TAKRAW FOOTWEAR! *SEPATAKU* CONSULTATION: OOYAMA SEPAK TAKRAW CLUB - HTTP://OSC.S140.XREA.COM
THE OLDEST SEPAK TAKRAW CLUB IN JAPAN, BASED IN THE OOYAMA NEIGHBORHOOD OF ITABASHI WARD IN TOKYO. WE HAVE BEEN DEPENDING ON THEIR HELP AND GUIDANCE WITH THE RULES AND CUSTOMS OF SEPAK TAKRAW SINCE BEFORE *MY GIRLFRIEND'S A GEEK* WAS OFFICIALLY PUBLISHED.

*INFORMATION CURRENT AS OF NOVEMBER 2008.

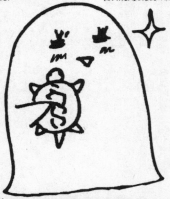

READY TO START ON THE REAL SEPATTE TAKURO? TURN TO THE NEXT PAGE!!

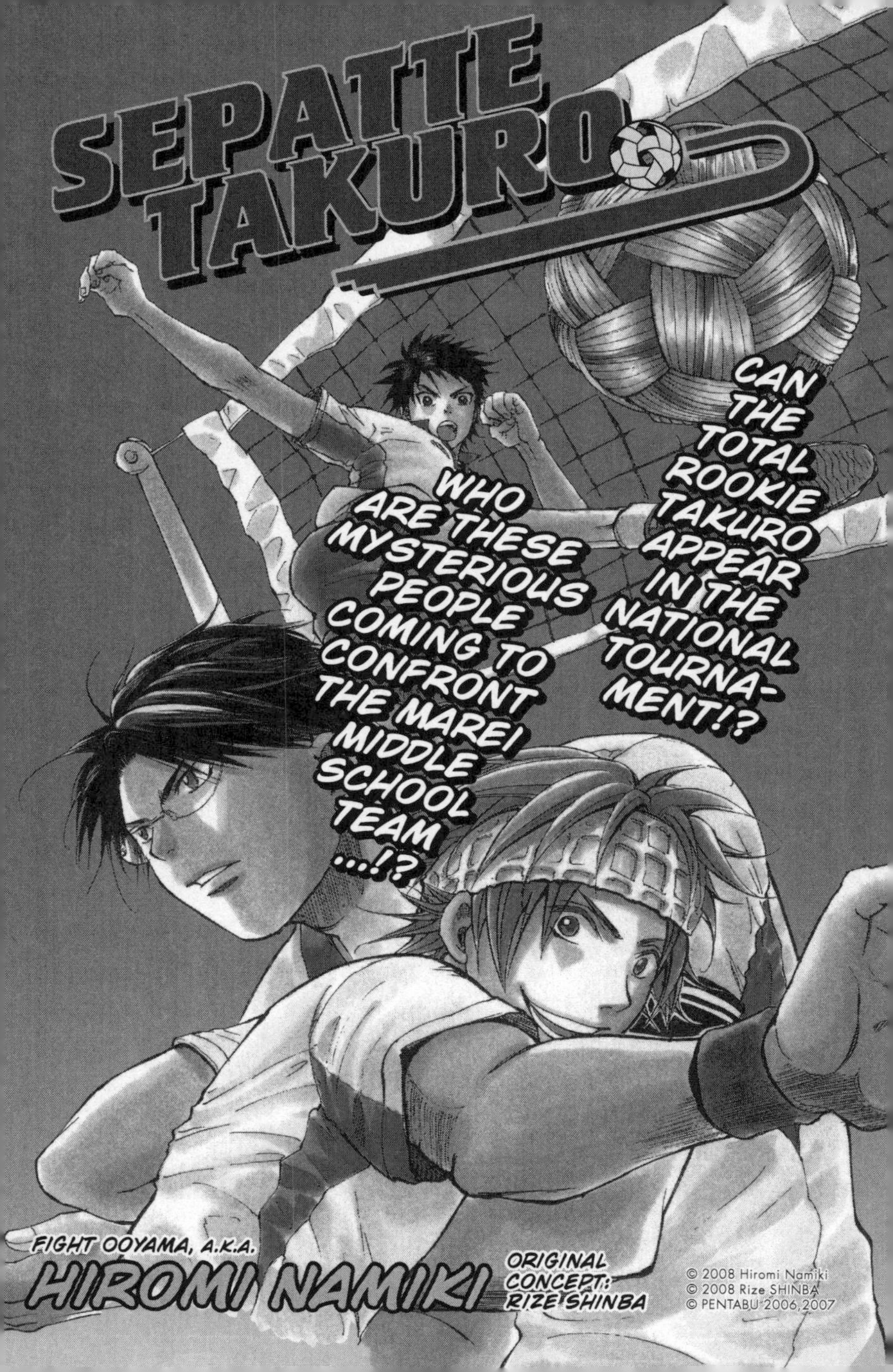
SEPATTE TAKURO
CAN THE TOTAL ROOKIE TAKURO APPEAR IN THE NATIONAL TOURNA-MENT!?
WHO ARE THESE MYSTERIOUS PEOPLE COMING TO CONFRONT THE MAREI MIDDLE SCHOOL TEAM ...!?
FIGHT OOYAMA, A.K.A.
HIROMI NAMIKI
ORIGINAL CONCEPT: RIZE SHINBA

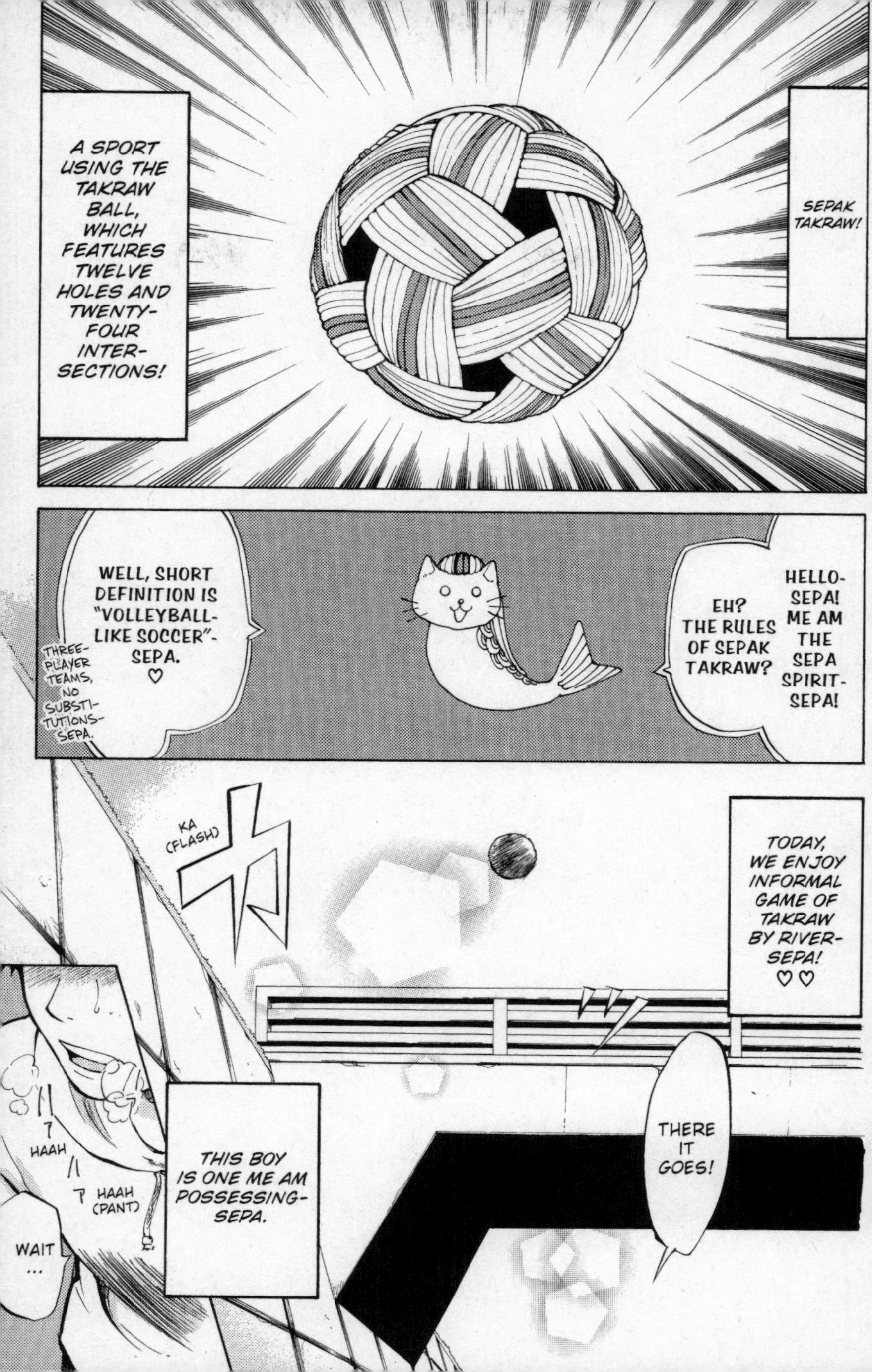
SEPAK TAKRAW!
A SPORT USING THE TAKRAW BALL, WHICH FEATURES TWELVE HOLES AND TWENTY-FOUR INTER-SECTIONS!
HELLO-SEPA! ME AM THE SEPA SPIRIT-SEPA!
EH? THE RULES OF SEPAK TAKRAW?
WELL, SHORT DEFINITION IS "VOLLEYBALL-LIKE SOCCER"-SEPA. ♡
THREE-PLAYER TEAMS, NO SUBSTI-TUTIONS-SEPA.
TODAY, WE ENJOY INFORMAL GAME OF TAKRAW BY RIVER-SEPA! ♡♡
THERE IT GOES!
KA (FLASH)
THIS BOY IS ONE ME AM POSSESSING-SEPA.
HAAH
HAAH (PANT)
WAIT ...

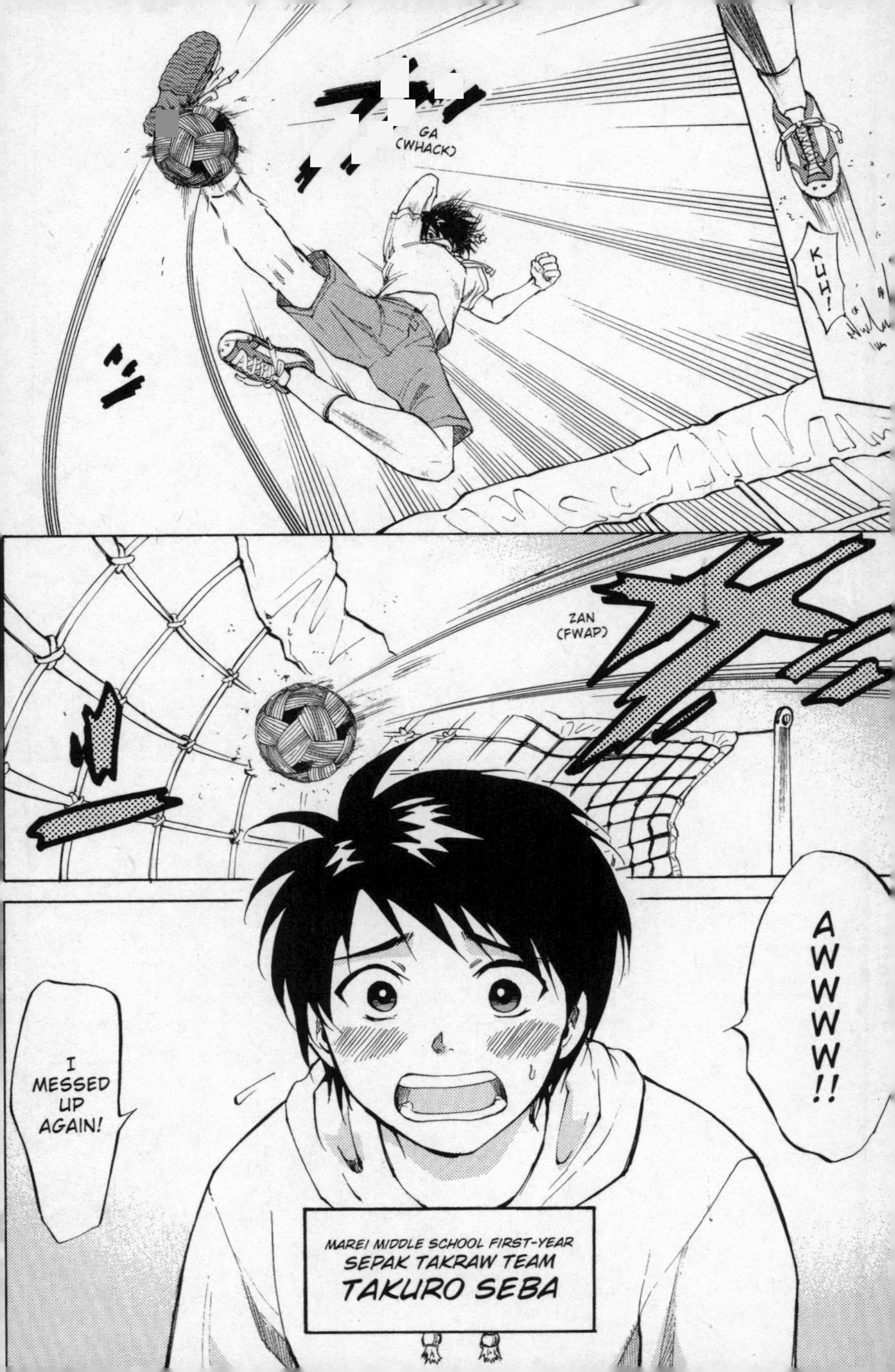
KUH!
GA (WHACK)
ZAN (FWAP)
AWWWWW!!
I MESSED UP AGAIN!
MAREI MIDDLE SCHOOL FIRST-YEAR
SEPAK TAKRAW TEAM
TAKURO SEBA

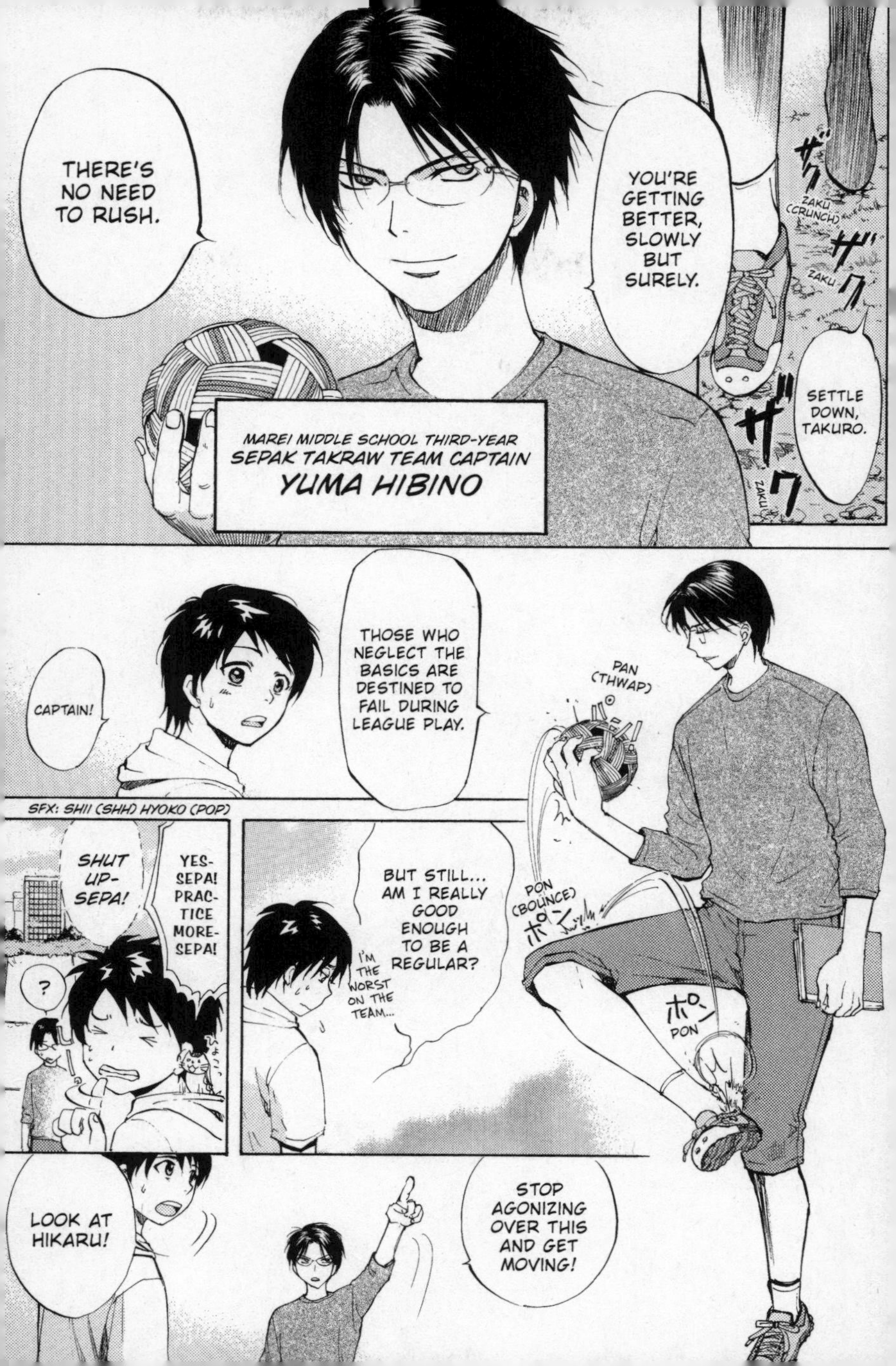
ザク
ZAKU (CRUNCH)
ザク
ZAKU
ザク
ZAKU
SETTLE DOWN, TAKURO.
YOU'RE GETTING BETTER, SLOWLY BUT SURELY.
THERE'S NO NEED TO RUSH.
MAREI MIDDLE SCHOOL THIRD-YEAR SEPAK TAKRAW TEAM CAPTAIN YUMA HIBINO
PAN (THWAP)
PON (BOUNCE)
PON
THOSE WHO NEGLECT THE BASICS ARE DESTINED TO FAIL DURING LEAGUE PLAY.
CAPTAIN!
SFX: SHII (SHH) HYOKO (POP)
BUT STILL... AM I REALLY GOOD ENOUGH TO BE A REGULAR?
I'M THE WORST ON THE TEAM...
YES-SEPA! PRACTICE MORE-SEPA!
SHUT UP-SEPA!
?
STOP AGONIZING OVER THIS AND GET MOVING!
LOOK AT HIKARU!

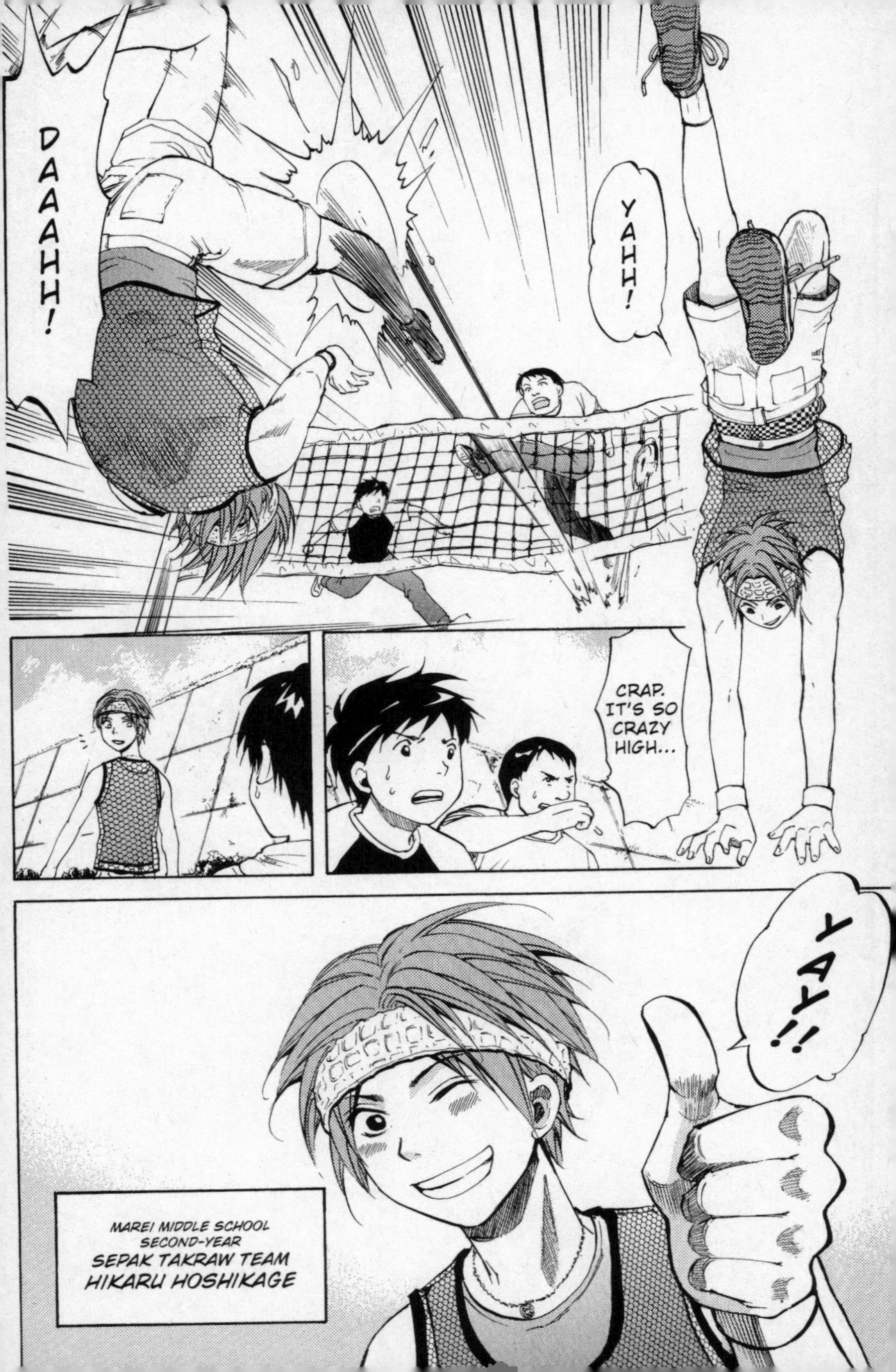
YAHH!
DAAAAHH!
CRAP. IT'S SO CRAZY HIGH...
YAY!!
MAREI MIDDLE SCHOOL SECOND-YEAR
SEPAK TAKRAW TEAM
HIKARU HOSHIKAGE

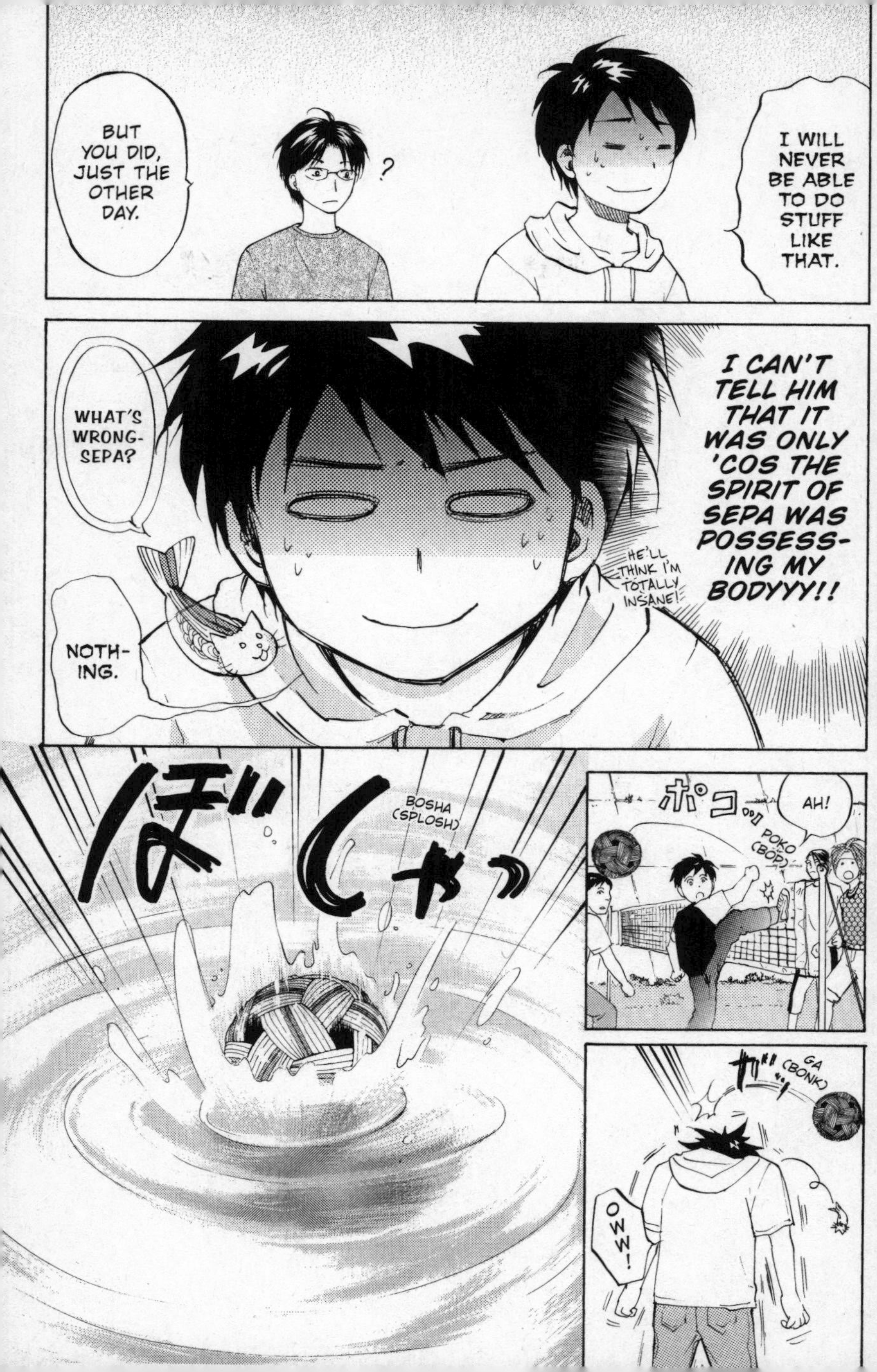

I WILL NEVER BE ABLE TO DO STUFF LIKE THAT.
?
BUT YOU DID, JUST THE OTHER DAY.
I CAN'T TELL HIM THAT IT WAS ONLY 'COS THE SPIRIT OF SEPA WAS POSSESS-ING MY BODYYY!!
HE'LL THINK I'M TOTALLY INSANE!
WHAT'S WRONG-SEPA?
NOTH-ING.
AH!
ポコ
POKO (BOP)
ガッ
GA (BONK)
OWW!
ぼしゃっ
BOSHA (SPLOSH)

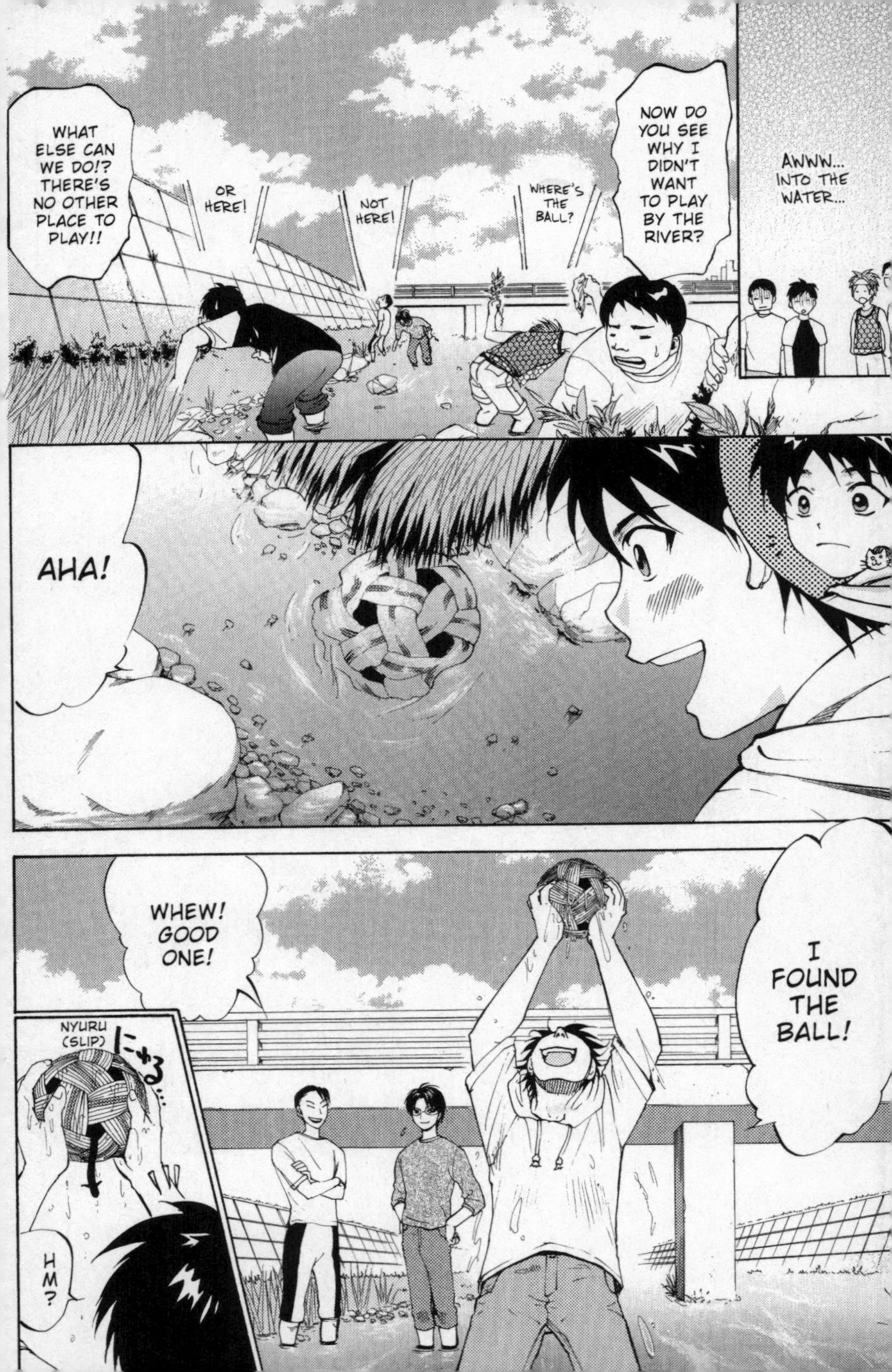
AWWW... INTO THE WATER...
NOW DO YOU SEE WHY I DIDN'T WANT TO PLAY BY THE RIVER?
WHERE'S THE BALL?
NOT HERE!
OR HERE!
WHAT ELSE CAN WE DO!? THERE'S NO OTHER PLACE TO PLAY!!
AHA!
I FOUND THE BALL!
WHEW! GOOD ONE!
NYURU (SLIP)
にゅる...
HM?

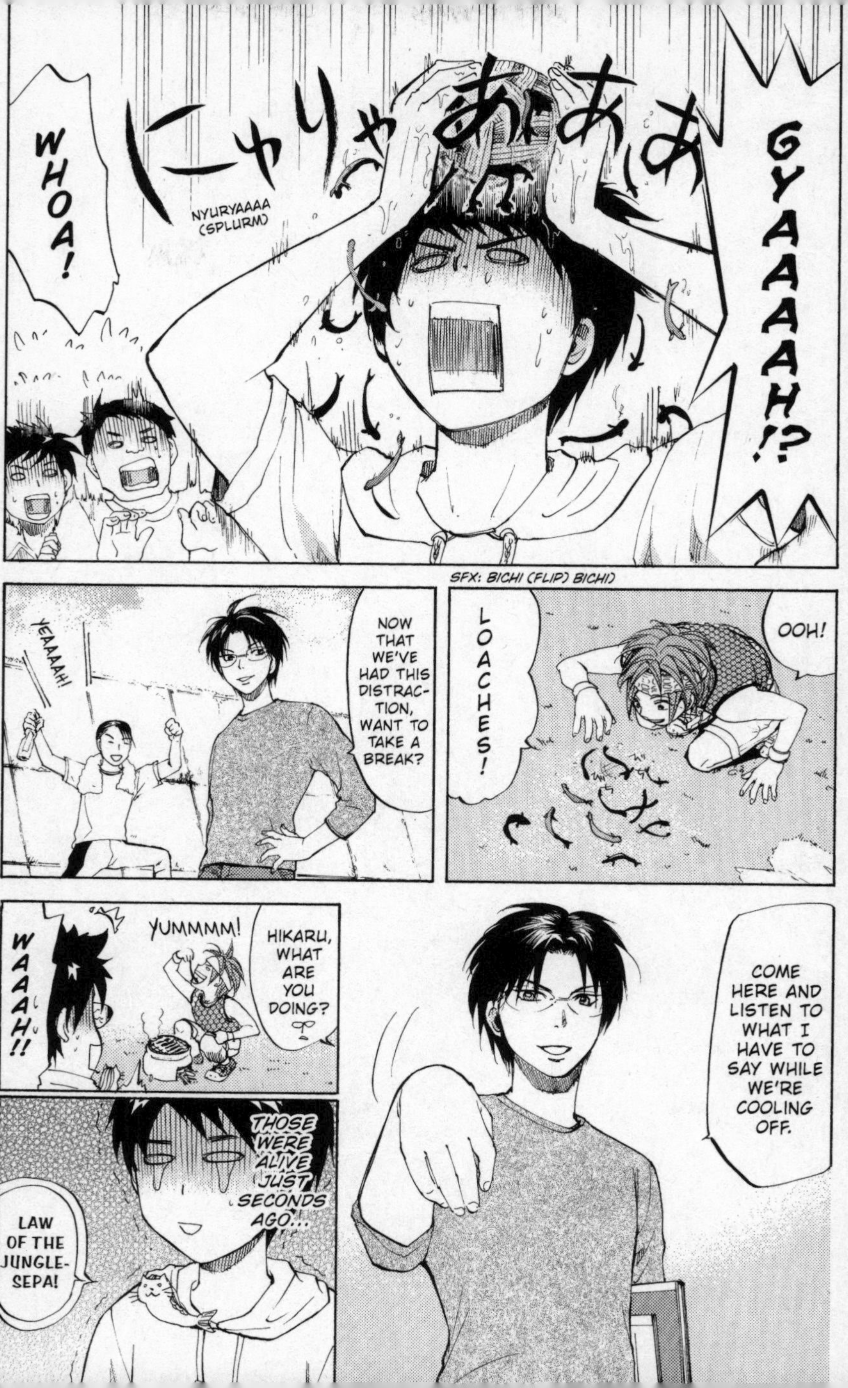
GYAAAAAH!?
にゅりゃあああ
NYURYAAAA (SPLURM)
WHOA!
SFX: BICHI (FLIP) BICHI)
OOH!
LOACHES!
NOW THAT WE'VE HAD THIS DISTRACTION, WANT TO TAKE A BREAK?
YEAAAAH!
COME HERE AND LISTEN TO WHAT I HAVE TO SAY WHILE WE'RE COOLING OFF.
HIKARU, WHAT ARE YOU DOING?
YUMMMM!
WAAAAH!!
THOSE WERE ALIVE JUST SECONDS AGO...
LAW OF THE JUNGLE-SEPA!

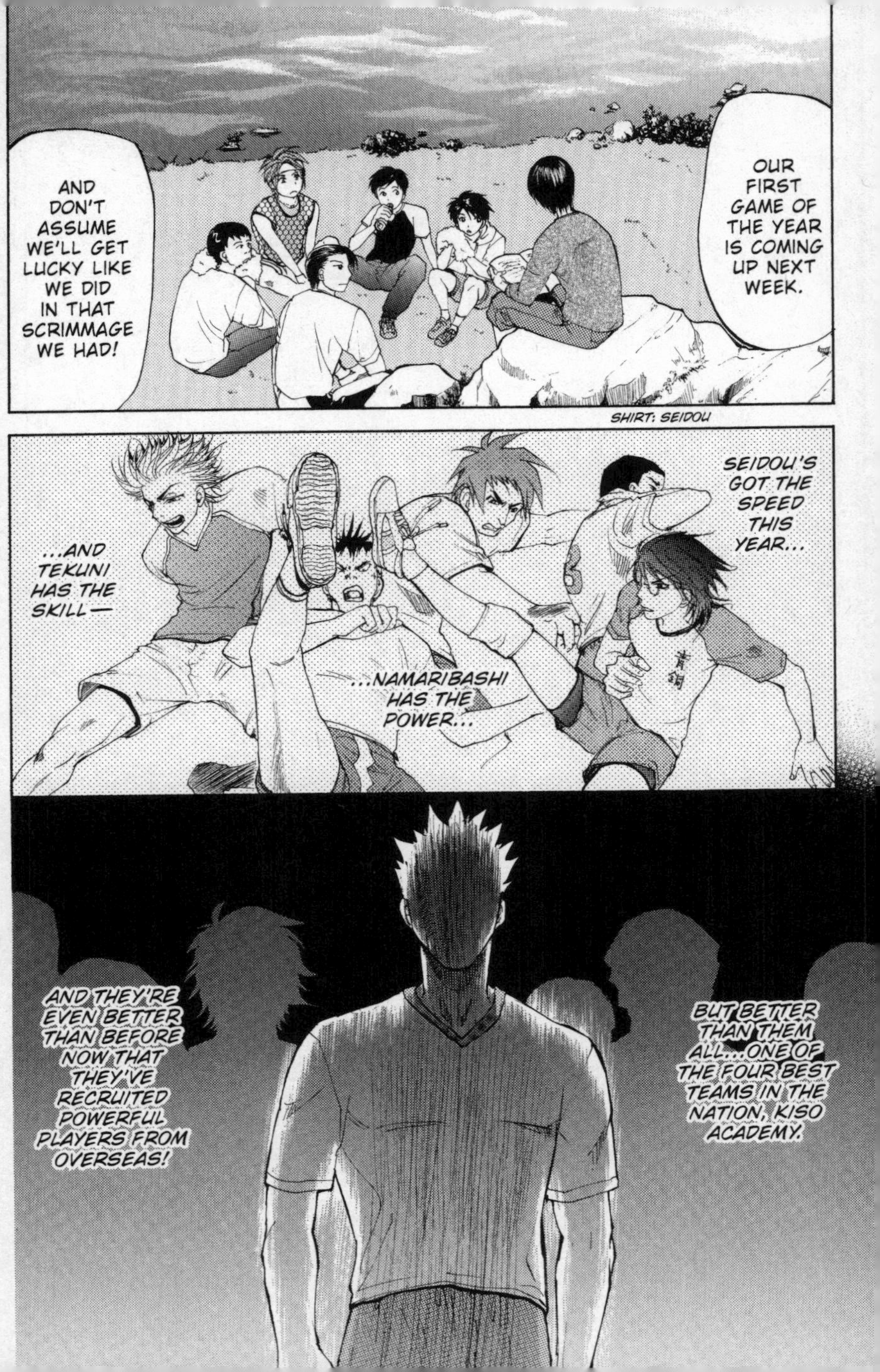
OUR FIRST GAME OF THE YEAR IS COMING UP NEXT WEEK.
AND DON'T ASSUME WE'LL GET LUCKY LIKE WE DID IN THAT SCRIMMAGE WE HAD!
SHIRT: SEIDOU
SEIDOU'S GOT THE SPEED THIS YEAR...
...NAMARIBASHI HAS THE POWER...
...AND TEKUNI HAS THE SKILL—
BUT BETTER THAN THEM ALL...ONE OF THE FOUR BEST TEAMS IN THE NATION, KISO ACADEMY.
AND THEY'RE EVEN BETTER THAN BEFORE NOW THAT THEY'VE RECRUITED POWERFUL PLAYERS FROM OVERSEAS!

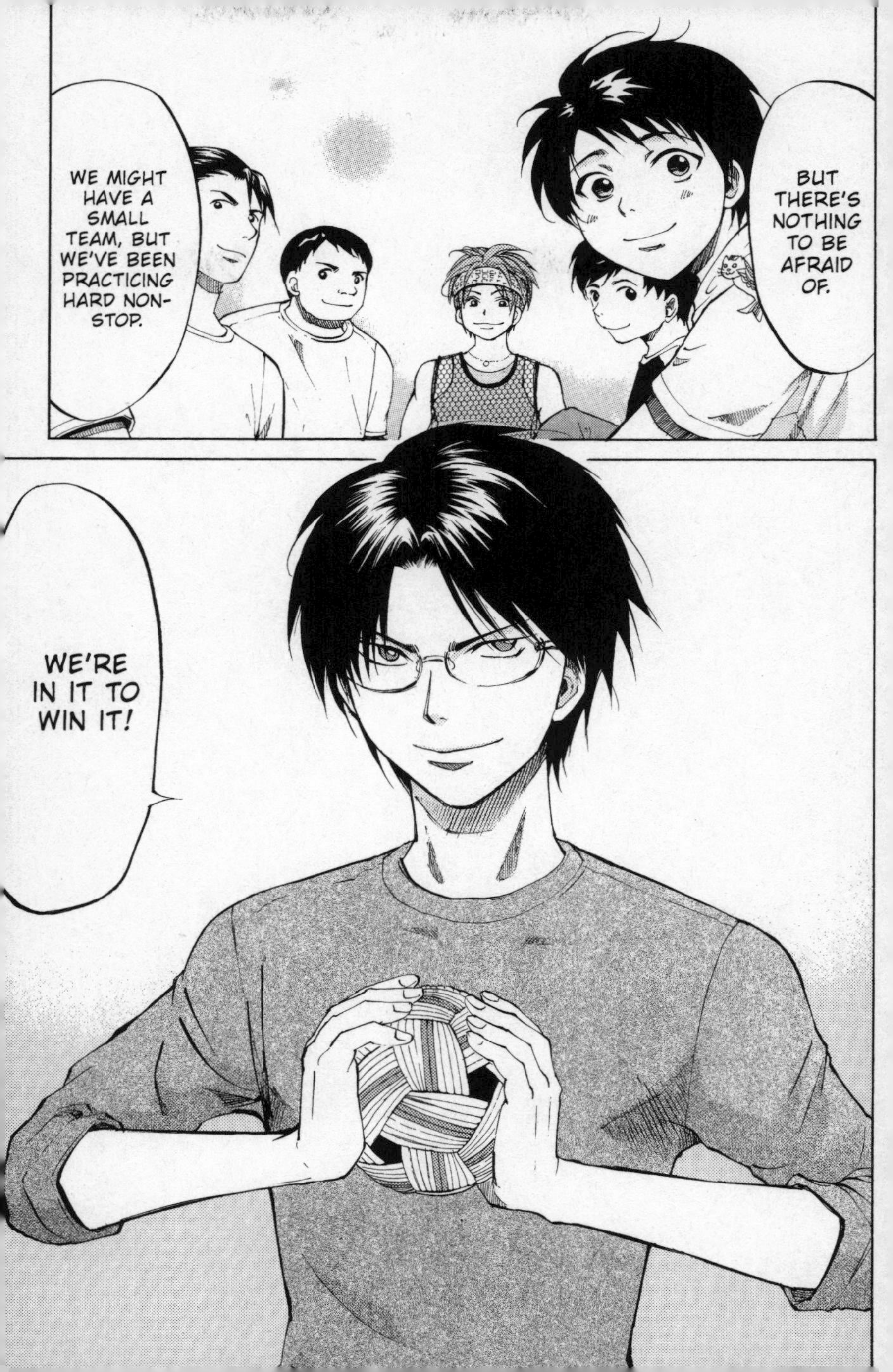
BUT THERE'S NOTHING TO BE AFRAID OF.
WE MIGHT HAVE A SMALL TEAM, BUT WE'VE BEEN PRACTICING HARD NON-STOP.
WE'RE IN IT TO WIN IT!

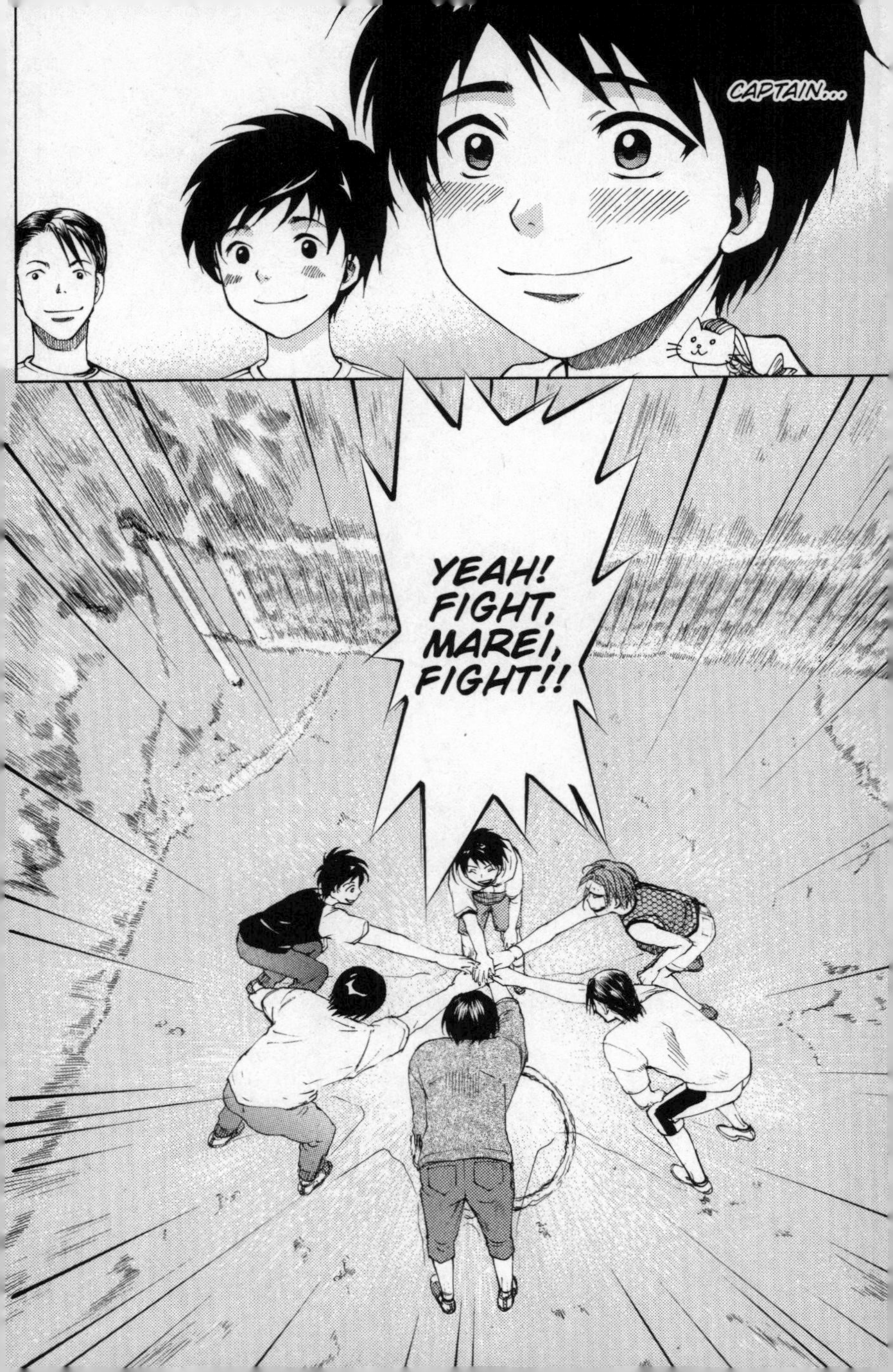
CAPTAIN...
YEAH! FIGHT, MAREI, FIGHT!!

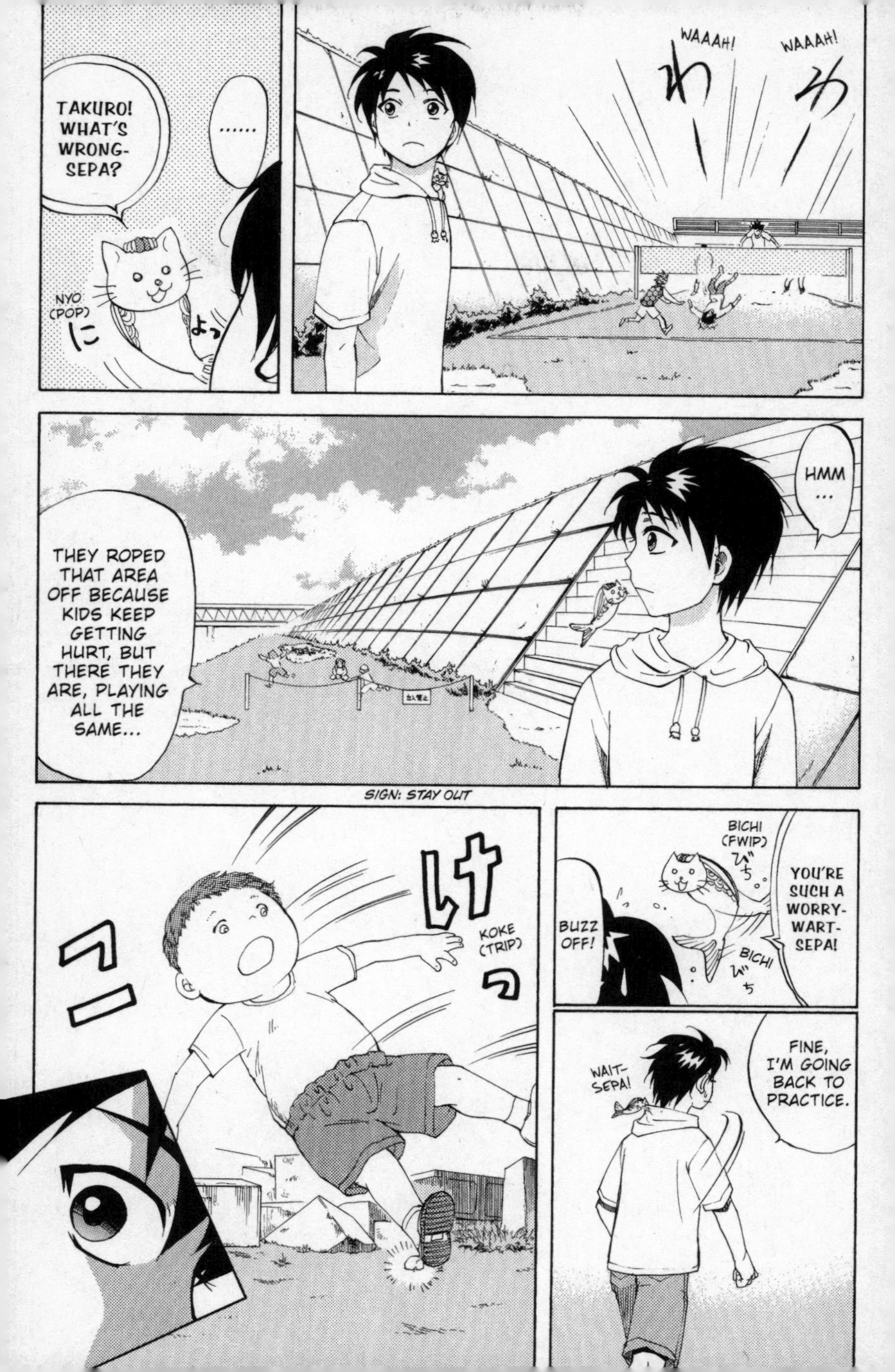

WAAAH!
わー
WAAAH!
ろー
......
TAKURO! WHAT'S WRONG-SEPA?
NYO (POP)
に
よっ
HMM...
THEY ROPED THAT AREA OFF BECAUSE KIDS KEEP GETTING HURT, BUT THERE THEY ARE, PLAYING ALL THE SAME...
SIGN: STAY OUT
YOU'RE SUCH A WORRY-WART-SEPA!
BICHI (FWIP)
びち
BUZZ OFF!
BICHI
びち
FINE, I'M GOING BACK TO PRACTICE.
WAIT-SEPA!
KOKE (TRIP)

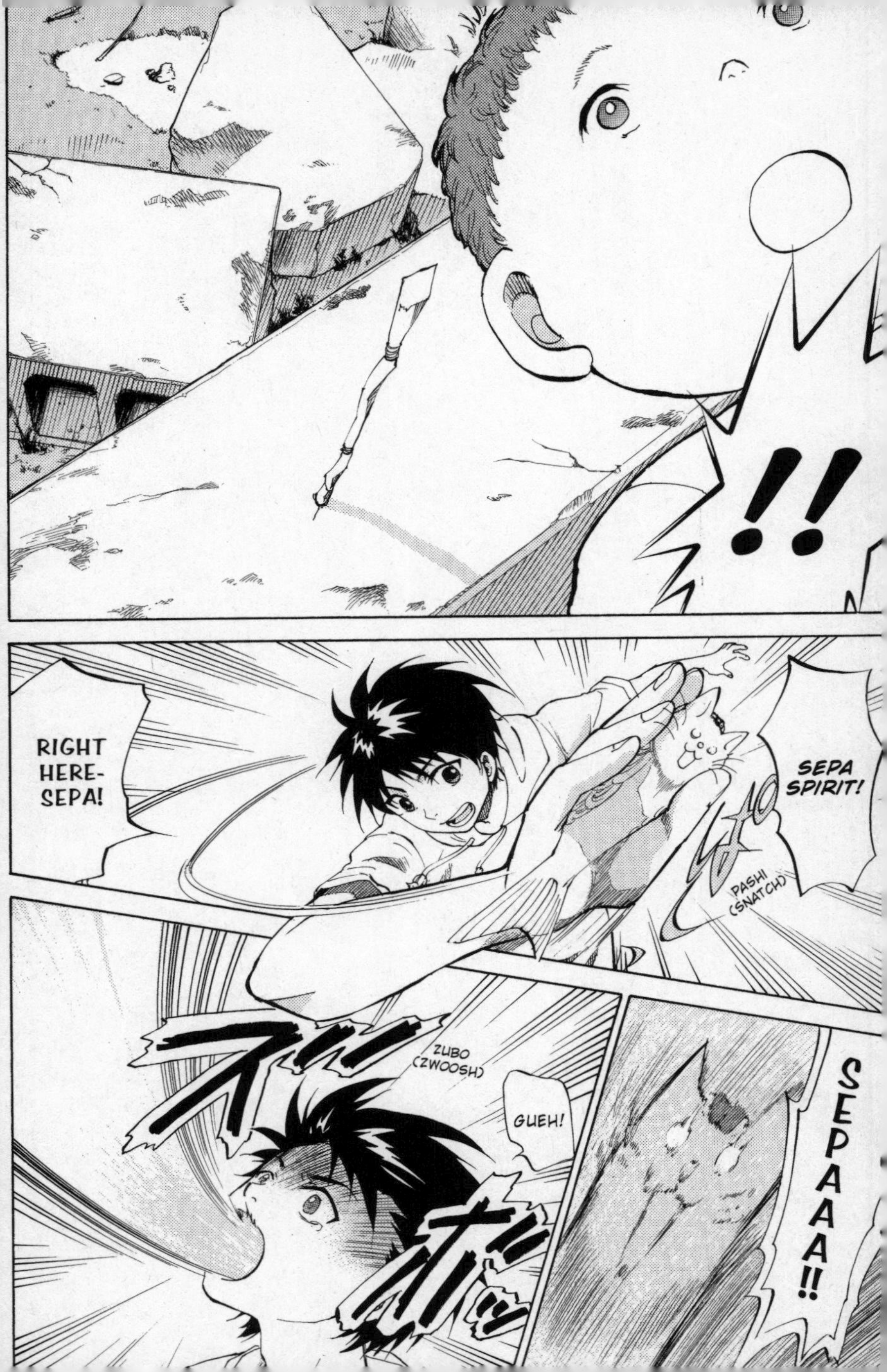
!!
SEPA SPIRIT!
RIGHT HERE-SEPA!
PASHI (SNATCH)
SEPAAAA!!
ZUBO (ZWOOSH)
GUEH!

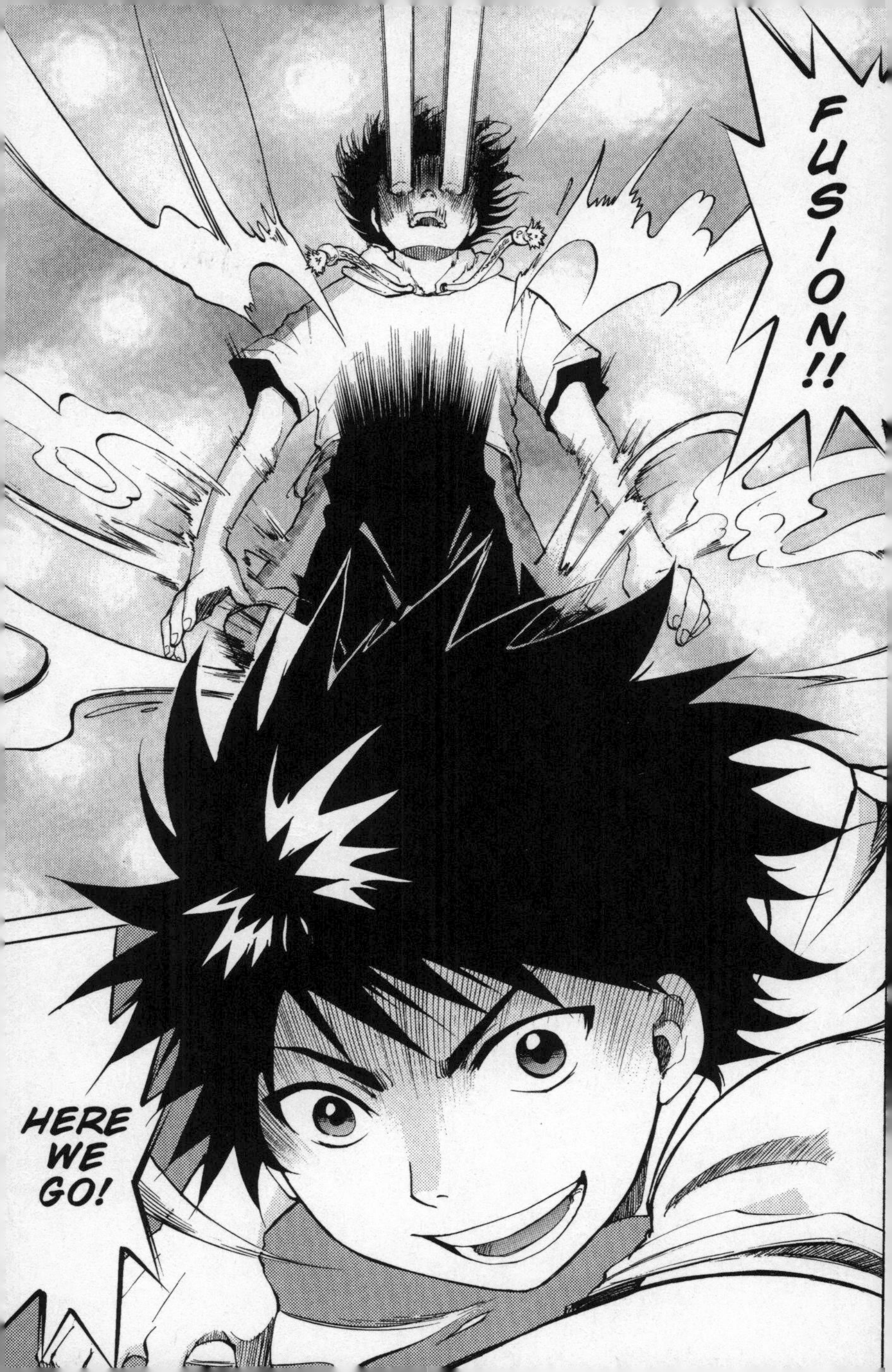
FUSION!!
HERE WE GO!

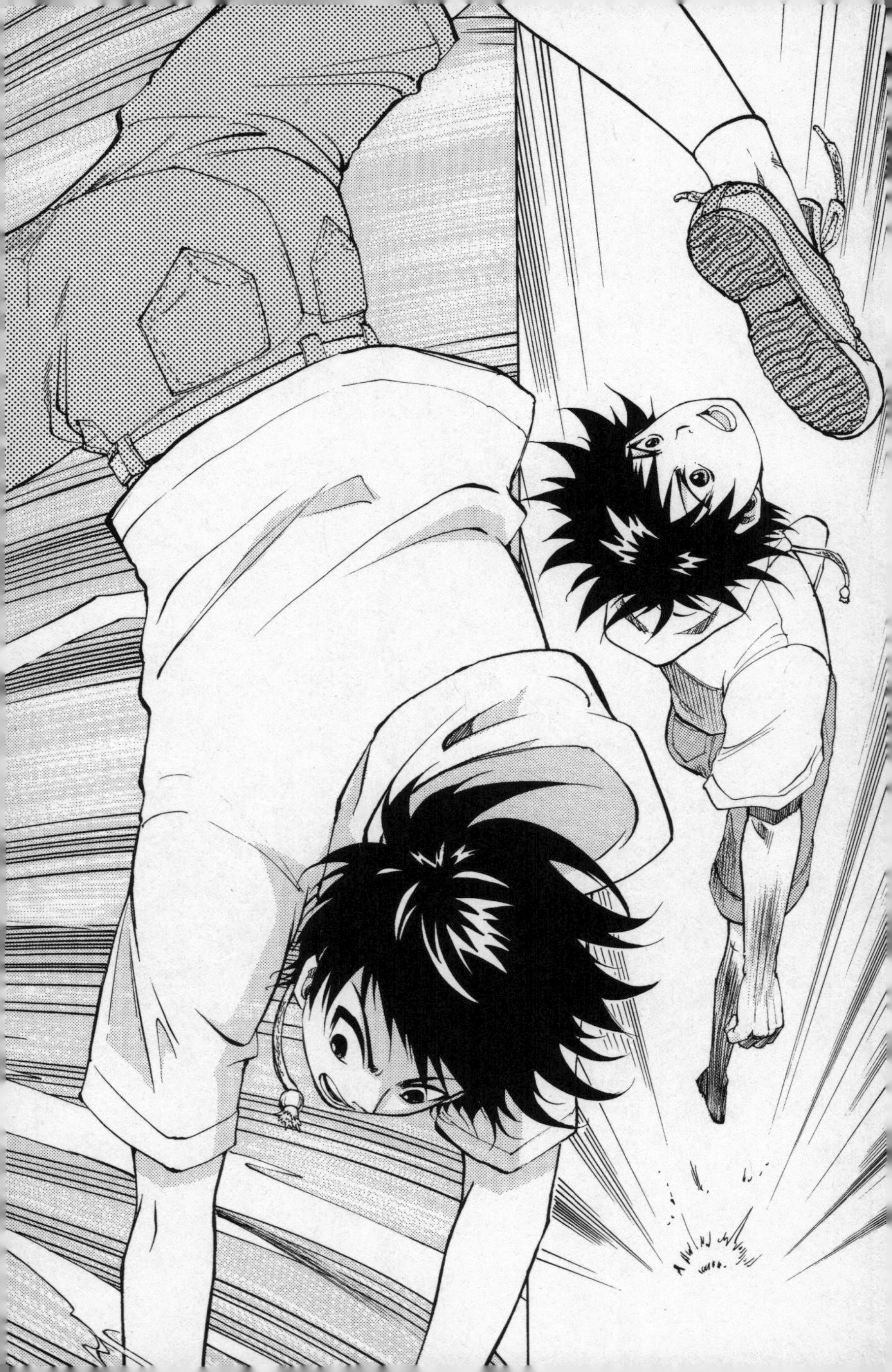

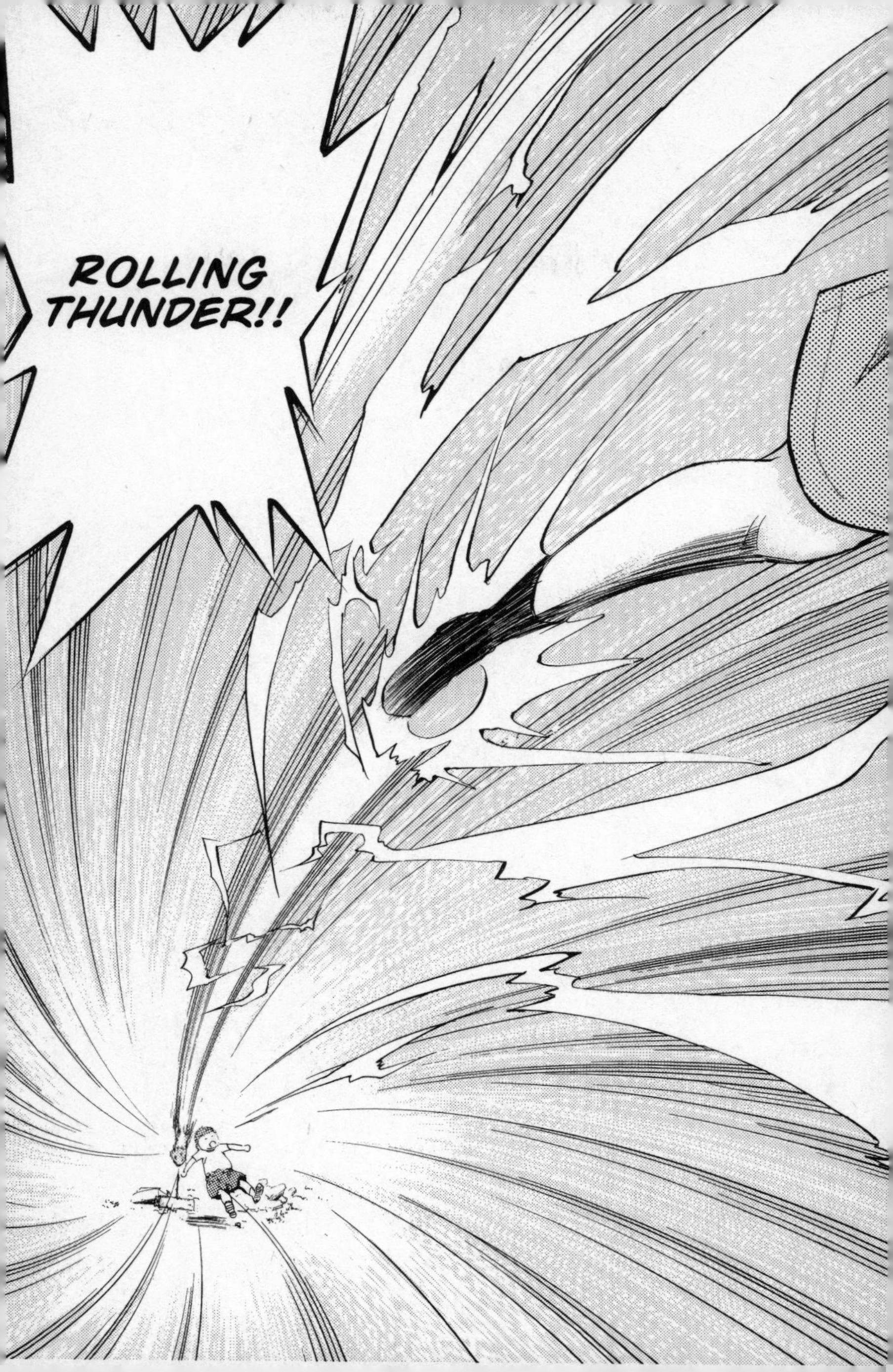
ROLLING THUNDER!!

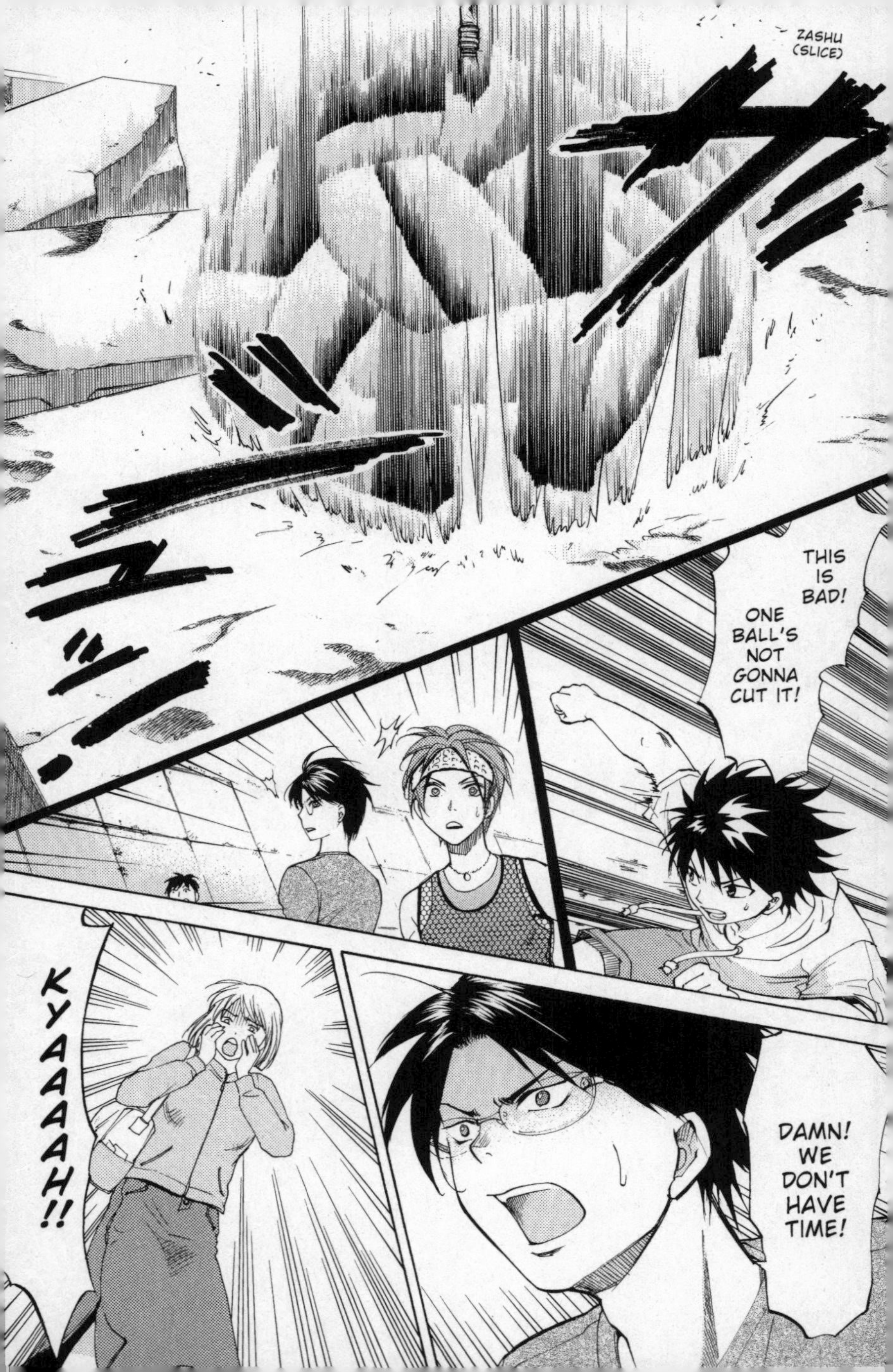
ZASHU (SLICE)
THIS IS BAD!
ONE BALL'S NOT GONNA CUT IT!
DAMN! WE DON'T HAVE TIME!
KYAAAAAH!!

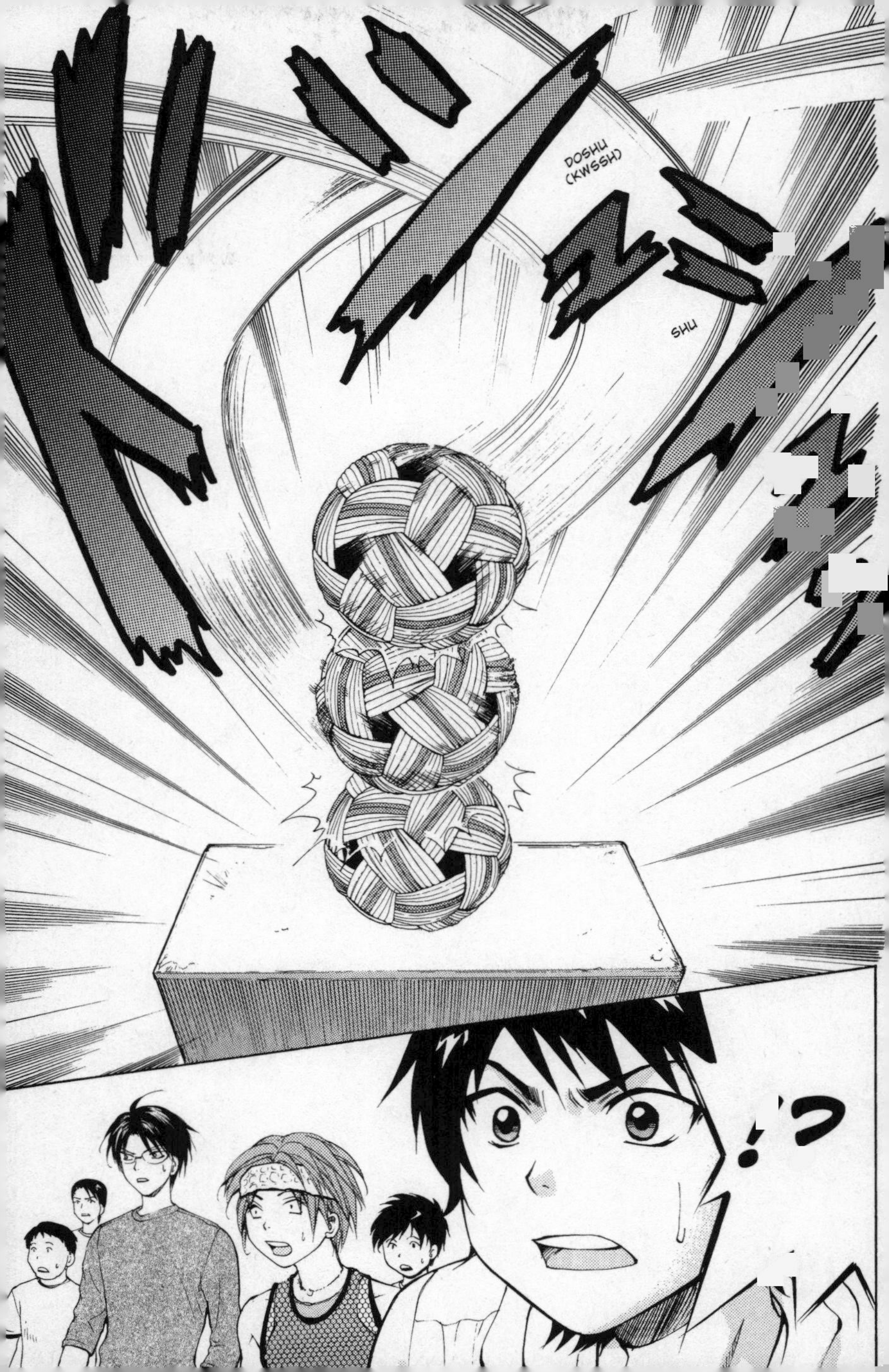
DOSHU (KWSSH)
SHU

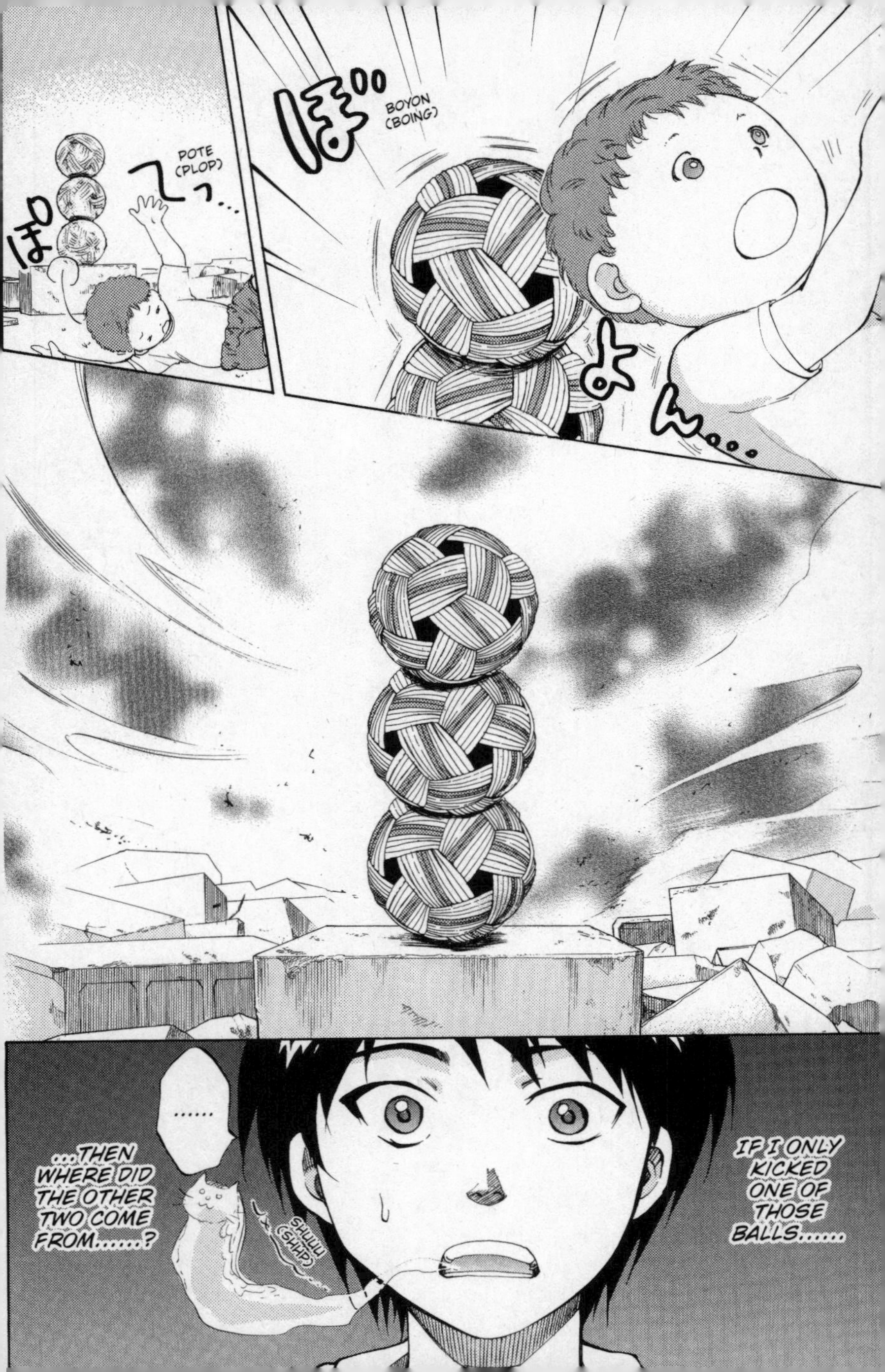

ぼよん...
BOYON
(BOING)
ぽてっ...
POTE
(PLOP)
IF I ONLY KICKED ONE OF THOSE BALLS......
......
...THEN WHERE DID THE OTHER TWO COME FROM......?
SHUUU
(SHHP)

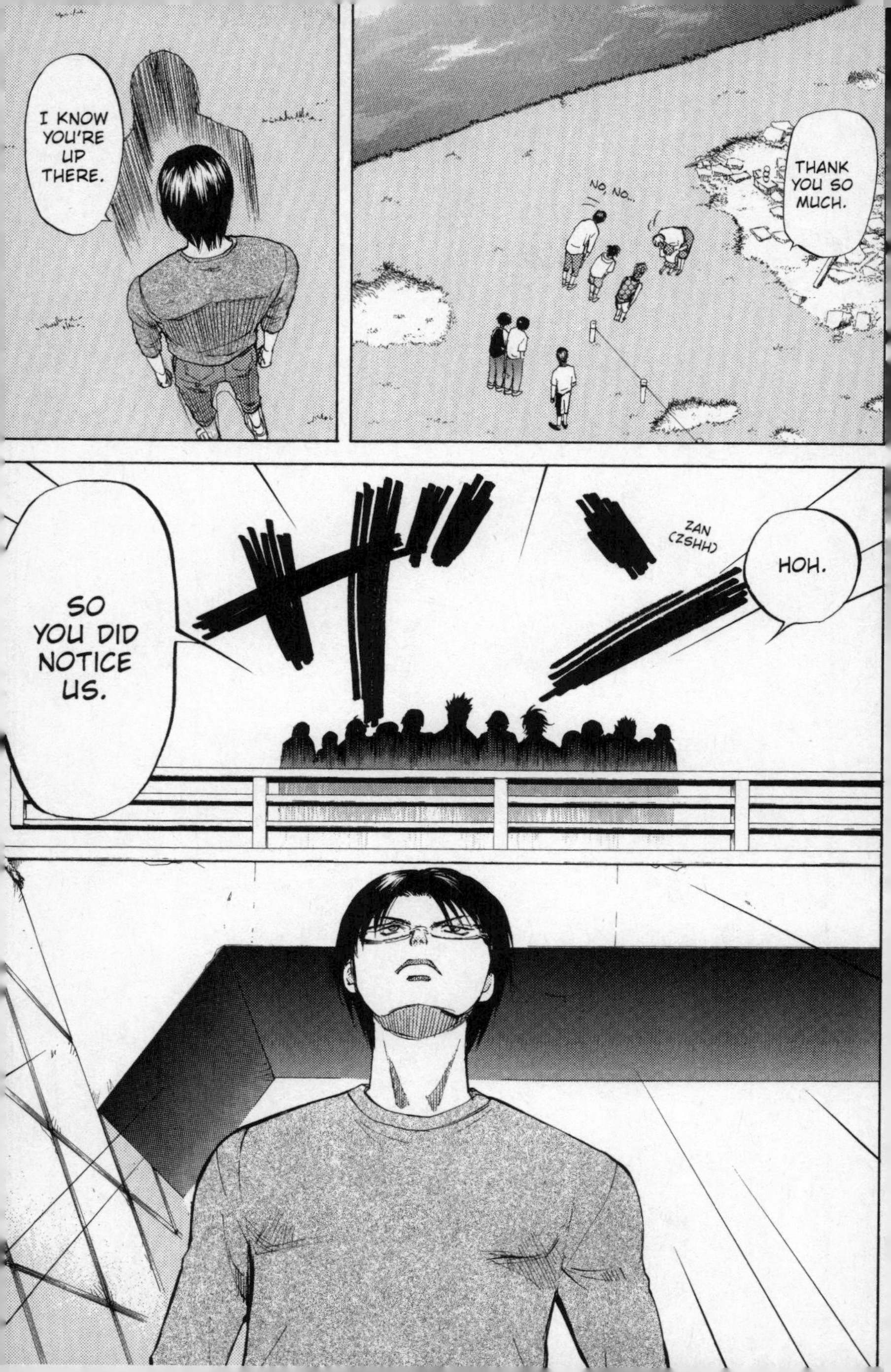
THANK YOU SO MUCH.
NO, NO...
I KNOW YOU'RE UP THERE.
HOH.
ZAN (ZSHH)
SO YOU DID NOTICE US.

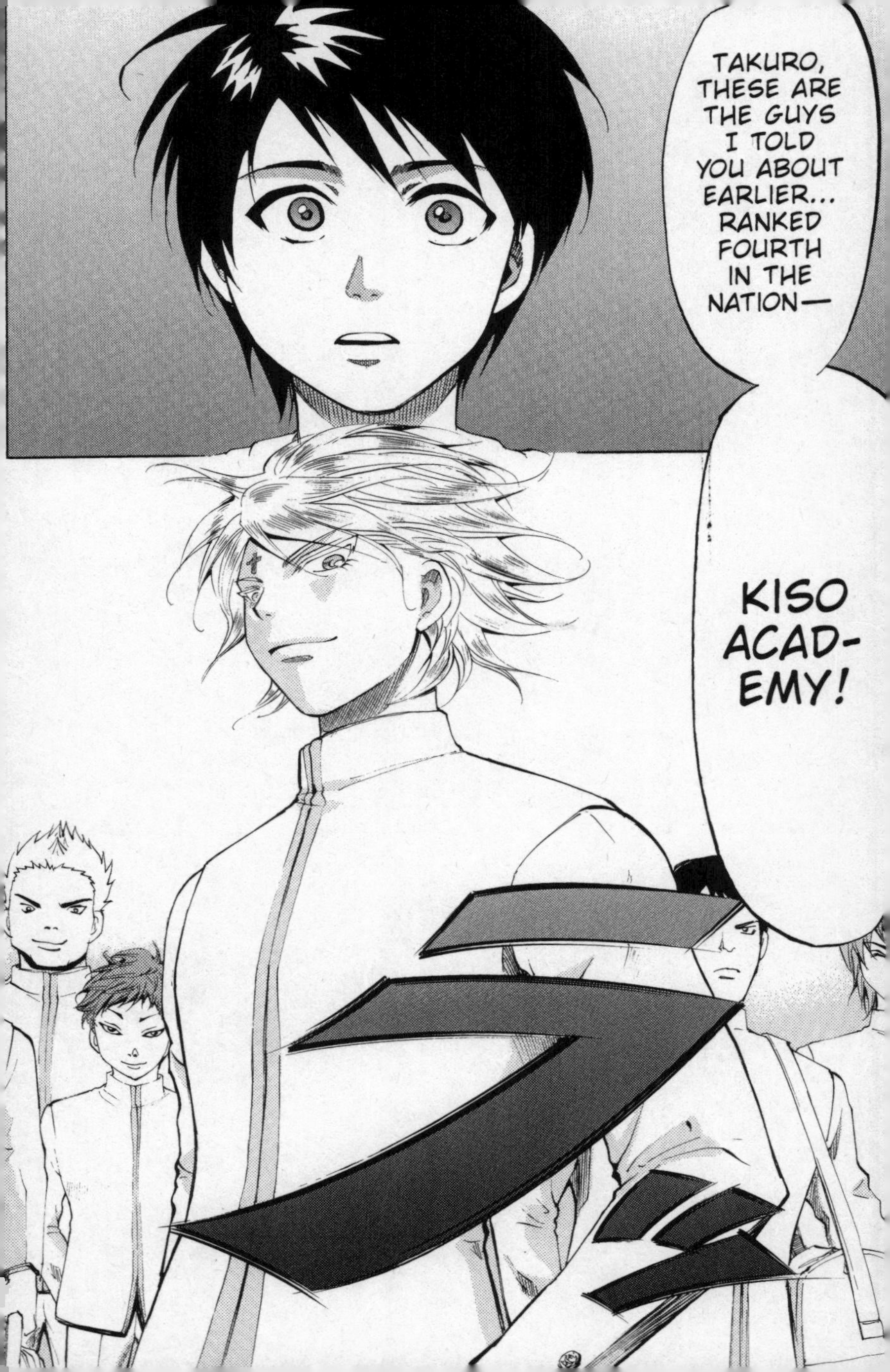
TAKURO, THESE ARE THE GUYS I TOLD YOU ABOUT EARLIER... RANKED FOURTH IN THE NATION—
KISO ACAD-EMY!

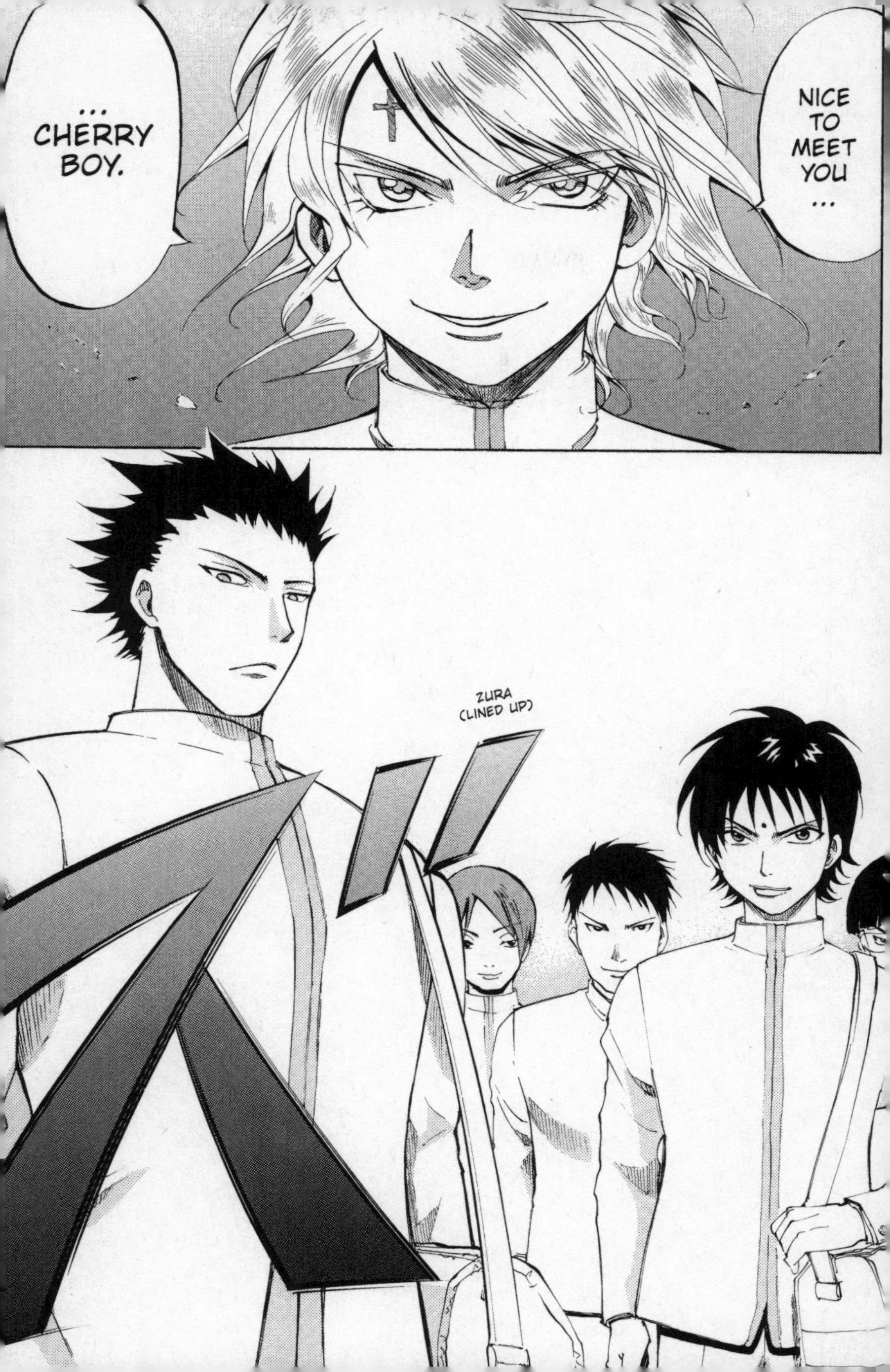
NICE TO MEET YOU ...
... CHERRY BOY.
ZURA
(LINED UP)

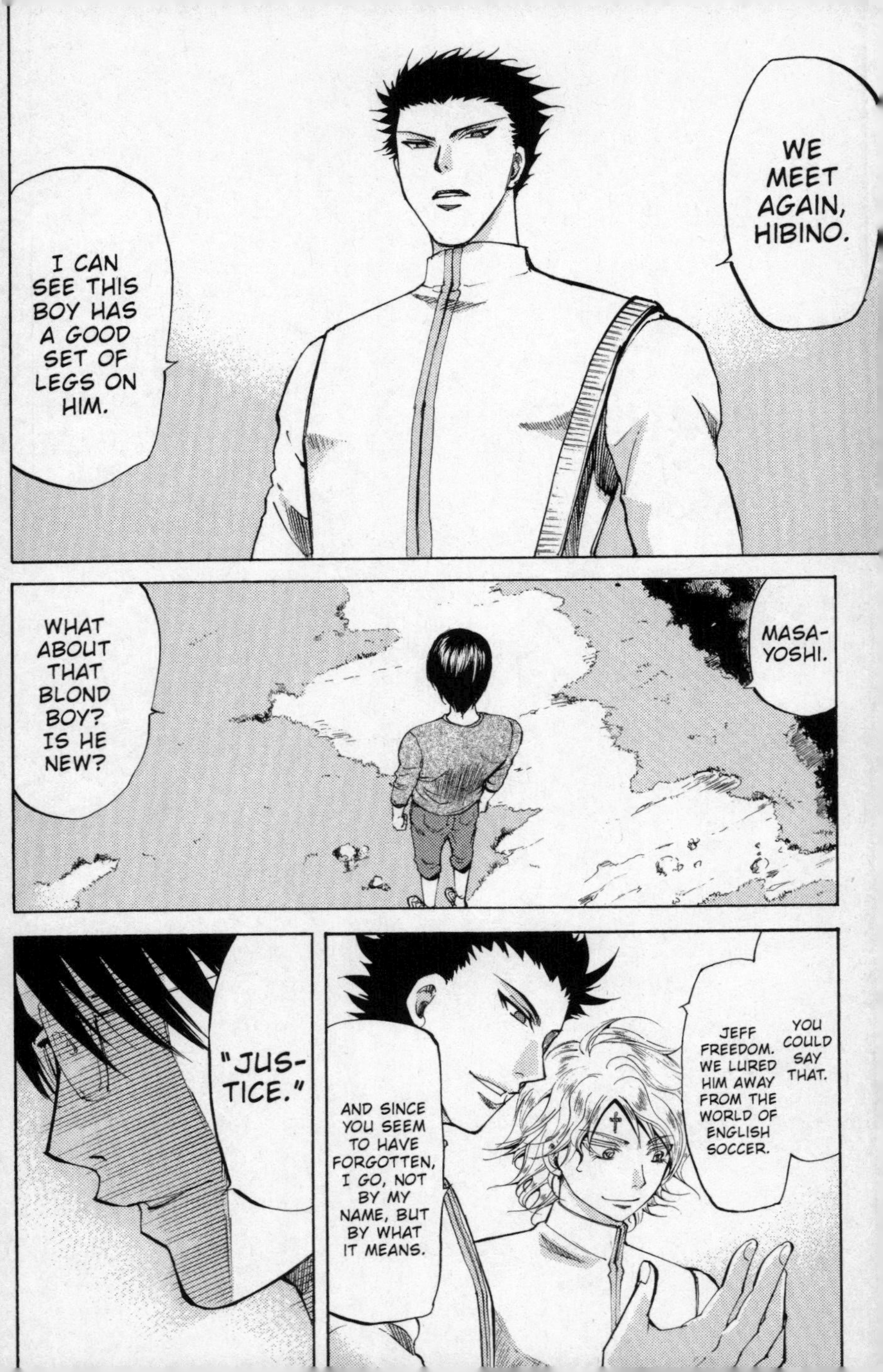
WE MEET AGAIN, HIBINO.
I CAN SEE THIS BOY HAS A GOOD SET OF LEGS ON HIM.
MASA-YOSHI.
WHAT ABOUT THAT BLOND BOY? IS HE NEW?
YOU COULD SAY THAT.
JEFF FREEDOM. WE LURED HIM AWAY FROM THE WORLD OF ENGLISH SOCCER.
AND SINCE YOU SEEM TO HAVE FORGOTTEN, I GO, NOT BY MY NAME, BUT BY WHAT IT MEANS.
"JUS-TICE."

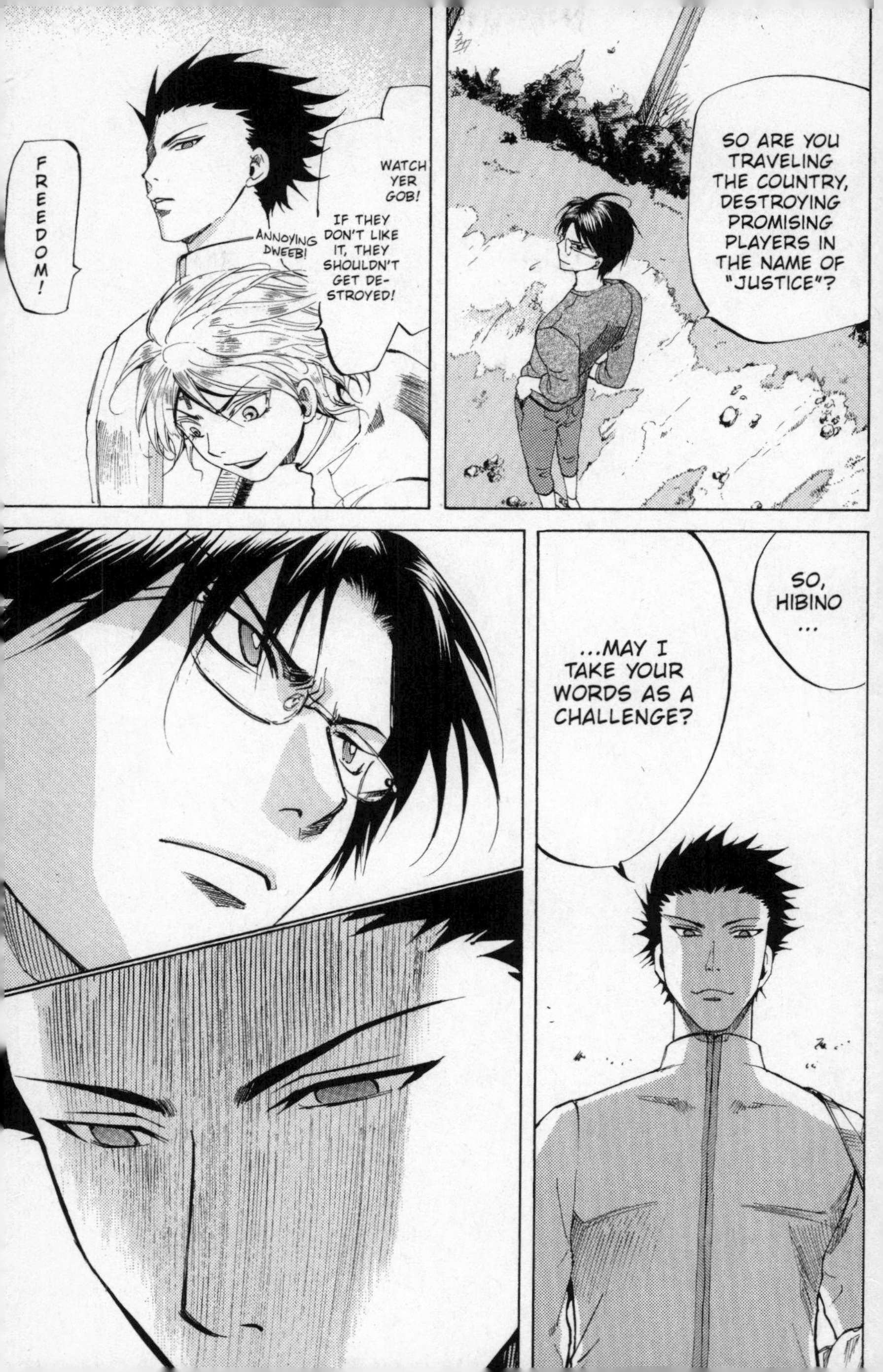
SO ARE YOU TRAVELING THE COUNTRY, DESTROYING PROMISING PLAYERS IN THE NAME OF "JUSTICE"?
WATCH YER GOB!
IF THEY DON'T LIKE IT, THEY SHOULDN'T GET DE-STROYED!
ANNOYING DWEEB!
FREEDOM!
SO, HIBINO...
...MAY I TAKE YOUR WORDS AS A CHALLENGE?

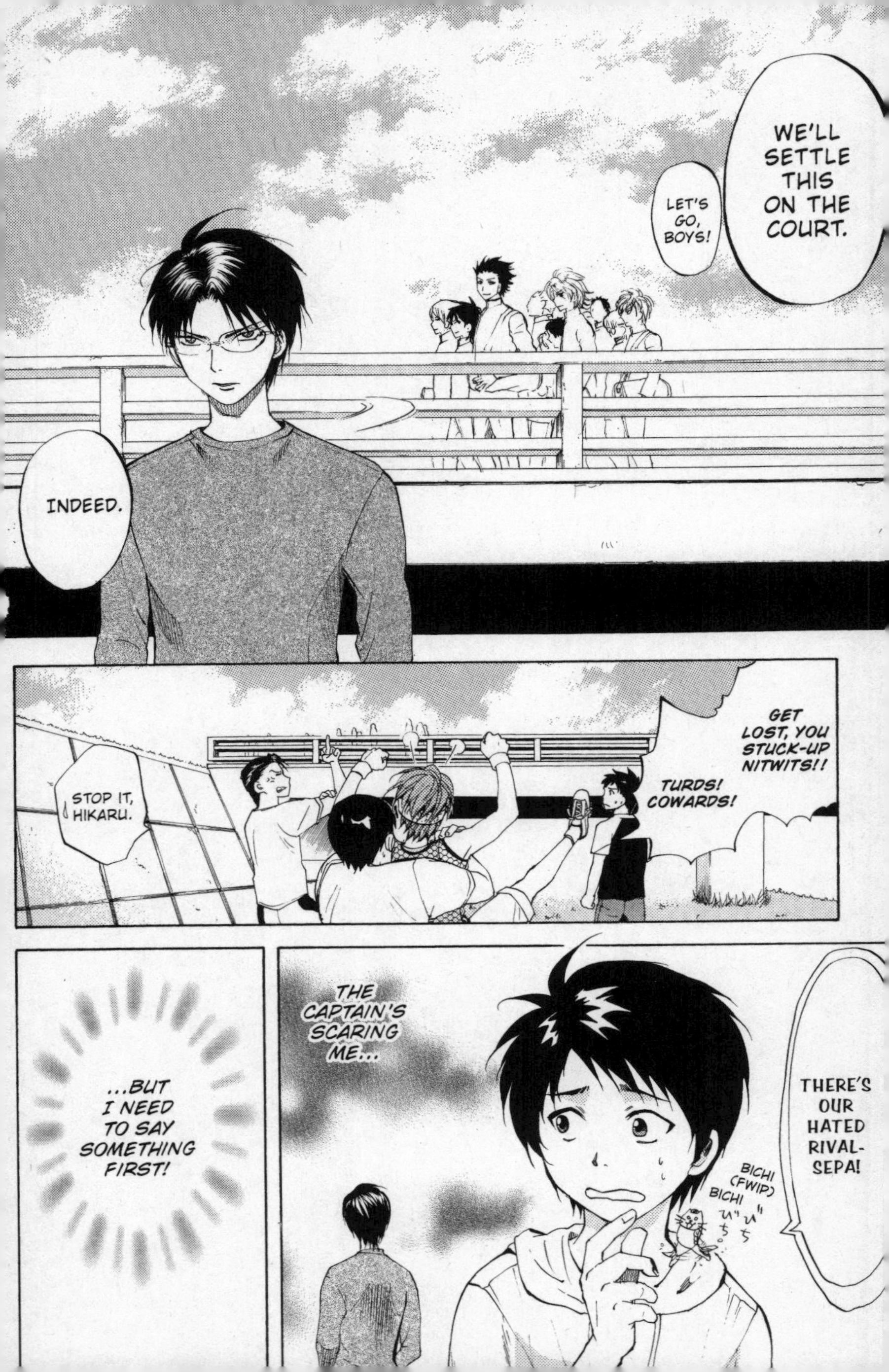
WE'LL SETTLE THIS ON THE COURT.
LET'S GO, BOYS!
INDEED.
GET LOST, YOU STUCK-UP NITWITS!!
TURDS! COWARDS!
STOP IT, HIKARU.
THERE'S OUR HATED RIVAL-SEPA!
BICHI (FWIP) BICHI
THE CAPTAIN'S SCARING ME...
...BUT I NEED TO SAY SOMETHING FIRST!

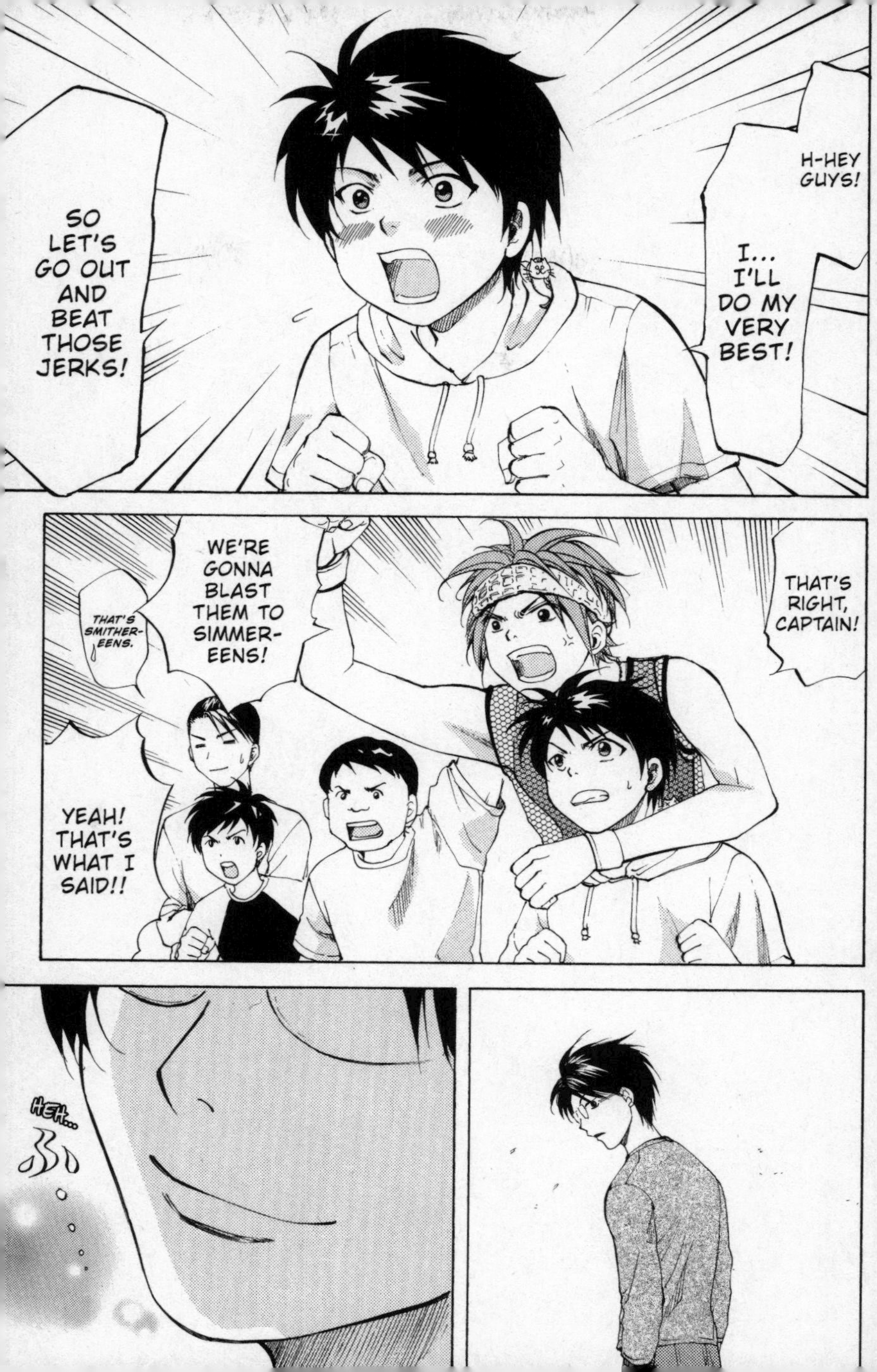

H-HEY GUYS!
I... I'LL DO MY VERY BEST!
SO LET'S GO OUT AND BEAT THOSE JERKS!
THAT'S RIGHT, CAPTAIN!
WE'RE GONNA BLAST THEM TO SIMMER-EENS!
THAT'S SMITHER-EENS.
YEAH! THAT'S WHAT I SAID!!
HEH...
ふ

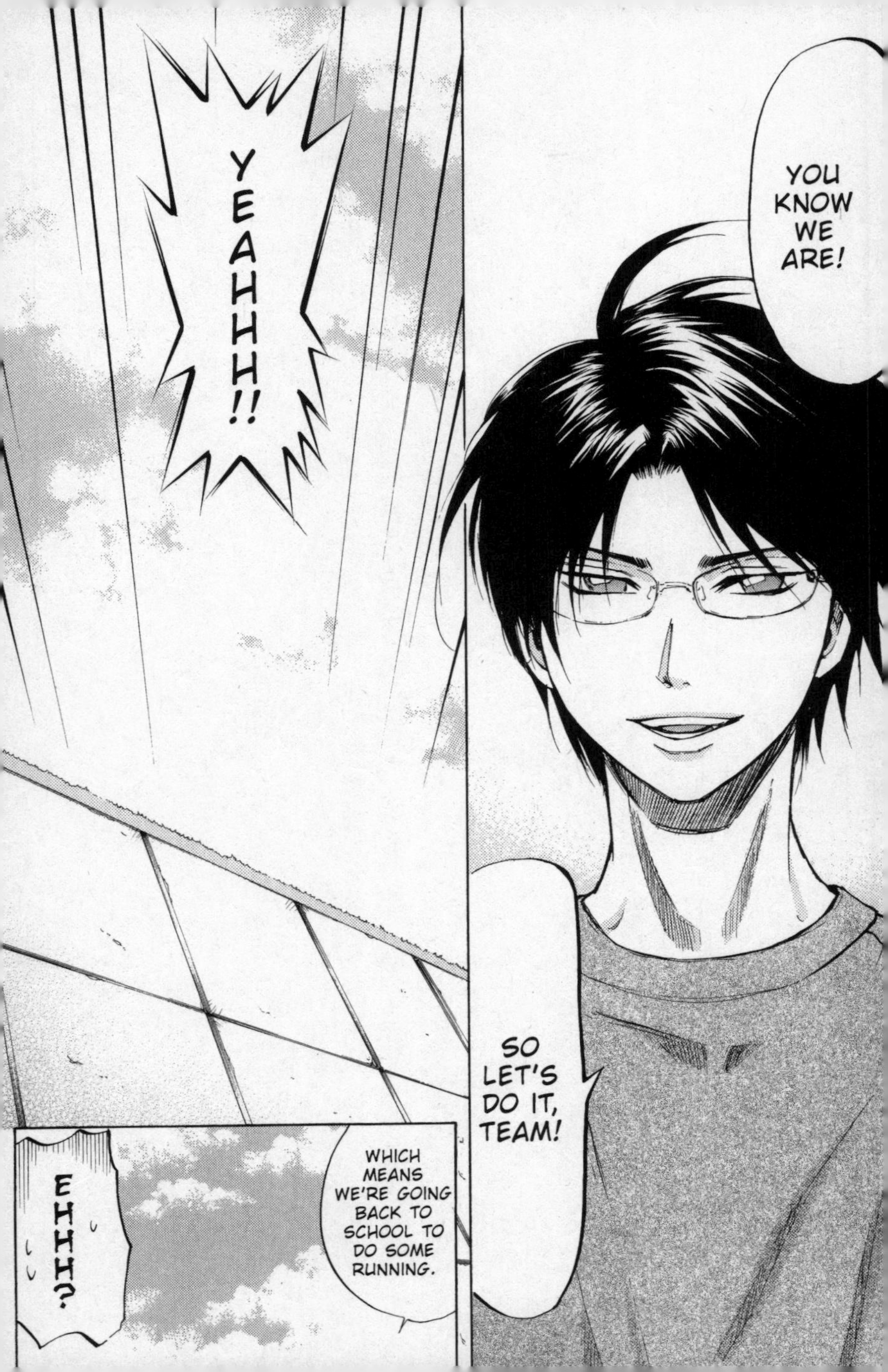
YOU KNOW WE ARE!
SO LET'S DO IT, TEAM!
YEAHHH!!
WHICH MEANS WE'RE GOING BACK TO SCHOOL TO DO SOME RUNNING.
EHHHH?

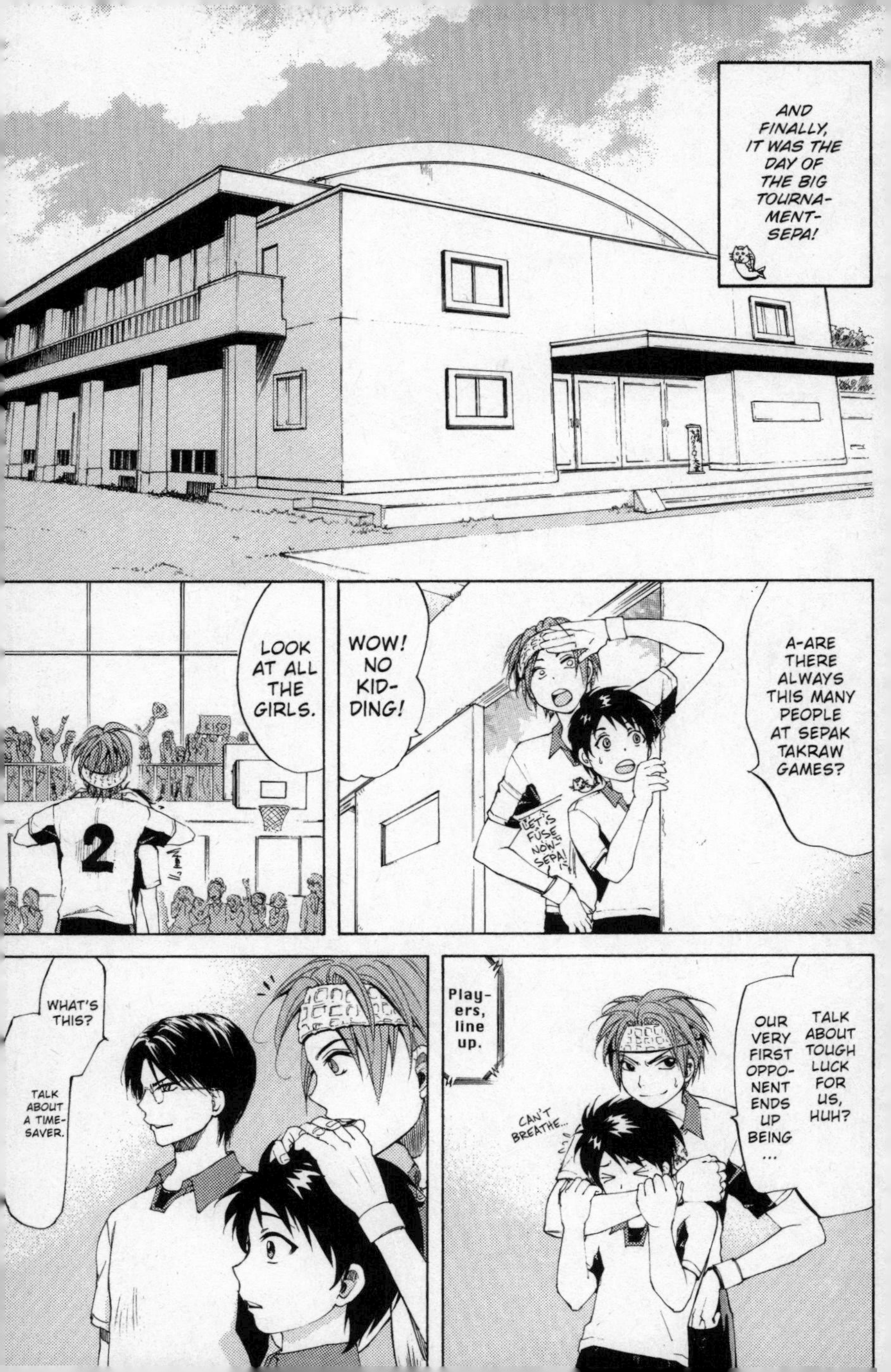
AND FINALLY, IT WAS THE DAY OF THE BIG TOURNAMENT-SEPA!
A-ARE THERE ALWAYS THIS MANY PEOPLE AT SEPAK TAKRAW GAMES?
LET'S FUSE NOW-SEPA!
WOW! NO KIDDING!
LOOK AT ALL THE GIRLS.
2
TALK ABOUT TOUGH LUCK FOR US, HUH?
OUR VERY FIRST OPPONENT ENDS UP BEING ...
CAN'T BREATHE...
Players, line up.
WHAT'S THIS?
TALK ABOUT A TIME-SAVER.

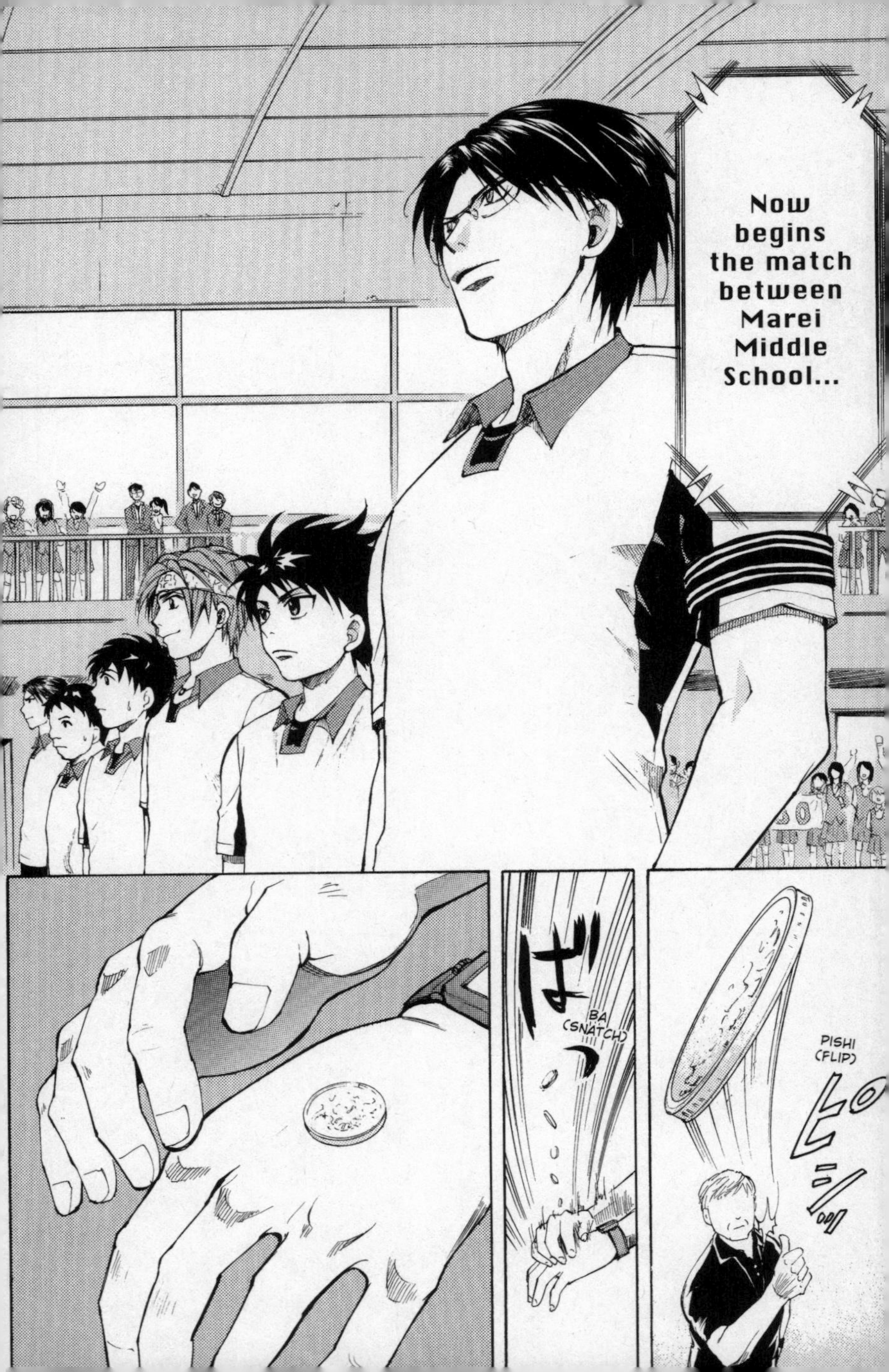

Now begins the match between Marei Middle School...
PISHI (FLIP)
ばっ
BA (SNATCH)

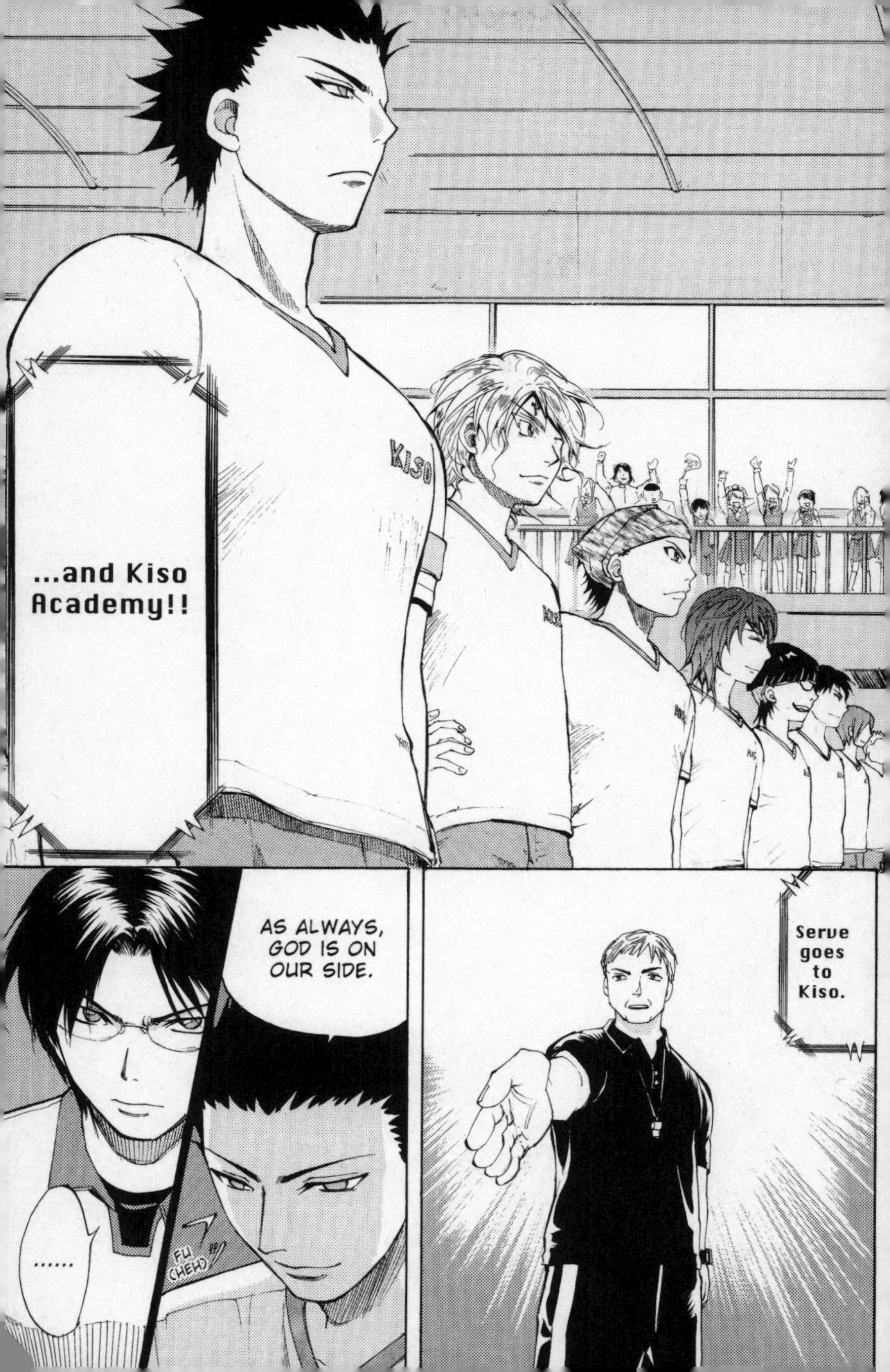
...and Kiso Academy!!
Serve goes to Kiso.
AS ALWAYS, GOD IS ON OUR SIDE.
FU (HEH)
......

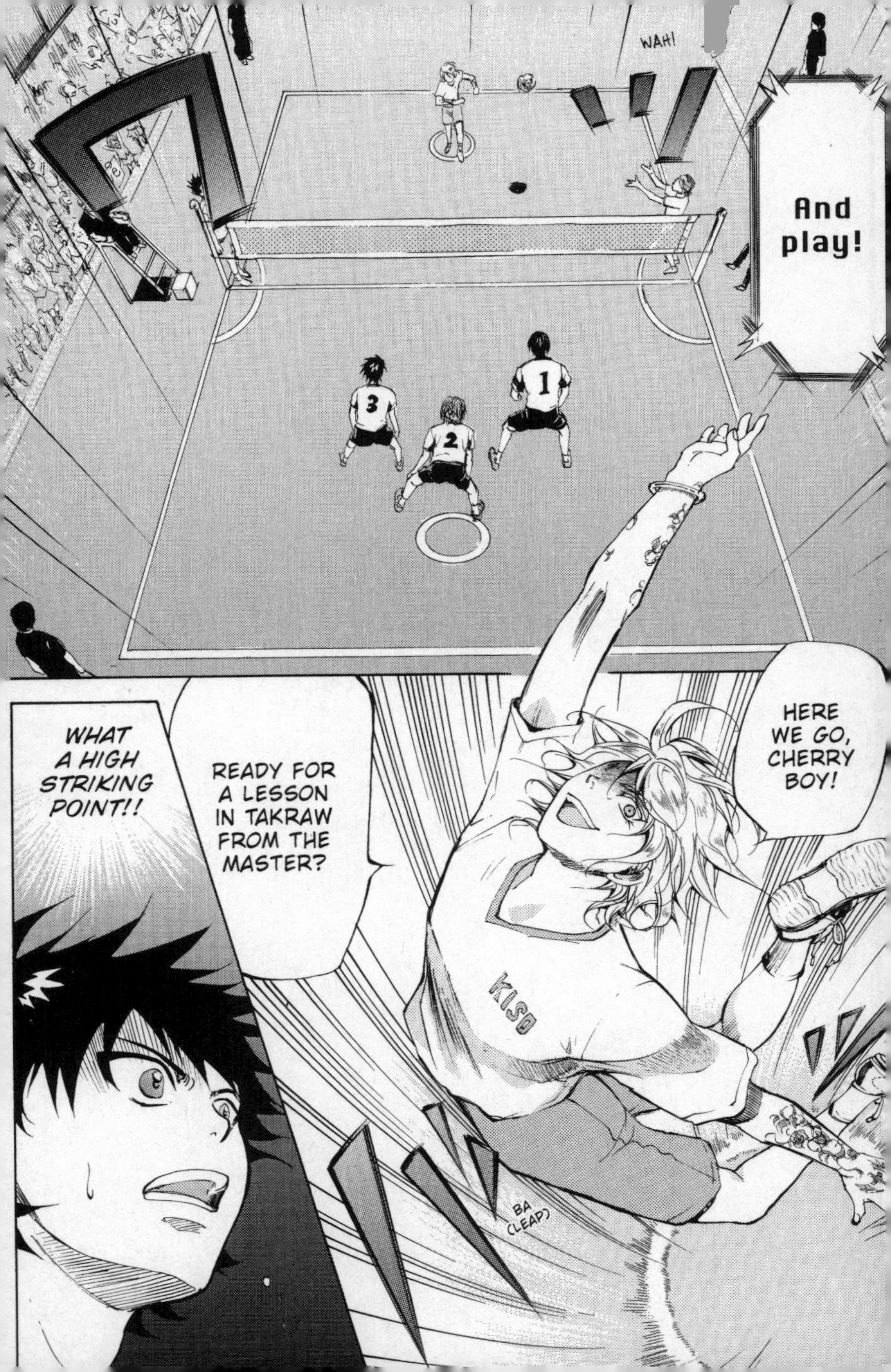

And play!
WAH!
HERE WE GO, CHERRY BOY!
READY FOR A LESSON IN TAKRAW FROM THE MASTER?
WHAT A HIGH STRIKING POINT!!
BA (LEAP)
KISO

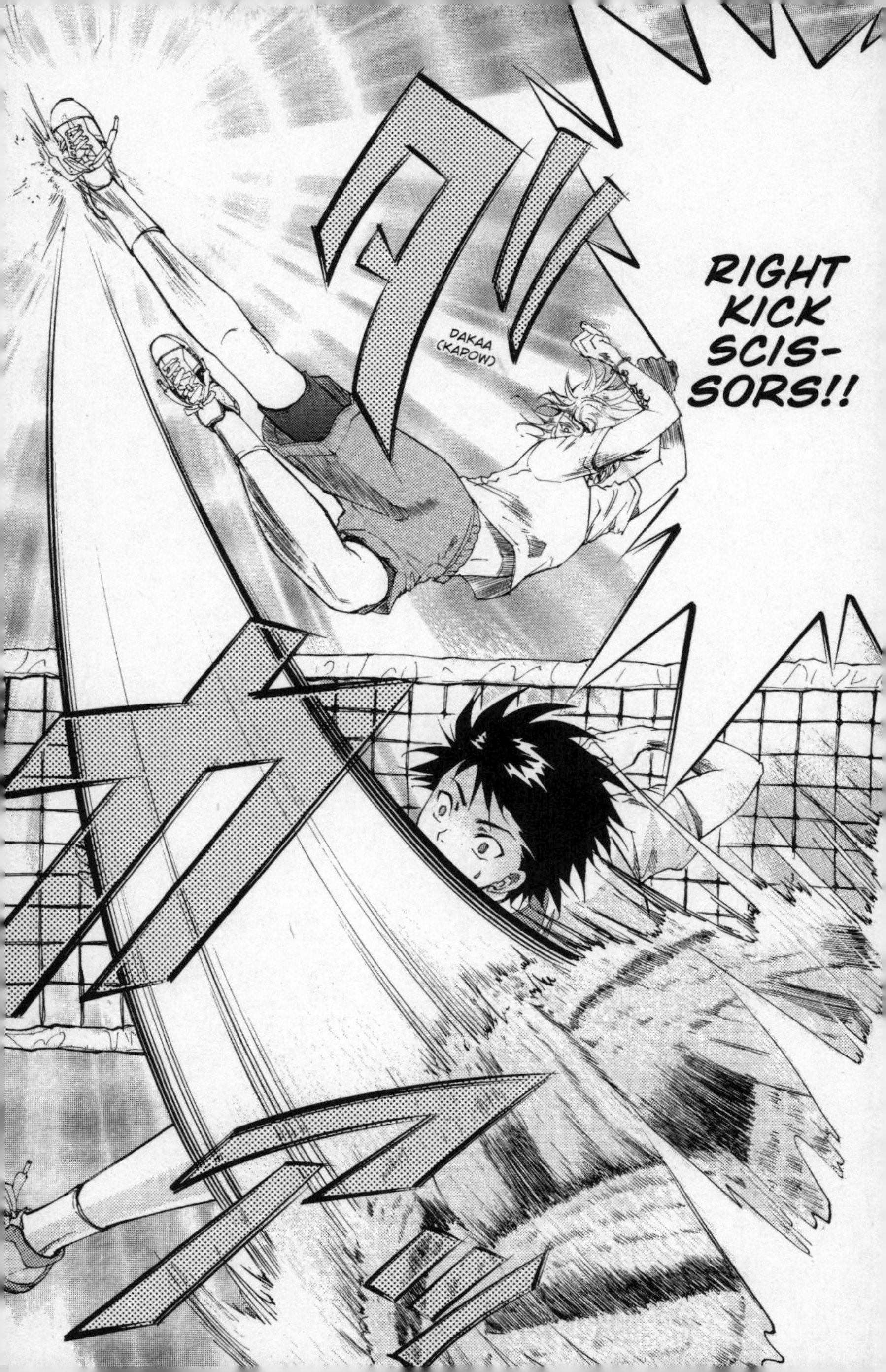
RIGHT KICK SCIS-SORS!!
DAKAA (KAPOW)

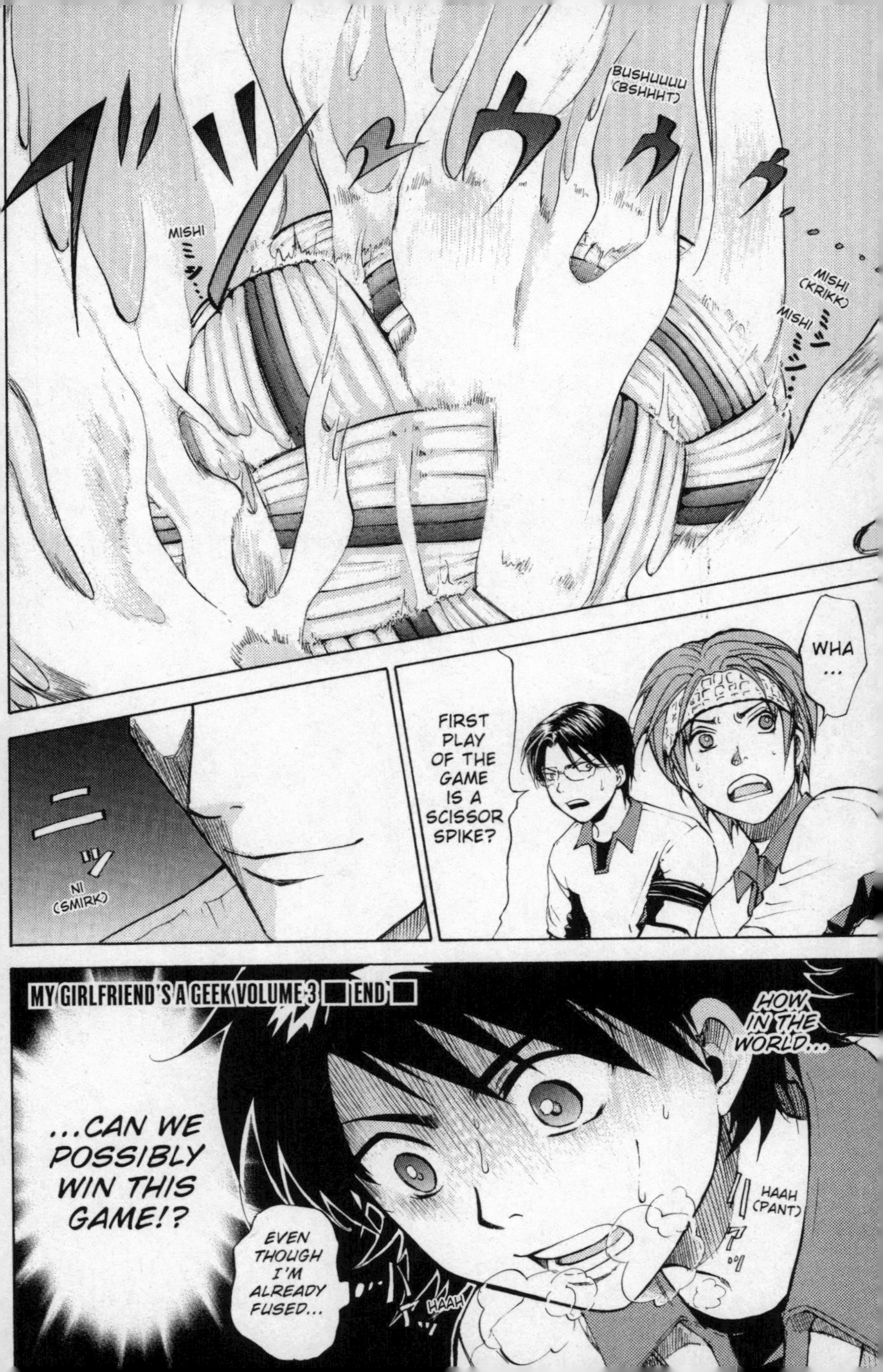
BUSHUUUU (BSHHHT)
MISHI (KRIKK)
MISHI
MISHI
WHA ...
FIRST PLAY OF THE GAME IS A SCISSOR SPIKE?
NI (SMIRK)
MY GIRLFRIEND'S A GEEK VOLUME 3 END
HOW IN THE WORLD...
HAAH (PANT)
...CAN WE POSSIBLY WIN THIS GAME!?
EVEN THOUGH I'M ALREADY FUSED...
HAAH

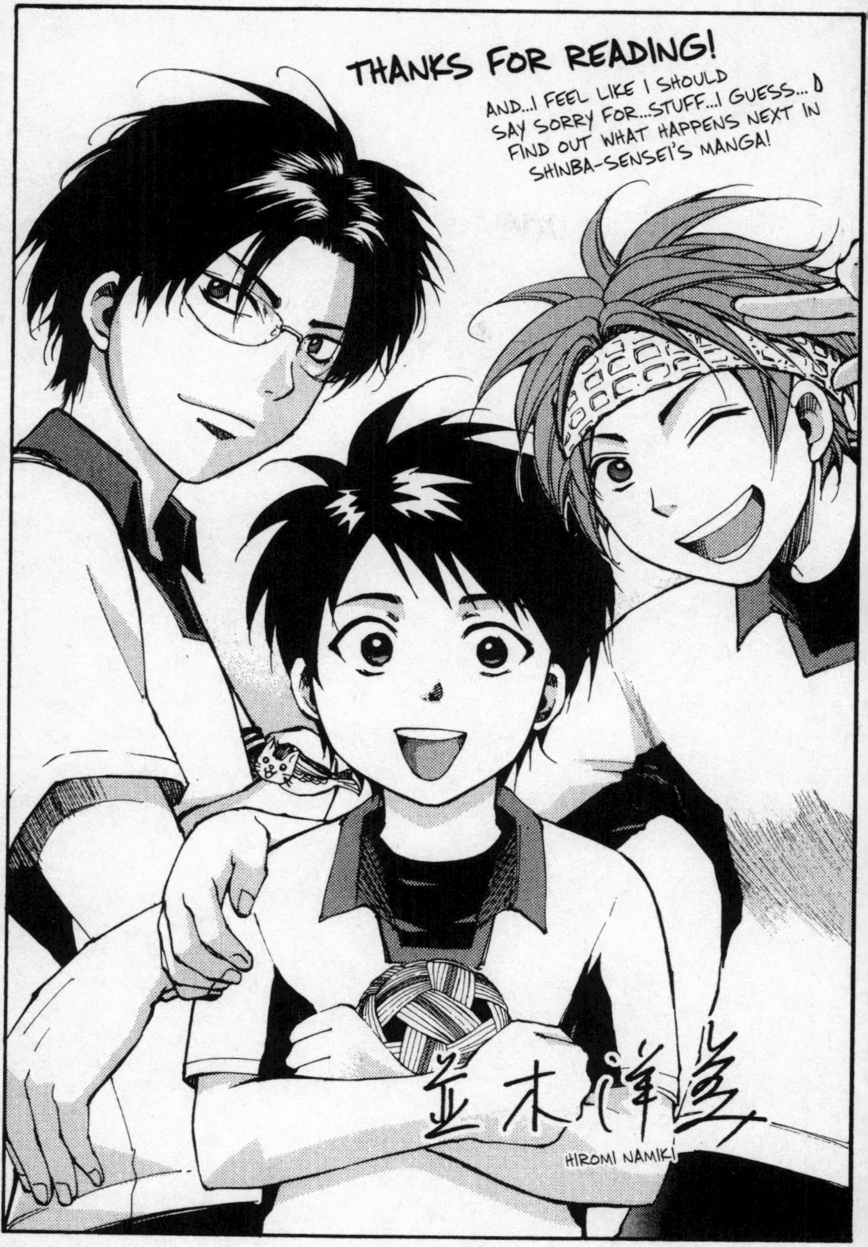
THANKS FOR READING!
AND...I FEEL LIKE I SHOULD SAY SORRY FOR...STUFF...I GUESS...
FIND OUT WHAT HAPPENS NEXT IN SHINBA-SENSEI'S MANGA!
HIROMI NAMIKI

Can't wait for the next volume? You don't have to!

Keep up with the latest chapters of some of your favorite manga every month online in the pages of YEN PLUS!

Visit us at www.yenplus.com for details!

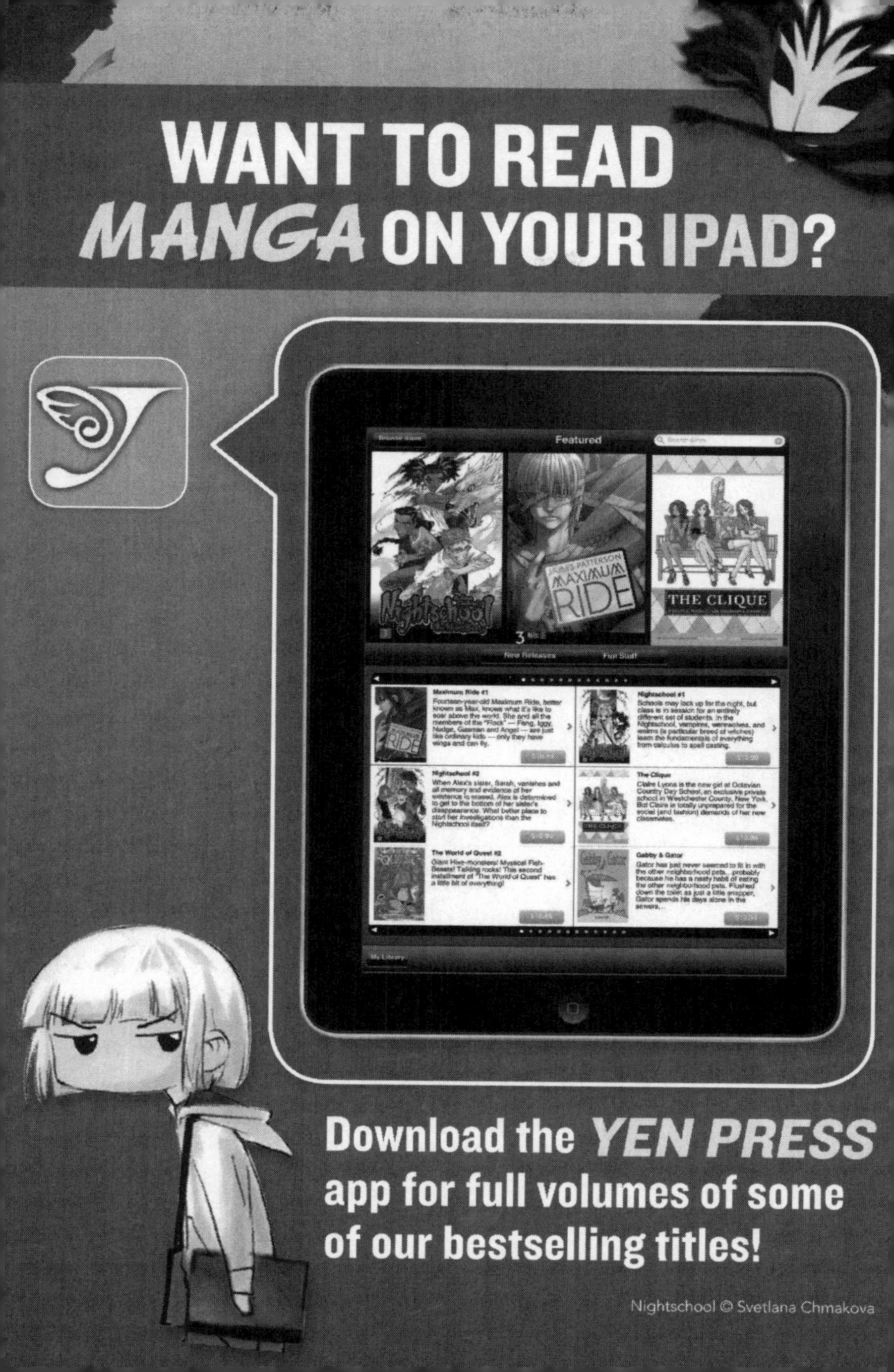
WANT TO READ
MANGA ON YOUR IPAD?
Featured
JAMES PATTERSON
MAXIMUM RIDE
THE CLIQUE
Download the YEN PRESS
app for full volumes of some
of our bestselling titles!
Nightschool © Svetlana Chmakova

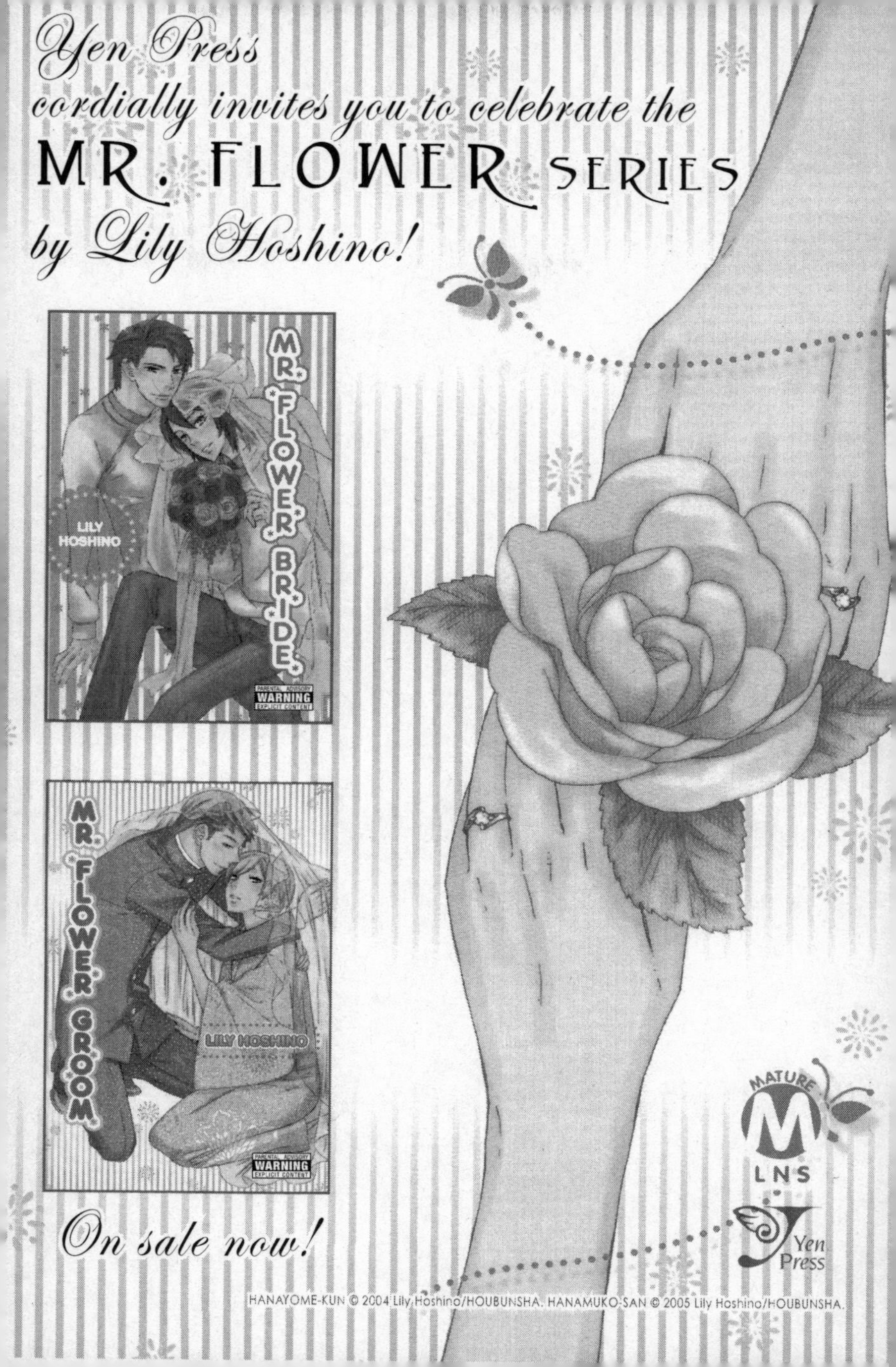
Yen Press
cordially invites you to celebrate the
MR. FLOWER SERIES
by Lily Hoshino!
MR. FLOWER BRIDE
LILY HOSHINO
PARENTAL ADVISORY WARNING EXPLICIT CONTENT
MR. FLOWER GROOM
LILY HOSHINO
PARENTAL ADVISORY WARNING EXPLICIT CONTENT
On sale now!
MATURE M LNS
Yen Press
HANAYOME-KUN © 2004 Lily Hoshino/HOUBUNSHA. HANAMUKO-SAN © 2005 Lily Hoshino/HOUBUNSHA.

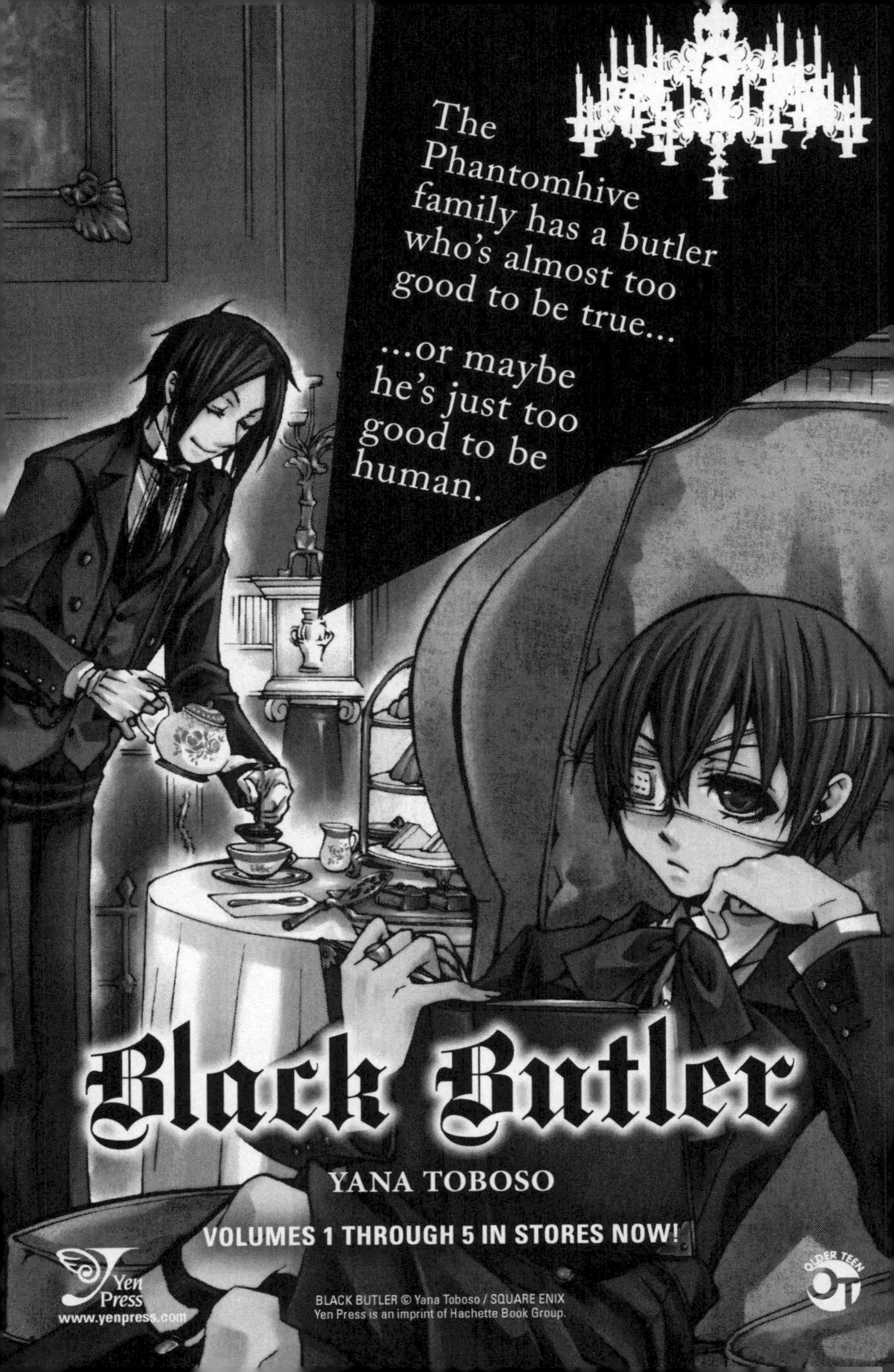
The Phantomhive family has a butler who's almost too good to be true...
...or maybe he's just too good to be human.
Black Butler
YANA TOBOSO
VOLUMES 1 THROUGH 5 IN STORES NOW!
Yen Press
www.yenpress.com
BLACK BUTLER © Yana Toboso / SQUARE ENIX
Yen Press is an imprint of Hachette Book Group.
OLDER TEEN
OT

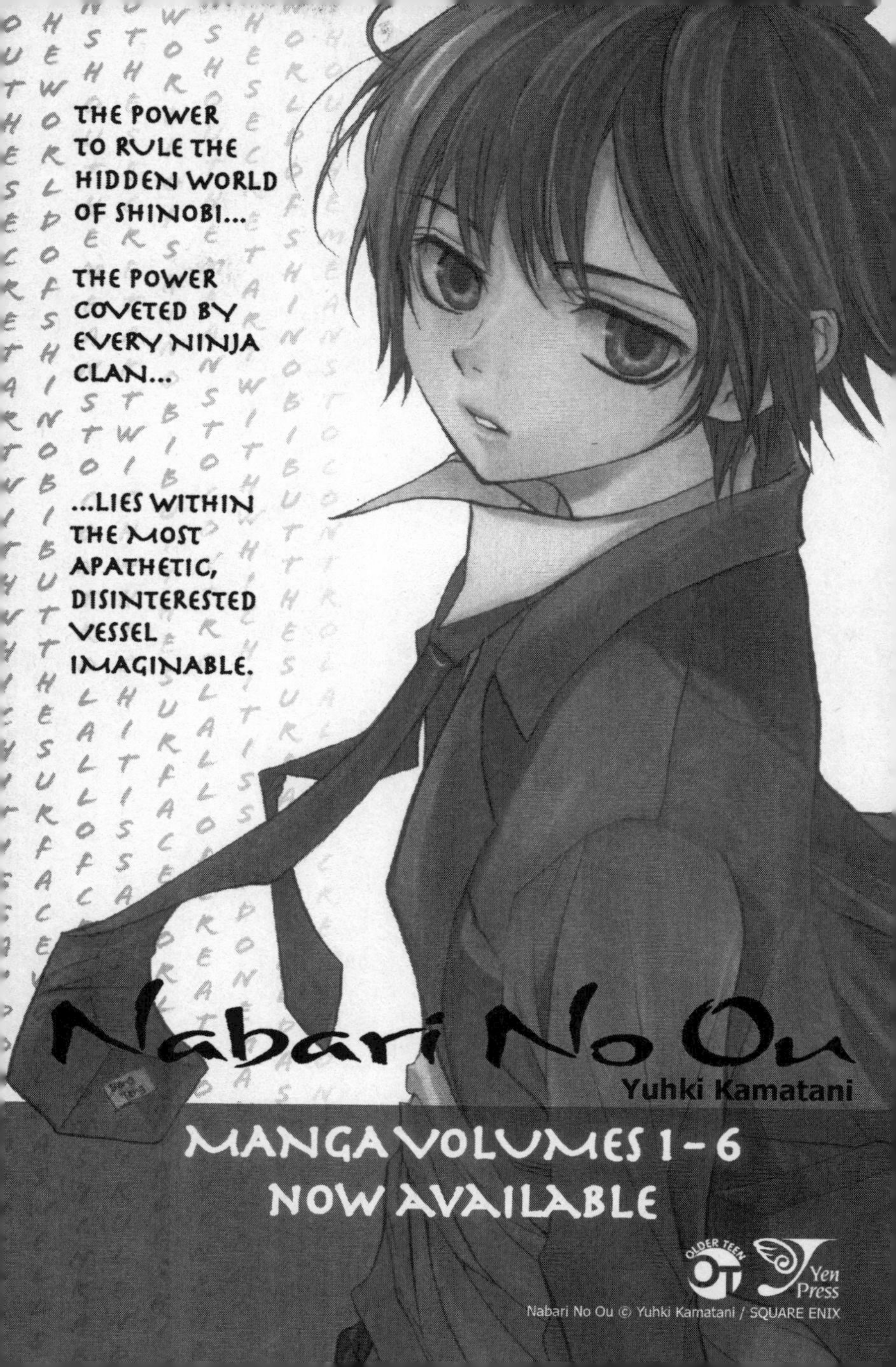
THE POWER TO RULE THE HIDDEN WORLD OF SHINOBI...
THE POWER COVETED BY EVERY NINJA CLAN...
...LIES WITHIN THE MOST APATHETIC, DISINTERESTED VESSEL IMAGINABLE.
Nabari No Ou
Yuhki Kamatani
MANGA VOLUMES 1-6 NOW AVAILABLE
OLDER TEEN OT
Yen Press
Nabari No Ou © Yuhki Kamatani / SQUARE ENIX

A totally new Arabian nights, where Scheherazade is a guy!

Everyone knows the story of Scheherazade and her wonderful tales from the Arabian Nights. For one thousand and one nights, the stories that she created entertained the mad Sultan and eventually saved her life. In this version, Scheherazade is a guy who disguises himself as a woman to save his sister from the mad Sultan. When he puts his life on the line, what kind of strange and unique stories will he tell? This new twist on one of the greatest classical tales might just keep you awake for another ONE THOUSAND AND ONE NIGHTS!

Yen Press
www.yenpress.com

Available at bookstores near you!

One thousand and one nights 1~11 final

Han SeungHee·Jeon JinSeok